CANADA AND THE TWO WORLD WARS

CANADA AND THE TWO WORLD WARS

Jack Granatstein
and
Desmond Morton

KEY PORTER BOOKS

National Library of Canada Cataloguing in Publication Data

Granatstein, J. L., 1939–
  Canada and the two world wars / J.L. Granatstein and Desmond Morton.

Contents: Marching to Armageddon : Canadians and the Great War, 1914–1919—A nation
forged in fire : Canadians and the Second World War, 1939–1945.
ISBN 1-55263-509-0

1. World War, 1914-1918—Canada. 2. CanadaæHistory—1914–1918. 3. World War,
1939–1945—Canada. 4. CanadaæHistory—1939–1945. I. Morton, Desmond, 1937–
II. Title.

FC543.G72 2003   940.3'71   C2003-903372-4

The publisher gratefully acknowledges the support of the Canada Council for the Arts and
the Ontario Arts Council for its publishing program.

We acknowledge the financial support of the Government of Canada through the Book
Publishing Industry Development Program (BPIDP) for our publishing activities.

First published by Key Porter Books in 1989 under the titles: *Marching to Armageddon:
Canadians and the Great War 1914–1919* and *A Nation Forged in Fire: Canadians and the
Second World War 1935–1945*

We acknowledge the support of the Government of Ontario through the Ontario Media
Development Corporation's Ontario Book Initiative.

Key Porter Books Limited
70 The Esplanade
Toronto, Ontario
Canada M5E 1R2

www.keyporter.com

Design: Don Fernley
Maps: Jonathon Gladstone, j.b. geographics
Electronic formatting: Jean Peters

Printed and bound in Canada

03 04 05 06 07 5 4 3 2 1

To Gael and Elaine

ACKNOWLEDGEMENTS

In any collaboration, readers may wonder how the authors shared the work. Since we have known each other since our days at le Collège militaire royal de St-Jean back in the 1950s, co-operation has come easily. Desmond Morton focussed on the First World War, and Jack Granatstein on the Second War, but both of us have researched and taught about both wars. And both or us shared the ideas and research of students and colleagues over many years. Some of them may recognize their contributions.

By giving us space, time and tolerance, our families are contributors too and an earlier version was dedicated to Elaine Granatstein and the late Janet Morton. Jan died as that version appeared but in this project, Elaine has been joined by Gael Eakin as inspiration and guide.

CONTENTS

INTRODUCTION
A Time of Catalytic Change

To some people, the world wars of 1914–18 and 1939–45 are ancient history, interesting perhaps to their survivors and to people hunting for their family tree, but irrelevant to modern life. Canadians are sometimes urged to forget about old wars. Yes, we participated, but, as Prime Minister Mackenzie King complained (just before taking Canada into the Second World War, "the idea that every twenty years this country should automatically and as a matter of course, take part in a war overseas for democracy or self-determination of other small nations ... seems to many a nightmare and sheer madness." To most, however, both wars were necessary. Victory was vital to Canada's existence as a civilized society.

That debate continues in Canada, and we wrote this book to give historical substance to those who wish to argue. More than any other sets of events, the two world wars of the twentieth century shaped our world. While much of the world, including Canada, escaped their violence, everyone on our globe was affected by the outcome of the world wars. The First World War not only contributed to its sequel in 1939 but created the bitter hatreds which still divide the people of the Middle East, Africa and Asia. The Second World War ended with a world divided between two hostile super powers. What avoided a Third World War? The best answer was the unmeasurable horror and limitless damage inflicted by modern war on combatants and civilians alike. Sixty years after atomic bombs shattered Hiroshima and Nagasaki, their mushroom-shaped clouds symbolized the "Mutually-Assured Destruction" or MAD which kept Soviet and American leaders from ending all our lives.

For our history as Canadians, the world wars were catalysts for every imaginable reform, from women's suffrage in 1918 to the right of workers after 1944 to bargain collectively and to share the wealth they had helped create. Wartime crises forced Canadian governments to solve financial, social and military problems they had never considered in peacetime. Canadians could finally see institutions they controlled with their votes respond to their interests. Whet we learned from a few years of war took many Canadians over sixty years of peacetime to forget.

The single biggest impact of the First World War on Canadians was our evolution from British colonials to citizens of a sovereign nation. When another great war brought great danger, we sought security from our southern neighbour. The same common sense that transformed a fortified American border into an undefended frontier evolved into one of the closest military partnerships in the world. Two world wars taught us why partnership mattered. Has sixty years of forgetfulness robbed us of the knowledge to protect ourselves?

In 1914, Canadians knew little of their past and nothing about their future. As bands played, flags waved and crowds cheered, thousands of young men marched off to Armageddon. "Same may not return," the Minister of Militia told the troops, "and pray God they may be few." One in ten of those who joined the wartime army died in its ranks. As many returned so maimed in body or mind that they never resumed their old lives. Some of that loss was due to our lack of military competence and a cultivated faith in military amateurism. At Ypres and the Somme, Canadian soldiers learned painful lessons. Improved tactics did not cut the losses but they turned Vimy, Passchendaele, Hill 70 and the "Hundred Days" of 1918 into a series of victories.

The Great War was a great divide. Afterwards, Canadians wanted to return to old ways but they could never do so. The war had cost us our innocence. Never again would Canadians share a universal faith in divine providence, our own perfectibility and the wisdom of Britain. Preachers had described war as "a fiery furnace" from which Canada would emerge purified. Wartime governments banned liquor, enfranchised women and conscripted wealth as well as manpower through a wartime income tax. Cynics pointed to bootleggers, "flappers" and profiteers. The long struggle divided Canadians and forced French- and English-speaking Canadians to serve as conscripts. Postwar Canada was a divided country, with bankrupt railways, a five-fold increase in the national debt, a huge pension burden, and a voice on the international stage most Canadians had neither the will nor the means to exercise.

Like others, the architects of the Treaty of Versailles in 1919 found that it is easier to make war than peace. Drowned in irreconcilable demands and reminded daily that victors were as exhausted as the vanquished, they postured, patched, compromised, and came home. They left a League of Nations to enforce peace but they had no will to do so themselves. As a new but minor power, Canada was as isolated as its American neighbour. We had not escaped the empire in order to allow a League to commit us to war. Only the chilling rise of Adolf Hitler forced Canadians back to the world. Without fervour or enthusiasm, Canada went to war on September 10, 1939. Again soldiers mobilized; sailors fought the North Atlantic and enemy submarines; thousands of youngsters filled Canadian skies in yellow training aircraft. Once again conscription shattered the fragile alliance of French and English Canadians.

This was a war waged in all the elements and across much of the globe. Canadians died at Hong Kong, in the Arctic and Indian Oceans, in Burma and Italy, over Berlin and in Normandy and the Netherlands. It was also a war of production. Men and women in overalls built trucks and guns, warships and bombers, radar and wireless sets. They found and processed the enriched uranium for the atomic bombs that ended the war.

History is another word for experience. Canada's wartime policies bore the stamp of memory, from pay-as-you-go taxes and early price and wage controls to resist inflation to Mackenzie King's earnest if unavailing efforts to avoid another conscription crisis. Perhaps the key lesson was that Canada could not dodge a war most Canadians had sworn to avoid. Again no one wanted to admit it but Canadians and their allies paid with their lives for an improvised and often amateur war effort.

Desmond Morton and J.L. Granatstein

I
OVER BY CHRISTMAS

A HOT AUGUST WEEKEND

The murder of an Austrian archduke and his wife in a small Bosnian city was hardly big news anywhere in Canada in 1914. Balkan crises and wars had been brutal perennials for a generation. Canadians with a taste for foreign news followed, instead, the trial of Mme Caillaux, wife of a former French premier, who had shot the editor of *Le Figaro* to stop his slanders. A jury set her free. Across the channel, the "Curragh Mutiny" had seen senior British army officers defy a constitutional government and win. If Herbert Asquith, Britain's Liberal prime minister, wanted to force the Protestant North into a self-governing Ireland, he could fight the Ulster Volunteers himself. An army officered largely by Irish Protestants would do little to help him.

That summer, Canadians had enough concerns of their own. On the prairies, a second year of drought turned wheat fields to parched desert. The two new transcontinental railways, the Grand Trunk Pacific and the Canadian Northern, plunged deeper into debt, while the thousands of men who had built them drifted into the army of unemployed. Those ranks swelled; Canada that summer was adjusting to the worst depression since the 1890s. Ontario employers complained that they were working at half-capacity. Still, outdated immigration propaganda drew shiploads of young Britons to win their fortunes in "The Last Best West". Others were not as welcome. Some were not welcome at all. In Vancouver harbour that July, Canada's only available cruiser, HMCS *Rainbow*, cleared for action against a defiant immigrant ship, the *Komagata Maru*; when the two hundred Sikhs abandoned their resistance British Columbians had won another battle against Asian immigration.

There was no way, in Canada, in 1914, to count the unemployed or to poll public opinion, but most barber-shop pundits could predict the fate of Sir Robert Borden's Conservative government. Three years of failure, mismanagement, and bad times would bring back the Liberals and their trusted old leader, Sir Wilfrid Laurier. Liberals were sure of it. Conservatives, of course, could argue that railway bankruptcy was a legacy of Laurier's folly, that Liberal senators could be blamed for blocking Borden's gift of $35 million to pay for three badly needed British battleships, and that, in June, Ontario's Tories had won a powerful new mandate — largely because their Regulation 17 would partially strip Franco-Ontarians of their French-language schools.

A country so preoccupied had little thought for the outside world. When the Toronto *Globe* wrote, on July 22, of "The Nation's Defences", it was referring to germs and the need for vaccination and chlorination. As for Europe, the great powers would surely keep the peace. "Let us hope," *La Presse* serenely observed, "that they will use their influence for a prompt settlement of differences." A cartoon in the *Vancouver Sun* had a more jocular view: "Hi mates," John Bull and Uncle Sam call to the German Kaiser and the Russian Tsar. "Come and sit on the fence with us an' we'll see if we can't settle this dispute without mussin' up your pretty uniforms."

Certainly the great powers had kept the peace in a dozen earlier disputes in the century. Even the assassination on June 28 of the heir to the Habsburg monarchy raised no insoluble problems. Two generations had passed since 1870, when Europe's power structure had been defined on one side by a triumphant Prussia and on the other by a vengeful France. Weaker than the newly proclaimed German Empire, France had bided her time, rebuilt an army, and, in 1894, forged an alliance with Russia. It was a marriage of questionable convenience. The Tsar's army was enormous, and Russia was the one continental power no one had ever defeated. But was there really a community of interest between the Third Republic and a vast, underdeveloped Russian autocracy? For all her enormous and powerful armies, Germany too felt threatened. In the ramshackle, disintegrating Austro-Hungarian Empire, she found her only dependable friend.

Alliances are often controlled by their weakest, not their strongest members. While the Archduke Franz Ferdinand was little mourned, his death at the hands of Bosnian terrorists had to be avenged or the Dual Monarchy would look feeble. Since Serbian plotters had helped hatch the assassination at Sarajevo, Serbia must be punished. That was the judgement of General Conrad von Hötzendorf, the chief of staff of the Habsburg armies, and neither his eighty-eight–year–old master, Emperor Franz Josef, nor any mere civilian opposed him. On July 23, Vienna issued its little neighbour an ultimatum so stinging that it was sure to be rejected. When the Serbs swallowed almost all of it, the tiny exception became the pretext for war. On July 28, Austrian artillery opened fire on Belgrade.

Conrad von Hötzendorf was not the only general who supplanted diplomats. Russian pride and dynastic survival dictated that Serbia had to be defended. Russia mobilized, but her generals had only a single plan, directed at Germany as much as at Austria-Hungary. Berlin commanded that the Russian mobilization cease in twelve hours. That ultimatum, too, was a pretext: Kaiser Wilhelm II and his generals had given up on peace. Indeed, it was the German generals who had the tightest grip on their country's choices. General Count Alfred von Schlieffen, chief of staff of the Kaiser's army, died in 1913, but he had left a plan that could give Germany victory in a two-front war. Not Russia but France would be the target. While a few divisions held off the slow-moving Russians, the highly developed road and rail system of Western Europe would carry more than a million Germans west across Belgium and northern France to envelop the French armies, much as Hannibal had swept up the Romans at Cannae. If the Belgians did not like their role as doormat for the German armies, they could, as the German ambassador politely explained, lump it. Belgium's King Albert I neither liked it nor lumped it: he mobilized his little army and called for help. On August 3, France and Germany went to war.

So far, the British Empire had no need to get involved and, in the view of many of Asquith's Liberal colleagues, no wish to do so. Germany had been a traditional friend — Kaiser Wilhelm was a cousin of King George V — France and Russia, the old enemies. But times had changed. The British and German monarchs detested each other. So did their countrymen. The Prussian victories in 1870 had alarmed Britain, as had Germany's remarkable industrial growth and trading rivalry. Most serious was the Kaiser's determination to challenge Britain's naval and imperial dominance with his own high-seas fleet and colonial empire. During the Boer War, 1899–1902, Britain had felt her isolation when Germany joined other European powers in righteous sympathy for the Boers. Painfully, the British had come to an understanding or "entente" with, first, the French, then the Russians. Unofficially, Colonel Henry Wilson met with Colonel Ferdinand Foch in 1907 to discuss what a British army might do if war came. The French now counted on British divisions on their northern flank. To match the Kaiser's growing array of battleships, the Royal Navy brought most of its fleet back from the Mediterranean. The French would look after Britain's interests while Britain would safeguard the English Channel coast. Of course, there were no written promises.

There was, however, a half-forgotten treaty. In 1839, Britain, France, and Prussia had all agreed to protect Belgian neutrality. Dividing the ownership of the European coastline was a vital British interest, but would it really matter to a peace-loving government with a small, troubled army? Would Britain embroil herself in a European war for the sake of what one German dismissed as "a scrap of paper"? The reluctant answer was yes. As German shells began to pound King Albert's frontier fortresses, a British ultimatum commanded the Kaiser to withdraw. At midnight, August 4, 1914, the ultimatum expired. The British Empire was at war.

In Canada, August 1 to 3 was widely observed as the Bank Holiday weekend. Only a wealthy minority, of course, escaped to cottages. Most crowded the beaches, amusement parks, or downtown streets, where excitement grew hourly. Prime Minister and Lady Borden had long since fled the aftermath of a tiresome parliamentary session for a few weeks of golfing at Port Carling. They were there as the vague Balkan crisis took shape. On July 31, Borden returned to Ottawa. That day, copies of the *Globe* reminded readers that the money-lenders would be the final arbiters of war: "If they refuse to finance it, it cannot be carried out." By Saturday, war news had finally captured Canadian newspapers. On Sunday, a few papers brought out special editions, the *Manitoba Free Press* apologizing for breaching the Sabbath and explaining that it had permission from the provincial government. On Monday, holiday crowds jammed the streets in front of newspaper offices to read the bulletins. Most Canadians waited for Britain's decision.

A few Canadians were already busy. On July 29, Britain warned its colonies to take precautions. Recent wars, notably the Russo-Japanese War, had begun with surprise attacks. Soldiers and Canada's few sailors manned the Halifax fortifications and dragged some guns to command the St. Lawrence below Quebec. The *Rainbow* headed south, mindful of German cruisers but determined to warn a couple of tiny British warships that had no wireless. At Victoria, Premier Richard McBride signed a cheque for $1,150,000 and bought two submarines from a Seattle shipyard. British Columbia's coast would not, now, be utterly defenceless. On Sunday, August 2, armed militia mounted guard on bridges, canals, tunnels, and railway stations. Crowds cheered them. Reporters visited local consulates to watch Austrian, Serbian, and French reservists arrange passage home. The Austrians, reported the Montreal *Gazette*, were "slightly undersized as to height, but sturdy specimens". In Winnipeg, Bishop Nicholas Budka reminded his Ukrainian flock of their duty to their Habsburg emperor, a message Canadian patriots would not allow him to forget.

In Ottawa, the Minister of Militia, Colonel Sam Hughes, was almost out of control. For most of his sixty-one years he had dreamed of leading Canadians to war. Immune to persuasion and ridicule, he had preached and prepared for war with Germany. Now he had to wait on London. The worst feature of the British Empire was that it was run by the English. "They're going to skunk it," he raged. An aide was ordered to haul down the Militia Department's Union Jack. The octogenarian quartermaster general, Major-General Donald Alexander Macdonald, persuaded Hughes to be patient. At 8:55 P.M., Ottawa got the news; Hughes was ecstatic.

"When Britain is at war, Canada is at war," Sir Wilfrid Laurier had explained in 1910; "there is no distinction." Nor was there consultation. No one in 1914 cared. In Quebec City, Montreal, Toronto, excited crowds filled the downtown streets. In Winnipeg, where the Knights of Pythias had gathered for an international convention, local citizens made certain that American delegates could report the patriotic fervour. The pleasure was marred when "some unknown maniac" drove his high-powered car into the crowd. In Vancouver, local militia regiments had time to organize a parade. The Associated Canadian Clubs cheered when Talbot Papineau, a Montreal lawyer and a descendant of the Patriote leader of 1837, rose to assure them "that there would be as many French Canadians as English Canadians to take up arms in defence of the Empire in this crisis". W.J. Bowser, a future B.C. premier, rejoiced that the pacifists had been driven from power in Britain: "fortunately the spirit of the people pushes such undesirables into the background when the honour of the nation is to be maintained...."

"READY, AYE, READY!"

Canadians, that August, were united. Immediately Laurier summoned journalists to pledge a party truce for as long as Canada was in danger. Dissidents in his caucus agreed to hold their tongues. Borden summoned Parliament for August 18 and then met for endless hours with cabinet colleagues to wrestle with a hundred unfamiliar problems. For the MPs, the prime minister struggled to rise to the rhetorical occasion, pledging Canadians "to put forward every effort and make every sacrifice necessary to ensure the integrity and maintain the honour of our Empire". As usual, it was Laurier who found the magical phrase. Recalling what he had said in 1910, he asked what Canada must do: "When the call comes, our answer goes at once, and it goes in the classical language of the British answer to the call of duty, 'Ready, aye, ready!'" Without division or significant debate, members approved an overseas contingent of 25,000 men, with Canada bearing the full cost: a war appropriation of $50 million and a Canadian Patriotic Fund to support the families of men who would fight for the Empire.

The government needed more. In the days before Parliament met, the Cabinet wasted hours trying to devise adequate emergency legislation. Exasperated, Borden handed the task to W.F. O'Connor, a Halifax lawyer. "Make absolutely sure that you omit no power that the government may need," insisted a Liberal MP, and O'Connor's draft War Measures Bill met the challenge. The Cabinet, it decreed, would have full authority to do anything it deemed necessary for "the security, defence, peace, order and welfare of Canada".

Canada, of course, was not ready for war. Indeed, no belligerent was prepared for the kind of struggle that began in 1914. Only old men could even remember the last real European war of 1870 or the American Civil War of 1861–65. A single Canadian officer had seen the Russo-Japanese War for himself. For soldiers and civilians alike, images of war were shaped by peacetime manoeuvres, colonial forays, and romantic lithographs of sword-waving heroes leading attacks. Experts and amateurs agreed that, if the generals did not end the war by Christmas, the financiers would. No national economy could stand the strain for more than a few months. European armies had patiently planned and organized to make their full strength available in the first few weeks. Building reserves of men and munitions was unnecessary and unwise.

There were dissenters. Field Marshal Lord Kitchener, summoned by Herbert Asquith to take over the British War Office on August 5, shocked his cabinet colleagues by predicting three years of war and a British army of a million men. As usual, the conqueror of dervishes and Boers gave no reasons. A generation earlier, Warsaw financier Ivan Bloch had predicted that modern weapons would lead to mass casualties, military stalemate, and ultimate exhaustion for one or both sides. Only the Tsar had listened to Bloch, and his arguments left their mark on two Hague conventions to limit such horrors of war as the use of poison gas. The generals were unimpressed; generals did not like to take military lessons from Polish-Jewish bankers.

By her own modest standards, Canada was better prepared in 1914 than for any earlier or later war. The South African War had given Canada some experienced officers and an incentive to think about war. Prosperity in the Laurier years made it easy to expand, rearm, and reform the militia. In 1907, the British had won agreement from their dominions to standardize military training, organization, and equipment. Keen militia officers had learned from able British instructors. For a few pre-war years, militarism had been in fashion in Canada, as a conservative response to urbanization, industrialization, and immigration. "The school mistress with her book and spectacles has had her day in the training of boys," boasted Professor Andrew Macphail of the *University Magazine*, "and sensible parents are longing for the drill-sergeant carrying in his hand a good cleaning rod or a leather belt.... That is the sovereign remedy for the hooliganism of the town and the loutishness of the city." In 1909, most provinces, including Quebec, agreed to institute cadet training in their schools. The Canadian Defence League, headed by a galaxy of clergy, physicians, professors, and business magnates, urged universal military training.

In such a setting, Sam Hughes was a model Minister of Militia. Borden had had misgivings about him in 1911 and had warned him that he was beset by two unceasing enemies, his tongue and his pen. Hughes, an editor and militia officer from Lindsay, was the pride of Ontario's Orange Lodge, a charming braggart with just a hint of mental imbalance. In 1899, he had bullied his way to South Africa and had come home strengthened in his faith in citizen-soldiers and his contempt for military professionals, popular prejudices widely shared in Canada. In 1902, Hughes had persuaded the Laurier government to order the Ross rifle. A marksman, Hughes knew it was a fine target rifle. Sir Charles Ross agreed to build his factory in Quebec, close to Laurier's constituents. However, the Ross was also a foot longer, a pound heavier, and a third more costly than the British Lee-Enfield, and it jammed easily and seized up when fired rapidly. The faults, shown up at the first trials, were never corrected. Hughes treated them as irrelevant or fabricated by British rivals, and the Liberals were happy to agree.

As Minister of Militia, Hughes ignored the constraints imposed on all civilian ministers. Borden, he believed to be "a most lovely fellow, gentle as a girl" — easily bullied. The militia prospered under its new minister's bullying and charm. In 1904, 25,000 volunteers had drilled; under Hughes, in 1913, 55,000 militiamen and 44,000 cadets went to camp. Militia spending rose from $7 million in 1911 to $13.5 million in 1913. Orders were issued for new guns and equipment to land in Canada as fast as British factories could deliver them. That was not very fast: in 1914, Canada had modern artillery for only two of the six divisions in its paper organization. Hughes ignored criticism, whether it was for equipping militia staff officers with Ford cars; banning liquor from training camps; or escorting a bevy of officers and their wives to the British, French, and Swiss manoeuvres in 1913. One pre-war Swiss notion, a shield-shovel with a stubby four-inch handle and loopholes for sighting and firing a rifle, he judged to be ideally suited for modern warfare. He patented it in the name of his secretary, Ena MacAdam.

Fashions change. By 1913, the depression had taken the starch out of Canadian militarism. "Drill Hall Sam" had become an embarrassment. His constant warnings that war with Germany was imminent cost votes in German-Canadian ridings. Even Conservatives began to wonder if Hughes might be crazy. But, on August 4, he suddenly looked very sane.

Hughes, though not a man of system, had better subordinates than he deserved. An able British officer, Major-General Willoughby Gwatkin, served as Chief of the General Staff. Thanks to him, a mobilization plan for a force of 25,000 to fight "in a civilized country in a temperate climate" was on file. By mid 1914, an interdepartmental committee had finally completed a "War Book", detailing all the precautions, from censorship to guarding cable stations, that the country must take on the outbreak of hostilities. Across Canada, the militia was more a social and political organization than a military force, keener on bands, dress uniforms, and mess dinners than on dusty manoeuvres, but scores of officers, professional and amateur, had done all they could to prepare themselves for war, often at the cost of income, careers, and ridicule. Their turn had come.

In one respect, the Borden government left Canada less ready for war than it had been in 1911. Conservative candidates had won votes by promising to scrap Laurier's "tin-pot" navy. Quebec voters, at least, had never grasped Borden's alternative: a $35-million gift to Britain to buy three of the huge Dreadnought battleships. When they did, a Liberal Senate sank the Naval Aid Bill. As for the navy, Borden let it wither to a few hundred men. Ironically, on August 5, the navy was Canada's front line. HMCS *Rainbow,* lacking crew and ammunition, narrowly missed the German cruisers that would have sunk her off San Francisco. Naval reservists were hurriedly mustered to man McBride's submarines. When the Germans sank Sir Christopher Cradock's squadron off the Chilean coast on November 1, four of his midshipmen became Canada's first war dead.

"THE WORLD REGARDS YOU AS A MARVEL"

If the war was to be over by Christmas, Canadians would have to hurry to share in the glory. In 1899, it took Ottawa two weeks to recruit and despatch a regiment of 1,000 men. In 1914, Britain had accepted the Canadian offer of an infantry division with supplementary units, a force of 25,000. It was what Gwatkin had anticipated in his plan, which, on July 31, Hughes cancelled. The minister would run the mobilization his way, free of interference from despised professionals. On August 6, hundreds of telegrams notified militia colonels to recruit volunteers aged eighteen to forty-five, physically fit, able to shoot, and, if married, armed with their wives' permission. Later, Hughes explained that his mobilization was "like the fiery cross passing through the Highlands of Scotland or the mountains of Ireland ... in a short time we had the boys on the way for the first contingent, whereas it would have taken several weeks to have got the word round through ordinary channels." This was nonsense; it took weeks to sort out the confusion. For maximum effect, the minister insisted that "his boys" would assemble at Valcartier, a sandy plain twenty miles north of Quebec City, designated earlier that year as a future militia camp. At once special trains went into service, ferrying workers, equipment, and building materials to the site. Units of the tiny permanent force arrived to help. Within days, the beginnings of roads, a water system, and a 1,500-target rifle range appeared. By the end of August, so did volunteers.

Recruiting was as easy as Hughes had expected, though not for his reasons. British immigrants flocked to enlist. So did the unemployed. Ontario, hard-hit by the depression, produced almost a third of the recruits; the western provinces almost half. Two-thirds of the volunteers were British-born. Few came from the Maritimes, and just over a thousand were French-speaking. Most came from the cities: Toronto, Montreal, and Winnipeg each sent enough men for two battalions, Vancouver sent one and a half, and Edmonton's 101st Regiment arrived at full strength. By September 4, there were 32,000 men and 8,000 horses in camp, far more than expected. Across the St. Lawrence, at Lévis, was a separate unit, the Princess Patricia's Canadian Light Infantry. Raised at the expense of Hamilton Gault, a Montreal millionaire, the unit was filled with British Army reservists, diverted from their regiments. The officers were Canadian, among them Lieutenant Talbot Papineau.

Even cynics were impressed by Valcartier, with its acres of tents, its showers, and its large rifle range. What he wanted, Hughes insisted, were men who could "pink the enemy every time". Hughes was everywhere, on horseback and in uniform. Ostensibly, Colonel Victor Williams, the militia's adjutant-general, a permanent-force officer, was in command, but the minister was in charge, greeting cronies, bellowing abuse, boasting of his achievements to admiring journalists.

"Pipe up, you little bastard, or get out of the service," Hughes bellowed at a captain. Another, whom he addressed as major, was promoted on the spot. Having created chaos, he alone would create order, forming ad hoc battalions and shifting them when fresh troops arrived. Four Ontario battalions formed the 1st (Provisional) Infantry Brigade under Colonel M.S. Mercer, a Toronto lawyer. Four Western battalions were grouped in the 2nd Brigade. Hughes's son Garnet recommended an old friend for the command: Arthur Currie was a Victoria real-estate dealer, a Liberal, and a former militia gunner who had commanded the 50th Highlanders. The third brigadier, Colonel Richard Turner, was a Quebec City merchant and a Tory. Slight and bespectacled, Turner gave no hint in his appearance of the heroism that had earned him a Victoria Cross in South Africa. To command the artillery, Hughes chose another South African veteran, Colonel E.W.B. Morrison — "Dinky" to his friends — the editor-in-chief of the Ottawa *Citizen*.

Uniforms, equipment, and weapons had to be found. The Ross Rifle Company factory in nearby Quebec worked overtime. So did textile mills and clothing factories because no one had thought to stockpile the new khaki serge uniforms that the Empire's armies had gradually adopted since 1900. Farm wagons, their paint still damp and the green timber already warping, were delivered as divisional transport. A bewildering variety of motor vehicles arrived as well: Hughes and the auto manufacturers agreed that the Contingent would be a showcase for Canadian products. In the South African War, soldiers had suffered miseries from Canadian-made Oliver pattern leather equipment but thousands of new sets arrived in Valcartier. Hughes believed in it. MacAdam shield-shovels also appeared, but most of the Colt machine guns, ordered from American factories, were delayed. Even Hughes admitted that the British water-cooled Vickers was better but the American gun would have to do.

Except for the governor general, the Duke of Connaught — an old soldier — and a few other veterans, visitors to Valcartier found it all marvellous. Never had Canadians seen so many soldiers or such purposeful confusion. With so many responsibilities, surely Canada's War Minister could be forgiven occasional rudeness to an Anglican bishop or a Humane Society official. Soldiers, after all, were supposed to be abrupt men of action. Only one cloud hung over Hughes's joy: how could he choose the units to go overseas? When Sir Robert Borden solved his problem, saying that all could go, Hughes wept with gratitude.

Embarkation was a nightmare. Ignoring the few professionals he had available, Hughes put William H. Price, the contractor who had built Valcartier, in charge of the docks. Extra ships were chartered to carry the additional men. Some arrived loaded down with private cargo and with 132,275 bags of flour — Canada's special wartime gift to Britain. Battalions were marched aboard only to be marched off again when they did not fit. Units ignored orders and schedules and crowded to the docks to avoid waiting. When the last of 30 ships had cleared Quebec harbour, 863 horses; 4,512 tons of baggage, vehicles, and ammunition; and a few soldiers remained. Price hired an extra ship.

At the Gaspé basin, the armada stopped to form convoy. The transports in their long lines looked to spectators like a vast battle fleet. On October 3, Hughes passed through the convoy on a final visit, delivering bundles of his farewell message. "Soldiers," it proclaimed, "The World regards you as a marvel." Crumpled copies soon dotted the dark surface of the St. Lawrence.

IVAN BLOCH'S NIGHTMARE

By the time the First Contingent reached England on October 14, the Polish banker had proved to be a better prophet of war than most of Europe's generals. The law of uncertainty still governed human affairs. The war would not be over by Christmas.

More than any other power, Germany had gambled on quick success. By the end of August, that gamble was paying off. The Belgian forts, expected to resist for months, were pulverized in a few days, thanks to huge guns borrowed from the Austrians. A campaign of terrorism discouraged even the slightest civilian resistance. At Dinant, almost seven hundred people, including a three-month-old baby, were shot. At Louvain, the university was sacked and burned. German soldiers, enraged that anyone dared oppose their desperate mission, added scores of smaller private atrocities. The purpose was clear: terror was the fastest, cheapest way to neutralize resistance. Dusty columns of infantry poured through Belgium and into France at an exhausting thirty miles a day. King Albert's army was shoved back to Antwerp.

Von Schlieffen's plan had discounted French resistance, an expectation the French fulfilled. Their strategy, Plan XVII, seemed designed to help the Germans. France almost ignored its northern frontier; huge armies were mobilized opposite the lost provinces of Alsace and Lorraine, poised to hurl themselves at the Germans. That was what von Schlieffen had hoped for when he had ordered the defenders to pull back, drawing the French deeper into a trap and making it easy for the huge German attack force to surround them. For years, French officers had concentrated only on the attack. French courage, willpower, *élan*, would overcome anything. In the Battle of the Frontiers, an almost metaphysical faith in the *attaque à outrance* would be tested. Instead, the French army proved only that it could die. Led by officers in immaculate white gloves, masses of infantry in old-fashioned blue coats and red trousers raced forward to be massacred by German artillery and machine guns. In the rugged terrain of Alsace, the wonderful French 75-millimetre guns were useless. High velocity and rapid loading meant nothing if a hill stood in the way of the shell. In a few days, 140,000 of France's best soldiers were killed or wounded and one officer in ten was dead. With no training or equipment for defence, the survivors reeled back from the frontier, a beaten army.

The British, unlike the French and Germans, had no plan. On August 5, Asquith met with Kitchener; Winston Churchill, the First Lord of the Admiralty; and Britain's generals and admirals to make one. Could Britain's little army be sent to Belgium? Perhaps it might be landed on the German coast?

Should it go to Amiens to build up its strength from reservists and Territorials, the British counterpart to the militia? Sir Henry Wilson, now a general, gave a chilling answer. His conversations years ago with Ferdinand Foch left Britain no choice: the French expected the British on their left flank. On August 23, five divisions of British regulars, 100,000 superbly trained troops, moved up to the Mons canal, just inside Belgium, in the path of sixty-one advancing German divisions. For a day, the British held their ground. That afternoon, pilots from the new Royal Flying Corps reported that the Germans were lapping around the British flanks. Sir John French, the aged and mercurial British commander, ordered a headlong retreat. A few days later, too exhausted to move, Sir Horace Smith Dorrien's II Corps gave further battle, beating back the Germans. Otherwise the British were out of the fight.

German victory seemed certain. Or did it? Belgium had collapsed but not before its railways had been sabotaged. German troops could march but could they be fed? Von Moltke's army was a horse-powered juggernaut; his cavalry divisions and artillery batteries were immobilized for lack of horseshoe nails. Troops were hungry. The French army had fallen back in defeat, away from its trap. To the east, Russia's "steamroller" had rumbled into Germany territory sooner than expected. Prussian *Junkers* demanded protection for their rural estates. Surely the victorious armies in the West could spare a few army corps. By the time help arrived, the crisis was over. A brilliant staff officer, Colonel Hoffmann, noted that the Russian armies had been split by the Masurian Lakes. Intercepted wireless messages told him the Russian plans. Railways concentrated the German defenders against one of the invading armies and, by August 30, the Russian general had shot himself, and 90,000 of his men were prisoners. By then, the battle in France had turned.

On August 29, the French general next to the British redirected his army and administered a stinging set-back to the weary, advancing Germans. If Sir John French had followed up, the Allies might have had a stunning victory. But, in his view, the British were too tired. The Germans, too, were growing cautious. With several of their divisions sent to Prussia, the Germans decided to shorten their swing, passing east of Paris. For weeks, with ox-like imperturbability, General Joffre, the French commander-in-chief, had watched events unfold, quietly gathering his reserves north and east of the German flank. The new air arm changed history. Pilots spotted German columns pushing east of the French capital, not beyond it as von Schlieffen had intended. Suddenly, it was the Germans who were in the bag. From Paris, General Galliéni sent his garrison in taxis and buses to spring the trap. To the south, the French retreat ended as Joffre attacked a hungry, exhausted invader. Even the British rejoined the battle, moving cautiously from the Marne to the hills overlooking the Aisne. There, faced by a German army corps too weary to move, their advance stopped. Much the same thing happened along the line, and both sides dug in. The chance for rapid victory had passed.

By October 10, the German guns had smashed Antwerp's defences. The Belgians and a few British marines fled along the coast to the Yser. There, just inside his country's border, King Albert ordered his army to fight. Pursuing Germans found the sluice gates opened and the land flooded. The Germans then sent troops to outflank the Belgians through the railway town of Ypres. On October 21, they ran into Sir Douglas Haig's I British Corps, bent on the same mission of out-flanking the enemy. For twenty days, the best of the British and German armies battled each other on the low ridges that surrounded Ypres. On November 11, the fighting died away, and both sides dug in. The Germans, remembering whole battalions of university students sacrificed in the struggle, called it the *Kindermord von Ypern*, the "child-murder of Ypres". The British knew only that 58,000 men, the best of their peacetime regular army, had been lost. Entire battalions had been virtually annihilated. The Ypres salient might be a useless excrescence in a line of trenches that now extended five hundred miles from the Channel to the Swiss frontier. Officially, the blood-soaked ground would be justified as a remnant of the Belgium for which Britain had joined the war. To British generals, whose sons and friends had died in the rain and mud, Ypres also was sacred soil. Canadians would come to know and curse those memories. They, too, would die at Ypres, among the millions who would perish in a war only Ivan Bloch had truly foreseen.

II
DOING YOUR BIT

A German triumph or a diplomatic compromise might have ended the war in 1914. Neither was possible. The generals had failed; compromise was unthinkable. By Christmas, France had 900,000 dead and maimed soldiers to avenge. Germans remained convinced that war had been forced on them, with the British, perversely, as the chief culprits. When the British learned of the atrocities in Belgium, some of them touched up by clever journalists, they knew that there could be no peace with the barbarian Hun. The Belgian horrors, sometimes corroborated by American reporters, were also a useful lever to shift neutral opinion, particularly in the United States.

In August, it had been enough that England was in danger; by early 1915, the war was a moral crusade. Canadians were a church-going people; among Protestants, crusading was a congenial act. If mankind was hard to perfect, society could certainly be improved, and the task might even be easier overseas than close at hand. In his day, Sir Wilfrid Laurier had warned Canadians against "the vortex of European militarism". Now, J.W. Dafoe of the *Manitoba Free Press* insisted that Canadians were in the war to defeat Prussian militarism. C.W. Gordon, the Presbyterian cleric who wrote popular novels under the name of Ralph Connor, put in verse what countless clergymen were to thunder from their pulpits:

> O Canada, What answer make to calling voice and beating drum
> To sword gleam and to pleading prayer of God
> For right? What answer makes my soul?
> Mother, to thee! God, to thy help! Quick, my sword.

A moral crusade transcended mere politics and government. Canadians, on the whole, expected little from their political rulers, and that little would be badly done. For a hospital, a college, or a waterworks, people looked to civic and business leaders. Apart from the alleged wastrels of the permanent force, even the Canadian militia was essentially a network of regimental clubs financed by wealthy families like the Gooderhams, the Pellatts, and the Olands. It was natural that Hamilton Gault should finance a regiment. A Yukon millionaire, Joe Boyle, raised his own machine-gun battery. So did Sir John Eaton, heir to the Toronto merchandising empire. Jack Ross, another scion of wealth, transferred half a million dollars to the Patriotic Fund, lent his yacht to the navy, and went off to war in command of HMCS *Grilse.*

A government with little idea of what to do about the war and, fearful of doing too much, found voluntarism a blessing. The Canadian Patriotic Fund (CPF) was a marvellous start. In the War of 1812, its forebear had financed pensions and a campaign medal; in 1914, under Sir Herbert Ames, a Montreal MP and businessman, the CPF was content to support soldiers' families. Admittedly, the government could have increased a private's pay from $1.10 a day but, as Borden explained, "It would be most undesirable to discourage private enterprise." In three months, the CPF collected $6 million. With the slogan "Give 'til it hurts", Toronto gathered $312,551; Montreal promptly raised $750,000. Led by the example of the Canadian Pacific Railway, employees of large companies were persuaded to donate a day's pay. The CPF continued to grow. By 1916, the national fund supported 55,000 families; in 1919 Ames reported a total income of $47 million. The fund did more than raise and spend money; organizers congratulated themselves on teaching thrift to soldiers' wives, discouraging foolish purchases, and depriving immoral mothers of their children. No state agency, Ames boasted, could have done as much or as economically, and none would have been able to discriminate against the undeserving.

Soldiers' families were not alone in sharing in wartime generosity. Christie Brown and Co., the biscuit-maker, offered full salaries to employees who enlisted. Ottawa, most provinces, and many employers followed suit. None realized how long the war would last. In 1915, it appeared that the war would end sooner if Canadian soldiers had more machine guns. With some Toronto judges as inspiration, service clubs, businesses, and school children launched an informal Machine Gun Fund. By the time Sam Hughes put a stop to it — on the grounds that factories were over-booked with government orders — fund collections had reached $731,000. An attempt to divert part of the money to launch a Disablement Fund to care for wounded soldiers was scotched by Sir Herbert Ames: the Patriotic Fund wanted no major competition as the biggest claimant on public generosity. Realism was intruding.

Other war charities were busy enough. Canadians were besieged by tag days for causes ranging from Belgian or Serbian relief to hospitals for wounded horses. The YMCA needed money to provide soldiers with stationery and sports equipment. The Red Cross collected $21,271,000 in cash and supplies. The Canadian Field Comforts Commission needed money to ease the lot of soldiers in the trenches. Late in 1915 Colonel William Hamilton Merritt, a passionate convert to the new dimension in war, launched a Canadian Aviation Fund to help would-be aviators finance flying lessons and to buy aircraft for the British flying services. In Montreal, a Khaki League opened hospitals for returning invalids. In Winnipeg, the same task was assumed by the Imperial Order Daughters of the Empire. The Boy Scouts volunteered to run messages. In Toronto, for a time, school children were required to salute soldiers; elsewhere, they collected scrap metal; and everywhere they were alert in looking for behaviour that would betray a German spy or saboteur.

Churches took a lead in patriotic causes. Before the war, reform-minded clergy had often declared themselves to be pacifists: since militarism was now the enemy, it took only a slight twist of convictions to preach war. "If ever a war in all history was seeking first the kingdom of God," S.D. Chown reassured Methodists, "this is, so far as we are engaged in it." "War is never wrong," declared the *Presbyterian Record*, "when it is a war against wrong." Preachers found a unifying theme in the image of the fiery furnace, in which society would be purged of its impurities. While theological reformers and conservatives differed over the list of evils, all promoted the cause. "If a man cannot conscientiously declare himself a patriot," warned W.B. Creighton of the *Christian Guardian*, "he has no business in any Church that prides itself upon its patriotism."

Thanks to Michael Fallon, the Catholic bishop of London and a fervent supporter of Regulation 17, most Irish Catholics refused to be distracted by the Easter Rising of 1916 in Dublin or its bloody aftermath. More than one in ten of those who joined the Canadian Expeditionary Force was an English-speaking Catholic, a figure comparable to that for Presbyterians. The thousands of English immigrants helped swell the Anglican ratio to almost one in five. Methodists lagged at one in twelve.

Like Creighton and Chown, pre-war feminists had denounced war. Votes for women, they insisted, would be votes for peace. Like the clergy, most women changed their minds when war came. The British suffrage leader Sylvia Pankhurst travelled across Canada, giving them reasons. "If this struggle is lost," she warned, "civilization that is based on right and justice will disappear...." War offered Canadian women some new roles. Almost three thousand were commissioned as nursing sisters; others went overseas to manage field comforts. Tens of thousands, after 1915, worked in an expanding munitions industry, sometimes in trades traditionally performed by men. A few went too far for conventional opinion. The Toronto women who bought uniforms, drilled, and learned to fire rifles were soon ridiculed into oblivion.

For most Canadian women, voluntarism largely confirmed traditional roles. Men collected the money for the Patriotic Fund; women distributed the charity and delivered the lectures on thrift and domestic economy. Women worked for the Red Cross, rolling bandages, knitting socks, packing food parcels, and serving meals. When the Militia Department wanted convalescent homes for invalid soldiers, women answered the call. When the businessmen who formed the Military Hospitals Commission in 1915 realized that discipline, not "a motherly touch", brought faster recovery, the women were thanked and the homes were closed. Certainly there were women who issued white feathers to men in civilian clothing or publicly denounced "slackers" and "shirkers", but such tactics were notorious, not effective, and male officials did their best to discourage them. In recruiting, women's real role was to persuade wives and mothers to release their men for war. Even when women took jobs as "conductorettes" on streetcars or as members of Ontario's Women's Emergency Corps, special uniforms and rates of pay maintained an "appropriate" distinction between the sexes.

The war would be won, a popular slogan insisted, if all Canadians "did their bit". Men, women, and children would, of course, do their best "bit" if they performed in their own spheres.

NOT QUITE UNANIMOUS

A national crusade is more natural if a nation is united. In 1914, French and English, Liberal and Conservative, Catholic and Protestant were united on the issue of Canada's role in the war. Dissenters were silent or inaudible, and foreigners, as the *Manitoba Free Press* noted on August 5, "made themselves scarce".

The war created acute tensions. After the British and French, Germans contributed Canada's third-largest ethnic element, with roots as deep as the 1780s. Immigration in the Laurier years had brought tens of thousands more from Germany and even more from the Habsburg Empire. Berlin, in western Ontario, prided itself on being a German city, complete with a statue of the Kaiser. Most Ukrainians, despite Bishop Budka's advice, remembered that they had fled Habsburg rule. In the circumstances, the government urged tolerance for all newcomers. "Having invited them to become citizens of this country," Sir Robert Borden explained, "we owe to them in the trying circumstances in which they are placed the duty of fairness and consideration."

Weeks passed before "enemy aliens" were ordered to register and it was October before internment of Germans and Austrians of military age began — long after the few Canadians in Germany had been confined. When a Montreal judge decreed that a German had no rights in a Canadian court, he was swiftly overruled.

Public opinion was not satisfied. The pre-war naval debate had conditioned many Canadians to believe that Germans were dangerous. The troops posted at public buildings and along the Welland Canal fed expectations of sabotage, probably in alliance with that traditional Irish-American bogey, the Fenians. In one of the more bizarre episodes of the war, rumours of an air raid from Ogdensburg in February 1915 blacked out Ottawa's government buildings. In fact, boys in the United States had released balloons to commemorate the centennial of the end of the War of 1812! In British Columbia, where thousands of militiamen were mobilized at the outset of war, local businesses found hysteria was an ally in keeping a profitable arrangement going. Troops meant public spending in a province hard hit by depression. Racial prejudice and unemployment fed hostility to Ukrainians. At Nanaimo and in the Crowsnest Pass, miners struck until "foreigners" were interned. At the Lakehead, municipal officials demanded that Ottawa lock up and feed hundreds of unemployed "enemy aliens" who otherwise required local charity. By the end of 1914, the government found itself guarding six thousand men in a dozen internment camps. Magistrates, acting on information gleaned from gossip or neighbourhood malice, daily added to the number. Under the War Measures Act, internees had no recourse to appeal. In May 1915, mobs reacted to the torpedoing of the *Lusitania* by pillaging German businesses in Victoria, Winnipeg, and Montreal. More "enemy aliens" were locked up. By the summer, more than eight thousand were confined. Economy, labour shortages, and common sense led to the release of most of the so-called Austrians so that, by the end of 1916, only a couple of thousand internees, most of them German, remained at Amherst, Nova Scotia; Kapuskasing, Ontario; and Morrissey, British Columbia.

Public passions were not satisfied. At Berlin, Ontario, on February 15, 1916, a crowd led by unruly soldiers threw the Kaiser's statue in a local lake. Resentful citizens fished it out. In May, the threat of a boycott of the city's industries forced Berlin to change its name to Kitchener, even though the margin was only eighty-one votes. In 1917, when a newly elected council proposed to restore the old name, riots and a boycott changed its mind. Across Canada, persecution spread. German-born officials and civil servants were fired and university professors and teachers were driven from their jobs. Patriotic Winnipeggers agreed that hamburgers would henceforth be known as "nips". Orchestras stopped playing the works of Wagner and Beethoven. In 1918, the government banned all publishing in "enemy" languages and then relented, provided that English translations were run alongside the foreign text.

On the scale set by European horrors, such persecution was minor but it left ugly memories and uglier precedents. Apart from a few trivial incidents, there was no sabotage and pathetically little espionage in Canada. When the Parliament Buildings burned on February 3, 1916, only the most ardent patriots blamed enemy agents.

Amid the patriotic consensus in English-speaking Canada were a few voices of dissent. Not all pacifists had changed their minds. In Toronto, Alice Chown argued with her prominent uncle that Methodists had been duped by militarism. Laura Hughes, the Minister of Militia's niece, came home from the International Congress of Women at the Hague in 1915 and joined Chown in forming the Canadian Women's Peace Party. In Winnipeg, Fred Dixon condemned the war from his seat in the Manitoba legislature, with moral backing from a dwindling handful of journalists and friends. In time, he was overshadowed by the Reverend James Shaver Woodsworth, a Methodist minister and expert on urban social problems. In contrast to Chown or Creighton, Woodsworth had been converted to pacifism by the war. He was appalled by its pointless cruelty and shocked when clergy turned their pulpits into recruiting platforms. In 1917, Woodsworth's convictions cost him his job and forced him, middle-aged and underweight, to find work loading ships on the Vancouver docks. Less famous was the case of Harry Erland Lee, a Toronto teacher whose attempt to explain both sides of the war led school trustees to rule that he was "unfit to discuss the war before loyal British children". Driven to enlist, Lee became the first Toronto teacher to be killed in the war.

Opponents of the war could hear a discreet supporting chorus of Canadian labour leaders. More had been expected in 1911 when, in sympathy with European socialist and union organizations, the Trades and Labor Congress (TLC) pledged itself to a general strike against war. As happened in Europe, labour's anti-militarism was washed away on the tide of patriotic euphoria. In 1914, so many trade unionists enlisted that some union locals collapsed. J.C. Watters, the TLC president, and his supporters retreated to a position of cautious but persistent criticism of a national war effort that offered neither consultation with labour leaders nor protection for working people. When war fever and wartime wages were forgotten, union officials hoped, members might again follow their chosen leaders.

Neither unions nor pacifists had much impact on French-Canadian opinion. Foreigners of any description found as cold a shoulder in Quebec as anywhere in Canada. In 1914, cheering crowds, political speeches, and earnest twinning of the Union Jack and the French *tricolore* suggested that Henri Bourassa, leader of the *nationalistes*, might be right about his *Union sacrée*. "There are no longer French Canadians and English Canadians," rejoiced *La Patrie*. "Only one race now exists, united by the closest bonds in a common cause." Lorenzo Prince of *La Presse* called for a French-Canadian regiment to join France's heroic army.

It was not to be and the government should have been the first to know it. In 1911, Conservative funds had helped elect *nationaliste* MPs, on the specious grounds that Laurier was subservient to Britain and that his navy would lead to conscription for British wars. Settled into their minor portfolios, Borden's French-Canadian ministers might change their views but their supporters would not. Nor did the France of the Third Republic, secular and corrupt, command more than a superficial affection in Quebec. To a Canadien, France was as foreign a country as England was to a Rhode Islander. As for moral crusading, it was not a Quebec style.

Besides, Quebec had an issue closer to home: Ontario's Regulation 17. "The enemies of the French language, of French civilization in Canada, are not the Boches...," thundered Bourassa, "but the English-Canadian anglicisers, the Orange intriguers, or Irish priests." If Borden wanted national unity for the wartime struggle, let him persuade Ontario to restore the educational rights of Franco-Ontarians. Borden insisted that he could do nothing: education was a provincial matter. Indeed, by 1916, Manitoba had followed Ontario's oppressive lead. Wartime patriotism was making it easier for English Canadians to insist on a homogeneous, English-speaking, British Canada. In Quebec, Bourassa's following grew correspondingly.

It was not yet dominant. Crowds cheered in October 1914 when Laurier invoked the memory of Adam Dollard des Ormeaux, the saviour of Montreal from the Iroquois, to raise recruits for the war. In 1916 a Conservative minister, Arthur Sévigny won his rural seat in a hard-fought by-election. There was more talk than money when Bourassa appealed for aid for *les blessés de l'Ontario*. If Quebec's Cardinal Bégin did little to conceal his suspicions of the Borden government and the war effort, Montreal's Archbishop Bruchési was openly sympathetic to the Conservatives. At root, most French Canadians felt little engagement with the issues of the war or of Ontario schools. Few enlisted in the Canadian Expeditionary Force; few sent money to the numerous Franco-Ontarian appeals. Bourassa spoke most eloquently for Québécois when he insisted that the first duty of all Canadians was to themselves. Canada should profit from the war, like its American neighbours, by sending food, shells, and other supplies, and keeping strict account of the bills. To send more and more men to the war was "to reduce the number and influence of...real Canadians, whether of British or French extraction, and to increase the power of the foreign element, especially of German and Slavs".

In March 1916, Talbot Papineau, now a captain, tried to counter Bourassa's growing leadership of French Canada by pleading for a common devotion to Canada. "At this moment as I write, French and English Canadians are fighting and dying side by side. Is their sacrifice to go for nothing, or will it not cement a foundation for a true Canadian nation?..." It was a message without meaning for Quebec. Bourassa dismissed it as a fake, from someone "utterly unqualified" to speak for French Canada.

It was a view that extended beyond Quebec. French Canadians were not the only people whose links to a mother country were attenuated by centuries. Middle-class crusading patriots did not speak for all Canadians. The war was a long way off. "Doing your bit" could mean profiting from soaring food prices, collecting wartime wages, or bidding on a profitable munitions contract as well as buying a tag for Belgian relief. It need not mean risking life or limb in Flanders. Canadian-born recruits had been scarce at Valcartier; they took time to convince.

JOINING UP

When the Canadian Contingent reached England in mid-October, the famous recruiting posters — Lord Kitchener, grim and finger-pointing, with the words "Your King and Country need you" — were rain-soaked and fading. By January 1915, Kitchener had collected 1.2 million volunteers for his New Army. Sam Hughes believed that Canadians would do just as well. At New York, as he boarded a liner for England, he boasted to reporters, "We could send enough men to add the finishing touches to Germany without assistance either from England or France." A Second Contingent, twelve more battalions, was authorized on October 9. In November, after militia cavalry complained of being overlooked, the government approved thirteen new regiments of Canadian Mounted Rifles. In January, Hughes announced a Third Contingent: "I could raise three more contingents in three weeks," he added. Promoted to major-general — out of British gratitude for not trying to command the Canadians in France — Hughes covered seven thousand miles that month, making recruiting speeches. "We are coming, General Kitchener, 500,000 strong!" he shouted. Audiences roared. Hughes was sublimely happy.

Hughes had a simple view of recruiting: he wanted the largest army imaginable. A thousand recruits meant a battalion; half that made a cavalry regiment. In early 1916, he promised audiences an army of twenty-one divisions, five of them from Toronto alone. The draining away of manpower through sickness, desertion, unsuitability, and battlefield casualties did not interest him. How Canadian divisions in battle were to keep their ranks full when every recruit joined a new battalion was not his concern. Perhaps, as one of Hughes's biographers suggests, his mind "could not handle these sorts of details". They were left to the weary General Gwatkin, armed with British figures showing that each division in the field needed between 15,000 and 20,000 new men each year. At that rate, Gwatkin advised, Canada could support two, perhaps three, divisions: "who shall say how long this war will last," he warned.

Hughes paid no heed. Neither did Borden. Canadian men would "do their bit". At Halifax, in December 1914, the prime minister insisted: "There has not been, there will not be, compulsion or conscription." By the end of 1914, the Canadian Expeditionary Force (CEF) had enlisted 56,584 men. In June 1915, the government set the authorized strength at 150,000. In November, after a discouraging visit to England and France, Borden raised the total to 250,000. An even grander gesture was needed. In his New Year's message for 1916, "in token of Canada's unflinchable resolve to crown the justice of our cause with victory and with an abiding peace," Borden announced that the CEF would rise to 500,000 men.

For a country of eight million people, it was a bold promise. For once, there was criticism from the government's side. Lord Shaughnessy, president of the CPR, warned that so large a commitment might endanger Canada's productive strength. "Piffle," said Hughes. In 1915, monthly enlistments rose from 9,363 in January to 22,581 in December. Of seventy-one battalions authorized by the autumn of 1915, all but two raised their full complement and thirty-four sent extra reinforcement drafts overseas. Not only were young Canadians eager to enlist, the government's recruiting methods proved the cheapness of voluntarism. Without asking for a penny from Ottawa, militia units paid the costs of raising new battalions from their own regimental funds. With expenses ranging from advertising to band instruments, reported the *Toronto Daily Star*, the price of recruiting a battalion averaged $13,384. To back up the effort, women's organizations, recruiting associations, and a Speakers' Patriotic League held meetings, raised money, and spotted likely prospects. Hundreds of young men, eager to join the exciting new war in the air, learned that both the Royal Flying Corps and the Royal Naval Air Service demanded prior qualifications. When J.A.D. McCurdy, Canada's aviation pioneer, opened a school for pilots in 1915 at Lakeview in present-day Mississauga, he charged $400 for 400 minutes of flying. Hundreds lined up for a chance. Hundreds more went to the United States for pilot training. By 1917, 750 young Canadians had left Canada to join the British flying services; others joined overseas.

It went without saying that voluntary recruiting and enlistment guaranteed a CEF that would make Canadians proud. Colonels could choose who joined their battalions. Germans, of course, were banned after the rumour that a former RNWMP sergeant had been found dead in a German uniform. Native Indians were welcome despite official fears that they might not enjoy "the privileges of civilized warfare"; Asiatics were not welcome, though a handful of Japanese Canadians fled B.C. prejudice to enlist in Alberta battalions. Despite occasional support from Hughes, blacks found it impossible to enlist. In 1916, "coloureds" were finally allowed to join a labour company that went to France to chop trees. Some battalions had a harder time finding men. A company of Russians and other assorted naturalized "foreigners" filled out the ranks of the 41st French-Canadian Battalion.

Despite Borden's pledges and Hughes's optimism, there soon were warning signs. As early as January 1915, results from the hinterland led the Toronto *Globe* to ask: "Is rural Ontario losing its imperial spirit?" Recruiting lagged in the Maritimes and, more notoriously, in Quebec. In July, the Militia Department cut its standards for height and chest measurement. In August married men no longer needed a wife's permission to join up; men who had enlisted lost the right to buy their way out for $15. By the autumn, even wealthy militia regiments had exhausted their funds. Increasingly the recruiting leagues turned their fire on a government that was doing nothing to help. Patriotic rallies heard demands for conscription or at least national registration so that "slackers" and "shirkers" could be identified and prodded to "do their bit".

Hughes briskly turned the tables on his critics. If the militia was failing, civilian organizations could do far better. Colonels did not have to be soldiers; what he wanted were "strong men who have successful business or professional training". Between the autumn of 1915 and the summer of 1916, 150 new battalions were authorized. Recruiting entered its most frenzied phase. In Toronto, by early 1916, eight battalions competed for men; in Winnipeg there were six; in Edmonton, three. Colonel Vaux Chadwick's 123rd Battalion led the way in "shaming" tactics, urging women to refuse their favours to lily-livered men who would not fight for their country; Colonel Kingsmill's 124th Battalion, in contrast, invited "pals" to enlist. Both Toronto units got their quota. Three battalions invited Irish recruits; a score offered the attraction of Highland kilts and bagpipes. A Winnipeg battalion got its quota by promising strict temperance; a similar Toronto battalion collapsed when its colonel suffered a nervous breakdown. Two western battalions sought Scandinavians; three Ontario units insisted upon having "Men of the North"; and five looked south of the border — to the dismay of the British Foreign Office — to recruit an "American Legion" (about a thousand joined, though half of them deserted; among those who stayed, four earned the Victoria Cross). Two battalions accepted "Bantams" — men below the minimum height of 5'2"; two others appealed for "Sportsmen". Five companies enlisted university students; they were used to fill the depleted ranks of Princess Patricia's Canadian Light Infantry.

No one had ever claimed that Hughes's recruiting system was efficient. Gwatkin had pleaded in vain for recruiting depots, with proper medical inspection, training, and discipline to fill the ranks of existing units. The minister dismissed such notions as military red tape. Under the pressure of time, sympathy, or a demanding colonel, doctors passed thousands of men as fit who promptly became medical and pension burdens. Elderly patriots who broke under the strain, tubercular cases, and sufferers from insanity added nothing but trouble to the CEF. One man, Wilfrid Lavalée, joined six times and got to England twice though he was variously described as "vagrant", "violent", "alcoholic", and "a dangerous moron" in his numerous discharge papers. He and others like him helped explain why, after 400,000 enlistments, close to one-quarter had "wasted away" without seeing action. The 210th Battalion, "Frontiersmen" raised around Moose Jaw, Saskatchewan, enlisted 1,020 men, paraded 782 for inspection, and embarked only 505 of them for England: 59 had deserted and 152 had been discharged. The high-spirited 118th Battalion, responsible for most of the anti-German riots at Berlin-Kitchener, managed to take only 231 soldiers to war.

On April 14, 1916, leaders of the recruiting leagues brought their frustrations back to Ottawa. Something a lot like coercion was wanted. When a meeting with the prime minister proved futile, they created a Canadian National Service League, with John Godfrey, a Liberal lawyer from Toronto, as chairman. Encouraged by Sir George Foster, Minister of Trade and Commerce, Godfrey identified Quebec as the stumbling block to successful recruiting, voluntary or compulsory. Godfrey also had an answer: a "Bonne Entente" movement to iron out the differences between the French and English. "The Freudian philosophy can be employed with races," he explained, "...the best method of getting rid of interracial differences is by the process of psychoanalysis."

Godfrey was by no means wrong in his observations. While recruiting in the Maritimes also proved disappointing, Quebec's poor results were too obvious to be missed. A more sensitive minister than Hughes might have addressed the problem. If recruiting depended on strong militia regiments, French Canada had very few of them. The few French-speaking senior officers were mostly long past their prime. As for fervent wartime patriotism, it hardly existed outside English-speaking Montreal. In the First Contingent, a single French-speaking company represented Quebec's majority. In October 1914, a delegation of fifty-eight leading Quebeckers persuaded the government to include a French-Canadian battalion in the Second Contingent, but it took wearying months to find the men. When the 22nd French-Canadian Battalion left in May, it took most of French Canada's military spirit with it.

By 1916, eleven battalions were hunting for French-speaking recruits in Quebec; a few more sought Acadians and Métis in the Maritimes and the West. Figures are unreliable since enlistment forms did not indicate a soldier's language, but Militia Department statistics for June 1917 reported 14,100 French-speaking members of the CEF; fewer than half had been recruited by Quebec battalions. More than half the province's infantry recruits were English-speaking. With distinguished exceptions, as the historian of the 22nd Battalion discovered, the quality of French-speaking recruits was dismaying. Olivar Asselin, a wayward disciple of Bourassa, found fellow idealists for the 163rd Battalion, the "Poil-aux-Pattes", and the 189th Battalion found tough, hard-fighting farmers and fishermen from the Gaspé. Other recruits had too evidently been attracted by the promise of regular meals and a warm overcoat, or by the 206th Battalion slogan, "le dernier régiment à partir; le premier à profiter de la victoire".

Justifications for French Canada's dismal performance flowed easily. Hughes's Orange bigotry, refusal to form a French-Canadian brigade, failure to give commands to Major-General Lessard (aged fifty-five) or the stone-deaf Colonel Pelletier, and the choice of a Methodist clergyman to inspire recruiting in Montreal were all charges reiterated by Liberals. Later observers noted that, like Maritimers, Canadiens married young and stayed on the farm, two of many arguments against enlistment. The plain fact was that French Canadians felt little identity with the war, and very few in French Canada attempted to change their minds. Laurier gave speeches of remarkable eloquence, once in 1914 and once again in 1916. When Borden's ministers spoke, they were reminded of their *nationaliste* speeches of 1911. In 1916, the Militia Department finally recognized that Quebec was not a province like the others, appointed a patriotic pharmaceutical manufacturer, Arthur Mignault — not a Methodist! — as chief recruiting officer, and gave him staff and a budget. The effort utterly failed. The luckless Mignault only added his recriminations to those that flooded into the government's mail.

Outside Quebec, Borden's 1916 appeal and the recruiting leagues had some effect. January 1916, with 28,185 recruits, was the best month ever, until March, with 33,960. Then the totals fell — 10,059 in June, 5,717 in September, 4,930 in December. Almost no one had volunteered for the infantry. Kilts, white feathers, displays of German atrocities, speeches by war heroes — nothing made any difference. Instead of 500,000 men, the CEF ended 1916 with 299,937 men and women in its ranks. Most who joined after mid-1916 enlisted in the Canadian Forestry Corps or the fast-growing Corps of Canadian Railway Troops, not the infantry battalions.

Bonne-Ententism led to a couple of talkative meetings with prominent Quebeckers, but no change of policy or attitude. Appointment of Montreal financier Sir Thomas Tait as Director General of National Service led only to his indignant resignation when his choice of staff was criticized. In the fall, R.B. Bennett, a millionaire lawyer and Calgary MP, reluctantly agreed to chair the National Service Board. Its role was to conduct a national registration through the distribution of cards, although their completion and return was not compulsory. Voluntarism died hard. Only in June 1917 were the cards fully counted: four out of five had filled them out; perhaps 286,976 could be available for service. A little more hard work by the recruiting leagues showed that *available* did not mean willing to enlist. Those Canadians who would "do their bit" in the war had done it. Voluntarism was over.

ORGANIZING SIDE-SHOWS

By 1915, the war in France and Belgium had settled into a stalemate. The Western Front stretched along a five-hundred–mile belt of trenches and barbed wire. The Eastern Front, vast, more sparsely fortified, and mobile, offered no greater hope of easy victory. The victors of Tannenberg had advanced cautiously into Poland but their Austrian allies had suffered only defeats. Habsburg forces had dissolved before the advancing Russians, leaving 350,000, either dead or captured, and falling back to the Carpathians. Even the Serbs had found the strength to hurl the Austrians from their soil. Everywhere the generals and politicians faced the new year with promises of early victory and secret quandaries about how to achieve it.

The French and Belgians saw few options. King Albert had to cling to the little strip of Belgium that remained, preserve his army, and hope that it would be strong enough to justify renewed Belgian independence if the Allies ever won. The French, too, were almost wholly preoccupied with regaining the ugliest, coldest, wettest, and most valuable part of their country. General Joffre's strategy, faithful adherence to Plan XVII had cost France most of its iron, its coal, and a great many of the factories that could produce the munitions of war. He and his generals promised that it could all be won back. The French faith in the offensive was unbroken. If the French allowed themselves any distraction, it was to coax, bribe, and bully Italy into the war. One of their paid agents was an ex-socialist agitator named Benito Mussolini. On May 23, 1915, the French had their way; Italy declared war on Austria-Hungary.

The Russian Tsar and his generals had no plans at all. At the end of 1914, Grand Duke Nicholas, the commander-in-chief, let his allies know that Russia could do no more. Victory and defeat alike had exhausted Russia's reserves of ammunition, artillery, and even rifles. Without weapons, the Russian steamroller could not move. In October 1914, after years of German influence, Turkey entered the war against the Entente. Not only did the Russians face a new enemy, but their only warm-water ports were cut off from the Mediterranean. Getting supplies from Arctic ports or from Vladivostok was a near-hopeless expedient, though a few Canadians were sent to help build railways. Without massive Allied help, the enormous potential power of Russia would be lost.

Perhaps because they had thought harder about war than other people, German leaders were even more desperate. They found themselves in the two-front war their strategists had always predicted they would lose. Britain's maritime blockade, proclaimed at the outset of war, reminded Germans that their faith that the war would end quickly had kept them from stockpiling scarce materials. German divisions would also be needed to prop up her hopeless Habsburg ally. Germany's magnificent fleet sat impotent in harbour. An early brush with the Royal Navy off Heligoland had cost three cruisers. "The Emperor," reported Admiral von Tirpitz, "did not want losses of this sort."

Germany's battleships were not quite useless. As the American naval theorist Alfred Mahan had taught both German and British admirals, a "fleet in being" was a powerful threat. In case the Germans ever came out, Britain was forced to keep her Grand Fleet, twenty-seven Dreadnoughts strong, ready and waiting at dreary Scottish naval bases. The British also discovered another danger. On September 22, 1914, in a couple of hours, a single German submarine torpedoed three elderly British cruisers. The Grand Fleet headed to sea in panic; its wartime bases had yet to be protected against the u-boat menace. Germany could open a new front: on February 4, 1915, neutrals and belligerents alike were notified that their ships might be sunk on sight: Germany was blockading Britain. The British were appalled. There was virtually no effective countermeasure against submarines; they could not even be detected unless they surfaced. There was, however, one weapon: public opinion. Sinking ships without allowing the crews to find safety was shockingly contrary to the rules of war. On May 7, 1915, the Germans were taught a lesson when a U-boat sank the British liner *Lusitania*, sister-ship of the *Titanic*. Many American passengers were aboard; 128 of them were among the 1,195 who drowned. British propaganda, shrewdly managed, amplified American indignation. In August, the Germans ended their unrestricted blockade.

For the most part, the Kaiser's far-flung empire and naval bases proved useless. The German China squadron, hurrying home, had demolished Admiral Cradock's obsolete cruisers off Chile only to be utterly destroyed off the Falklands on December 7 by a more powerful British squadron. By 1915, almost all of Germany's commerce-raiding cruisers had been destroyed, one of them by an Australian cruiser. In South Africa, Louis Botha and Jan Smuts forgot the bitterness of the Boer War, crushed a revolt of fellow Afrikaners who did not, and rewarded themselves by acquiring German South West Africa. Other German colonies fell as easily, from Tsingtao, captured by the Japanese, to Togoland. The sole exception was German East Africa, where General Paul von Lettow-Vorbeck smashed a British landing force at Tanga on December 5 and then led his tiny army inland to out-run and out-fight vastly superior British and South African forces for the rest of the war. Von Lettow-Vorbeck's 3,500 white and 12,000 black troops kept 372,950 of the enemy engaged until November 1918. It was Germany's most economical and successful side-show.

The Germans' second most economical side-show opened January 19, 1915, with the first Zeppelin raid on England. The Kaiser had forbidden attacks on residential areas and "above all on the royal palaces" but, at 11,000 feet, bombing was indiscriminate. Forty airship raids killed 537 people and injured 1,358. That was trivial by the standard of other losses but more than enough to persuade editors and politicians to denounce government negligence while Anglican bishops demanded condign vengeance. When the Royal Flying Corps's few planes utterly failed to drive off the invaders, fliers on leave were mobbed. In 1917, when the Zeppelin threat had been beaten by improved fighters, the Germans sent twin-engined Gothas at 15,000 feet. Again civilian casualties mounted, frightened crowds packed London's Underground stations, and factory production on the night shift fell 73 per cent. As the Germans had hoped, the Royal Flying Corps (RFC) was forced to bring its best pilots from France and to build up an air-defence organization that absorbed 200 first-line aircraft and 15,115 men. Thousands of young Canadians were trained for the new air war, particularly in 1917 and 1918, after a few Canadians had proved their courage and skill as pilots and aerial fighters. German bombing and British reaction forced a doubling of the RFC and, ultimately, the creation of a single flying service, the Royal Air Force, as the means of organizing retaliation on Berlin. A Canadian, Colonel W.R. Mulock, commanded the force designed to begin attacking the German capital in December 1918.

In London, most British generals were as scornful of "side-shows" as their French counterparts. Wars could be won, they insisted, only by destroying an enemy's army. Some politicians were equally insistent that there must be a more ingenious way. The solution pointed to Turkey. The British were outraged that an old, if despised, ally had lined up with the enemy. Yet the Ottoman Empire, with its corrupt leaders and hopeless army, surely offered a chance of easy victories unavailable in France. The point was made when the Turks launched an army of 90,000 into the Russian Caucasus; only 18,000 frozen, beaten survivors straggled back. A smaller Turkish army attacked at Suez. A weak British garrison, backed by the newly arrived Australian and New Zealand Army Corps (ANZAC), drove them off. Dreams of conquering Palestine and Syria blossomed in British minds. A force from India landed at the Persian Gulf and captured Basra. Soon the British edged north, up the Tigris towards Mesopotamia and Baghdad.

No one could claim that winning Palestine and Mesopotamia would defeat Germany but they were irresistible prizes to a country that had always used war to add to its empire. Once launched, the British campaigns could not be limited. Nor could they be easily won. The Turkish army was ill-equipped and horribly administered but its troops were brave, German-led, and provided with artillery, machine guns, and shovels — the implements of the Western Front war. British generals assigned to the Turkish campaigns were old, stubborn, and often second-rate. Their armies were savaged by sickness, heat, maladministration, and a sense of futility. The British finally took Baghdad in 1918 but not before 889,702 British and Indian troops had gone to the Persian Gulf and only after a British division was forced to surrender at Kut-el-Amara in April 1916 and marched into a horrible captivity, which few survived. The Palestine campaign won Jerusalem at Christmas 1917, but not until a series of humiliating defeats had first drawn 1,192,511 men from Britain, India, and the Antipodes.

Only one thrust at Turkey promised a war-winning dividend. By forcing the Dardanelles, the straits that separated European and Asiatic Turkey, Russia's allies could open a way to the Black Sea. Russian wheat could then pay for Allied munitions and the Russian military steamroller could move again. Forcing the Straits was no new idea; the Royal Navy had repeatedly planned such an operation before the war and it had regularly concluded that the job *could* be done — but only if troops were landed to neutralize the Turkish guns. At the Admiralty, an ambitious Winston Churchill was bent on building his reputation. There were no troops: Lord Kitchener refused to provide them. Churchill demanded action anyway. A fleet of obsolete British and French battleships twice silenced the Turkish forts, only to withdraw for rest. The Turks rebuilt the forts, mined the Straits, and, on March 18, sank four old Allied battleships and damaged others. It was all they could do. The rest of the fleet could have sailed on to Constantinople. Instead, it turned back. The Allied admirals had had enough: they would not proceed without an army.

Another month passed. A German general, Otto Liman von Sanders, took command of the defences. On April 25, a small army of ANZACs and British regulars poured ashore at the tip of the Gallipoli peninsula; they met barbed wire, machine guns, artillery, and valiant resistance from Turkish troops, commanded in part by Kemal Pasha, the future creator of modern Turkey. The survivors clung to a couple of narrow beach-heads. Through the heat of the summer, sickness and snipers took a terrible toll. Both sides attacked with huge losses and no more success than assaults on the Western Front. On August 6, the British landed more divisions, at Suvla Bay. Inexperienced troops and hopelessly unenterprising generals turned a near-victory into another stalemate. In December, in the only brilliant operation of the campaign, the British and ANZACs slipped away from Gallipoli and Suvla without leaving a man. They had lost 213,890 casualties, a majority of them through sickness, a few from frostbite. For Australians, the suffering, losses, and futility of ANZAC Beach and Gallipoli became a unifying national memory.

The fiasco had other consequences. Bulgaria watched the disaster, waited for its 1915 harvest, and, on September 6, joined Germany and Austria. Vengeance was a motive: in 1913, Serbia had robbed her of Macedonia. In October, as German and Austrian divisions drove south into Serbia, the Bulgarians struck from the east. Serbian resistance collapsed. Half the Serbian army and tens of thousands of refugees perished in a winter retreat across the mountains to Albania and the Adriatic. The starving, frost-bitten survivors were taken to Corfu to recuperate.

There was almost nothing more the Allies could do for land-locked Serbia. The French dictated the response: a landing at Salonika with 150,000 troops to force neutral Greece into the war, and to drive north against Belgrade and Bucharest. The drive failed at the Vardar: the despised Bulgarians turned out to be tough soldiers, with machine guns too, if not very many of them. The usual stalemate followed. The British suggested withdrawal; the French insisted on staying: by 1917 more than half a million British, French, Serbian, and Russian troops were camped at Salonika, facing a Bulgarian army that had no intention of moving. Like Gallipoli, the Salonika front was hot in summer, cold in winter, disease-ridden, and hopelessly miserable. The Germans boasted that it was their biggest internment camp. They were right.

Brigadier-General Sir J.E. Edmonds, the British official historian of the war, dismissed the "side-shows" as "a drain on the resources of the British Empire without being a corresponding embarrassment to Germany". They were certainly not the route to victory in 1915. Was there another way?

III
LEARNING WAR

Liverpool was the normal destination for Canadians crossing the Atlantic but the Admiralty's new fear of submarines sent the Canadian convoy to the little West Country port of Plymouth. At dawn on October 15, welcoming crowds saw the first mist-shrouded ships enter Plymouth Sound. The welcome turned chilly. After days on board ship, officers and men broke ranks to try the potent English beer. Captain J.F.C. Fuller, an officer sent by the War Office to help with disembarkation, was told that Canadians were not "coolies" and would not unload their own ships. He managed it in nine days with a thousand British "New Army" recruits. A nightly "Drunkards' Express" delivered Canadian stragglers to their new camp on Salisbury Plain. Their equipment was piled along a country road near Plymouth for units to sort and collect. With six months' training, Fuller told his mother, Canadians would make fine soldiers "if all their officers were shot".

The Canadians had less than four months to become an infantry division. At Salisbury, conditions were ideal — for a week. Of 123 days the Contingent spent in England, it rained for 89. Gales flattened tents, rain turned to sleet and snow, and the thin topsoil turned to mud. Soldiers learned the dilemma of whether to sleep in a sodden uniform or to put it on again in the morning. Some officers joined their wives in nearby hotels or fled to London. The men stayed put or went absent without leave. Under the driving rain, with a handful of British instructors, battalions practised route marching, bayonet fighting, and, when the few ranges were available, shooting. Much of their equipment was gratefully abandoned. Canadian boots dissolved in the mud, Bain wagons collapsed under a full load of ammunition, and MacAdam shovels — impossible to carry and by no means bulletproof — were left to rust. For all its defects, the Ross remained: with fourteen Territorial and eighteen

A C.E.F. battalion, escorted a potential soldier for the next world war, undergoes he only useful training it could get in Canada in 1915, a route march. The lack of weapons and equipment was no accident. Canada had nothing but Canadian-made uniforms to give its soldiers, and even they would be replaced by better-made, more serviceable British uniforms once the soldiers reached England.

A heavy gun of a Canadian siege battery was an impressive sight when fired at night. While its shell might pulverize a poorly-built German dugout, its accuracy and range made it more useful as a weapon to destroy German field artillery, a skill Canadian gunners began to master in 1917.

Departing soldiers and "the girls they left behind them." Until 1915 wives had to give written permission for their husbands to depart— but the mood of the times favoured sacrifice for king and country, and the Patriotic Fund promised to compensate for a soldier's meagre pay.

Artillerymen, in a motley collection of uniforms, practise on an 18-pounder field gun. In patriotic passion, Colonel Sam Hughes shipped all the modern guns in Canada to Britain, leaving none for later contingents or for training.

Hughes watches "his boys" off the Gaspé coast in 1914. As a minister Hughes had an imperfect grasp of the separation of civil and military powers. He also had supreme confidence in his own judgement.

A practice trench in Winnipeg would have looked ridiculous to any veteran of France or Flanders, but Canadians were trained by officers and soldiers whose only knowledge of war came from manuals, newspapers, and perhaps memories of service in South Africa.

Motor vehicles for the First Contingent parade the mechanized
modernity of Canada's army. Nine different manufacturers provided
140 cars and trucks for the Contingent. Hughes boasted that they
would show Canada's industrial potential, but because of a lack of
parts or poor design most never got farther than England.

Toronto's Mayor Tommy Church bids farewell to Italian reservists after Italy joins the Allied side in 1915. Thousands of immigrants returned to their European homelands to fulfil reserve commitments—including a good many who slipped out via the neutral U.S. to fight for Germany or the Austro-Hungarian Empire.

By 1916, new CEF battalions had to struggle for recruits. The 198th Battalion—"The Canadian Buffs"—rented a Toronto streetcar as a mobile recruiting station. "Drumming up" recruits was an older tradition.

In the First World War, recruiting was utterly dependent on local initiative and funds. For the government this was a cheap and congenial solution. This recruiting station in rural Halton county was typical of many.

A C.E.F. battalion, escorted a potential soldier for the next world war, undergoes he only useful training it could get in Canada in 1915, a route march. The lack of weapons and equipment was no accident. Canada had nothing but Canadian-made uniforms to give its soldiers, and even they would be replaced by better-made, more serviceable British uniforms once the soldiers reached England.

A heavy gun of a Canadian siege battery was an impressive sight when fired at night. While its shell might pulverize a poorly-built German dugout, its accuracy and range made it more useful as a weapon to destroy German field artillery, a skill Canadian gunners began to master in 1917.

Departing soldiers and "the girls they left behind them." Until 1915
wives had to give written permission for their husbands to depart—
but the mood of the times favoured sacrifice for king and country,
and the Patriotic Fund promised to compensate for a soldier's
meagre pay.

Artillerymen, in a motley collection of uniforms, practise on an 18-pounder field gun. In patriotic passion, Colonel Sam Hughes shipped all the modern guns in Canada to Britain, leaving none for later contingents or for training.

Hughes watches "his boys" off the Gaspé coast in 1914. As a minister Hughes had an imperfect grasp of the separation of civil and military powers. He also had supreme confidence in his own judgement.

A practice trench in Winnipeg would have looked ridiculous to any veteran of France or Flanders, but Canadians were trained by officers and soldiers whose only knowledge of war came from manuals, newspapers, and perhaps memories of service in South Africa.

Motor vehicles for the First Contingent parade the mechanized modernity of Canada's army. Nine different manufacturers provided 140 cars and trucks for the Contingent. Hughes boasted that they would show Canada's industrial potential, but because of a lack of parts or poor design most never got farther than England.

Toronto's Mayor Tommy Church bids farewell to Italian reservists after Italy joins the Allied side in 1915. Thousands of immigrants returned to their European homelands to fulfil reserve commitments—including a good many who slipped out via the neutral U.S. to fight for Germany or the Austro-Hungarian Empire.

By 1916, new CEF battalions had to struggle for recruits. The 198th Battalion—"The Canadian Buffs"—rented a Toronto streetcar as a mobile recruiting station. "Drumming up" recruits was an older tradition.

In the First World War, recruiting was utterly dependent on local initiative and funds. For the government this was a cheap and congenial solution. This recruiting station in rural Halton county was typical of many.

"New Army" divisions to equip, the British had no better rifles to spare, even if Hughes had allowed them.

By January, the best twelve battalions of the First Contingent had been selected and their organization was set, for the third and final time, at four companies each. Days of drill and polishing climaxed on February 4, 1915, in a review for King George V. A week later, the Canadian Division had left for France.

Raising a second contingent took longer. Most of the experienced officers and almost all of Canada's tiny stock of modern weapons had gone in October. The British pleaded a lack of accommodation. It was spring before the infantry battalions left Canada and August before the last artillery batteries reached England. Sensitive to Canadian outrage at the conditions on Salisbury Plain, the War Office evicted a British division from huts at Shorncliffe Camp near Dover and installed the Canadians. As scores of new battalions were authorized in Canada that summer, more and more units were despatched overseas. Canadian camps spread to Witley, Bramshott, Seaford, Hastings, and other towns of southern England. Scores and ultimately hundreds of surplus officers, left over from contingents and broken-up battalions, manoeuvred themselves into staff positions.

Men in the ranks rarely had that kind of influence. Whatever his high patriotic motives, once a man mumbled his oath of allegiance and signed his attestation papers, he had lost most of the rights he had ever enjoyed as a civilian. Under military law he could suffer "death or lesser penalty" for a score of acts, from cowardice in the face of the enemy to sleeping while a sentry. Lesser penalties ranged from extra drill to "Field Punishment No. 1" — being lashed to a wagon wheel for an hour each morning and evening for such offences as "absence without leave", forgetting to shave, or "dumb insolence". A soldier forfeited privacy, dignity, and autonomy. Obey orders was the general principle; ask questions later — or never — was the army's rule. Drill, with sergeants bellowing personal abuse, attempted to turn a soldier into an obedient automaton. In 1914, Hughes had insisted that "his boys" could choose whether to be inoculated for typhoid fever. That kind of choice faded fast. By 1916, medical officers regularly instructed men to drop their pants so that their genitals could be inspected for symptoms of gonorrhoea. In camp, soldiers were jammed ten or fifteen to a tent twenty feet in diameter; in barracks, they were crowded into ill-heated frame huts, occasionally two to a bed.

Canadians modelled their army on what they had learned from childhood was Britain's greatest military institution, the infantry battalion. Pre-war militia units had painstakingly imitated the uniforms, customs, and traditions of British regiments; under their drab khaki uniformity, CEF battalions did the same. Militia Headquarters issued a standard maple-leaf badge but battalions designed and purchased their own. Kilts and bonnets for would-be Scottish battalions, black buttons for the Winnipeg and Nova Scotia "Rifles", even the white goats some units boasted as mascots were borrowed from British regimental traditions in hopes of instant *esprit de corps.*

Canadian volunteers inherited less traditional features of Queen Victoria's armies. Peacetime soldiers had been recruited from the bottom of society, from men who were presumably unfit for better work. Even in the army's idiom, "soldiering" meant shirking. Endless supervision and brutal punishments were necessary because peacetime soldiers could be counted on to dodge work, malinger their way to hospital, and do the least possible. In army language, any chore was a "fatigue". Even in wartime, a soldier's pay, clothing, and food ranked him among society's poor. At $1.10 a day, a Canadian private was better off than any Allied soldier but he earned half the rate paid a Canadian unskilled labourer in 1915. In camp, his meals consisted of a few monotonous staples: porridge and tea for breakfast; stew and a pudding for dinner; bread, cheese or jam, and tea for supper. Over longjohns or a cotton vest and underpants, a soldier wore a coarse grey-flannel shirt, khaki serge jacket and trousers, heavy boots, and puttees — long strips of wool that an infantryman wound up from his ankles to his knees (a cavalryman or gunner wound them down his legs).

Officers, in contrast to "men", were gentlemen, a breed apart. They were commissioned, not enlisted. They wore tailored uniforms, with a collar and tie, and a leather Sam Browne belt carefully polished by a soldier-servant or "batman". Soldiers saluted officers, called them "sir", and spoke to them only when spoken to. Striking an officer was a capital offence. Officers — and sergeants, too — lived and ate separately. Table manners and an ability to abide by "mess etiquette" were among the expectations imposed on a would-be officer. The sergeants' mess aped the officers'.

Over time, the CEF evolved its own style. It was a slow process. Until October 1916, Canadian soldiers were part of the British army, disciplined by the Army Act. Officers were issued British as well as Canadian commissions. The affinity was more than legal. Every senior officer in the CEF and a quarter of the men in the ranks had belonged to the pre-war militia, with its British-style uniforms and procedures. Almost 20,000 had served in the British regular army. Next to the colonel, the most important figure in many new CEF battalions was an elderly British veteran who acted as regimental sergeant-major. He and the sergeants, chosen from those with any prior military experience, indoctrinated raw Canadians in their new way of life. British soldiers were the backbone of many CEF units, passing on the customs and language of Indian cantonments a decade earlier. A "chit" was any army form, a "dekko" was a look-see, a "wallah" was anyone of importance.

In Canada, soldiers discovered that "kicking" and complaining would win public sympathy against harsh conditions or over-zealous officers. At Camp Borden in June 1916, anger at the heat, blowing sand, and shortage of water produced a noisy demonstration against Sam Hughes that no hurriedly imposed censorship could suppress. Once in England, there was no audience for such protests. Soldiers also found that they had spent months and even years in Canada without adequate training. Officers appointed because they could attract volunteers usually had no time, knowledge, or inclination to be instructors or disciplinarians. In England, British instructors usually rated newly arrived Canadians as two-week recruits. Drill, route marches, and shooting began again. Once in England, battalions raised on the pledge that friends would fight shoulder to shoulder with friends were ruthlessly dissolved. By 1916, the army in France needed only privates and lieutenants.

In Canada or in England, soldiers learned that they were part of a complex organization. In the infantry, a soldier knew his section best: ten to fifteen men under a corporal or lance corporal. A lieutenant commanded a platoon of four sections, with a sergeant as *alter ego* and second-in-command. Four platoons formed a company, under a major or captain. A battalion of four companies, with a lieutenant-colonel in command, was a soldier's "unit", the "family" to which he returned from hospital or a course. That was why breaking up any battalion was traumatic. Soldiers soon formed new loyalties to the 8th "Little Black Devils" from Winnipeg; the 29th Battalion, "Tobin's Tigers" from Vancouver; or the elite 42nd, one of three CEF battalions raised by Montreal's Royal Highlanders. A division — 18,000 to 20,000 men — was commanded by a major-general and included three infantry brigades of four battalions, each commanded by a brigadier-general. Two or more divisions formed an army corps under a lieutenant-general. An army controlled several corps. Staff officers, with red tabs on their collars and a red band around their caps, were a hated and despised by-product of the army's higher organization.

A battalion was the limit of most soldiers' horizon, but a growing range of supporting arms, services, and specialist organizations developed during the war, from cyclist battalions to a veterinary corps. Just behind the infantry were batteries of field artillery with 18-pounder guns. Much farther back was heavier artillery — 4.5-inch howitzers and 60-pounder guns, with shells able to collapse dug-outs or shatter concrete. Trench mortars, throwing a few bombs and rushing away to leave retaliation to fall on the infantry, were both effective and deeply disliked. In time, machine-gunners became a specialist corps, with their heavy Vickers guns. By 1918, each infantry platoon had its own temperamental Lewis gun. Men specialized as snipers, machine-gunners, rifle grenadiers, and "bombers". Sick and wounded depended for evacuation and treatment on the Army Medical Corps, while the unloved but essential Army Service Corps delivered food, ammunition, and fuel — usually at a safe distance from the fighting.

The British, and some Canadians who should have known better, imagined that Canadians (and Australians) adjusted well to soldiering because of their customary robust, outdoor life. In fact, barely a quarter of the CEF came from farming, mining, or frontier occupations. Almost as many were from clerical, sales, or professional backgrounds and more than a third were recruited from urban manufacturing, construction, and labouring jobs. What such men brought to the army was the rigid discipline of pre-1914 industrial society. Teachers, parents, foremen, and employers had exacted conformity and obedience. The army reinforced what society had begun in the home, school, factory, or office. Civilians also enjoyed fewer creature comforts in 1915; it was no sudden hardship to be cold, wet, or hungry. If there was a British accent to the CEF it was also, conveniently, the accent of most of the men in the ranks of the Canadian Corps until 1916.

That did not guarantee that "soldiering" came easily. Canadians resented the "coolie" burden of large pack, haversack, greatcoat, spare boots, water-bottle, rifle, bayonet, 150 rounds of ammunition of "full marching order", when transport could easily halve the eighty-pound burden. Grudgingly and seldom did Canadian soldiers accept the special privileges of junior officers when they knew that a commission in the CEF usually rewarded social or political "pull" or a few extra years of education. Until 1916, commissions were awarded to men who could persuade a militia colonel in Canada to make them officers. Even officers promoted from the ranks were suspect, perhaps all the more so because they had abandoned their comrades for a life of relative privilege. Like army food and the weather, officers were accepted by soldiers as part of a temporary and unnatural existence, but some day there might be a reckoning. Robert Correll, a quiet, friendly soldier with two more months to live in the summer of 1916, explained to his sister: "I guess you will notice that a number of officers have been killed or wounded. It seems a hard thing to say but from what we can learn the ones that used the men dirty over here sometimes get 'accidentally' shot during a charge...."

TRENCH WARFARE

A legend that Hughes stopped the break-up of the Contingent by bearding Lord Kitchener at the War Office is colourful fantasy. The British had intended, from August 1914, to use the Canadians as a division. To ensure that Sam Hughes would not take command, they offered a choice of their available generals. Hughes settled for Sir Edwin Alderson, a conscientious fifty-five–year–old veteran who had commanded Canadians during the South African War.

By no means all those who had landed at Plymouth went to France with the 1st Canadian Division. Newfoundland's contingent, raised in a dominion with no better peacetime army than the popular Church Lads' Brigade, reached England without rifles, equipment, or even military caps. To safeguard their separate identity, the Newfoundlanders left the CEF in December 1914, went north to Scotland, joined the British 29th Division at Gallipoli in September 1915, and returned with it to France in 1916. The Princess Patricia's Canadian Light Infantry (PPCLI), with its trained British reservists, went to France on December 20, 1914, as part of the 27th Division. Canada's two permanent-force cavalry regiments and a brigade of Royal Canadian Horse Artillery formed most of the Canadian Cavalry Brigade. To Hughes's indignation, the War Office gave the command to Colonel J.E.B. Seely, a British amateur soldier, adventurer, and politician who had been Kitchener's predecessor at the War Office until the "Curragh Mutiny". Never again, Hughes insisted, would Canadians be denied a voice in choosing their commanders.

Normally, British troops crossed the Channel from Dover or Folkestone to Le Havre. Fear of losing a shipload of Canadians to a U-boat persuaded the Admiralty to order a longer, rougher journey from Avonmouth to St. Nazaire, on February 16. Officers climbed into battered coaches; other ranks squeezed into tiny French cattle cars with the familiar markings: "Hommes — 40 Chevaux — 8". Two days' journey across France took them to Hazebrouck on the Belgian border, headquarters of General Sir Horace Smith-Dorrien and his new Second British Army. By the end of the month, twinned with British units, most of the battalions had experienced trench warfare in a quiet sector near Armentières.

The worst of a bad winter was almost over by the time the Canadians arrived, but the British trenches along the Flanders plain were as wet, muddy, and dreary as any on the Western Front. Water lay only a couple of feet below the surface. An army that believed its own legends was convinced that it was un-British to retreat to dryer and more defensible ground, even if it could be found. The French and Belgians, whose ground it was, agreed. British defenders did their best in appalling conditions, made worse because no one had foreseen the vast quantities of tools, lumber, barbed wire, and duck-boards, to say nothing of flares, grenades, and artillery ammunition, that trench warfare consumed. A virtual truce at Christmas 1914 helped the British even more than the Germans to improve their defences, but generals, far from the line, punished fraternizers and preached the "offensive spirit". The PPCLI, in the line by December 1914, had won early distinction by launching one of the first trench raids of the war in February 1915.

Canadians learned that front-line defences ideally consisted of three lines of trenches behind a barbed-wire entanglement. A fire trench faced the enemy; a second or "support" trench lay behind it; and a reserve trench was a third line of defence. The French put few men in the front line and counted on destroying attackers with a storm of shells from their famous 75s, followed by a counter-attack. The British insisted on doggedly holding every inch. Brigades manned their sectors with two battalions in the trenches, a third in reserve, and a fourth back under the control of the Division.

Trench routine turned day into night. At dawn and dusk, the likeliest times for an attack, every soldier stood to, fully armed, for an hour. At night, work began: repairing barbed-wire entanglements; shoring up trenches after artillery fire or erosion; fetching and carrying up food, water, ammunition, and building materials. A few men, faces blackened and armed with clubs, knives, and grenades, set out to patrol no man's land, perhaps to seize a prisoner or collect identification from a dead enemy. Periodically, flares lit the sky, machine guns emptied belts of ammunition into the darkness, and artillery would join in until quiet returned.

After the dawn stand-to, most of the troops could rest. Officers could authorize an issue of SRD ("service rum, diluted") after a cold or particularly unpleasant night. Rations, brought up in a sandbag, with tea and sugar tied into separate corners, were distributed—a can of bully beef or Maconochie stew between two or three men, a can of jam or butter between five, a few hardtack biscuits for each man. It was a diet, historian Denis Winter has noted, that left men hungry, flatulent, and afflicted with boils. British generals did not believe in comfort in the trenches: after all, troops should remember that they would be moving on in the spring or summer offensive. Dug-outs were reserved for headquarters and officers' quarters. Soldiers built a shelf or burrowed a "funk-hole" in the trench wall, rolled themselves in a greatcoat and a waterproof sheet, and tried to sleep.

Common sense and military values came into frequent conflict. To the dismay of sergeant-majors and the stuffier officers, soldiers took the stiffening from their caps and hacked off the long skirts of their greatcoats so that mud would not cling to them. Though men in kilted battalions suffered from the cold and from cuts inflicted on the back of their knees from mud-encrusted cloth, pride denied them trousers. In 1916, long after the French and Germans, the British provided their men with steel helmets. The goatskin jerkins and leggings and the washbasin-shaped helmets made soldiers resemble medieval pikemen.

Day and night, soldiers lived in the miasma of rotting corpses and latrines, turned acrid by the odour of chloride of lime. Rats prowled the trenches and gorged on human flesh. Within a few days of reaching France, officers and men alike were infested with lice. Such was the misery that men woke up bleeding from scratches gouged to relieve the itching. In the foul conditions, infection often followed. Only in 1918 was trench fever — "pyrexia of unknown origin", or PUO — traced to body lice. Standing for hours and even days in freezing water produced trench foot, akin to frostbite. Rubbing feet with whale oil and changing socks regularly seemed to curb the swelling. That took systematic discipline: officers of units that reported too many cases of trench foot were warned and then fired.

Armentières was a quiet part of the trench line, where both sides had learned to live and let live. It was a style, British historian Tony Ashworth claims, Australian, Canadian, and Scottish divisions rarely adopted. Letters and memoirs suggest little of the front-line comradeship that purportedly united trench soldiers of both sides against all staff officers, generals, and gunners. Canadians certainly saw the staff as enemies, but they hated Germans too. War was too cruel to love one's opponents.

Even a few days in the front line cost a battalion a dozen or more killed and wounded. On both sides, snipers hid themselves and waited for the unwary. The Germans, who stayed in the same sector for months, were better at their job. Machine guns were no threat to men under cover, but night patrols and wiring parties were easily caught in the open by flares. The worst threat was from mortars and artillery: more than half of all Canadian casualties were the victims of shelling. Until 1917, infantry were the main victims of artillery duels. Under shelling, soldiers could join in a deadly game, dodging from traverse to traverse to escape a slow-moving mortar bomb. More often, men developed a carapace of fatalism; they were safe until that inescapable shell or bullet "with their name on it" arrived. Under a heavy barrage, with the earth shaking and the sky hidden by smoke and dust, there was no fatalism or even courage. It was then that brave men cried, fouled themselves, waited for a sordid death. Charles Yale Harrison, an American in the CEF, recalled a German *minenwerfer* barrage:

I am terrified. I hug the earth, digging my fingers into every crevice, every hole.
A blinding flash and an explosive howl a few feet in front of the trench.
My bowels liquefy.

Acrid smoke bites the throat, parches the mouth. I am beyond mere fright. I am frozen with an insane fear that keeps me cowering in the bottom of the trench. I lie flat on my belly, waiting....

Suddenly it stops.

No single weapon transformed war as much as aircraft. Few foresaw what airplanes — barely eleven years old when the war began — would do, although all the belligerents had them. A single plane had changed the outcome of the Battle of the Marne in 1914. As trench war developed, aircraft and balloons became the only means of seeing beyond the enemy's front line. From the sky, observers spotted artillery targets and guided fire. Air photos became instant maps and the best source of information for army staff officers. Aircraft forced armies to move and work at night and to hide under camouflage. Anti-aircraft guns became a new form of artillery. By the end of the war, they had shot down more planes than the specialized fighter aircraft that caught the public's eye.

The Germans had a technological lead, as in much else, in aircraft engines and frames. By adapting a primitive device on a captured French plane, Anthony Fokker devised an interrupter gear that allowed machine-gun bullets to get past propeller blades. By adapting this to his *Eindekkers*, Fokker created the first real fighter plane. Pilots could merely point their craft at the slow-moving two-seater observation planes, fire, and score a kill. In self-defence, pilots learned the violent evasive manoeuvres their instructors had forbidden because, until 1916, no pilot knew for certain how to pull out of a spin. Fighters became instruments in a struggle for supremacy in the sky. For the winner, the reward was uninterrupted aerial observation and the kind of help Canadians needed on the Somme and at Vimy Ridge to locate German guns and troop movements.

In 1915, Lord Kitchener had invited the dominions to set up their own squadrons. The Australians did so, but a Canadian government that had rejected its own navy wanted no air force. Air-minded Canadians flocked to join the Royal Flying Corps and the Royal Naval Air Service. Though the British tried to reserve their pilot ranks for "officers and gentlemen", Canadians, with their ambiguous class status, met fewer obstacles. Britain's reward was some of its most skilled pilots. Of twenty-seven top Empire "aces" who downed thirty or more aircraft, eleven were Canadians. The best was Lieutenant-Colonel W.A. "Billy" Bishop, who ranked third among all the aces of the war, with seventy-two victories. Lieutenant-Commander Raymond Collishaw of the RNAS was fifth with sixty. Without the Canadians, historian Denis Winter concedes, the British record of victories would have been thin.

Despite legend, few Canadians escaped the trench war into the flying services. In 1916, a shortage of good, experienced infantry officers led the CEF to ban transfers. Instead, ordinary soldiers and their officers faced the alternation of terror and boredom as long as the war — or their lives — continued.

The "front" was only part of their lives. Within battalions, companies rotated from the fire trench to support and reserve. Even in 1915, a division had only four of its twelve battalions in the trenches at one time. Once relieved, almost always at night, troops filed their weary way back through a maze of communications trenches to form up and march to billets, perhaps in a battered farmstead, in rain-sodden tents, or even in prefabricated huts. "Rest" was a relative term. The infantry was the army's labour force, compelled to dig trenches, repair roads, bury the dead, or load supplies, usually under the supervision of men from other corps, such as the Engineers, whose work it might have been. Generals chose rest periods to inspect troops: that meant that soldiers spent time practising drill, polishing buttons, and burnishing steel. Out of the line, soldiers were paraded to baths and waited, naked and shivering, for a minute of tepid and sometimes scalding water. Shirts and underwear were handed in to be laundered, disinfected, and returned — usually with the lice and their larvae intact. Not until 1918 did a Canadian, Colonel J.A. Amyot, devise adequate sterilization equipment for the British army.

At each relief, a few men earned a brief escape. Ordinary soldiers could expect a week's furlough to England once a year; officers went three or four times as often. Perhaps no grievance in the ranks was more bitter. Courses were another escape. Brigade and divisional schools taught sniping, signalling, patrolling, or the new-fangled Stokes trench-mortar. A few weeks of spit and polish was a small price for learning new weapons, tactics, or techniques and to escape the trenches.

Soldiers dreamed of a more enduring escape, a "Blighty", borrowed, like so much army language, from Hindustani, for "a country across the sea". With rare, Victoria-Cross–winning exceptions, wounded men dropped out of the battle. If they could, they made their own way back; if they were lucky, comrades or stretcher-bearers would help. Army doctors, faced with mass casualties, practised a ruthless sorting of those they could help and those who must be left to die — discreetly concealed by its French name, *triage*. A lucky man with a "Blighty" could be in an English hospital by nightfall. The less fortunate might convalesce just behind the lines. The luckless died in slow misery, beyond the help of medicine or friends. Stomach wounds and fractured thighbones were agonizing and usually fatal.

Courage, whatever the original stock, is a wasting asset, exhausted by too many hours of anxious stand-tos, earth-crunching bombardments, and night patrols. Over time, the letters and diaries of Canadians in the trenches reflect the strain and deepening despair. Some men sought death. Some fled it. Some deserted; a few wounded themselves; so many thousands were diagnosed for "shell shock" that the Medical Corps banned the words and boasted of cures by massive electro-shock. In the end, discipline and military law held soldiers to their appalling duty. In all the wars of the Victorian era, only three British soldiers had been shot for military offences; in France and Flanders, the British Expeditionary Force executed 304 men, 265 for desertion or cowardice. The CEF followed suit: by the end of the war, 25 Canadians had been shot, 2 for murder and the rest for failing the test of courage in battle.

"SAVING THE SITUATION"

The Canadians entered the line near Neuve Chapelle in March. Though a handful of Territorial battalions had reinforced the over-strained British regulars, the Canadians had preceded all but the regular army divisions raised in England since August 1914. Now they were on the fringes of their first battle. For weeks Sir Douglas Haig's First Army had rehearsed, studied the unfamiliar new air photos, collected ammunition, and waited. On March 10, British and Indian troops attacked at Neuve Chapelle behind a short artillery barrage. The British took much of the German front line on schedule and waited for the second phase. Hours passed. A merciless rain of German shells cut telephone lines and smashed into waiting troops, as reinforcements rushed into place. When their attack resumed, the British were slaughtered. Further attacks on March 11 and 12 met the same fate. When the fighting ceased, Haig's army had lost 12,892 men, 100 of them Canadians, caught in incidental shelling. Perhaps the French and the Germans had an improved opinion of the BEF but it was a costly lesson in "enterprise and initiative" in the attack.

In early April, the Canadians marched back to Smith-Dorrien's Second Army. By April 17, they had replaced a French division in the Ypres salient, with the British 28th Division on the right and a French Algerian division on the left. The Algerians and a division of French Territorials linked up with King Albert's Belgian army. It was a quiet sector with historic memories of famous regiments and the brutal fighting six months earlier. Ypres — "Wipers" to the troops — had survived almost intact and it was easily visible from the low ridges the Canadians occupied. The immediate concerns were prosaic ones: the French trenches were "filthy" and "in a deplorable state" and the Canadians must bring them up to British standards. However, the weather was getting warmer, the skies were clear, and the enemy was quiet.

Duke Albrecht, of the German Fourth Army opposite, had no grand plans but he had been given a chore. In 1909, the Germans had signed the Hague Convention against asphyxiating gases, but war was war. Germany's chemical industry produced vast quantities of chlorine, a deadly gas that was heavier than air and would certainly invade enemy trenches and dug-outs. Albrecht had been given six thousand cylinders of the gas and orders to try it out. There was one problem: as flyers were already discovering, the prevailing winds blew from the west into the German lines. From January to April, the Germans waited. Finally, they lugged the cylinders to the north side of the Ypres salient, facing the French. If the cylinders worked — and sensible people doubted it — the Germans could collapse the salient and win a reassuring little victory. If they didn't....

On April 11, the Germans were ready. Belgian spies sent word. German prisoners reported the cylinders. Joffre's headquarters was contemptuous: "All this gas business need not be taken seriously." The British headquarters was no more concerned.

Thursday, April 22, was a beautiful day with a gentle westward breeze. Two brigades, Brigadier-General A.W. Currie's 2nd on the right, R.E.W. Turner's 3rd on the left, held the Canadian line. M.S. Mercer's 1st Brigade was far to the rear, training for a possible future attack. For a week, German shells had battered Ypres. The Cloth Hall was soon in flames; fleeing civilians and their possessions crowded the few roads out of the town. At 3:00 P.M., Turner's headquarters got orders to collect a hundred mouth organs from the Division. An hour later, the German guns began pounding the French lines. In minutes, the shelling spread to Turner's trenches. At 5:00 P.M., observers saw two greenish-yellow clouds rise from the German lines, merge, and roll forward like a dawn mist. Minutes later, stricken Algerians, choking and crying from the gas, poured from their trenches. A few fell into trenches held by the 13th Battalion, Royal Highlanders from Montreal. Most poured back towards Ypres. French guns burst into action, slowed, and stopped as the cloud of chlorine reached them. Behind the cloud German troops, protected only with face-masks purchased days before in Brussels, picked their cautious way over Pilckem Ridge, past Langemarck, and towards Kitchener's Wood where British gunners abandoned their heavy guns. Little but their own caution remained to keep the Germans from Ypres.

Brigadier-General Turner grasped the situation. His flank was open. Neither he nor anyone else could realize that fully four miles of defences lay unmanned because of the gas cloud. Reserve companies were ordered into St. Julien, a village on the Canadian flank. As dusk fell, Sir Edwin Alderson ordered an attack to retake Kitchener's Wood and the British guns. The surviving Algerians, he was told, would help. In the darkness, the 10th Battalion, from Alberta, and the 16th Canadian Scottish, from B.C. and Ontario, formed a dense mass. At 11:30 P.M. they moved forward. Half-way, five hundred yards from the wood, flares suddenly lit the sky and machine guns spat fire. The survivors rushed the woods but the Germans kept fighting. The French never came. By dawn, only one-third of the 1,500 Canadians had crawled back to form a thin line of defence. The rest were dead or captured.

The Canadian attack had at least stalled the German advance. All night and the next day, British and Canadian battalions rushed up to plug the gap. Alderson found himself struggling to control a score of units. By now, Ypres was a burning ruin. German artillery pinpointed roads forward to the battle, where they crossed the Yser Canal and the reserve trench lines, to kill the reinforcements. On April 23, more battalions were poured in piecemeal in an attempt to drive the Germans back. All they could do was stabilize the line. At St. Julien, Lance Corporal Fred Fisher of the 13th Battalion lugged his heavy Colt machine gun forward to fight off German attackers. His heroism earned him the first 'Canadian' VC of the war. He died on the 24th. Sergeant-Major Fred Hall of the 8th Battalion was killed trying to haul wounded men to safety. He also earned a VC.

On Saturday, April 24, the Germans turned on the two Canadian brigades that still held out in the salient. At 4:00 A.M., shells blasted the shallow ditches where the Canadians waited. A few minutes later, gas was released. The 8th Battalion, Winnipeg's "Little Black Devils", and the 5th Western Cavalry had been issued cotton bandoliers to cover their mouths. Dry or soaked in urine the cloth made no difference. Scores of men lay coughing and gasping, faces black from asphyxiation. Survivors opened fire on the mass of advancing Germans. As their over-heated Ross rifles seized, cursing soldiers slammed open the bolts with their boots or shovels. Colt machine guns, heavy, awkward weapons, jammed or ran out of their special ammunition.

Captain Edward Bellew of the 7th Battalion fought his gun until the Germans overran his position. Out of ammunition, he smashed the mechanism and was taken prisoner. His VC was announced only after he returned to Vancouver in 1919. On the right, most of Currie's brigade clung to their trenches. On the left, remnants of the 3rd Brigade fell back. Germans on their flank blasted them with enfilade fire and closed in on St. Julien. In the wild confusion of his headquarters, Turner and his brigade major, Garnet Hughes, misinterpreted Alderson's order to hold the village as a directive to withdraw to a stronger line. By 3:00 P.M., St. Julien's defenders, left to their fate, had been overwhelmed. On the right, with his men clinging to the apex of a shrinking triangle, Currie told his two colonels, Lipsett and Tuxford, to pull back to the reserve line and then walked back through the shell fire to get help. The British commander of the 27th Division, Major-General T.D'O. Snow, treated Currie to contempt and outrage, appalled that a brigadier would leave his headquarters on such an errand. If the Canadian had got his men into trouble, said Snow, he could get them out again. Currie walked back with a handful of Canadian stragglers to find that his two colonels had ignored the order to retreat. Their men would have been slaughtered if they had moved.

The battle continued in utter disorder. On Sunday, British and Canadian battalions kept struggling to regain the lost ground. A British brigade of regulars lost half its men in a valiant, unsupported bid to retake St. Julien. Virtually isolated and assailed by two German brigades, Currie finally pulled his men back to join the remnants of the 3rd Brigade on Gravenstafel Ridge. By April 27, Alderson's Canadians had withdrawn to count their losses. In the salient, the battle continued with growing ferocity. On May 8, as part of the 27th Division, the PPCLI valiantly held the shoulder of a German drive on Frezenberg Ridge. Of 550 Patricias who began the day, only 150 remained that night. Somehow they had held their ground.

Second Ypres was no triumph. In a savage defensive battle, the Canadians had fallen back two miles and lost 208 officers and 5,828 men. The inexperience of a raw division had shown; so had its courage. Survivors would argue about Turner's remoteness from the battle and the British official historian would condemn Currie's decision to go back for help. One battalion commander, Lieutenant-Colonel J.A. Currie, MP, was removed for drunkenness and cowardice in the battle (and, once back in Canada, promoted). Men sent into battle with a bad rifle had every reason to be bitter and demoralized. However, in a brutal baptism of fire, the Canadians had not broken. They had done all they could be asked to do and more. Four Canadians won Victoria Crosses for their courage in the fight or in risking their lives for wounded comrades. One of them, Captain Francis Scrimger, a medical officer, had risked his life rescuing wounded men as Germans shelled his dressing station. Another doctor, Lieutenant-Colonel John McCrae, would win immortality for a poem he scribbled in the wake of the battle, as he remembered how the wrecked bodies of men he had known had been dragged into his field hospital.

In Flanders fields the poppies blow
Between the crosses, row on row,
That mark our place; and in the sky
The larks, still bravely singing, fly
Scarce heard amid the guns below.

We are the Dead. Short days ago
We lived, felt dawn, saw sunset glow,
Loved, and were loved, and now we lie
   In Flanders fields.

Take up our quarrel with the foe:
To you from failing hands we throw
The torch; be yours to hold it high.
If ye break faith with us who die
We shall not sleep, though poppies grow
   In Flanders fields.

Canadians would come to curse the Ypres salient and the battered ruins it now surrounded. Thousands more would fight and die for muddy fields that their generals should cheerfully have abandoned. But in April 1915, Canadians wanted to be proud of their sacrifice at St. Julien and Kitchener's Wood and of the terse words in the British official communiqué: "The Canadians had many casualties but their gallantry and determination undoubtedly saved the situation."

A Dreadful Equilibrium

The second battle of Ypres ended, like the first, in a bloody stalemate. For a few square miles of ground and the odium of adding poison gas to the battle-field horrors, the Germans had lost 35,000 casualties; to preserve a largely symbolic salient, the British had sacrificed 59,275, of whom only a few dozen actually died from the gas. In its outcome, the battle reflected the war in 1915.

For the Germans, Ypres had never been more than an incident. Having missed victory in the west in 1914, it was time for the generals to turn eastward. With France's falling pre-war birthrate, French military manpower would only shrink in number. Russia's immense manpower could only be disarmed. Germany's strategy, insisted the Kaiser's new chief of staff, General Erich von Falkenhayn, must be to destroy the Russian army without invading Russia. More Austrian setbacks in early 1915 confirmed that the Habsburg armies would now be little help, but a new German army, thrust into the midst of their line, might find a complacent as well as ill-equipped Russian opposition. So it proved. On May 4, 1915, some 700 German and Austrian guns opened fire. Russian defences collapsed. By the end of the month Field Marshal August von Mackensen's Eleventh Army had collected 153,000 prisoners.

It was just a beginning. In Poland, Warsaw fell to von Hindenburg's armies on August 5, 1915. By the end of the month, Brest-Litovsk was in flames. Then, to the dismay of subordinates and allies, von Falkenhayn reined in his armies and suggested a separate peace. The Russians had lost two million soldiers, half of them as prisoners; three thousand guns; and uncounted rifles. Men could be found; the weapons never would be. At Petrograd, the Tsar ignored the peace offer and clung to his European allies. Henceforth, he announced, he would command his armies in the field. As much as the politicians in France and England, the Russian autocrat realized that only victory would satisfy his people.

Von Falkenhayn had won a victory, not the war. Thanks to Nicholas II, Russia would fight on. In the south, Serbia was conquered, and the road to Constantinople again lay open through Bulgaria but only to drain off more German men, money, and equipment. The Italian front gave the Germans more comfort. Having declared war in return for secret Allied promises, Italy had launched her armies towards Trieste. Her fourth battle for the Isonzo River ended like the first three and the next seven, with cruel losses and no gains. At the end of 1915, a quarter-million Italians were dead or wounded.

In the West, it was France that insisted on early victory; the British were content to wait until their armies were ready in 1916. Joffre's faith in the offensive was unmarred by experience, and his target stared from the map. The German trench line formed a huge bulge into France; it would be pinched out of existence from its two flanks, the Artois and the Champagne districts. The British, feeble fighters if their 1914 performance was any evidence, could best help by occupying more miles of trenches and by making diversionary attacks.

It was what the Germans had expected. Unlike that of their enemies, their pre-war planning had included defence. They knew they would need picks, shovels, and millions of miles of barbed wire. They had huge trench-mortars and heavy artillery too, while the British depended on obsolete naval guns so inaccurate that the troops christened them "Strictly Neutral". When Joffre launched his first attack in the Champagne, the Germans were ready and waiting. The resulting disaster cost France 200,000 men. Neuve Chapelle in March won the British a little grudging respect, but Ypres in April was a distraction. In May, General Ferdinand Foch launched his Artois offensive with fifteen divisions. A couple of them almost captured Vimy Ridge. Canadians found the dead bodies two years later. They were among 100,000 French casualties.

The British helped out with their own attack at Festubert. The Canadian division, hurriedly filled with men who had been left behind in February, sent the 2nd and 3rd brigades into assaults across open ground on May 23 and 24.

German machine guns opened fire, troops stumbled into uncut wire, and the price was 2,468 Canadian dead and wounded. A month later, at Givenchy-lez-la-Bassée on June 15, it was the turn of Mercer's 1st Brigade to attack. A British mine exploded prematurely and the 2nd Battalion, which tried to attack across uncut barbed wire, lost 366 men in a few minutes.

Through the summer, Joffre demanded renewed offensives. Russia's plight and the growing disaster in the Balkans were added arguments. By the time the French moved, von Falkenhayn had brought four divisions back from the east. On September 25, Haig's First Army attacked at Loos. The lessons of Neuve Chapelle were absorbed. A far heavier bombardment and careful rehearsals allowed some of the British, at enormous cost, to struggle through to the German second line despite huge losses. Others were trapped when their poison gas blew back on them. Haig appealed for reserves. Reluctantly, Sir John French sent him two New Army divisions. Hungry and weary after struggling along jammed roads, the raw British troops were still in mass formation when German shells tore into their ranks. Losses were appalling. Whole battalions broke and fled. The Guards Division plugged the hole but the British had few gains. Sir Douglas Haig had his revenge. His friends at court spread word of Sir John French's incompetence. By Christmas, Haig had taken his place.

The new British commander did not entirely fit the stereotype of a mindless ex-cavalry officer. Except in French, which he spoke well, Haig was painfully inarticulate, acutely unimaginative, and conventional; he shared a military contempt for politicians and their art but he was no fool. At fifty-four he was young enough to learn both politics and war. Neither was Haig a genius: the pre-war British army would not have accepted him if he had been. Haig's chief eccentricity was a profound Christian faith and a calm conviction of divine mission. He was proof against a general's worst enemy, despair. Haig knew that he would succeed and, if one means failed, he would find another.

Both Joffre and von Falkenhayn had failed to break the stalemate in 1915; perhaps Haig would succeed in 1916.

IV
WAITING AND WORKING

SHELLS AND FOOD

B ritish generals had an explanation for their failures in 1915: an acute shortage of artillery shells. In March, British field guns were rationed to eight rounds a day; in April, they could fire ten. When senior officers leaked the truth to sympathetic newspapers, the public outrage in Britain forced Asquith into a coalition with the Conservatives. Blame fell on Lord Kitchener; a War Office wrapped in peacetime red tape; and an in-grown, obsolete munitions industry. Lloyd George, the foe of pre-war preparedness, was chosen as national saviour. As the new Minister of Munitions, he discovered to his surprise that Canada was part of the problem, and might also be part of a solution.

The problem began with Hughes and political patronage. The outbreak of war had escalated Canada's depression. Buyers cancelled orders, construction stopped, and factories closed. Anticipating economic collapse helped cause the problem; war contracts offered salvation from it. Businessmen and their agents pestered Hughes wherever he went, pledging their patriotism and party loyalty. Hughes made some of them honorary colonels. "I could get hold of them," he explained, "in case they did not play the game square." The British preferred to place their overseas orders with their New York agent, the banking firm of J. Pierpont Morgan. Sir Robert Borden was angry: people were wondering why men were "going without bread in Canada", he warned his high commissioner in London, "while those across the line are receiving good wages for work that could be done as efficiently and cheaply in this country."

That efficiency and cheapness was not apparent. Hughes had fitted out the Canadian Contingent as a testimonial to Canadian manufacturing; much of the resulting equipment had been left behind as useless. Two million boots,

49

ordered by the War Office for New Army recruits, became a byword in Britain for bad fit and quality. Canadian greatcoats were rejected as too thin and shoddy for British use. Rumours that cardboard had been used in the boots issued to the CEF offered the Liberals such a scandal that they abandoned party neutrality. In April 1915, Borden dismissed two of his back-benchers for gross profiteering. In May, he created the War Purchasing Commission to remove from Hughes and his department a function the minister and his cronies had obviously abused.

In the sorry mess of Canadian war procurement, Hughes deserved credit for one glowing accomplishment. At Valcartier in September he had summoned a few industrialists and, on the basis of a pencilled note, constituted them a Shell Committee, with authority to carry out any contract the War Office cared to place. Within weeks, the British had ordered 200,000 shells; by May 1915, the Shell Committee had distributed $170 million in contracts to 250 firms, large and small, across Canada.

Canada, of course, had no real munitions industry. In 1914 a single government factory at Quebec produced enough shells and rifle ammunition for the annual militia camps. A shell, the cast-steel projectile that delivered high explosive or shrapnel to the enemy, was not complicated but it had to be machined to a fine tolerance, and any flaw in the casting could lead to a premature explosion, demolishing gun and gunner. In all of Canada there were half a dozen experts and only ten sets of gauges. The War Office, to add to its problems, had its own version of an inch, 0.010 smaller than anyone else's. Workers had to be trained, machinery purchased, and costs estimated on the basis of a war that might be over in months.

It was a typical Hughes venture. Politicians demanded and got favours for constituents, from a job as inspector to a contract for a firm that needed business. Sir Alexander Bertram, the Shell Committee chairman and a major contractor, tried to run the business from his Montreal office. Hughes ordered a transfer to Ottawa; there Bertram's son struggled with the mounds of paperwork while waiting contractors perched on ammunition boxes. To spread the work, shells shuttled back and forth across Canada so that small firms in Lethbridge or Lindsay could add a little polish or paint. The British, after all, would pay. But were the British getting deliveries? Lloyd George discovered that, of the $170 millions' worth of shells on order, Canada had delivered $5.5 millions'. Without reorganization, the Canadians would get no more business.

Hughes was defiant. D.A. Thomas, a Welsh colliery-owner sent to investigate, reported on the Shell Committee's costly chaos and left without results. Four months passed without orders. That was enough. Over Hughes's objections, the Shell Committee was shoved aside and, by December 1915, Borden had approved a new Imperial Munitions Board (IMB), responsible solely to the British but run by a Canadian, Joseph Wesley Flavelle, a Toronto millionaire whose management skills as a bacon exporter were respected on both sides of the Atlantic. Flavelle picked a team of skilled managers and backed them as they cut prices, tightened quality, and resisted political pressure.

Flavelle made himself few friends and some well-earned enemies. A Toronto firm had counterfeited inspection stamps. A Montreal manufacturer tried to slip through a batch of faulty shells by painting over the pinholes. To keep peace, Flavelle granted contracts to prairie and B.C. firms, despite high prices, and then was denounced for keeping IMB business in Ontario and Quebec. When unions demanded the fair-wages clause guaranteed in other government contracts, Flavelle insisted that they were working for Britain and their members should be glad to have jobs. In June 1916, Hamilton and Toronto machinists walked out. Flavelle broke the strike and, with backing from the War Measures Act, banned reporting of the dispute. Lloyd George had opened the way for hundreds of thousands of women to work in British munitions factories. The IMB followed suit, promising equal pay, female inspectors, and separate lunchrooms. By 1917, more than 30,000 women were employed. The War Measures Act was again used to suppress any reports of discontent, bad working conditions, or sexual assaults on women munitions workers.

The Imperial Munitions Board was easily the biggest business Canada had known, with six hundred factories in 1917, a quarter of a million workers, and production worth $2 million a day. From producing shells, the IMB expanded to fuses, brass casings, and propellants. Close to a third of the shells fired by the British army in 1917 were Canadian-made. When contractors proved greedy, incompetent, or recalcitrant, Flavelle took them over or built his own factories. British Munitions loaded shells at Verdun. British Explosives bought out ill-managed companies at Renfrew and Trenton. Canadian Explosives built its own factory at Nobel near Parry Sound during the harsh winter of 1917. British Acetones took over the Gooderham and Worts distillery at Toronto. Nearby, at Ashbridge's Bay, British Forgings was Flavelle's answer to the price-fixing "buccaneers" of the Canadian steel industry. In 1918, the IMB added a shipbuilding department and, by the end of the year, launched 103 steel and wooden vessels.

Late in 1916, as the Royal Flying Corps (RFC) struggled to find pilots to replace losses from superior German aircraft, months of negotiations with Canada finally jelled. Thousands of Canadians had already joined the British flying services; it made sense in the crisis to go to the source. In weeks, the IMB bought the Curtiss operation from its Canadian promoters. Its tiny aircraft factory became the nucleus for Canadian Aeroplanes Ltd. By the war's end, the IMB had produced 2,600 Curtiss JN-4 trainers and 30 F-5 flying boats.

In British Columbia, the IMB employed 24,000 workers to hunt for the prime spruce and fir needed by British aircraft factories. Flavelle did more. IMB agents scoured the countryside around Toronto for bases and developed airfields at Camp Borden, Beamsville, Hamilton, Armour Heights, and Deseronto. The British created RFC Canada as a training organization, recruited 9,000 cadets and 7,500 mechanics, and graduated 3,372 aircrew at a cost of 129 lives. In all, 22,812 Canadians served with the British flying services in every role from trying to spot submarines to piloting heavy bombers over Germany. Of 13,160 Canadians who served as aircrew, 1,388 were killed, 1,130 were wounded or injured, and 377 became prisoners of war. Canadians were 6 per cent of British flying casualties in 1915 and 16.8 per cent in 1918. The IMB had contributed more than shells.

If the IMB was the most spectacular creation of Canada's wartime economy, it was not unique. Textile mills rolled out khaki serge for uniforms, flannel for hospital sheets, and miles of canvas for tents and tarpaulins. Paper and woodpulp production doubled with the appetite for war news and propaganda. With wartime prosperity, an automobile became a luxury a lot more Canadians could afford: car registrations rose from 74,416 in 1914 to 342,433 in 1919. Only construction stayed in a wartime slump.

For the common cause, Canada's new industries mattered less than her old export staples. With French farms stripped of manpower and Russian wheat blocked in the Black Sea, Allied countries needed all the food Canada could produce. As usual, Ottawa looked to voluntarism. A "Patriotism and Production" campaign in 1915 urged farmers to grow all they could. With the promise of wartime prices, farmers obliged by planting a record 40 million acres. The climate obliged. By November 1915, Canadian farms had yielded 393.5 million bushels of wheat at an average of 26 bushels an acre. It had never happened before — nor would it again. In 1916 and 1917, acreages grew and yields fell. Heat, drought, a late frost in 1917, and the relentless results of soil exhaustion cut wheat production to only 189 million bushels in 1918, 11 bushes to the acre. Canada's wheat exports fell 238 per cent between 1915 and 1918.

The 1915 bumper crop kept prices close to 1914 levels but, from 1916 on, scarcity shaped the market. When Italy led Allied attempts to corner the 1916 crop, Ottawa helped dealers form the Wheat Export Company. In 1917, the government went further, closing the Winnipeg Grain Exchange and handing wheat-marketing to a new Board of Grain Supervisors. When prices rose from

$1.70 to $2.40 a bushel, farmers and politicians learned the delights of orderly marketing. Much of the new wealth was spent on automobiles. For a lot of prairie farm families, cars bought from wartime incomes ended rural isolation.

Wheat, of course, was only one crop and the prairies were only one region. Until the war, Canadian cheese and meat had fought a losing battle in British markets. With the Danes and Dutch briefly cut off by the conflict, Canadians had a fresh opportunity to compete. In the war years, Canadian fishermen doubled their landings and their exports. By 1917, Canadian pork exports tripled and beef exports grew sevenfold. Food processors packed pork and beans, bully beef, and all the cheese they could produce. Ontario was the main beneficiary. Its farmers also had their frustrations. Ideal growing seasons in 1917 and 1918 fulfilled all the hopes of "Production and Thrift" campaigns, but who would harvest the crops? The spirit of voluntarism turned women into "farmerettes" and boys into "Soldiers of the Soil". Civil servants, teachers, retail clerks, and clergy sacrificed annual holidays for harvest duty. Farmers soon discovered that city folk did not make efficient harvest labourers. Much of the crop rotted in the fields.

FINANCING THE WAR

Canada entered the war as a debtor nation. In 1913, its balance of payments was $408 million in the red. While patriotic crowds marched and cheered, the Montreal stock markets closed to forestall a panic. An order-in-council took Canada off the gold standard. To reassure the banks, Ottawa for the first time printed its own dollar bills. Fiscal prudence was not universal. Despite solemn pledges to respect strict accounting procedures, the War Appropriation Act became a licence to print money. By the war's end, the original $50 million had grown to $1,069 million, by no means all of it wisely or honestly spent. After a vigorous year in 1915 pursuing malefactors, Parliament's public-accounts committee lapsed into exhaustion. A year later, the ailing auditor general, John Fraser, also abandoned his struggle. To its dismay, the Department of Finance found itself compelled to hand over huge sums with little to say in their use.

Almost every issue of wartime finance and politics was entangled in the fate of the two transcontinental railways Laurier had helped create as rivals to the CPR. The Canadian Northern had given cheap, popular service to the prairies until its promoters, William Mackenzie and Donald Mann, persuaded the Bank of Commerce and Laurier to finance a line from Vancouver to Toronto. Charlie Hays of the Grand Trunk talked his British shareholders into similar folly before he drowned with the *Titanic*. Laurier had helped by offering to build a line through the northern Quebec and Ontario bush and a bridge across the St. Lawrence at Quebec City for the GTR's convenience, all at public expense. Perhaps symbolically, the Quebec bridge collapsed twice, in 1907 and 1916. The Liberals had basked in the glory of big spending; the Conservatives inherited the bills: two unfinished railways on the verge of collapse, and a disastrous national credit rating.

The war was the railways' salvation and their ruin. Borden's finance minister, Sir Thomas White, had long condemned the railway deals and their promoters but he understood that railway bankruptcy could wreck Canada's credit, to say nothing of that of the prairie provinces and the wealthy Torontonians who had given their money to Mackenzie and Mann. In wartime it was easy to argue that every railway was needed and, grudgingly, money was found for the Grand Trunk and the Canadian Northern. However, the war was also a patriotic excuse for the Board of Railway Commissioners to hold down freight rates. The CPR grumbled publicly but quietly rejoiced at the spectacle of despised rivals being squeezed to death by low revenues. As costs soared — the price of a freight car tripled — the Grand Trunk and the Canadian Northern gradually crumbled. By 1917, the majority of members of a royal commission recommended a solution Borden had urged since 1904: nationalization.

Whatever their fate, the railways devoured money. So did the war. In relative terms, the war took only 15 to 16 per cent of the gross domestic product — far less than the 1939–45 war — but a nation that had spent $13 million on defence in 1913 was shouldering a military budget of $311 million three years later. Even in 1915, shocked officials calculated that Canada was spending half a million dollars a day for military purposes; by 1917, the daily outlay was close to a million dollars. Raising the money from taxpayers, White concluded, was out of the question. Investors and immigrants would shun a country with high taxes. Of course, as he admitted in his 1915 budget, both rich and poor would have to make sacrifices. That meant increased tariffs, and a range of duties on bank notes, cheques, telegrams, railway tickets, and insurance premiums. In 1916, Ottawa cautiously levied its first direct tax — a business war-profit tax — designed less for revenue than to demonstrate government indignation at profiteering. Public cries for the conscription of wealth drove White against his will to an Income War Tax in 1917: 3 per cent for a family earning over $3,000 or an individual earning over $1,500. The prime minister, one of only 31,130 Canadians who paid, would have owed about $80 on his official salary. The income tax, White promised, would end with the war.

The real money would have to be borrowed. War, White and his advisers agreed, was "an extraordinary expense", to be financed like a railway, a waterworks, or a bridge. "We are justified in placing upon posterity the greater portion of the financial burden of this war," White explained, "waged as it is in the interests of human freedom and for their benefit in equal if not in greater degree than for our own." In short, the children would pay, but who would lend the money?

Not the British. By 1915, they were struggling to finance their own war effort. To the dismay of Canadian bankers, White turned to New York: it was costly but he saw no alternative. By the summer of 1916, Canada had borrowed $220 million. Sir Joseph Flavelle, White's former boss at the National Trust, shoved the minister in another direction. Canada, he pointed out, was recovering. There was money to borrow. White's officials protested that there was no precedent. In November 1915, the finance minister nervously floated a domestic war loan for $50 million at 5 per cent, tax free and fully convertible. In a week, big investors had subscribed $100 million. Smaller investors took $79 million. Flavelle got his cut: since the IMB would create still more wealth, White could advance him the surplus from the loan to finance more British munitions purchases.

The 1915 war loan set a durable pattern in Canadian public finance: Canadians would lend to their own government. In September 1916 and March 1917, the government asked for a total of $250 million and took in $460 million. For the fourth loan, in November 1917, White tapped small investors with Victory Bonds at 5½ per cent. A sea of posters in French and English helped attract 820,035 subscribers and $398 million. A fifth loan a year later raised $660 million from 1,067,879 Canadians. The sixth and final war loan, in November 1919, produced $680 million. Between them, the war and the railways quadrupled Canada's national debt; four-fifths of it was owed to Canadians.

Flavelle's deal, by helping the British to borrow, also helped fill the IMB's order books and expanded its contribution to the wartime economy. By 1917 Britain's credit was nearing exhaustion, its own munitions factories were running full out, and Canadian shells were becoming a luxury. Luck and Flavelle's ingenuity came to the rescue. On April 7, the United States entered the war. Flavelle collected his staff and headed for Washington. Americans welcomed him as a fellow spirit. As unready for war as Canada had been three years earlier, the United States needed just about anything the IMB factories could produce. If the Canadians tendered at least 7 per cent lower than U.S. contractors, they could have the business. With trained workers and most of their machinery paid for by the British, most of the IMB's companies could compete. IMB activity in 1918 slumped by about a third from the 1917 peak but American orders helped diversify its operations into shipbuilding and additional aircraft manufacturing.

For the rest of his natural days, Sir Thomas White insisted that his fiscal policies had not contributed to inflation. Economists would disagree. Until late 1919 the Canadian and U.S. dollars remained virtually at par and banks bought relatively few of White's bonds but, as an improvised central bank, the Finance department was generous with its paper. As the money supply grew from $1,108 million in 1914 to $2,091 million in 1920, Ottawa printed the notes. Borrowing on the future heated an economy that, by 1916, had more money than ways to spend it. Inflation indexes were even more imperfect in 1914–18 than now, but they told a story. The Department of Labour family budget index, set at 100 in 1913, fell to 98.7 in 1915, reached 147.2 in 1918, and climbed to a height of 184.7 in 1920. A price-level index based on 100 for the 1935–39 period was 85.4 in 1914, 166 in 1918, and 203.2 in 1920. Simply put, purchasing power in the war years was halved.

Inflation was not necessarily a disaster. Tight money, when the rest of the world was on a spending spree, would have priced Canadian food and munitions out of competition. Exports paid for the war. Britain's bill — $252,567,942.03 — for providing food, clothing, transportation, munitions, and just about everything but pay to the Canadians overseas, was more than offset by what Britain owed the IMB. Nor was inflation solely a result of fiscal policy. Bad harvests tightened food supplies and raised prices. The U.S. entry into the war and a harsh 1917 winter produced fuel shortages. Though governments did nothing to restrict the output of consumer goods, wartime affluence encouraged higher prices. Wages slowly followed inflation, with the usual noisy accompaniment of strikes and lock-outs. Then further increases could be justified to meet the added labour costs. There was no such relief for the elderly, the poor, and those on fixed incomes. They tightened their belts and suffered, often in silence.

Three-quarters of a century later, it is easier to understand the wartime inflation. Historians have argued that Canadian prices and wages, after half a century of remarkable stability, had actually started to climb in 1907. No one took strong objection until the increases soared in late 1916. Nor were the causes easily grasped. Fiscal policy, labour shortages, and crop failure were too banal or complex. The public wanted a scapegoat: greedy profiteers satisfied the need.

Canada Regenerated

Profiteers especially fitted the demonology of a moral crusade. Canada's leaders in mobilizing a voluntary war effort were predominantly English-speaking middle-class Protestants, often with rural roots. Like most people, they thought their own ideas should fit just about everyone. In the struggle against Kaiserism, all people of goodwill must surely agree on the need to purge Canadian society of greed, corruption, partyism, vice, and the liquor evil. Wartime solidarity left no room for the arrogance of capital, the violence of revolutionaries, or the selfishness of sects. Middle-class feminists who had led the struggle for the vote found a fresh argument in the war: if victory depended on moral regeneration, the most moral members of the race must extend their power beyond the family. "Women have cleaned up things since time began," declared Nellie McClung in 1916, "and if women get into politics there will be a cleaning up of pigeon-holes and forgotten corners in which the dust of years has fallen."

By no means all Canadians, not even middle-class Protestants, saw the war as a crusade. For politicians in 1914, it was business as usual. Ontario's "Doc" Reid; Manitoba's Bob Rogers, the notorious "Minister of Elections"; and George E. Foster, a passionate patronage-monger, constituted themselves a cabinet committee to ensure that the War Appropriation was spent to the Conservatives' advantage. Hughes did not want their help. As an aide, John Bassett, explained to an enquiring friend: "Contracts are sent to a great extent to those firms who have political pull...." If the friend wanted a share, he could line up with the others. Another aide, Harold Daly, helped guard the minister's door. "I was particularly good to lawyers," he recalled, "because I knew what business I was going into when I got out of the army."

The Tories needed friends in 1914. After three years of "Bad Luck" Borden, Laurier and the Liberals were convinced that voters would undo the cruel injustice of 1911. Conservatives feared that legislative fiascos and the 1913-14 depression might prove the Liberals correct. Would the war give the Tories a renewed chance? Rogers and the rest of the old guard were eager to try a snap election in November 1914. Borden finally drew back: it was too opportunistic. The spring of 1915 would be better. Meanwhile, over Laurier's objections, soldiers were given the right to vote and Harold Daly sailed on the *Lusitania* in May to manage the overseas campaign. He survived the sinking and reported from London: "I am still glad to die for the Conservative Party but I am glad I didn't drown for it." By then, Borden had changed his mind. A stack of letters and renewed pressure from colleagues persuaded him that an election would be inappropriate while Canadians digested the casualty lists from Ypres and Festubert. Laurier had drawn applause from a Toronto audience when he proclaimed: "I do not care...so long as the war lasts, to open the portals of power with that bloody key." In September, the two leaders negotiated a one-year extension of Parliament until 1917. Surely the war could not last that long.

Laurier's motives were clear. He knew what had happened to British Liberals in the patriotic "Khaki Election" of 1900; he could easily have guessed Bob Rogers's proposed slogan for the campaign: "Vote Conservative for Borden backs Britain". The Liberals had much more work to do in revealing just how corrupt and patronage-ridden Borden's patriotism really was. In 1915, they exposed boots, binoculars, and spavined old horses. For 1916, private detectives helped untangle the affairs of the Shell Committee, Sam Hughes, and his favourite honorary colonel, J. Wesley Allison. By threatening to "rawhide" his critics and by claiming that Allison had "more honour in his little finger than the Auditor-General had in his entire carcass", Hughes added colour to the language and deepening embarrassment to the government. Ministers distanced themselves from the hero of Valcartier. A particularly righteous speech by George Foster led an amused Borden to note that his veteran minister "has no more political sense than a turnip".

In fact, Foster, and Borden too, sensed that Canadians would no longer tolerate a war effort run on traditional lines. In 1914 the Patriotic Fund had given business-like management to what should have been a government function. The pattern was repeated in 1915. The War Purchasing Commission, the Military Hospitals Commission, and, pre-eminently, the Imperial Munitions Board involved businessmen and business methods. Politics, as the War Purchasing Commission files reveal, were by no means forgotten but they were buried under business-like efficiency. Through the IMB, Joseph Flavelle gained a powerful influence on policy inside the government and on attitudes of the Canadian public. At the end of 1916, after a visit to England and France taught him what defective shells meant in war, Flavelle was in no mood for Toronto contractors who pestered him about their profit margins: "Profits?" cried a suddenly animated Flavelle. "I have come straight from the seat of a nation where they are sweating blood to win this war and I stand before you stripped of many ideas. Profits! Send profits to the hell where they belong."

If the war could do that to a Methodist millionaire, it could do much. It could persuade Stephen Leacock, a deeply conservative economist, to insist that government must intervene to end "silly and idle services or...production that is for mere luxuries and comforts". It convinced Newton Rowell, Ontario's Liberal leader, that Robert Borden, a Conservative, might even be a better national leader than a man who played politics with the war effort and who pandered to Quebec prejudices in Regulation 17. Had Sir Wilfrid Laurier really followed the new gospel of "service above self"? Late in 1916, the young Ernest Lapointe had insisted on dividing Parliament on a question beyond Ottawa's powers — Ontario schools — and Laurier had not controlled him. MPs had split by language, not by party, western Liberals had abandoned Laurier, and Rowell had encouraged them. The war gave him reasons to do so again and again.

The war and the cause of regeneration fed on each other because lines were so often shared. Whatever the views of most Canadian women, their self-appointed leaders were tireless for both sacrifice and reform. In 1914, the corrupt Roblin regime in Manitoba survived the joint onslaught of Liberals and feminists; in 1915 it fell, possibly because several thousand potential supporters had left for the war but even more because its easy morals were at odds with the wartime mood. Early in 1916, the feminists got their reward: votes for Manitoba's women. Alberta and Saskatchewan followed within months; British Columbia and Ontario adopted the change in 1917. Almost automatically, the prohibition cause shared in the triumph. Saskatchewan, which had bravely banished the bar in 1915, found itself the prairie laggard a year later when it was the last to end any sale without benefit of prescription. The old counter-arguments, government meddling, personal freedom, job protection, lost their weight in the wartime mood of sacrifice and discipline. What better example of the excesses of personal freedom, cried Nellie McClung, than the Kaiser, "William Hohenzollern". Manitobans were commanded to use "ballots for bullets and shoot straight and strong in order that the demon of drink might be driven from the haunts of men". By 1917, every province but Quebec had banished booze. Thirsty souls with credit and a fixed address could summon "liquids" by mail order from Montreal.

As usual, Quebec seemed to be the exception: recalcitrant on liquor, demanding on French-Canadian rights elsewhere, uninterested in the rights of women, and indifferent to the world struggle against Kaiserism. Were the French better than the "enemy aliens" who also seemed as "unenlightened" about women, liquor, and the war? Organized labour was another reluctant warrior. The Trades and Labor Congress had waited (like the National Council of Women) until 1913 to endorse female suffrage but among its leaders only the socialist Jimmy Simpson backed prohibition and neither he nor the others showed the patriotism of "the best" British and French trade unionists by denouncing strikes. Instead they had resisted the war, resisted national registration, and would resist conscription. How did this serve the soldiers who were making the supreme sacrifice to build a purer and better Canada?

The answer, as ever in Canada, was that there was more than one perception of the new world. Those whom middle-class reformers found wanting had no common cause. Bourassa and the *nationalistes* despised the pre-1914 European immigrants as cordially as any English Canadian. No argument against the war effort seemed more compelling to their eyes than the fear of handing over Canada to "foreigners" by draining strength to serve some Imperial behest. Leaders of organized labour, predominantly British in ethnicity, saw the "foreigners" as competition for scarce jobs. Nor could they possibly cross the barriers of language and social philosophy to make common cause with the *nationalistes*. On language and culture, labour leaders were as unresurrected as the Orangemen they sometimes were.

Save for those who take character and circumstance as they find them — almost always a taciturn and placid crowd — both regenerators and their opponents could agree about the evils of profiteering. So could the government. On November 10, 1916, after public clamour, Borden announced that a cost-of-living commissioner, the useful W.F. O'Connor, would have the power to pursue and publicize offenders. The food-processing industry, intermediary between the selfless farmers and the innocent consumer, was an obvious target for investigation — and a profitable one. There were few larger or more successful firms than the William Davies Company. Its well-known president had been raised to a baronetcy in June 1917. In August, when O'Connor's report revealed that the company had earned 85 per cent on its capital in the previous year, Sir Joseph Flavelle became the most reviled man in Canada — "His Lardship", the "Baron of Bacon". "To hell with profits" indeed!

GENERALSHIP BY DEATH

From December 6 to 8, 1915, Allied generals met at Chantilly. For all its setbacks, 1915 had not been a complete disaster. Russia had survived, Italy was still fighting, France's army was strong, and, by 1916, the British would at last field the military strength of a nation of forty million. Germany, it was agreed, must be close to exhaustion. Berlin had also retreated from unlimited submarine warfare just when it was becoming dangerous to the Allies. Victory in 1916 could be achieved by co-ordinated, simultaneous attacks around the circumference of the Central Powers. That, at least, was "Papa" Joffre's view, and who could argue the principle? Practice was another matter. When would the time come? Would the Russians be able to help? Above all, where on the Western Front should the attacks be made?

The details were still far from resolved on February 21 when a German naval shell landed in the heart of Verdun. In a few minutes, 1,220 German guns, some of them the heaviest any army had ever used, had begun to devastate the old French fortress. A *Trommelfeuer* or drum-fire, designed to annihilate the French garrison, opened a year-long battle. The Germans had a strategy, too.

In 1915, General von Falkenhayn had tried to drive Russia from the war. Now it was the turn of France. "If we succeeded in opening the eyes of her people to the fact that in a military sense they have nothing more to hope for...," he argued, then "England's best sword" would be lost. Operation *Gericht* or "Doomsday" would slaughter Frenchmen for the ultimate purpose of beating Britain. The technique was simple: seize a position the French would have to recapture, have enough heavy artillery on hand to smash the counterattacks, and destroy the French army. Verdun was the place. A year earlier, Joffre had reflected on the uselessness of the Belgian fortresses and stripped Verdun of its heavy guns to give his armies more firepower against German trenches. A colonel complained; National Assembly deputies worried; Joffre was calm. Verdun, an exposed salient, should probably have been abandoned but somehow it did not seem appropriate to vacate native soil. In February 1916, Verdun became all that von Falkenhayn could wish: the most sacred soil of France, the key point in the French line, the symbolic reminder of Charles Martel's defeat of the Huns a millennium earlier.

On February 25, Fort Douaumont, key to Verdun, fell. On the same day, General Henri-Philippe Pétain took over. A cool master of defensive war, Pétain eventually used almost every French division in his struggle to hold Verdun. "Ils ne passeront pas" became France's slogan. A single road, crammed night and day with truckloads of supplies and troops, became *la Voie sacrée*. Von Falkenhayn had his strategic wishes fulfilled but the slaughter was not one-sided. Germans were drawn deeper into the battle as attack followed attack. Typically, French regiments lost a third of their strength in eight to twelve days; German regiments lost even more. A new, more terrible gas, phosgene, was introduced. It only added to the horror. Through the spring, summer, and fall, the battle ground on. In October, Pétain's subordinates, generals Robert Nivelle and Charles Mangin, persuaded him that a major counter-attack could work. French factories were now pouring out artillery shells. It was the French turn to flood down fire by the ton. "When the trench is well turned over, off we go," explained Mangin. "Any Boches who are still there are ours." On October 24, the French retook Douaumont. In November, the Germans fell back. In three days in mid-December Nivelle took 11,000 prisoners. "We know the method and we have the Chief," boasted Mangin. "Success is certain."

That was premature. Von Falkenhayn's strategy had cost the French 362,000 men but, even by their own questionable statistics, Verdun cost the Germans 336,831. On August 29, more than a month after he had ordered the hopeless attacks to stop, von Falkenhayn was gone, displaced by his enemies, von Hindenburg and von Ludendorff.

Von Falkenhayn's other failure was in Italy. He had yielded to Field Marshal Conrad von Hötzendorf. Both of them had sent some of their best troops to attack in the Trentino in the hope that Italy, too, might be driven from the war. On May 15, the offensive began with impressive gains. Italian regiments, badly armed and worse led, crumbled. But General Luigi Cadorna found reserves and shoved them into the line. A twelve-mile advance was all the Germans and Austrians were allowed, at a cost of 80,000. Italian losses were far higher — 250,000 in dead, wounded, and prisoners — but on June 16 Cadorna began to push back. The Austrians lost almost all they had won.

The Austrian retreat was wholly unexpected. So was the reason. The Russians, by the end of 1915, had been counted out of the war. Instead, they had found a general, and their despised munitions industries had worked miracles. General Alexei Brusilov took over the Carpathian front and staged a series of small methodical attacks to discover, as he explained, which part of the enemy line was stone and which part lath and plaster. On June 4, Brusilov attacked and the Austrians — the lath and plaster — collapsed. By September the Russians had 450,000 new prisoners. Romania, which had hesitated in June 1916, joined the Allies in August. Then Brusilov's victory fell apart. The Tsar's high command did nothing. The Germans, as usual, rushed to rescue their Habsburg allies. By the time Brusilov's campaign was over, the Russians had lost a million men. Next, Germany turned on Romania. The campaign was a consolation prize for von Falkenhayn. By early December, he and Field Marshal von Mackensen marched their soldiers in triumph through Bucharest.

In the West, no one on either side knew whether the Somme was a victory or a defeat. It was certainly a tragedy. Now in command of an army of a million men — forty-three divisions and nineteen more to come — Sir Douglas Haig believed that the time had come for Britain to win the war. His army was still imperfect — "a collection of divisions untrained for the Field" — but it was in better spirits than the French. Like von Falkenhayn, Haig believed that the French were near their limit. They must be helped, but the British must take the lead. By choice, Haig would have attacked in Flanders, on ground he had come to know, but co-operation with the French dictated an attack near the British-French juncture. Joffre insisted on the Somme valley, a German salient with trenches that rose on limestone ridges beyond the river. It was hard to find a tougher German sector but its capture would be a German disaster.

Verdun altered the Allied battle. Joffre had promised two armies; he could now spare only one. Haig proposed to wait until a new British secret weapon, the "tank", was available. Joffre was almost frantic: the French armies could not hold out that long. The British must proceed. General Sir Henry Rawlinson's Fourth Army was filled with raw New Army divisions, the elite of Britain who had hurried to volunteer in 1914. For two years they had suffered from the lack of equipment, training, experience, and competent officers. Now, at last, they could begin their march on Berlin. By June 1916 there were guns and shells enough for seven long days of bombardment.

By 7:30 A.M. on July 1, 1916, 1,738,000 British shells had turned the German positions above the Somme into a cratered dusty desert. The forward battalions of eleven British divisions, dazed after the week-long storm of fire, rose at blasts from officers' whistles. Men, burdened with eighty or a hundred pounds of equipment, heaved themselves out of the trenches, formed lines, and walked forward. The officers in one New Army battalion kicked footballs. They did not reach the enemy line. Nor did most attackers. For all the barrage of British shrapnel, the German wire was only partly cut. When shelling ceased, hundreds of German machine-gunners scrambled from dug-outs twenty feet underground, adjusted their sights, and opened fire. Thousands of British soldiers fell in a few dreadful minutes.

The Newfoundland Regiment, in its first real battle, had moved up in support. At 9:05 A.M., after a report that the lead brigade had won its objectives, the Newfoundlanders were sent into the attack. The reports were false. As the men bunched at the few gaps in the wire entanglements, like cattle in a pen, the German machine guns found them. In a few minutes, 684 Newfoundlanders had fallen; 310 were dead. Along the British front, 57,470 men were casualties; 19,240 were dead. The Germans lost 2,000 prisoners and 20 guns in the first day at the Somme.

The Germans had been prepared. With such obvious British preparations in front of them, it was hard not to be. British shelling sounded fiercer than it was. Of heavy shells 30 per cent were duds; one in a thousand high-explosive shells was "premature", likely to explode in the gun barrel. British batteries called themselves "suicide clubs" and kept firing. No British shells could hurt dug-outs thirty or forty feet underground; no shrapnel — a collection of small bullets in a casing — was going to cut barbed wire. On the right, where a French attack was unexpected and the front-line trenches were close, the British attack succeeded. Elsewhere, the attackers died utterly in vain. Philip Gibbs, whose "Eyewitness" reports were the official British hand-outs to the press, reported: "It is, on the balance, a good day for England and France." History, in contrast, has judged the first day on the Somme as a military tragedy of epochal dimensions.

The battle went on. On July 14, a night attack by 22,000 raw New Army troops took the German front line. German counter-attacks almost wiped out the gains. Each gain was contested, with the Germans as committed as the British had been at Ypres, to hold every inch. Through July and August sacrificial death engraved placenames on a generation's consciousness: Pozières for the Australians; Delville Wood where a South African brigade died; Beaumont Hamel for the Newfoundlanders and British.

September 15 had become the target date for Joffre's concentric attacks. The "tanks" Haig had wanted for July 1 might be available, but only 49 of them, not 150. Canadians were available, too; three divisions of them, and a fourth coming. The Canadians proved more certain at Flers-Courcelette than the tanks. Only thirteen of the secret weapons crossed the trenches into action. Myth and excited German reaction gave them the credit for any gains that day; the reality was a brutal struggle of men against fire in the ruins of farms and villages. Techniques had improved from bloody experience. There was more heavy artillery than in July, and it now fired timed barrages so that infantry, if they could keep up, were on top of German trenches and dug-outs before the machine-gunners could emerge. Artillery could also blast the counter-attackers as they formed up. But German artillery could do so too, and both sides pummelled the ground into a moon-like landscape. Men on foot were exhausted by the scramble across no man's land; guns, tanks, and wagons were trapped by the churned, cratered earth.

In October came rain and the first signs of the coldest, bitterest winter Europe had known since 1880–81. Earth and chalk, blasted by artillery shells, turned to a glutinous, pale-coloured mud that trapped feet and wheels. The battle went on. Fighting in October cost the British 60,000 casualties. By November 14, conditions made more fighting impossible. For 419,654 British and 194,541 French casualties, Haig and his French partner, Ferdinand Foch, could boast of a strip of France thirty miles long, seven miles wide. The Germans admitted to 465,525 losses at the Somme. Doomsday had come to both sides.

V
THE CANADIAN CORPS

SAM HUGHES'S ARMY

A Royal inspection always told a division it was ready for France. The turn of the 2nd Canadian Division came on September 2, 1915. The summer had been warm and dry, a contrast to the misery of Salisbury Plain, and the twelve battalions looked fit and proud as they swept past the King, Lord Kitchener, and a beaming Sam Hughes, proud in his major-general's uniform.

Within two weeks, the Canadians were at Hazebrouck. Only the division's artillery brigades remained in England; the lack of guns in Canada and the shortage in Britain had delayed their training. The whole division needed training too, but there was no time. A British division was desperately needed for the offensive at Loos. By September 13, the raw Canadians were in the trenches, looking up at the jungle of wire that marked the German line along the Messines-Wytschaete ridge. Through the cold, wet winter of 1915–16, the Canadians would guard the southern flank of the sacred and cursed Ypres salient.

Sam Hughes had done more than smile on his boys. Major-General Sam Steele, the original commander of the division, had been imposed by the Honourable Bob Rogers: the West, after all, was entitled to its general, even if Steele was sixty-five and a veteran of the Red River Expedition. The British, horrified at Steele's age and inexperience, offered the Canadians any available general. Alderson proposed Arthur Currie, in recognition of his outstanding performance at Ypres. Hughes insisted on Richard Turner. His son Garnet, Turner's brigade major, reported well of him. Moreover, among the Canadian brigadiers, only Turner had spoken up for the Ross rifle. So had Lieutenant-Colonel Dave Watson, whose battalion had done so well at Ypres. He could have the 5th Brigade in place of Colonel J.P. Landry, who lacked a forceful word of command. Critics immediately noted that Watson, publisher of the Quebec *Chronicle,* was an old Hughes crony while Landry's father, the Conservative leader in the Senate, had made trouble for the government over Regulation 17. General H.D.B. Ketchen, a Winnipegger, could keep the 6th Brigade but the 4th must go to Lord Brooke, son of the Earl of Warwick and a fine fellow. The minister insisted on it.

Two Canadian divisions would form a Canadian Army Corps. The Australians and New Zealanders had set the precedent of a Dominion formation. In April, Hughes's loyal agent in England, Brigadier-General John Wallace Carson, had urged formation of a corps "with your good self in command". Colonel J.J. Carrick, a Quaker businessman and MP from Port Arthur whom Hughes had despatched as his representative at General Headquarters, urged the idea on Sir John French. The Corps was welcome, but the commander must be Sir Edwin Alderson. When Borden and Hughes visited England in the summer of 1915, the arrangements were completed. Alderson could have the Corps, Currie would inherit the 1st Division, and M.S. Mercer, also promoted to major-general, would command the Corps Troops, a collection of units that came to include the Canadian Cavalry Brigade, two unassigned infantry brigades, six regiments of Canadian Mounted Rifles, and supporting units. After a firm hint from the minister, Mercer's 1st Infantry Brigade was given to Garnet Hughes. For his helpfulness, Sam Hughes received a knighthood.

In June 1915, the War Office had asked Canada for a third division, in addition to the monthly quota of five thousand reinforcements needed to complete the Canadian ranks. In Ottawa, Major-General Willoughby Gwatkin, the long-suffering chief of the general staff, warned that Canada might not be able to find enough men. Hughes overruled him and reassured an anxious prime minister: General Alderson had explained to him that the third division in an army corps was almost always in reserve and immune from casualties. At Christmas, Mercer's command became the nucleus of the 3rd Canadian Division. The six Mounted Rifle regiments were reorganized as four infantry battalions, the PPCLI came back from their British division, and the Royal Canadian Regiment of the permanent force ended its exile on Bermuda. The other battalions were chosen from the growing number in England. Since the division had no artillery, Mercer was temporarily lent the British gunners of an Indian army division that had returned to a warmer climate. The cavalry brigade went off to the British cavalry corps to await the great breakthrough.

Sir Sam had no intention of leaving the British or even his own officers to manage promotions or organization overseas. In England, Hughes preserved control by preserving confusion. At Shorncliffe, Brigadier-General J.C. MacDougall, a timid permanent-force officer, commanded the Canadian

Training Division but Major-General Steele, given command of the Shorn-cliffe District by the British as a consolation prize, insisted that he had authority over MacDougall. The two men appealed to the minister's friend and agent, General Carson, who, for his part, assured the War Office that he was responsible for Canadian affairs in England. As a further complication, when Lord Brooke had to give up his brigade, Hughes gave him command of a big new Canadian camp at Bramshott, independent of both Steele and MacDougall. The net effect was that every decision, serious or silly, had to be referred to the minister.

Since Canadians in France were under full British control, exercising influence there was more difficult. Carrick quit in August, leaving his business partner, Major J.F. Manly-Sims, in charge. The real successor was Sir Max Aitken, a New Brunswick–born son of the manse who made himself a millionaire during the Laurier boom by managing corporate mergers. In 1910, Aitken had moved to England, bought the *Daily Express*, and entered Parliament as a Conservative. Sir Max was a busy man but his stock-in-trade was information. Canada could help. The British barred reporters from the front and issued cheerfully misleading communiqués through an "Eyewitness". Hughes promptly appointed Aitken as "Canadian Eyewitness", added him to the list of honorary colonels, and thus provided the publisher-politician with the rank and status to go and come as he pleased between London, GHQ, and the front. In September, Hughes added the title of "General Representative for Canada at the front".

The minister could hardly have been better served. Aitken was an ingenious publicist, eager to glorify Canadian military exploits and ready to lavish his wealth on preserving Canadian war records. His organization in London sponsored writers, photographers, and some of Britain's most talented painters. The Canadian War Memorials Fund employed artists as diverse as Paul Nash, Augustus John, and Wyndham Lewis as well as such Canadians as David Milne and A.Y. Jackson to depict Canada's war effort. Without Aitken's patronage, this book and others like it would have been difficult to illustrate. Though a Tory, Aitken had little respect for Britain's ruling class and his contempt for its military branch developed into a vendetta. Long before the prejudice became conventional, Sir Max had concluded that the British army was led by donkeys and that Canadians could manage as well with native-born generals who had been publishers, farmers, and stockbrokers. Aside from his personal favourites, such as Lord Brooke, Hughes entirely agreed.

The dramatic expansion of the Canadian Contingent in France from a single division to an army corps with three divisions was a challenge for Aitken and Hughes. Alderson took most of his staff with him to the new corps headquarters. Dozens of Canadian colonels and majors, left behind in England, eyed the new vacancies and besieged their superiors and the minister. Officers sent home as drunks or failures insisted that they had learned their lesson or, more often, that they were victims of snobbish British prejudice. Hughes needed little prompting from Aitken to take their side: "it is the general opinion that scores of our officers can teach the British Officers for many moons to come.... There is altogether too much staff college paternalism and espionage abroad...."

It is hard to find evidence for the charge. Apart from Brooke, whom Hughes insisted on again appointing to the 4th Division, every division and brigade in the Canadian Corps had a Canadian commander with one exception: Brigadier-General L.J. Lipsett, a British instructor in Canada at the outbreak of the war, had commanded the 8th Battalion at Ypres. His men later remembered him as the most approachable and popular general in the Corps. The British sent some of their best staff officers to the Canadians. Charles Harington, Alderson's Brigadier-General, General Staff, went on to become the legendary chief of staff of Sir Herbert Plumer's Second Army, the one formation BEF divisions longed to join because of the excellence of its staff work. Harington's successors and the British officer who served as the Corps's deputy-adjutant and quartermaster general, Brigadier-General George Farmar, were of comparable stature. So were the British staff officers who played similar key roles under Canadian divisional commanders. Since the Canadians became as well known for meticulous staff work as for courage and ingenuity, "staff-college paternalism" deserves some of the credit.

Perhaps the problem was Alderson. Hughes never forgave him for abandoning the Canadian-made equipment on Salisbury Plain. He also blamed Alderson for Canadian losses at Ypres and Festubert. He remembered that Alderson had balked at giving his son Garnet a brigade. When Canadians were accused of indiscipline, Hughes complained that Alderson was too gentle to manage real men; when Alderson scolded the Nova Scotians of the 25th Battalion for panic during a German raid, he was too harsh. Alderson's greatest crime was allowing the 1st Division's Ross rifle to be replaced by British Lee-Enfields in the summer of 1915. When Hughes learned that Alderson had invited his officers to comment on the rifle, the minister was livid. The resulting replies were a loyalty test. Garnet Hughes, Turner, and Watson supported the Canadian-made rifle; Currie, Mercer, and a majority condemned it. "[It] is nothing short of murder," wrote an anonymous colonel, "to send our men against the enemy with such a weapon." After Ypres, a third of the 1st Division had rearmed themselves with Lee-Enfields. In the summer of 1915, armourers did what they could to improve the Ross. Turner threatened harsh punishment for any member of his division found with a Lee-Enfield. Mercer had to explain why the PPCLI still carried the British rifle. As for Alderson, Hughes sent him a blistering letter accusing him of undermining confidence in the Ross and failing to provide the right ammunition. Copies were distributed to every colonel. Men in the ranks could decide for themselves whether Hughes or Alderson best defended their interests.

BLOODING THE NEW DIVISIONS

Canadians knew about winter but only veterans of Salisbury Plain were prepared for Flanders. A driving, relentless, continual rain filled every trench and shell crater. Mud liquefied and oozed from sandbags. From their higher ground, Germans added their drainage to the shells and sniper bullets they poured on the Canadian trenches. Sleet, snow, and bitter winds were countered only by the morning tot of rum.

In the French sector armed neutrality was the rule between battles; but Haig's headquarters insisted that the British "dominate" no-man's land with snipers, patrols, and constant raids. The Germans responded, usually with more skill, almost always from better ground. In November, two Canadian battalions, the 5th and 7th, practised ninety-man raiding parties for ten days. On the night of November 16–17, they crossed a little creek called the Douve and one of the parties captured prisoners and a new kind of German gas mask. Both groups escaped casualties but the less successful battalion had to try again a few nights later. Haig, newly in command, was delighted. Canadians found themselves celebrated and studied as leaders in what a less enthusiastic British officer later called "the costly and depressing fashion of raiding the other side". Costly it certainly was. From its creation on September 13 to the end of 1915, the Canadian Corps suffered 2,692 casualties, 688 of them fatal.

In the new year, the 3rd Division extended the Canadian sector until the Corps held six miles of waterlogged mud south from St. Eloi. The raids and counter-raids continued. Tunnellers from both sides drove mines and counter-mines in a claustrophobic struggle to blow up enemy trenches. The Germans went deep, the British went deeper, to sixty feet. By the end of March, the Corps had lost another 546 killed and a total of 2,760 casualties from battle, sickness, and accident.

The adjoining British corps had lost a small salient on February 14. Plumer, whose Second Army controlled the salient, ordered the corps to avenge the defeat by cutting off the German salient at St. Eloi. The British 3rd Division, weary and depleted, attacked on March 27. Mud and water leaped skyward from the bursting of six British mines. The huge explosions

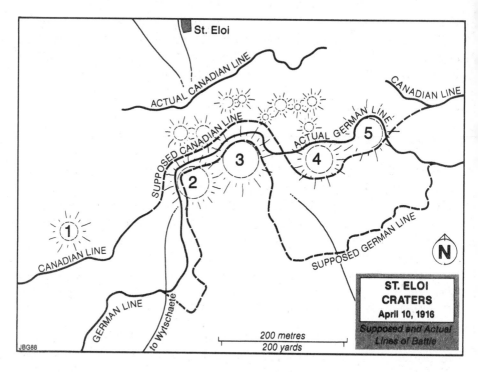

St. Eloi

ACTUAL CANADIAN LINE

SUPPOSED CANADIAN LINE

CANADIAN LINE

ACTUAL GERMAN LINE

CANADIAN LINE

1

2

3

4

5

CANADIAN LINE

SUPPOSED GERMAN LINE

GERMAN LINE

to Wytschaete

N

ST. ELOI CRATERS
April 10, 1916
Supposed and Actual
Lines of Battle

200 metres
200 yards

JBG88

transformed the landscape and buried the German defenders. A British brigade on the right took craters 1, 2, and 3. Machine guns held up the other assaulting brigade. More attacks followed, and by day's end the British claimed that craters 4 and 5 were occupied. In fact, lost in the sodden, devastated landscape, the British had actually occupied crater 6 and a seventh from an earlier explosion. The Germans had three days to prepare before the exhausted British discovered their error and completed the attack. Throughout the battle, German artillery saturated the tiny patch of mud and, on the night of April 3–4, when the British moved out of the line, there was not much left of their 3rd Division. Turner's 2nd Canadian Division took over.

The St. Eloi sector fell to the westerners of Ketchen's 6th Brigade. The battered British had left almost no trenches. The mine craters were now small lakes, the biggest of them 180 feet across and 50 feet deep, all of them an obstacle to supplies or reinforcements. By noon on April 4, half of the 27th Battalion were dead or wounded by German shellfire. That night, Ketchen sent up the 29th Battalion to relieve them as the German counter-attack struck. It was the disaster every officer feared: trenches packed with men, confusion of command, pitch darkness split by flares and exploding shells. Within three hours, the Germans had taken back almost everything the British had captured. Ketchen's counter-attacks failed. The Albertans of the 31st Battalion regained craters 6 and 7 but, like the British a week earlier, they believed they were at craters 4 and 5. From the heights of Messines, the Germans knew better; Canadian staff officers, peering up at the muddy ridges on their skyline, did not. Geysers of spray and mud from German shells kept them from going closer. Eight days of fog and mist kept British aircraft from checking from the sky.

Turner proposed to withdraw from St. Eloi, blast the Germans as they had blasted his men, and retake the lost ground. Alderson agreed. Sir Herbert Plumer, advised that the Canadians still held key craters 4 and 5, told them to stay put. Only on April 16 did air photos finally tell Turner the truth. It was too late. On the afternoon of April 19, a crushing bombardment buried the defenders of crater 6 and then 7. "Our men were glued in the mud," wrote one of them. "The survivors were in no condition to offer fight being dazed and shell shocked. The rifles were clogged and useless, only two or three being capable of firing." The few survivors surrendered. The Germans claimed 483 casualties; Turner's division had lost 1,373. It was not a victory.

Plumer fired his chief of staff and the officers found wanting in the 3rd British Division. Turner and Ketchen, he insisted, must also go: it was inexcusable that they had not known what was happening on their front. Alderson agreed. He had not forgotten Turner's strange inactivity at Ypres a year before. Sir Douglas Haig had more political sensitivity. In his diary, he weighed "the danger of a serious feud between the Canadians and the British" against "the retention of a couple of incompetent commanders". If Turner stayed, Alderson would have to go. Aitken, when he arrived, was delighted to oblige. In Ottawa, Borden and Hughes had prepared to defend their officers: Aitken's message was a relief. On May 28, Alderson was shuffled to the wholly nominal post of inspector general of the Canadians in England. His successor was Lieutenant-General the Honourable Sir Julian Byng, a cheerfully unintellectual cavalryman known to his colleagues as "Bungo". Byng had also turned out to be, to some people's surprise, a cool and effective field commander, who had personally managed the bloodless British evacuation at Gallipoli.

When Haig concentrated his troops for the Somme offensive, the Canadians remained in the Ypres salient. The 3rd Division, more confident and at full strength, now occupied almost the only high ground the British had retained from the year before; a hill called Mount Sorrel and Observatory Ridge, which ran from Tor Top in the east a thousand yards deep into the Canadian sector. It was key ground and the Germans wanted it, not only to make the rest of the salient untenable but to hold the British troops from their coming offensive.

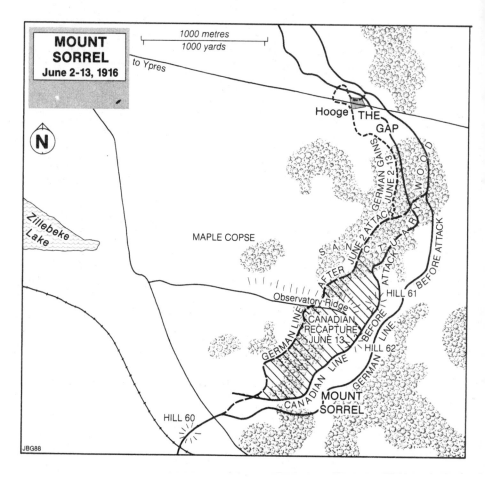

In May, British pilots spotted signs of German rehearsals behind their lines. Others saw guns and mortars in profusion. Then bad weather stopped systematic observation.

At night on June 1, German shelling stopped. Canadians were alerted but, in a few hours, when German troops had cut the Canadian wire, the shelling resumed. Next morning, Mercer and Brigadier-General Victor Williams of the 8th Brigade walked out to see the 4th Canadian Mounted Rifles position on Mount Sorrel and Tor Top. They were there when German shelling burst out with a dense fury no British troops had yet experienced. From Mount Sorrel to Sanctuary Wood, Canadian trenches and their defenders vanished. German observers saw dirt, trees, weapons, and human bodies hurled into the air. Four mines exploded under Mount Sorrel. Then, almost calmly, waves of German infantry walked forward. Dazed survivors offered little resistance. Of

702 men of the 4th Canadian Mounted Rifles, 76 survived unscathed. Two of the four Mounted Rifles colonels were killed; a third surrendered, as did the remnants of his headquarters, and a badly wounded General Williams. General Mercer, twice wounded, was found dead. In Sanctuary Wood, the PPCLI lost more than 400 men as it held the flank of the German attack. Elsewhere, scattered reserves rushed up to hold the line. With little barring them from Ypres, the attackers unaccountably stopped after a 600-yard advance and dug in.

That evening Byng ordered: "all ground lost to-day will be retaken tonight". The task was given to Brigadier-General E.S. Hoare-Nairne, commander of the 3rd Division's British artillery and Mercer's successor. With his own reserves and a couple of brigades from the 1st Division, Hoare-Nairne did his best. It was a second disaster. Signals misfired. Attacking troops, packed in trenches, were slaughtered by German guns. Artillery support, hurriedly improvised, was feeble. Machine guns swept away attackers. At dawn, the Germans still held their gains. On June 6, four more exploding mines slaughtered the Canadian defenders of Hooge, a little to the north. The Canadians had lost another piece of the salient. The Germans were two miles from Ypres. "This...goes to prove," Haig sourly noted, "that men with strange equipment and rugged countenances and beards are not all determined fighters."

Corps commanders who lost ground were "degummed" — fired. Byng deserved a second chance and time. Haig refused troops: they were needed for the Somme but he could lend some guns. This time the Germans would face a bombardment as good as their own. Like Alderson, Byng had soon spotted Currie as his best general: retaking Mount Sorrel would be his test. Losses from the earlier attack forced Currie to organize his division into two composite brigades. Assaulting battalions moved into the front lines, learned the terrain, and withdrew to rest and rehearse. A gunner in his militia days, Currie insisted on knowing the artillery plan and adding a little ingenuity. Four times, the bombardment reached a crescendo and stopped. Each time, the Württembergers opposite scrambled to defend themselves only to be blasted when they were in the open. On June 12, at 8:30 P.M., the guns reached a fifth crescendo. This time the Canadian infantry advanced. They found little resistance and two hundred prisoners. In an hour they had regained the losses of June 4. Then, it was the Germans' turn to fight, with a hurricane of shells and waves of counter-attacks. Both sides lost heavily, but no ground changed hands. On June 14, the firing died away.

In ten days, the Canadians had lost 8,000 men; the Germans 5,765, but it was the Canadians who felt victorious. They had also learned some useful principles for future victory: patient preparation, limited objectives, planned artillery support. The shaken 3rd Division soon recovered under the human touch of Major-General Louis Lipsett. Best of all, Mount Sorrel confirmed a lesson of St. Eloi: Canadians could not be expected to fight Germans with the Ross. On June 21, the War Office authorized an exchange of rifles and from Ottawa, in Hughes's absence, the government cabled its consent. Among the troops, it was a vindication of Alderson: for years the myth persisted that opposing the Ross had cost him his job.

THE BLOODY SOMME

If Haig had had his way, the British offensive in 1916 would have started in Flanders and Canadians might have been involved. It was General Joffre who insisted on fighting among the hard limestone ridges and the overgrown villages that rose from the valley of the Somme. Perhaps he had spared Canadians from the horror of July 1 and the dreary, grinding battles that followed through the summer but their turn came soon enough when Haig prepared for the vast, co-ordinated Allied assault on the Central Powers, timed for September 15.

The Somme had become Haig's *Gericht*: von Falkenhayn's insistence on contesting every inch with remorseless counter-attacks matched the British tactical faith that three and four lines of infantry could swamp any defence. For the September offensive, GHQ had two innovations: enough shells for the artillery to fire "rolling barrages", leading the infantry on to their objectives so that Germans would have no time to man their machine guns; and "tanks", tracked, armoured monsters that could flatten any machine gun that did emerge. This time, Haig believed, the exhausted Germans might finally crack and his three divisions of cavalry could pour through.

The Canadians came south in late August, fifty miles along dusty roads. They would replace the Australians and New Zealanders who had struggled, with futile valour, to take the Pozières ridge, the long limestone slope that commanded the British lines. On August 31, Currie's division took over the Australian line and on September 2, his 13th Battalion shared in a last Australian attempt on Mouquet Farm. That was a distraction. Sir Hubert Gough, once the leader of the "Curragh Mutiny", now commanded the Corps in the Reserve Army. His orders were to seize Courcelette and the ridge beyond. The Canadians must do it. On the right, Turner's 2nd Division would capture Courcelette; Lipsett's 3rd, on the left, would finish with Mouquet Farm and take the long German trench, Fabeck Graben.

At 6:20 A.M. on September 15, British and Canadian guns, parked wheel to wheel, opened fire. Turner's men reached their first objectives in half an hour.

Only five of the seven tanks assigned to the Canadians started; four were blasted by German shells and a sole survivor struggled to its objective at the maximum speed of a mile an hour. Five frightened infantrymen, assigned to clear wounded from its path, found none. Though an excited British "Eyewitness" boasted that tanks had given the British a sweeping victory and that cheering British troops followed one down the main street of Flers, German generals dismissed the new devices as a toy. Haig, more far-sighted or optimistic, ordered a thousand more from the Ministry of Munitions. Canadians, on the whole, tended to the German view, though one soldier remembered that a sole tank, named *Crème de Menthe,* had allowed his company to get moving when machine guns had pinned it down.

At dusk on the 15th, Byng ordered the next attack. On the left, battalions of Lipsett's 3rd Division fought a savage battle at Mouquet Farm and along the German trench line. On the right, the 22nd and 25th battalions struggled through Courcelette and into the fields beyond only to be cut off when German defenders emerged from cellars and tunnels in the sheltered village. The New Brunswickers of the 26th Battalion, followed through Courcelette, were caught in a desperate house-to-house battle. Almost isolated, the French Canadians and Nova Scotians fought off eleven counter-attacks in two days. "Si l'enfer est aussi abominable que ce que j'ai vu," Colonel Thomas Tremblay of the 22nd Battalion recorded in his journal, "je ne souhaiterais pas à mon pire ennemi d'y aller" (If hell is as bad as what I saw, I would not want my worst enemy to go there). At Mouquet Farm, Captain George Pearkes recalled, more prosaically, that he went around stopping up German tunnels with bombs from a trench-mortar. Only when he had completed the job would a British battalion agree to take over. Private John Kerr of the 49th Battalion, wounded and losing blood, led a squad of grenade-throwing Canadians deep into German trenches and brought back sixty-two prisoners. He lived to collect his Victoria Cross.

Days of pouring rain soon dragged the fighting to a stop. Always there were more German positions farther up the slope, with fortified redoubts that commanded every approach. On the 25th, the Fourth Army, adjoining, drove its weary men forward, to Morval, Lesboeufs, and, on the 26th, Gueudecourt. That day, at Gough's insistence, the Canadians advanced as well. Now it was the 1st Division's turn to lead. Its battalions found that the Germans, to escape the shelling, waited with their machine guns in front of their trenches, crouching in craters and ditches. The Canadians fought their way through two German lines but beyond the ridge, at Regina Trench, the few weary survivors turned back. Brigadier-General G.S. Tuxford found only seventy-five men left in the 14th Battalion but he sent them back for another try at 2:00 A.M.

German flares and machine guns caught them. Turner, on the right, tried piecemeal attacks and then belatedly co-ordinated them, but each assault ended in failure.

To higher commanders, Regina Trench had become the symbol of a victory they desperately wanted. It was also a desperately difficult objective, tucked behind the ridge line, fronted by tons of concertina wire which the Germans rolled out each night to fill gaps. Byng's orders were blunt: Turner's division, slightly rested but not rebuilt, would stay in the line until it had taken Regina Trench. Lipsett's division would help. October 1, 3:15 P.M., was zero hour.

It was hopeless. Driving rain turned the cratered ground to clinging, grey mud. Faulty British shells fell among the struggling infantry. Among the Canadian Mounted Rifles of the 8th Brigade, whole companies were slaughtered against uncut wire. A company that broke through was annihilated; another was driven back. In this sector, Turner depended on the depleted 5th Brigade. The 22nd Battalion struggled for half a mile through shells and machine-gun fire to find the wire uncut. "From this moment," its war diary recorded, "the attack failed." The 25th Battalion got thirty of its two hundred men to Regina Trench, and the 24th Battalion, the Victoria Rifles from Montreal, did better but the Germans drove in the Canadian flanks. The 2nd Division could manage no more than to collect its seven hundred losses.

Byng turned to Currie's 1st Division again. A week of foul weather gave both sides a little miserable time to prepare. Currie chose to attack at dawn with eight battalions in line. It made no difference. The line of German Marines, who now held the trench, was impregnable behind their wire. The 3rd Battalion, the "Toronto's", somehow got through. So did a hundred men of the 16th after an eighteen-year-old piper, James Richardson, strode up and down before the wire. His body was found later. On the 3rd Division front, some of the Royal Canadian Regiment cut their way through the wire but the Germans killed the attackers or drove them out. The cost of the day was 1,364 casualties for no gain. The post-mortems were bitter. Heavy artillery had failed to batter the German defences; shrapnel would not cut wire; the few men who broke into enemy trenches ran out of the grenades they needed to fight their way from traverse to traverse and there was no way to get them more. Replacements fresh from England, complained Currie, were virtually untrained and there were too few of them.

The reason, of course, was the chaotic Canadian organization in England, with its competing commanders and its distant, erratic overlord. Of 19,500 Canadians at Shorncliffe, more than a quarter had been diverted into odd jobs as orderlies, mess waiters, or bandsmen. Potential reinforcements were channelled into a 4th Canadian Division and then a 5th. Hughes came to England at the end of July to guarantee the command of the 4th for his old friend Dave Watson. Brigades were reserved for his brother, W. St. Pierre Hughes, of the 21st Battalion and for Lord Brooke. A hard-bitten prohibitionist newspaper owner from Vancouver, Victor Odlum of the 7th Battalion, got the third. "Big drive expected," Hughes cabled Canada, "and great desire Canadians should be first in Berlin." He planned four more divisions; Borden should send 80,000 more men.

In mid-August, Watson took the 4th Division to France. A few weeks at Ypres trained his battalions in trench fighting and a week at St. Omer allowed them to exchange their Ross rifles for Lee-Enfields. Then the division moved south to the Somme. By October 17, an exhausted and depleted Canadian Corps had moved north from the Somme to the Arras-Lens sector and the raw 4th Division took over its line. It was a horrible introduction to war. The coldest winter in memory had begun early, with sharp winds and icy rain. The trenches on the Pozières ridge were mere ditches, already knee-deep in water. Soldiers who burrowed into the walls to escape the rain risked burial in waterlogged mud.

It was long past time to stop the battle but Haig was not satisfied. The Germans, he insisted, were exhausted too. The Allies, in trouble everywhere, desperately needed a victory. He would like to announce it when the generals met again at Chantilly in November. Sir Hubert Gough wanted to oblige. On October 21, Brigadier-General Victor Odlum's 11th Brigade rushed part of Regina Trench behind a figurative wall of fire. In three hours, Montrealers and British Columbians had blocked a sector of the trench and thrown back German counter-attacks. The cost was 200 casualties and the rewards were 160 prisoners. It seemed so easy that, on the 25th, Watson sent the 44th Battalion in a similar attack. It was a slaughter. Later, the brigadier, St. Pierre Hughes, claimed that he had warned Watson that the artillery had chosen that day to switch position. As a result the barrage was feeble. German machine guns and artillery caught the Manitoba battalion in the open and killed or wounded 200.

For two weeks, steady, remorseless rain pelted the battlefield. The rest of Regina Trench still had to be captured. Gunners demanded two clear days for bombardment. On November 9 and 10, they finally got them. At midnight on the 10th, four of Watson's battalions attacked, starting from 150 yards in front of their trenches, away from the German counter-barrage. By dawn, they controlled the whole of Regina Trench, now a shallow ditch, twenty feet wide, littered with debris and corpses. Gough wanted still more from the Canadians. A week later, amid the first driving snow of the winter, with mud freezing underfoot, Odlum's 11th Brigade attacked Desire Trench beyond Regina. Perhaps Haig had a point: 625 Germans surrendered and one counter-attacking group threw down its rifles and gave up. The 11th, however, was isolated. Attacks by the 10th Brigade and a British brigade failed. Finally the Canadians withdrew from their farthest advance. For them the battle of the Somme was over.

Haig and historians would argue about its value. The few who knew what the Somme had cost Britain in the quality of its young men as much as in the appalling numbers felt numb and then furious with frustration. Yet Haig had insisted that the war could not be won until the German army was defeated and was there another way? Against an Allied claim of 623,907 dead and wounded the Germans recorded 465,525 casualties, but their statistics ignored a quarter of the wounded who recovered near the front. Von Ludendorff understood exactly what the fighting had done to his enemy when he pleaded in November for a return to unrestricted submarine warfare: "we must save the men from a second Somme battle". The Germans had sent 93 divisions into the battle, half of them twice. Most emerged with their cadres destroyed; 1,500 or 2,000 casualties in a regiment of 3,000. The old German army was gone, much as the British regulars had perished at Ypres and Neuve Chapelle.

The Canadians, too, had suffered at the Somme. The 2nd Division would proudly remember Courcelette and the 4th Division Regina Trench but, for all of the divisions, the Somme was a memory of mass butchery ordered by generals who were all-powerful and never seen. The Somme cost Canadians 24,029 men. They knew there was little to show for it but painful lessons. Like other soldiers on the Western Front that year, Canadians digested cruel experience. Infantry needed fresh, flexible tactics. Artillery had to protect attacking troops from the merciless German guns. Above all, communications had to pierce the fog of war so that generals and colonels could help front-line soldiers. Overdue but necessary, a ferment of ideas would transform the tactics and technology of fighting.

A WINTER OF DESPAIR

A war that generals had expected to win in four months had lasted twenty-eight months by the end of 1916. Now its misery was aggravated by the harshest winter since 1881. There was starvation in German and Austrian cities. Britain, the banker to the world, had mortgaged its last credit. Lord Lansdowne, Conservative leader in the House of Lords and once a governor general of Canada, pleaded privately that only peace could preserve the fabric of civilization. On November 21, 1916, the ancient Habsburg emperor died.

His heir, a nephew of the victim of Sarajevo, contacted a brother-in-law in the Belgian army to see if peace could be arranged. In Berlin, the chancellor, Theobald von Bethmann-Hollweg, again proposed a separate peace with Russia. German generals scuttled such proposals by proclaiming an independent Poland. On December 12, Bethmann announced still broader peace overtures. The terms he wisely kept secret; Germany would keep her conquests, spread her empire, and collect huge reparations from her enemies. Nothing less was now acceptable to the generals, and perhaps to the suffering German people.

The Germans at least considered terms; the Allies still thought only of total victory. In Washington, President Woodrow Wilson had tried to be a peacemaker and now he tried again. Narrowly re-elected by Americans as "the man who kept us out of war", Wilson invited warring nations to consider "peace without victory". The Allies responded awkwardly, conscious of secret promises to each other, anxious to build an image of moral superiority that might draw Americans into the war. They wanted a return to the 1914 frontiers, reparations for Belgium, France, Serbia, and other victims and, in an unexpected flourish, "national self-determination" for the subject peoples of the Habsburgs and "the bloody tyranny" of Turkey. Americans were mildly pleased but Allied terms bound Turkey and Austria all the more tightly to their German ally.

The truth was that to most people in Germany, France, and Britain, peace talk still represented defeatism and a form of treason. British seamen refused to allow delegates to a peace congress at Stockholm to board their ships. In Paris, Joseph Caillaux, the ex-premier whose wife had been acquitted of murder in 1914, urged a compromise peace with Germany. So did Louis Malvy, an interior minister who slipped money to a defeatist newspaper, *Le Bonnet rouge*. Patriots scorned them.

In every warring country, civilian ministers had helped to glorify generals as the architects of victory. The public, far removed from the battlefield, now believed in them as military geniuses. Even the soldiers at the front, yearning for peace and well aware of failures of generalship, could not contemplate defeat. Bethmann had welcomed the enormous prestige of von Hindenburg and von Ludendorff as assets in his own search for negotiated peace only to find von Ludendorff empowered by his reputation, and von Hindenburg's, to pursue grander and more disastrous strategies. There must be victory in the East, von Ludendorff insisted, not peace. In the West, though, he cancelled von Falkenhayn's policy of holding every inch. Behind the German line, 50,000 Russian prisoners laboured on a shorter, painstakingly fortified new defence line, the *Siegfried-Stellung*. Once completed, the "Hindenburg Line", as even

Germans called it, would secure the West and release fifteen divisions for other, more decisive battles. Most of all, von Ludendorff demanded that Germany take up the weapon she had abandoned in 1915: unrestricted submarine warfare. Strategy meant winning, not worrying about neutrals. German admirals now had a good reason to agree.

On May 31, 1916, the German High Seas Fleet had finally clashed with the British Grand Fleet in the foggy waters of the North Sea off Jutland. Three times the German battleships had slipped through a British trap; once the British admiral, Sir John Jellicoe, had turned away from the enemy for fear of mines or torpedoes. That was not how Nelson had fought nor did it seem a British victory to lose three capital ships to two German battleships. Jutland was another of the blows 1916 brought to Britain. The truth about Jutland was caught by an American headline: "The German Fleet assaulted its jailer but it is still in jail". Within a couple of weeks, Jellicoe was back at sea. The fatal weakness of his battle cruisers was soon repaired. Apart from a single scurry from harbour in the summer of 1916, the German High Seas Fleet now stayed in port. A few of its marines had faced Canadians at Regina Trench; most seamen waited in mutinous idleness, a fatal diversion of resources that von Ludendorff insisted must be put to real use. German admirals agreed. Who cared if sinking every ship approaching Britain brought the Americans into the war? England would starve in six months. France would collapse without her ally and, by the time Americans had an army, it would have no place to land.

One man could match von Ludendorff in ruthlessness of purpose. Alone among British politicians, Lloyd George had built a popular following. He had preached a "knock-out blow" to cheering crowds and always he had seen that blow padded by amateurism, indecision, and the refusal to mobilize national and Allied strength. Andrew Bonar Law, the Canadian-born leader of the Conservatives, shared Lloyd George's frustration: Max Aitken, another Canadian Tory, was the go-between. The decent, drunken Herbert Asquith, in his own eyes "the indispensable man", was dispensed with when 102 Liberals joined with Conservatives to make Lloyd George prime minister on December 7.

At once, Britain's wartime management changed. A tiny War Cabinet — Lloyd George, three Conservatives, and a Labour member — took charge of the war effort, most without carrying ministerial burdens. A supporting staff — Lloyd George's "Garden Suburb" — was created to carry out a prime minister's will. Merchant shipping, food production, and manpower were controlled. Only the army seemed too much to control: like Bethmann, Lloyd George realized that wartime generals had vast popular followings. Conservatives protected Haig; the King made him a field marshal. Instead of being "a

While some women broke stereotypes to fill a variety of wartime jobs, most channelled their support into traditional female tasks. Knitting produced a phenomenal output of socks, scarves, wristlets, and other goods. Men overseas cherished them for their quality—and for the unexpected personal notes they sometimes found enclosed.

A militant minority of women joined quasi-military organizations, drilled, and learned how to shoot. Ridicule from both sexes soon drove such groups out of existence; in any case, there was plenty of more conventional patriotic work for them.

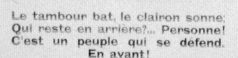

TOUS LES VRAIS
POIL-AUX-PATTES

S'enrôlent
au
163ᵉ C.-F.

Cᵗ en chef:

HENRI DES ROSIERS

ci-devant du 14ᵉ F. E. C.

Cᵗ en second:

OLIVAR ASSELIN

Comprend aussi:
le major RODOLPHE De SERRES,
le capitaine ROBERT ROY,
le lieut. Alain de Lotbinière Macdonald,
tous de retour du front;
le lieut. de JONGHE, Victoria Cross; etc.

Le tambour bat, le clairon sonne;
Qui reste en arrière?... Personne!
C'est un peuple qui se défend.
En avant!

QUARTIERS **MONTREAL** RUES Sᵗ DENIS
GENERAUX ET Sᵗᵉ CATHERINE

VICTOIRE!
les Poil-aux-Pattes
s'en viennent

The 163rd Battalion was one of the few successful recruiting efforts in Quebec after 1914. While Henri DesRosiers, a veteran of Ypres, was in command, the real attraction was Henri Bourassa's errant lieutenant, Olivar Asselin. While Asselin insisted that he was doing his duty for France, his memoirs show him responding to his yearning for adventure. The "Poil-aux-Pattes"—literally the "hairy paws"—appealed to the best and brightest in French Canada.

Native Indian parents and their newly enlisted son. Though military authorities worried that Germans "might refuse to extend to them the privileges of civilized warfare," native Canadians were eagerly sought as volunteers and many enlisted. Wartime service and sacrifice seemed to many native groups a solid argument for better treatment from the Canadian majority.

FRONT LINE TRENCHES

Wire

Forward Sap

Latrine

FXirebay

Traverse

Dug-Out

Dug-Out

Communication
Trench

Front Line

Coy. H.Q.

Medical
Officer

Support Line

To Reserve Trenches

A diagram of a trench system, showing the first two lines. Naturally, nothing on the ground was this systematic.

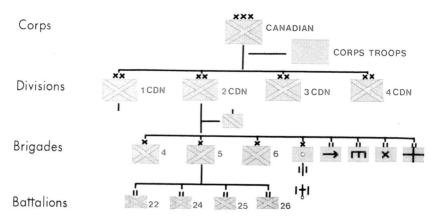

Corps

CANADIAN

CORPS TROOPS

Divisions

1 CDN   2 CDN   3 CDN   4 CDN

Brigades

4   5   6

Battalions

22   24   25   26

The organization of the Canadian Corps in 1917. By 1918 a brigade of engineers had been added to each division, and machine-gunners were grouped in a battalion for each division as well.

Colonel William (Billy) Avery Bishop was Canada's leading air ace in a realm where Canadians excelled. The top dozen aces in the war shot down 757 aircraft; the four Canadians among them, Bishop, Raymond Collishaw, Donald MacLaren, and William Barker, accounted for 247.

While officers slept in dug-outs, men in the ranks made themselves comfortable on narrow steps carved out of the trench wall. The mark of a veteran soldier was the ability to sleep anywhere.

First aid in the trenches. A wounded soldier grimaces as a comrade applies a dressing. The septic Flanders mud could make even minor wounds fatal. Gas gangrene was a terrible way to die.

This odd 1919 contribution from *The Veteran*, the publication of the Great War Veterans' Association of Canada, is a reminder that a few black Canadians crossed the CEF racial barrier and served gallantly with fighting units.

butcher's boy driving cattle to the slaughter" for Haig, Lloyd George tried to persuade the Italians to lead the attack. General Cadorna, the Italian chief of staff, prudently declined. Suddenly, Lloyd George found a better agent.

The French, also, had a new leader. Joffre's miscalculation over Verdun and the terrible casualties that followed were too much even for his reputation. His reward was a marshal's baton and retirement. Verdun had produced a handsome, articulate national hero who had thrown German armies back with seemingly trifling casualties. General Robert Nivelle surely had prestige enough to allow Aristide Briand's socialist government at least to explore peace. But no; Nivelle, an artillery officer, was a man with a plan. A tornado of artillery fire, an irresistible mass of manoeuvre, and a certain breakthrough, he promised: "Laon in twenty-four hours and then the pursuit." Other generals argued that the plan was hopeless and that the French army would not be strong enough — or were they merely jealous? Lloyd George was dubious too until he met the new French commander-in-chief. Thanks to his mother, Nivelle was more articulate in English than Douglas Haig. Even better, Nivelle wanted the French to do most of the fighting. Haig and his generals learned at Calais on February 26 that the War Cabinet had put them under Nivelle's command. In united fury, they forced the prime minister to back down: the subordination would only be during Nivelle's attack. They never trusted Lloyd George again.

There was other news from that bitter winter. In Petrograd in early March, rioters smashed into bread shops. Cossacks refused to ride them down. The Tsar returned to his capital only to be turned around by defiant railwaymen. On March 15, his generals persuaded him to abdicate. Committees or Soviets of workers and soldiers took power but the government passed to middle-class liberal politicians. Once the new Provisional Government agreed to carry on the war, there was enormous relief. In the Allied countries and in the United States, Tsarist autocracy had been the ugliest blemish on the Allied cause. Doubtless too, it was also to blame for Russian defeats. Democracy would surely refuel the Russian steamroller but even optimists knew it would take months, if not years. Von Ludendorff quietly arranged for a troublemaker named Lenin to travel home to Russia from Switzerland in a sealed railway car. Another Russian revolutionary named Leon Trotsky was released from a Canadian internment camp at Amherst, Nova Scotia, after pressure from Canadians sympathetic to Russia's new liberalism. Surely the new, democratic Russia needed men who had fought tyranny.

On January 31, 1917, Bethmann lost a bitter argument with von Ludendorff. Germany proclaimed unrestricted submarine warfare. Two days later, as he had promised, Woodrow Wilson severed diplomatic relations. He would go no further. U-boats ignored his restraint: more American ships were sunk. Alfred Zimmermann, a Bethmann subordinate, wired the German embassy in Mexico City to promise German aid if the Mexicans attacked the United States. British intelligence intercepted the message, diverted it neatly into American hands, and waited for the results. Wilson and the U.S. Congress obliged. On April 7, the United States went to war.

It was a triumph for the Allies but, like Russia's March revolution, American participation did not promise quick results. The American fleet of modern battleships made no difference to the U-boat war. The United States had no real army. To create one meant drafting, training, and equipping millions of young Americans, but only France and Britain could provide them with artillery, tanks, aircraft, and even rifles. American credit could sustain British and French finances but the American economy had all that it could do to support its own mobilization. The Yanks were coming — but not yet.

And they might not come at all if von Ludendorff was right. In March, U-boats sank 600,000 tons of British and neutral shipping. In April, the total reached 870,000 tons. No shipbuilding program could match such staggering losses. One out of four ships that left British ports never got back. In six months, the Germans had sent 3.75 million tons of shipping — and 3,833 seamen — to the bottom. The Admiralty had no answer. Since U-boats no longer surfaced to rescue crews, they were usually invisible and undetectable except when they had to charge their batteries. Admiral Jellicoe, now the First Sea Lord, dismissed convoys as impossible. Shipping companies agreed. Beginning in January 1917, Lloyd George imposed rationing. Even the rich, a visiting Canadian politician complained, could not get all they wanted to eat.

All that the French and British could hope was that General Nivelle was right.

VI
A NATIONAL CRUSADE

C anada's acting high commissioner in London understood the status of the CEF in 1914: "as soon as the Canadian troops arrive here they will be entirely under the authority of the War Office and become part of the Imperial army in every sense of the word." That was understandable from George Perley, an imperialist, an Ottawa millionaire, and a Tory minister without portfolio who had accepted a summer in London as an ideal reward for his unpaid chores. An official reason to keep the vulgar Sam Hughes away from "his boys" was an added bonus, but Perley was perfectly correct. The CEF was as much part of the British army as any Scots guardsman or Lancashire fusilier. Canada provided the men and the money but Britain, as Hughes himself admitted, gave the orders.

In 1914, that seemed appropriate. Sir Robert Borden, and most Canadians like him, revered Britain and its institutions. The war was a test of loyalty they proudly passed. In 1915 it was different. The casualty lists from Ypres gave Canada a direct stake in a war the British seemed to be bungling. Borden went to London in 1915 to help: he found himself treated as an intruder. The dull, seemingly phlegmatic Canadian had a temper. Unless he got information, he warned Bonar Law, "I shall not advise my countrymen to put further effort into the winning of the War." That did it. Lloyd George was summoned from a country weekend and poured out almost more than Borden wanted to hear: "During my recent visit to England," Borden wrote later, "a very prominent Cabinet Minister in speaking of the officers of another Department said that he could not call them traitors but he asserted that they could not have acted any differently if they had been traitors." The department, of course, was the War Office.

Once back in Ottawa, information and even gossip were unavailable. Borden could learn about the war only from his morning paper. Again he demanded to be informed. Well aware that the Canadian capital was a sieve for secrets, the British demurred. Bonar Law repeated what he had said in London: "if no scheme [to keep Ottawa informed] is practicable, then it is very undesirable that the question should be raised". Fury at that response fuelled Borden's New Year's pledge of half a million Canadians for the CEF. That would show the British what earnestness meant. His anger poured into a letter to Perley, to be shown to British cabinet ministers: "It can hardly be expected that we shall put 400,000 to 500,000 men in the field and willingly accept the position of having no more voice and receiving no more consideration than if we were toy automata.... Is this war being waged by the United Kingdom alone, or is it a war being waged by the whole Empire? If I am correct in supposing that the second hypothesis must be accepted, then why do the statesmen of the British Isles arrogate to themselves solely the methods by which it will be carried on?"

A few days later, when his temper and his lumbago had subsided, Borden cancelled the letter but he liked it well enough to include it in his memoirs twenty-five years later. It spelled out his assertion of a new status for Canada in the Empire and the war: henceforth she would be a junior but sovereign ally in the struggle, not a subservient colony.

From that, much would follow, but not right away. Through most of 1916, Borden was engulfed in the problems of war finance, bankrupt railways, the decay of Conservative support in the provinces, and, above all, rescuing the war effort from the tempestuous and terrifying Sam Hughes.

Nowhere was that effort more chaotic and embarrassing than in England. Some of the problems came from Canada. Scores of CEF battalions arrived only to be broken up, adding to the hundreds of surplus officers that had collected in England with the First Contingent. Battalions in France now preferred to fill vacancies from their own ranks rather than with colonels, majors, and captains who owed their rank more to politics than soldiering. Many such officers sacrificed rank and pay to serve; more helped expand the military bureaucracies that Carson, Steele, MacDougall, and lesser rivals created. In February 1916, when Alderson visited Shorncliffe in a hunt for men for the Corps in France, he found 1,476 officers and 25,085 other ranks — but only 75 officers and 2,385 men were even training to fight in France. Carson's staff in London had grown to 3,500 all ranks by the autumn of 1916.

By 1916, the War Office despaired of sorting out who was responsible for Canadian military administration in England. General Gwatkin, who understood that and most other problems, tried to let Borden know but the prime minister now regarded Gwatkin's messenger, the ancient Duke of Connaught, as a meddler. Twice Hughes left for England promising reform. In April, he was summoned back to face charges of double-dealing and profiteering in his Shell Committee. Exonerated by a royal commission that discreetly loaded all the guilt on the unlovely J. Wesley Allison, Hughes was free to return in the summer of 1916 for another try. In both cases, his solution was a council of his aged cronies and dependants, with authority only to submit every decision to him.

By the end of September, when Hughes returned to Ottawa, he was as certain as ever that a little bullying would make Borden accept his latest scheme. He was wrong. For one thing, the riot at Camp Borden in July, while Hughes was inspecting "his boys", not only underlined administrative failures, it dispelled the belief that the troops adored their minister. For another, his old enemy, Sir George Perley, had spent the summer in Ottawa. For more than a year Perley had pleaded for reform. With the war giving Canada a new influence, he had warned, "it is especially necessary that we should just now impress people here that we are both sane and capable in the management of our own affairs". Ships carrying Perley and Hughes had passed in mid-Atlantic. Borden had made up his mind. On October 27, Hughes learned how. A new Minister of the Overseas Military Forces of Canada (OMFC) would be based in London, with the powers of a Minister of Militia and more. Hughes was outraged. He would lose all control over "his boys". Then, more slyly, he suggested a nominee: Max Aitken. No, it would be his enemy, Perley. Again Hughes exploded. For once, Borden was firm. A final abusive letter from the militia minister was too much. On November 9, Hughes was fired.

Borden had never fired a minister before, and he feared huge wellsprings of popular support for Hughes from Orangemen, Tories, and, above all, from the troops. He knew the secrets a furious Hughes would reveal and the lies, which would be believed. In the long run, he was right. For the moment, only Hughes's enemies rejoiced. "I do not like to kick a man when he is down," wrote Colonel J.J. Creelman, an artillery officer in France, "but I am willing to break nine toes in kicking Sam." The public posturing, the political officers, and, above all, the Ross rifle had ended any Hughes identity with "his boys". In time, he would find defenders. Nationalists took pride in his pugnaciousness. Canadians yearn for larger-than-life figures; victims of his bullying, from the prime minister to permanent-force officers, should have stood up for themselves. Their failure made them wrong. Military red tape, his professed target, remains unpopular. Hughes's reputation will live as long as mountebanks are admired. That guarantees his historical longevity.

Sir George Perley had to clean up the mess. If he had known how much there was, he later told Borden, he would never have accepted the job. Perley found chaplains fighting each other, the Army Service Corps embedded in graft, and the Veterinary Corps in a mess. Surplus officers were everywhere. In France, there were 2,526 Canadian officers for 105,640 men; in England there were 7,420 for 128,980. Thousands of the men freshly arrived from Canada were unfit for service. The nastiest legacy was a report on the Canadian Army Medical Corps by a Hughes-appointed colonel. Dr. Herbert A. Bruce, founder of Toronto's Wellesley Hospital, was already a bitter critic of the overseas Director of Medical Services, Major-General G.C. Jones, when Hughes invited him to investigate medical matters overseas. After six weeks, Bruce had seen enough to blast Jones for toadying to the British. Canadian wounded had been sent to improvised English hospitals that were nothing more than "matrimonial agencies". Canadian hospitals had been sent to the Mediterranean where there were no Canadians. Too little was done to hurry Canadian wounded back to the front or to treat VD cases with severity. Some medical officers were even "drug fiends or addicted to alcoholism". A delighted Hughes had fired Jones, put Bruce in his place, and now used the report to attack Perley, who sympathized with the much-abused Jones.

Perley's strategy was to let proven officers from France run his Overseas Ministry. General Turner reluctantly gave up his division to come to London. Byng, delighted to be rid of an inadequate commander, gave the vacancy to General Harry Burstall, a permanent-force gunner. Perley faced his first crisis when Borden, anxious to pacify Sir Sam, demanded the vacant division for Garnet. A compromise was found by giving Garnet the new 5th Division, now designated, because of the lack of men from Canada, to be held for the home defence of Britain.

Once in England, Turner rapidly solved old problems. The seventy unused CEF battalions became twenty-four reserve battalions, linked to battalions in the Corps and soon to regions and provinces in Canada. Men from the same town would serve together. To Canadianize the Corps staff, the British agreed to provide vacancies in their staff courses. Carson, MacDougall, and Steele were eased out. Sir Max Aitken — now Lord Beaverbrook as a reward for helping Lloyd George into power — continued with the Canadian War Records Office but left Perley alone. In France, Colonel Manly-Sims would manage liaison with GHQ but, symbolic of a new regime, he soon had twenty-six pages of instructions to guide him.

The medical mess, Perley found, was "the most serious and difficult of all the many troubles here". Nothing would be more devastating to home-front morale than allegations that wounded heroes had been maltreated or neglected. At the same time, Bruce's exaggerated allegations so enraged the great Canadian physician Sir William Osler that he quit the game in disgust.

Just as furious and closer at hand were prominent ladies, from the Duchess of Connaught to Lady Perley herself, whom Bruce had impugned for their charity work in the hospitals. Perley promptly arranged for a report by Sir William Babtie, a prominent British army surgeon. When it criticized Bruce's snap judgements, General Jones was briefly restored and the senior medical officer with the Corps, Major-General G.L. Foster, was summoned as a permanent replacement. Bruce's fury would echo for a generation and at least some of his complaints were justified, but the Canadian Army Medical Corps was restored to relative calm.

Canadians had little idea why the OMFC was created. The government had no wish to advertise the mess. Front-line soldiers have a legendary contempt for the "bomb-proof" jobs at base, and Argyll House, the OMFC's London headquarters, soon became a soldier's shorthand for the insulated arrogance of a remote staff. The government, too, cautiously avoided publicizing the change of status that the Overseas Ministry represented. By reaching across the Atlantic to establish a department to control Canadian troops in England and on the continent, Ottawa had softly but firmly asserted that Canadians were no longer "part of the Imperial army in every sense of the word". "The Canadian Force," Perley explained to the War Office, "is an entity irrespective of where parts of it may be situated or serving...." It had not been so in 1914; it would be so in 1917.

VIMY RIDGE

The Canadian Corps that emerged from the winter of 1917 was different. On their shoulders men now wore "Somme Patches", big flannel rectangles in red, blue, grey, and green for the 1st, 2nd, 3rd, and 4th divisions, with other patches to distinguish infantry battalions. The voices were different too: the Old Originals and the Second Contingent, with their British accents, had been swept away at the Somme; flatter Canadian accents now dominated. Most battalions had been rebuilt; a few from Quebec and British Columbia showed the impact of Canada's recruiting crisis. When Colonel Tremblay returned to the 22nd Battalion from five months in hospital, such was the state of discipline because of unsuitable men from the depots that he felt obliged to approve three death sentences. Manitoba and British Columbia battalions, too short of replacements, were transferred to Ontario or New Brunswick where recruits were still adequate in number.

The bitter winter weather had brought frozen hands and feet. Veterans remember hot food freezing in their mess tins. Soldiers showed unusual enthusiasm for kitchen fatigues, with their shared warmth. But men who remembered Flanders in 1915–16 rejoiced in the dry, well-drained trenches and the dug-outs the French had left them. Vimy had been a quiet sector, dominated by a German-held ridge, running four miles north-west from Farbus Wood to the west of Givenchy-en-Gohelle, with an added hill in the Bois de Givenchy that soldiers christened "The Pimple". To the west, Canadians faced a gentle slope rising to two heights at opposite ends of the ridge, Hill 135 and Hill 145; to the east, the slope fell steeply, into thick woods. At 450 feet above sea level, Vimy Ridge would have been unremarkable elsewhere, but in flat country it dominated the landscape.

Twice in 1915, the ridge's German defenders had thrown back Foch's best troops; they had learned from the experience, creating a dense network of trenches, tunnels, concrete emplacements, wire, and dug-outs. One was so big it could hold a battalion. The German forward defences included three successive lines, and a second zone behind the crest was just as strong. Hills, farmsteads, and a couple of villages had been turned into small fortresses. Guns and mortars were hidden in the woods behind the ridge. Three divisions from General Freiherr von Falkenhausen's Sixth Army, two Bavarian and one Prussian, shared in defending Vimy Ridge, and they knew it was vital ground.

In February, British pressure on the Somme and Nivelle's approaching offensive convinced von Ludendorff that it was time for Operation "Alberich": a retreat to the Hindenburg Line after such systematic devastation of the intervening 2,000 square miles of France that the enemy could not pursue. After four days, March 15 to 18, the operation was complete. Not until April 5 could the Allies establish their new lines. The Somme salient, a key to Nivelle's plan, was gone. French politicians and generals invited him to reconsider his offensive. He threatened to resign. They gave way. The Germans had not abandoned his objective on the Chemin des Dames Ridge nor the objectives he had assigned to Haig: Arras and Vimy Ridge.

From November, General Byng had known that his Corps would be attacking Vimy though it was only on January 19 that he knew that the Canadians would have to do the job alone. If they failed, the British Third Army attack along the Scarpe River from Arras would be in serious danger. In six months Byng and his men had seen a lot, and they liked each other. "This is a soldier," wrote Andrew Macphail, now a medical officer, "large, strong, lithe, with worn boots and frayed puttees. He carries his hand in his pocket and returns a salute by lifting his hand as far as the pocket will allow." Canadians liked that.

Byng was slack about salutes but not about preparations. Since Nivelle seemed to have discovered the secret of attacks, he sent Arthur Currie to Verdun to find out. Currie came back skeptical of some French theories but with some important new ideas. Instead of attacking in line and in waves, as the British had insisted in 1916, assaulting troops should move as fast as they could, fighting their way forward in platoons, tackling resistance from the flank or in the rear. Maps and air photos belonged with front-line troops, not just with the staff. Remembering Regina Trench, Currie insisted that objectives should be obvious natural features men could easily find, not a map reference or a trench that might be obliterated or confused. And, above all, attacking units should be rested, fed, and happy. Other units should do the dirty work always assigned to the PBI — the "poor bloody infantry".

Perhaps the strongest image of the First World War is of bull-headed generals ordering their men into hopeless attacks. The memory of a generation was scarred by the sixty thousand dead and wounded on the first day at the Somme. Yet soldiers did manage to overcome barbed wire, machine guns, and artillery barrages — because generals and staff officers searched feverishly for weapons and tactics that could break the trench stalemate. Most of the devices offered by eager inventors were rubbish. Even the famous tank deserved most of the skepticism it collected from colonels and privates alike; it would not have survived without Haig's willingness to divert men and resources to the new arm. But artillery tactics were transformed by science and ingenuity, and the most dramatic changes have been the least understood. By 1917, when the Canadians attacked Vimy, troops fought in "platoons" of thirty or forty men. Specialist sections in the platoon carried a Lewis gun for firepower, bombs, and "rifle grenades". A Mills bomb on the end of a stick turned a soldier's rifle into a personal artillery piece to knock out a German pillbox or machine-gun post. At a horrifying cost, platoons of infantry could fight their way forward until they ran out of bullets and bombs. When victory eventually came, it was because soldiers — French and British as much as Canadian — learned, experimented, and learned again.

Byng had made other preparations as well. For three winter months, engineers and pioneer battalions — filled with men unfit for front-line service — built and repaired roads, laid twenty miles of light-railway track, buried twenty-one miles of signal cable, and laid sixty-six miles of telephone wire. Signal wires were "laddered" — separate lines with connecting links so that a single shell could no longer snap communications. Tunnelling companies burrowed eleven underground galleries to help infantry get to assault positions safely, wired them for lights, and added chambers for headquarters, dressing stations, and supplies. Just to water the fifty thousand horses needed to haul supplies and guns required forty-five miles of pipeline.

The key to success, Byng insisted, would be artillery. The Corps could count on 480 18-pounders, 245 howitzers and heavy guns, and 42,500 tons of shells, with new fuses that ensured that, this time, German wire could be cut. A young engineering professor from McGill, Lieutenant-Colonel Andrew McNaughton, had borrowed counter-battery techniques from the French and British and improved on them. Three groups of heavy guns, a squadron from the Royal Flying Corps under Major Charles Portal, and an elaborate network of spotters detected 83 per cent of the guns behind Vimy Ridge and targeted them for destruction.

Sir Edmund Allenby of the neighbouring Third Army had wanted two days of bombardment; Byng insisted on two weeks, doubling the rate of fire in the second week. German survivors, pinned in their dug-outs and starving because ration parties could not reach them, remembered it as "the week of suffering". At dusk on April 8, firing slowed. Germans emerged and then relaxed. Nothing happened. Far below them, gunners piled shells and fixed fuses for the next day. Infantry battalions, which had practised for days on a vast replica of the Ridge, filed past for the real thing. In assembly areas, men stopped for a hot meal and a tot of rum. It was bitterly cold.

In the black pre-dawn, men crawled from the forward trenches and waited on the frozen mud. At 5:30 A.M., April 9, Easter Monday, as a sudden storm of sleet and snow gusted from the west, almost a thousand guns opened fire. "Imagine the loudest clap of thunder you ever heard," Lieutenant E.L.M. Burns recalled, "multiplied by two and prolonged indefinitely." Sixteen battalions, eight thousand men, rose to move forward across cratered, debris-strewn ground. All four Canadian divisions advanced in line, from the 1st, opposite Thélus, to the 4th, facing Hill 145 and Givenchy.

Dazed Germans defenders emerged to face sleet and snow. Few of their own guns survived to support them. In the first couple of lines, only sentries and a few men stumbled out to offer resistance. Canadian assault troops hurried forward behind the barrage, visible now in the grey dawn with its white puffs of shrapnel and the oily black eruptions of high-explosive. Follow-up waves bombed German dug-outs or took the occupants prisoner. The third line was different. German machine-gunners sliced into advancing Canadians. Strong points had survived the awful barrage. Depleted platoons tried their new tactics. When officers and sergeants were gone, corporals and privates took over. Weary survivors struggled on to the next murderous battle.

At 7:00 A.M., the 1st Division was the first on its primary objective. The 3rd reported reaching the crest at 7:30 and the 2nd, with much heavier fighting, took another half-hour. For a few hours the attackers paused while supporting brigades moved up for the final phase. Currie's division was responsible for Farbus Wood; Lipsett's 3rd, with an attached British brigade to help, moved down the far slope to the woods below. Two battalions of the 2nd Division swarmed down the ridge with bayonets fixed to take 150 prisoners, including a German colonel. Captain Thain MacDowell of the 28th personally took two machine guns and, by bluff, persuaded 77 Prussian Guards to give up. The handsome university athlete won one of the four VCs earned that day. Of the four winners, he alone survived the war.

On the left, the 4th Division had some of the toughest objectives, made all the harder because two of its battalions had been almost destroyed in a disastrous trench raid on March 1. Watson's division faced Hill 145, the highest point of the ridge and the best defended. To help him, the colonel of the 87th asked the artillery to leave one German trench intact as cover for his men. Instead, the Canadians found it full of hard-fighting Germans. As the Canadian attack faltered, Germans to the rear had time to emerge. Survivors of the 102nd Battalion from northern B.C. got to Hill 145 and held on, but that meant that guns could not blast Germans without killing Canadians too. Watson had intended his reserve brigade to take The Pimple. It was sucked into the battle for Hill 145. It was after dark when a raw Nova Scotia battalion, the 85th, brought into the battle as a labour force, went up and took the German defences. The few Canadians who struggled as far as Givenchy were overwhelmed. For the moment, Watson could do no more.

By April 12, the Germans had pulled their line well back on the Douai Plain but they had thrown the Prussian Guard Grenadiers into the defences of Givenchy and The Pimple. Watson had given the objective to Brigadier-General Edward Hilliam, an Alberta rancher who had once been a British sergeant-major. With eighteen artillery batteries in support and driving snow and sleet behind him, the westerners of Hilliam's 10th Brigade attacked at 5:00 A.M. An hour later, though half of them were killed or wounded, the Canadians had won. Hilliam signed his report "Lord Pimple".

Vimy was a triumph: "Canada's Easter gift to France", wrote a Paris newspaper, with the ineffable assumption that the French were entitled to it. The King sent Haig his congratulations. Canadians then and later knew that they had done a great thing and that on such deeds nations are built. A victory so quick might also seem easy. At most, 40,000 Canadians shared the naked vulnerability of the infantry on April 9 and the days that followed. Almost all the Canadian losses — 3,598 killed, 7,004 wounded — came from that number. Most of the wounded would survive and many would return to their battalions but almost one in ten of those who fought at Vimy would live only as a name engraved on the soaring memorial that now stands atop Hill 145.

MILITARY SERVICE ACT

When the Canadian Corps scored its Easter Monday triumph, Sir Robert

Borden was in London, a hundred and fifty miles away. It was not by accident. Early in January, Lloyd George had announced to advisers that it was time to summon the Dominion premiers. "We want more men from them," he explained. "We can hardly ask them to make another great recruiting effort unless it is accompanied by an invitation to come over and discuss the situation with us."

The summons to discuss "great matters" at an Imperial War Conference was what Borden had wanted since 1915. The Canadian Parliament was summoned and adjourned within a month to free the prime minister for his historic journey. In London, ministers and lesser lights busied themselves with the conference while premiers and key advisers were closeted with Lloyd George in an Imperial War Cabinet. "When they are here," Bonar Law had warned his new chief, "you will wish to goodness you could get rid of them." Doubtless it was true when Borden, South Africa's Jan Smuts, and New Zealand's W.F. Massey led discussion into the future shape of the "Imperial Commonwealth" or the need for "an adequate voice" in foreign policy. Chiefly, though, the premiers learned of matters they had not read about in newspapers: the disastrous U-boat campaign, the collapse of Russia, the exhaustion of French and British manpower and, when the United States entered the war on April 6, the certain delay in American mobilization.

The message was clear: even if Russia recovered and the United States someday delivered vast armies, the brunt of fighting now fell on the Empire. To weaken was to lose. A prime minister who had preached earnestness needed no persuading. Tireless visits to Canadian wounded steeled Borden's heart: he saw men who would be sent again and again to battle until they were dead or too maimed to be used. Easter Monday and the news of Vimy Ridge brought reflected glory. Borden hurried to France to review the troops in pelting snow, to see the devastated field and to talk to officers. To keep the Corps up to strength required 75,000 men a year; there were 10,000 in England and 18,000 in Canada. Fewer than 5,000 had joined the CEF in March and almost none had chosen the infantry. In England, Lloyd George had asked him to match the five Australian divisions in France. That was impossible but, without men, could Canada even keep four divisions? When Borden returned across the U-boat–infested Atlantic in early May, his slow, systematic mind was made up.

No news in Canada would change it. National registration had failed. So had a last valiant effort by Pierre Blondin, the postmaster general, to raise a Quebec battalion. So had the attempt to raise a special home-defence force to release thousands of CEF men for the front. The efforts of Major-General Sydney Mewburn, aided in Quebec by Colonel Armand Lavergne, produced 200 men for a force intended to be 50,000 strong.

For months, even years, some Canadians had cried out for conscription: the Liberal lawyer J.M. Godfrey, the blind Boer War hero Colonel Lorne Mulloy, Manitoba's chief justice T.G. Mathers, a host of clergy, and the IODE. Clarendon Worrell, the Anglican archbishop of Nova Scotia, summed up their common argument: "Why men of infinite value to the community should be called upon to sacrifice themselves in order that a number of worthless and non-producing creatures may go on in their animal enjoyment is beyond comprehension."

Those were not Borden's arguments when he spoke to the Cabinet on May 17 or to the House of Commons on May 18. Nor was his argument based on Empire or on Britain's need. "I conceive that the battle for Canadian liberty and autonomy is being fought today on the plains of France and Belgium." The Canadian Corps had become "a new revelation of Canadian patriotism"; conscription was needed to fill its ranks and to keep faith with its members. "If what are left of 400,000 such men come back to Canada with fierce resentment in their hearts, conscious that they have been deserted and betrayed," he demanded, "how shall we meet them when they ask the reason?"

Liberals had answers. Conscription, they insisted, was being used as a popular issue to attract votes. Borden was trying to distract Canadians from the plight of the bankrupt railways. Anti-recruiting riots in Montreal on May 24 were another answer. A day later, Borden invited Laurier into a coalition of equals; he would vacate the prime-ministership if it helped. He would even defer conscription. On June 6, Laurier said no. He should have been consulted before Borden spoke on conscription, not after. It was now too late. If he joined, he would hand his province to Henri Bourassa and the *nationalistes*.

Laurier had other motives he could not share with Borden. A Liberal victory seemed imminent that spring. Conscription might not be so popular. Australia, more British by far than Canada, had rejected it in 1916 and would do so again. Farmers and trade unionists would oppose conscription, if more discreetly than had the Québécois. Borden knew the arguments, too, and he had no illusions of easy victory. On the goal he was clear; on the means he would be flexible and very patient.

Chief of the means was a Military Service Bill, drafted by Arthur Meighen, the coldly eloquent solicitor general, and modelled on the new U.S. selective-service law. Critics could note that young bachelors would be selected first, that there were exemptions for religious objectors, and that three layers of appeal had been included, from two-member local tribunals nominated by the opposing political parties to a Supreme Court justice. On June 11, the long, bitter debate began. "Do not tell me this is Canada's war," cried David-Arthur Lafortune, a Quebec Liberal. "Canada did not make war on anybody." Laurier, seeking above all to hold his party together, argued for a referendum. Even some Liberals dismissed the idea of delay. Conscription, Laurier declared, drove a wedge through the unit of Canada; it was "an obstacle and a bar to that union of heart and soul" on which Confederation was based. The listeners grew tired. Minds were made up. On July 6 the House voted. Nine Quebec Conservatives joined Laurier; twenty-five Liberals deserted him. One of them, the devoutly partisan Frank Carvell, had confessed to a friend: "There is something within me which abhors the idea of throwing up my hands when others are fighting my battles." He had to go home and think. He switched. The Senate took longer, but on August 29, conscription was law. The wedge had been driven. In a New York paper at the end of August, a future prime minister, W.L. Mackenzie King, reassured Americans: "it is perhaps not surprising that the rest of Canada sees in the Quebec attitude nothing but disloyalty, and is more determined than ever to make certain that Quebec shall not prevent the Dominion from doing its entire and splendid duty to the men at the front."

HAIG'S OFFENSIVE

The Canadian triumph at Vimy Ridge on April 9 was the overture to Nivelle's victorious strategy. Nivelle's ideas had contributed to the success: the massive bombardment, the care in destroying the German artillery, the flood of troops in the first wave. Fortunately the Canadians had not believed everything the French general preached: they had not raced on beyond the range of their artillery and they had discovered for themselves the weary, deadly business of dragging their guns, ammunition, and supplies across the cratered morass that any heavy bombardment left.

On the same day, General Sir Edmund Allenby's Third Army had driven south and west along the axis of the Scarpe River with almost comparable success: in a week the British had captured 13,000 prisoners and 200 guns. That was the help the British had promised. The rest was up to Nivelle — and the Germans.

Nivelle's tactical brilliance was an article of faith, at least among the war-weary junior officers and men of the French army. His strategic vision was almost as persuasive, at least to politicians who wanted to believe. The Germans occupied a deep salient stretching to the Somme. For six months, the

British and French armies had drawn German divisions in and destroyed them. Now, from Arras in the north and Champagne in the south, the Allied armies would strike with irresistible force, bursting the salient like a bubble. The trouble was that von Ludendorff in March had neatly pulled his troops back into his *Siegfried-Stellung*, creating a wasteland barrier to any heavy attack and saving himself thirteen divisions, which he promptly moved south. After all, anyone with a Paris newspaper knew when Nivelle's offensive was coming and a trench raid had even given the Germans a copy of the plan.

The Germans also had a new defensive strategy that topography and local stubbornness had not revealed at Vimy. German commanders thinned out their front lines, leaving them to be pulverized by the enemy's guns. The attackers were then channelled onto the "killing grounds" Germans themselves chose, to be slaughtered by concentrated fire from artillery and machine guns. Then German counter-attacks recovered lost ground.

On April 16, behind the fire of five thousand French guns, Nivelle's men found out for themselves how the new strategy worked. With the courage and conviction of men who believed in victory, the French rushed forward into a massacre. German guns knocked out the new French tanks. German fighters concentrated overhead to drive the French planes from the skies. By nightfall, the gains of the first day were lost. Nivelle poured in more divisions. French army medical services, told to prepare for ten thousand wounded, planned for fifteen thousand and got ninety thousand. In ten days, the French had gained four miles. On April 28, Nivelle was fired. The hard-headed hero of Verdun, General Henri-Philippe Pétain, replaced him.

Next day, an exhausted battalion, reduced to a third of its strength, refused to go back to the attack. On April 30, the ringleaders were shot and the remnant obeyed orders. On May 3, a whole division refused orders despite appeals and promises. Mutinies spread. Soldiers elected committees, raised the red flag, and sang the Internationale. Staff officers, the *buveurs de sang*, made themselves scarce. By June, most of the French army had been affected. Pétain moved efficiently to end the crisis. He corrected grievances about food, leave, and quarters. Discipline returned. Courts martial convicted 23,385 mutineers, and sentenced 412 to death. Pétain ordered 55 mutineers shot and sent hundreds more to penal colonies. There was no softness but there was understanding. The French army would defend France and the most mutinous regiments proved it in the line but soldiers would no longer be sent like sheep to slaughter.

The British army was not so lucky. Throughout April, Allenby continued the drive up the Scarpe against ever-tougher resistance. Sir Henry Horne, with the Canadians as part of his First Army, joined in. On April 28, Currie's division captured the Arleux loop of trenches south-west of Vimy. Nivelle's plight forced the British on. On May 3, Allenby's army failed almost everywhere along its line of attack. Currie's men alone made gains, taking Fresnoy: "The relieving feature," commented the British official history, "of a day which many who witnessed it considered the blackest of the War." By May 8, when the British called off their struggle, Fresnoy had fallen to a counterattack and the Scarpe battles had cost the British 158,660 casualties, far more than the official total of 137,000 French losses in Nivelle's attack on the Chemin des Dames.

Haig would have stopped the Scarpe battles sooner. Loyalty to Nivelle and Lloyd George's commitment of the British army to the common cause kept the losses mounting. Since 1916 and perhaps earlier, Haig had believed that Flanders was the right place for the British to fight. Ten miles beyond Ypres, at Roulers, he could cut the rail junction the Germans needed to supply their northern front. At Zeebrugge and Ostend, Admiral Jellicoe erroneously believed, were the submarines that were strangling England. Each Allied disaster, from Salonika to the French mutinies, was a fresh argument for action. In Russia, with brave folly, Alexander Kerensky had pushed Russia's army into a new offensive which, for a few days, succeeded and then failed more disastrously than any. Entire Russian divisions shot their officers and dissolved. In Italy, a tenth Isonzo offensive failed as tragically as all the others. Even the British suffered set-backs, in Palestine, where two battles at Gaza in March and April were so disastrous that General Allenby was sent to rescue the situation.

Haig's arguments for his offensive were defective. In early May, French and British generals had met at Paris and agreed that victory was impossible in 1917. When the French army crumbled, Pétain wanted his ally to take over more trenches, not to waste men. Even General Foch, passionate defender of the offensive almost anywhere, insisted that Flanders was not the place. Who, he demanded of Sir Henry Wilson, now the chief British liaison officer in Paris, was sending Haig on "a duck's march through the inundations to Ostend and Zeebrugge"? If it was Jellicoe, he was wrong: there were few German submarines on the Belgian coast. It was certainly not Lloyd George, yet the British prime minister was not protesting, either. He had been so wrong about Nivelle that his judgement was shaken. The prime minister had promised Britain a victory and Haig was eager to fight for it.

Even more, Haig delivered a triumph. On June 7, the roar of nineteen huge explosions under the Messines Ridge rattled windows in London. After almost three weeks of bombardment, British and Australian troops of Sir Herbert Plumer's Second Army swarmed up the ridge. There were more days of the inevitable shelling and counter-attacks but the Messines-Wytschaete ridge Canadians had known in 1915–16 was taken. For the first time, the casualty toll favoured the British: 17,000 to 25,000 Germans.

If Haig had wanted to fight in Flanders, the shattering victory at Messines should have been followed up. Instead, fighting stopped for a month. He needed to persuade Lloyd George again, at meeting after meeting. He had also promised his protégé, Sir Herbert Gough, that he would command the attack and it took weeks to move the Fifth Army headquarters north and to prepare plans while, on the spot, Plumer's headquarters waited in frustration. It was time the Germans did not waste; they tunnelled and dug and built yet more concrete pillboxes to hold the low ridges in front of Ypres.

On July 31, Haig's offensive began. For fifteen days, shells had pounded the earth to dust. As Gough's troops waited to attack, a gentle rain turned to a drenching downpour. For four days, before it literally bogged down in a sea of mud, the Fifth Army moved 3,000 yards at a cost of 31,850 casualties. Even the direction was wrong. Haig had wanted to move towards high ground; instead Gough had chosen to push north, and his commander had not interfered. The attacks resumed in a week as the rain kept bucketing down. Years of shelling had destroyed any natural drainage system. Roads, trees, buildings, all had been demolished, leaving a sea of mud marked chiefly by occasional ruins, derelict tanks and guns, and bottomless lakes over mine craters and shell craters. By the end of August, the British had lost 68,000 men to regain St. Julien and part of Pilckem Ridge.

At the end of August, Lloyd George might have called a halt; Haig probably should have. It was not in him to do so. There was no more talk of Ostend or Zeebrugge but there was insistence on a German army worn down at the Somme and now reduced to exhaustion. The French, too, must be spared, though a French diversionary attack at Verdun in August not only took 10,000 prisoners but showed the benefit of Pétain's nursing. Lloyd George came, saw what Haig's GHQ showed him — carefully selected, weedy-looking German prisoners — and returned to London.

There was an added reason for Haig's confidence. In September, the rain stopped, the ground dried, and Plumer, the best of Haig's generals, took over the attack. On the 20th, the attack began. A day's rain made no difference. As usual, Plumer's staff had watched the details. Tactically, the battle was as perfect as any in the war. Rolling barrages were timed to stay with soldiers floundering in mud. Infantry headed for fixed, visible objectives. Aircraft overhead kept in touch with movements. On September 20, the British had reached Menin Road; on the 26th, Polygon Wood; and Broodseinde, on October 4. The onslaught, von Ludendorff wrote, "proved the superiority of the attack over the defence". Australians, leading Plumer's advance, reported seeing German guns being dragged away. Beyond "were green fields and pastures, things of course we had never seen in the Ypres sector".

Then, on October 4, the rains returned, driving, drenching torrents that restored the churned soil to an endless sea of stinking mud, spotted with the bodies of horses, men, and all the detritus of war. Wounded drowned in it. When eight or a dozen stretcher-bearers were needed to move a single casualty, too few reached hospitals. For the first time, Germans found British soldiers eager to surrender and talking of killing their officers. The optimism went out of the British army, wrote Philip Gibbs, the former "Eyewitness". The generals and their apologists could explain Passchendaele as a series of climatic misfortunes. Posterity preferred Siegfried Sassoon:

> I died in hell —
> (They called it Passchendaele); my wound was slight
> And I was hobbling back, and then a shell
> Burst slick upon the duck-board; so I fell
> Into the bottomless mud, and lost the light.

VII
KILLING GROUNDS

LENS AND HILL 70

On June 6, 1917, a newly knighted Sir Arthur Currie was summoned to Corps headquarters and a week of rumours ended. Byng would replace Allenby in command of the Third Army and Currie would replace Byng. It all made sense. Vimy had proved Byng's competence. From Ypres to the recent vicious struggles at Arleux and Fresnoy, Currie had clearly emerged as the best of the Canadian generals. He was cool, innovative, with an instinctive eye for ground and tactics. A big, flabby real-estate promoter could also be a great field commander. Before Vimy, Currie and Byng had clashed angrily over trench raids, with the Canadian refusing to sacrifice his best officers and men. Currie remembered Byng circling him "like a cooper round a barrel", while he patiently explained why raiding hurt his troops, not the Germans. Currie had been right: his 1st Division, its battalions intact, had taken its objectives while the 4th Division, decimated by the raiding policy, had stumbled badly.

No set of Canadian appointments could be simple. Haig and Byng had forgotten that Perley now decided CEF promotions. In December, Turner had been promised the Corps if he went to London. On June 8 Colonel Manly-Sims arrived: "apparently wanted to suggest a dicker," Currie noted. It was not for Turner: promotion to lieutenant-general and status as senior Canadian soldier overseas sufficed for him. It was Sir Robert Borden who wanted to dicker: Currie must send a strong statement on conscription and he must give Garnet Hughes the vacant division to quiet old Sir Sam. The statement was easy but Garnet was unacceptable. Currie had already chosen Brigadier-General Archie Macdonell, a tough NWMP and cavalry veteran his men called "Batty Mac". In London, Currie and Hughes squared off in a three-hour shouting match. "I'll get even with you before I'm finished with you," Garnet finally shouted.

Perhaps he could. Back in August 1914, while Garnet had promoted Currie's virtues to his father, Currie had been busy paying off the worst of his business debts with a big government cheque intended to pay for his regiment's uniforms. For three years, Currie had hoped that his guilty secret was buried; meanwhile the regiment's creditors patiently tracked down their quarry. In June 1917, they succeeded. Just as Canadians learned that one of their own now commanded the Corps, the government got evidence that its new general was a thief. While Perley and A.E. Kemp, Hughes's successor as Minister of Militia, argued about what to do, Currie borrowed the missing money from Watson and General Odlum and paid back his old regiment. Whether or not the Hughes family knew Currie's secret, it could no longer blackmail Currie without implicating Sir Sam.

With a mind burdened by such problems, Currie returned to his new command and the war. His task, under Sir Henry Horne's First Army, was to hold German divisions that might otherwise stop Haig's Flanders offensive. From the first, Currie insisted on doing the job his way. Haig had ordered that attackers must hold any ground they took. To Currie, that meant exposing troops to needless casualties. His Canadians would raid, destroy, and return to their trenches before the Germans could catch them. In a series of carefully planned sorties, Currie showed how to hit without getting badly hurt. On June 8 and 9, brigades from the 3rd and 4th divisions drove deep into the German line south of Lens. The cost was 709 casualties, 100 killed, but the efforts paid off. Two weeks later, the Germans pulled back to Avion, well aware that their position was now hopelessly weakened.

What the British really wanted was Lens itself, a ruined coal-mining town that had defied them since the Battle of Loos in 1915. On July 7, Currie got his orders. On July 10, the Canadian replaced a British Corps in trenches that looked across at Lens and at the two hills, Sallaumines and Hill 70, that flanked it. Currie went out and climbed a hill behind the Canadian lines, the Bois de l'Hirondelle, and lay there for a morning, examining the ground. What he saw made him think. The Canadian troops could fight their way through the rubble of Lens but they and their supporting guns would be on low ground, easily commanded by Germans on the two hills. The smart answer was to seize one of the two hills, preferably Hill 70 to the north, and let the Germans waste their men trying to take it back. Corps commanders were supposed to obey orders, not change them, but Currie was different. To Horne, he explained his concerns: "if we were to fight at all," he insisted, "let us fight for something worth having." Haig was summoned, predicted that the Germans would not let the Canadians have the hill, and approved — provided the attack was under way by August 4.

Haig had a point. Hill 70 was a bald knob of limestone the British had taken and lost in 1915. Clumps of miners' cottages on the slopes of the hill had given the Germans a perfect covered approach for their counter-attacks. The shell-battered ruins, with a maze of cellars, trenches, and tunnels, would now be even better cover. Currie had an answer. His new machine-gun companies would follow the assault waves, dig into the hard chalk surface, and wait for the counter-attacks. His artillery, better and heavier than anything the British had had in 1915, would be waiting for the Germans in a killing ground of his choosing, not theirs.

Currie had no illusion that Hill 70 would be easy. The batteries of British guns available at Vimy had moved north to Flanders. General Morrison knew that many of the remaining guns in the Corps heavy artillery were worn out and no longer accurate. Germans had introduced frightening new weapons in July — *Flammenwerfers* or flame-throwers that threw a jet of fire fifty feet or more, and a new gas that smelled of mustard and raised agonizing blisters wherever droplets fell, especially in the crotch, armpits, lungs, or wherever the skin was damp. Weather was a misery at Lens as much as in Flanders, and rain washed out Haig's deadline. To Currie, it was far more important that rehearsals and preparation be perfect.

So far as they could be, they were. At dawn on August 15, ten Canadian battalions rose from their trenches and walked into the barrage. In front of them, Hill 70 erupted in explosions of flame and dirt. The Germans, alarmed at the Canadian threat, had sent troops forward but a diversionary attack by Watson's 4th Division on Lens distracted them. Thick black smoke from five hundred blazing oil barrels spread as a screen over Hill 70, blinding German machine-gunners. Even blinded Spandaus spat out five hundred rounds a minute to kill and wound, but in twenty minutes the surviving Canadians were on top of Hill 70. Battalions from the 2nd Division wheeled south, into the mining villages on the slopes, while Macdonell's 1st Division pushed east and north. On the far side Brigadier-General F.O.W. Loomis's 2nd Brigade faced a huge chalk quarry and German defenders unshaken by the bombardment. British Columbians and Winnipeggers of the 7th and 8th battalions fought from shell-hole to shell-hole but it was early on August 16 before they were in position. Most men of the battalions were dead or wounded.

Then the real fight for Hill 70 began. As early as 9:00 A.M. on August 15, the Canadians fought off their first counter-attack. Attacks kept coming. In the intervals, infantry and machine-gunners hacked holes for themselves and their guns or cared for wounded comrades. Artillery observers used wireless for the first time to zero in on advancing German columns. Private Harry Brown of the 10th Battalion died of terrible wounds after struggling back with word of a massing German counter-attack. He won a vc. At Corps head-quarters, intelligence officers had calculated how long it took German reserves to reach points along the road into Lens. Long-range artillery shells met the Germans as they marched. Aircraft spotted the results. Certainly the Canadian artillery suffered heavily. German mustard-gas shells lobbed at the gun positions cost two artillery brigades 178 casualties after gunners had yanked off their masks to see what they were doing. Somehow, the survivors kept the batteries firing.

Hundreds of Germans got through the storm of shrapnel and high explosives and hurled themselves forward with grenades, rifles, and the terrifying flame-throwers. Canadians fought back, sometimes hand to hand. Sergeant Fred Hobson wielded a Lewis gun until it was jammed, tossed it to a private to repair, and fought off Germans with his bayonet until it was back in action. His body was found surrounded by fifteen dead Germans. Major Okill Learmonth of the 2nd Battalion, desperately wounded, led his men from the parapet, catching German grenades and hurling them back. Both Hobson and Learmonth earned a posthumous Victoria Cross. In all, Canadians won five vcs at Hill 70.

At dawn on August 18, Learmonth's men stopped the twenty-first and last German counter-attack. The battle for Hill 70 was over. Taking the Hill cost the Canadians 3,527 men; holding it cost 2,316 more, including the hundreds of gunners who had suffered from German mustard gas. Currie's strategy had paid off: five German divisions had been thrown into the battle at a cost of 20,000 men: they could not go to Flanders. For Currie, it was "altogether the hardest battle in which the Corps had participated" but years later, he remembered it as his proudest. Like Plumer at Messines, Canadians had cost the enemy far more than they had paid and, in his first battle, Currie had shown the British professionals that he was a shrewder tactician than they were.

Hill 70 did not end the fighting for Lens. To clear Germans from more of the mining villages on the slope, Currie ordered a fresh attack on August 18. Ketchen's 6th Brigade ran into a German counter-attack and was stopped. So was part of Hilliam's 10th Brigade, but two of his battalions got forward, inspired by an ex-Russian army bayonet instructor, Corporal Filip Konowal, who took three German machine guns. Ahead lay the wreckage of a pit-head and a slag heap called the Green Crassier. To take them, Hilliam sent in a badly depleted 44th Battalion. The Manitobans relived their bad luck at the Somme. They moved forward, took both positions in bitter fighting, and found themselves facing two German battalions. In a few hours, the 44th lost 354 dead or missing and 87 prisoners of war — almost all the men who had gone forward. It was a grim, local tragedy of war.

Lens and Green Crassier stayed German and the Canadian Corps headed into an even uglier, more encompassing tragedy.

PASSCHENDAELE

On October 3, without prior notice, Sir Douglas Haig showed up at the Canadian Corps headquarters. Currie had been half-expecting his message: the Canadians were needed at Passchendaele. The reasons, at least to Haig, were sadly obvious. He had pushed his British and Australian divisions to the limit, and the Germans still held the ridge and the symbolic smear of brick dust that gave the battle its name. Currie protested. Like other Canadians, he knew the Ypres salient and hated it. Nothing good had ever happened there to Canadians or to the Allies' cause. Canadians, he warned, would lose sixteen thousand men they could not afford. Haig was firm: "some day I will tell you why," he told Currie, "but Passchendaele must be taken."

No British lieutenant-general could make terms with a field marshal but the Canadian Corps was no longer British. Currie had conditions. He would not serve in General Gough's Fifth Army: the Somme and Gough's mindless orders to attack hopeless objectives were not forgotten. Instead, the Canadians would replace the Australian Corps under Plumer. They must also have time to make thorough preparations. Well aware that delay had already cost him too many chances that year and eager to end the battle, Haig begrudged any added days but he agreed. Then the two men went out to meet the divisional commanders and Haig explained it all again — including Currie's protest and his conditions.

Currie had no illusions about the Corps's reactions; few of his men would know that he opposed the new commitment. He sent Lipsett and Odlum to look at the battlefield: it was, if possible, even worse than they expected. Odlum later recalled: "all you could see was shell holes with a group of men in them, and you could look perhaps two hundred yards over and see the Germans in the same position. Both sides were just finished."

While the British occupied the vast bog created by a creek called the Ravebeek, the Germans occupied slightly higher and drier ground. Their heavy artillery reached every part of the salient, from men huddled in shell holes to the reserves, resting under sodden canvas shelters in the rear. German defences were based on scores of circular concrete pillboxes with walls five feet thick, impervious to any available artillery and located for interlocking support. Only two roads led up through the salient to the front and the British had been forced to concentrate their artillery in dense clusters beside each of them, one for field guns, another farther back for the heavy guns. For lack of hard ground, engineers had built wooden platforms that became, in effect, rafts in the mud. To save time and the awful labour of moving guns, General Morrison agreed to take over the Australian Corps artillery where it sat. Canadian gunners reported that of the 250 Australian heavy guns they were supposed to take over, only 227 could be found and 89 of them were out of action. Barely half the 306 field guns farther forward were usable. A staff officer at Plumer's headquarters suggested that Currie submit a proper indent for the guns according to procedure. The Canadian general exploded: he could not kill Germans with indents. The paperwork was forgotten and the guns were brought forward.

There was everything to do. Brigadier-General W.B. Lindsay, the Corps chief engineer, a jumbo-sized man of proverbial resoucefulness, organized twenty-one companies of engineers and nine battalions of pioneers for the task of rebuilding roads, carving drainage ditches, constructing new gun platforms, and collecting supplies, all just a little faster than German artillery could destroy his work. Lindsay's men suffered almost fifteen hundred casualties before the fighting had even begun. The Germans, from their high ground, had easy targets. Men who fell off the roadways or the narrow duckboard tracks that snaked forward to the infantry positions risked drowning in the mud. Wounded men sank for ever in the foul soup. At Passchendaele, scores of German aircraft bombed and strafed troops and camps. Big two-engine Gotha bombers, designed to attack London, were diverted to the battle. Never had Canadians been hit so hard from the air. The dreadful weather provided one small compensation: German bombs and shells buried themselves in the deep mud, doing far less damage than on normal ground.

Currie's plan was simple: a succession of limited advances well within the range of his supporting artillery. At each stage, while the infantry consolidated, guns could be dragged up for the next advance. When he saw the ground for himself, Currie made another change. Traditionally, attacking troops rested in the rear, moved up just before zero hour, and advanced while they were still fresh. No man would be fresh after struggling through yards of knee-deep mud and there was no real rest anywhere in the salient. Currie's men would come up a couple of days before their attack, recover from exhaustion as best they could, and be ready to move when the barrage came down. Wireless, tried at Hill 70, would be used again to make sure that the shelling did not move beyond the floundering attackers. It was faster than carrier pigeons and telephone wire rarely survived enemy shells. It was all Currie could do for his troops.

The first attack was planned for October 24. Because preparations were so painfully slow, Currie postponed it to the 29th and then, at Haig's insistence, brought it back to the 26th. For ten days the weather had been dry; on the 25th it broke and, at dawn on the 26th, men of the 3rd and 4th divisions faced a sea of mud and flooded craters that blocked half their frontage. For two days and nights, Canadians struggled forward under German fire. A few valiant men discovered that the German pillboxes could be tackled if they could be isolated from supporting fire. The narrow slits, with thick walls, gave the defenders little visibility and the Germans did most of their fighting from trenches to the rear. The struggle depended on sodden, shivering heroes, coated in twenty or thirty pounds of slimy yellow mud, crawling close enough to lob grenades at an enemy who was in no hurry to give up or run away. By the night of the 28th, the attacking battalions had lost 2,481 men. Three Canadians had earned the vc. One of them, Private Tom Holmes, twice ran forward with bombs under heavy fire, to blast a German pillbox. Finally, 19 Germans surrendered to him.

At 5:50 A.M. on October 30, fresh battalions tried again. This time the weather was cold and clear; the shelling was harder and a thousand more yards cost 1,321 in dead and wounded, among them Major Talbot Papineau of the PPCLI, whose dismay at the conscription crisis had persuaded him to leave a safe staff job. He was blown to pieces by a shell. Another casualty was George Pearkes, an ex-mountie and a major in the 5th Canadian Mounted Rifles (CMR). He was hit in the thigh as he emerged from cover but he knew that his men would go back if he did. He clambered to his feet and plodded painfully forward until only a handful of men from his and an adjoining British battalion remained. Since it didn't seem to make sense to go back, Pearkes stayed, ignoring shells, counter-attacks, and the failure of attempts to rescue his tiny force. Late on the 30th, 200 men of another CMR battalion finally got through to relieve Pearkes and 35 survivors. Pearkes won the vc, as did three others that day.

Another officer did not survive. Meyer Cohen, a Toronto Jew, had not been welcome in the 42nd Battalion — the posh Royal Highlanders from Montreal — until he showed fellow officers that he could fight with his fists. At Lens in September, he took out a patrol, captured three Germans, waited, and captured three more. General Archie Macdonell came in person to congratulate him and to tell him that, henceforth, he was MacCohen. At Passchendaele, he took his platoon to take Graf House, a ruined farmhouse that had thrown back attack after attack. Cohen and his men took the post after dark and held it until only five men remained alive. Cohen was not among them. There is a tiny Star of David in the Royal Highlanders' memorial window in a Montreal Presbyterian church.

The 3rd and 4th divisions, exhausted and decimated, gave way in the first days of November to the 1st and 2nd divisions. The wounded, when they could be found alive, required twelve men in relays of six to struggle through the mud. There were not many German prisoners to help. The dead stayed where they were, adding to the special horror of Passchendaele. On November 6, Canadians launched their third attack. The sky was clear, the ground was higher and drier, and the barrage, which, despite precautions, had moved ahead of earlier attacks, had barely passed the Germans when the Canadians were among them with bayonets and grenades. A new German division should have provided a tougher resistance; instead the hand-over seems to have confused the defenders. Still, the Germans fought almost as relentlessly as ever, and Canadians in the open were still easy targets for shells and machine-gun bullets. The 31st Battalion reported double jeopardy. Its men had left their heavy greatcoats in long lines when they moved up to attack. German airmen mistook them for a line of troops and strafed the coats mercilessly. The real losses were 2,238 men, 734 of them dead. One of them, Private James Robertson, had gone out twice to rescue wounded under furious German fire. An unlucky shell got him on his second trip.

By noon, the 27th Battalion had overwhelmed the pillboxes that were all that remained of Passchendaele but Haig still needed the top of the ridge. On November 10, two Western Canadian battalions, the 7th and the 8th, opened the final attack. Conditions were vile but they got to their objective only to find that the adjoining British attack had utterly failed. The 10th Battalion, mostly Calgarians, took over the front line late in the afternoon. It was a narrow point, jutting deep into the German positions. "If the Canadians can hold that," an Australian observer commented, "they are wonderful troops." German guns hammered the Canadians from three sides. Fighters strafed anything that moved. Mud erupted in a storm of shells but the Alberta soldiers grimly endured. At dusk, counter-attacks faded and the line held.

For the Canadians, Passchendaele was almost over. On November 14, British divisions began to move into the Canadian trenches. By the 20th, Currie was once again in command of the Lens-Vimy sector. He had been right about Passchendaele. Canadians lost 15,654 dead and wounded in the battle, a thousand of them buried for ever under the Flanders mud. In Paris after the war, Haig did explain to Currie, as he had promised. The French mutinies and the German submarines were reasons, of course, but Haig's real concern was the spreading peace movement in London and Paris. Only a clear Allied victory in

1917 could stop the rot. The Canadians had done their part but, by mid-November, hardly anyone seemed to care.

On the way down the line or in billets behind the line, soldiers lined up to fill out a ballot in Canada's thirteenth general election. They wondered if it would make a difference.

UNION GOVERNMENT

In June 1917, Currie had cheerfully paid part of the price for his new command. Borden had wanted public support for conscription; Currie had provided it. Six months later, not a single conscript had appeared. Frustrated and feeling used, Currie felt very far from home.

In Canada, remote from the mud and the fear, the government played by political, not military rules. "Our first duty," Borden told his supporters, "is to win, at any cost, the coming election in order that we may continue to do our part in winning the war and that Canada be not disgraced." Without a mandate, there would be no conscription.

In England that spring, Lloyd George had offered an amendment to the British North America Act if Borden wished to prevent a wartime election. The Canadian had refused. Laurier, in turn, had refused a coalition but Borden did not stop with him. For years, while he played the political game, Borden had privately yearned for a government without the mean, corrupting squabbles of party politics. The conscription crisis had cracked party lines; might it unite all Canadians who saw the war as a national crusade — excluding the corrupt Bob Rogers as much as the unrepentant Liberal vote-mongers? Borden now had allies, among them the deaf but powerful Sir Clifford Sifton; his Winnipeg newspaper, the *Free Press;* and its respected editor, John Wesley Dafoe.

Coalition would not happen easily. Potential Liberal defectors were nervous, undecided, emotionally tied to their "plumed knight", Sir Wilfrid Laurier, and still hopeful of an election victory. In August, Borden turned back to Parliament and his Tory majority. A new Military Voters Act allowed men and women in uniform to vote for either the Government or the Opposition. Those without close links to a constituency in Canada could choose their own. Both parties, as the Minister of Justice gently explained, would want to persuade soldiers to put their votes where they would do the most good. No one doubted how soldiers would decide. Arthur Meighen, as a Manitoba minister, knew the rising Liberal strength among European immigrants: "to shift the franchise from the doubtful British or anti-British of the male sex," he suggested, "and to extend it at the same time to our patriotic women would be in my judgement a splendid stroke." Liberals howled, the *Vancouver Sun* called it a "Steal the Election Act", but closure and Conservative votes pushed Meighen's Wartime Elections Act through. Citizens from enemy countries, naturalized since 1902, lost their votes; the wives, mothers, and sisters of CEF members would be able to vote. The "patriotic women" would understand what conscription meant for their men.

Both laws had their effect. Liberal confidence faded. During the summer, hard-boiled Grit partisans had met in Toronto and Winnipeg to cheer for a leader who would bring them back to power. Now they had doubts. Frank Carvell, Newton Rowell, and others, to whom both Liberalism and the war were moral crusades, remembered how alienated they had felt by Laurier's perpetual concern for Quebec. By staying with him, were they not guilty of a corrupt "partyism" when the war called for sacrifice above self?

On October 6, Parliament was dissolved; Canadians would vote on December 17. On October 12, weeks of rumour and negotiation ended: Borden presented a Union government backed by every provincial premier but Quebec's Sir Lomer Gouin. Led by Newton Rowell, nine Liberals and a plump trade unionist, Gideon Robertson, joined twelve Conservatives in the biggest Cabinet Canada had yet seen. Outside Quebec all but a handful of Liberal papers endorsed the new regime. A delighted Tory confessed that he would match Borden against Job in a patience contest any day.

Now more than ever Borden needed patience. Tory ministers remembered the old bitter attacks from new colleagues. Rowell felt compelled to claim that a new purity had entered a once-corrupt regime. In scores of constituencies across Ontario and the West, nomination battles loomed between Conservatives and freshly converted Liberal Unionists. On October 18, the Unionists announced their platform. Some planks were predictable: full commitment to the war, reorganization of the railways, a crusade against political patronage. Other reforms were more controversial, though by 1917 their time seemed to have come: votes for all Canadian women, a total ban on the production and sale of liquor. On the tariff — a bitterly divisive issue between prairie farmers and most Tory supporters — the program was discreetly silent. Even Stephen Leacock, who despised women's suffrage as much as he cherished his whiskey, would hold his tongue.

To French Canada, such reforms were as much an anathema as conscription. They symbolized the Unionist rejection of the Canadian duality. Pierre Blondin had gone to England with the rump of his battalion; Albert Sévigny, who remained as almost the lone French-Canadian minister, needed police protection in Quebec. Few in the rest of Canada seemed to care what Quebec thought. "It is certainly not the intention of English Canada," warned *Satur-*

day Night magazine, "to stand idly by and see itself bled of men in order that the Quebec shirker may sidestep his responsibilities." No one asked, of course, whether Quebeckers had insisted on assuming those responsibilities.

In October, victory for the Unionists seemed easy. Laurier was shattered by the defection of life-long English-speaking colleagues. The Liberal organization was in ruins. Trusted party fund-raisers did not answer their calls. Then, as weeks passed, Unionist confidence began to ebb. In Nova Scotia, New Brunswick, and parts of the West, promises of Liberal backing proved worthless. In British Columbia, Liberals and Conservatives refused to co-operate. Soon both sides mistrusted the high-minded Rowell.

Liberals took heart. Candidates emerged, including Mackenzie King, oddly confident of victory in North York, the constituency of his rebel grandfather. An ailing and weary Laurier ventured west. Large, cheering crowds were a tonic. In Edmonton and Calgary, party organs had stayed faithful. If elected, Laurier told audiences, he would "increase, double and quadruple the output of all that may be necessary for marching and fighting armies". Conscription, he insisted, would be put to the people in a referendum and he would "carry out the wishes of the nation as thus expressed". Critics answered that Laurier's pledge was no more than Bourassa's policy of trying to get rich from war production but Unionists soon began to wonder if they would win a conscription plebiscite. At Kitchener, an anti-conscription crowd howled Borden from the platform for the first time in his political life. General Sydney Mewburn, the Hamilton Liberal who was now Minister of Militia, warned that Ontario farmers planned to vote for Laurier to keep their sons at home. Hurriedly, the government announced that farmers' sons would be exempted from conscription. So were the brothers of serving soldiers: ageing parents would not be robbed of their only breadwinner.

Desperation fuelled one of the ugliest election campaigns in Canadian experience. Laurier, Henri Bourassa, and the Kaiser were linked in speeches and cartoons. Quebec, declared George Allan, a Winnipeg Unionist, is "the plague spot of the whole Dominion". Clergy fed the hysteria. "Henry Bourassa is the real leader of Quebec," insisted Toronto's Archdeacon Henry Cody, "and I ask if that Province led by him, shall have the domination of the rest of this free Dominion which has sacrificed and suffered." The *Mail and Empire* warned on election day that a vote for Laurier was a vote for Germany, the Kaiser, von Hindenburg, and the sinking of the *Lusitania*.

Overseas, Sir Arthur Currie's neutrality was exceptional. Whatever their military limitations, surplus officers had political skills and they used them to organize military voters. The "Old Originals" of 1914 were promised a furlough home. The 5th Division at Witley was promised that it would stay together, perhaps even go to France. In France, Brigadier-General Manly-Sims abandoned GHQ to organize the Unionist campaign. There was no Liberal opposition. In England, Laurier's sole agent was an out-of-work patronage-seeker notorious in Ontario Liberal ranks as "Hug-the-Machine" Preston. His allegations of political manipulation were well founded, though his own record hurt Preston's credibility. Besides, any manipulation was irrelevant. Canadian troops needed no persuasion. Australian soldiers had rejected conscription because it would pollute their ranks with pressed men; Canadians had no such scruples. They were ready to share death with slackers. Yet, even overseas, government supporters wondered whether their efforts would pay off.

The early returns on December 17 justified the worst Unionist fears. Every seat in Prince Edward Island, nine of the twelve in Nova Scotia, and half the seats in New Brunswick went Liberal. In Quebec, Unionists clung to only three English-speaking seats in Montreal. Ontario farmers, targets of the special Unionist campaign, swung back but Borden's majority before polls closed in Western Canada was only eighteen seats. It was the West that gave the Unionists their victory, and the soldiers' votes when they were reported six weeks later. Military voters in Canada changed two seats; the overseas votes added a dozen more. In all, the civilian margin for the Unionists was a mere 97,065 of 1,650,958 votes cast; the CEF gave 215,849 votes to the government and only 18,522 to Laurier. Though the government's overseas organizers, with the full connivance of sympathetic officers, had done what they could to distribute loose votes where they were needed, the chief returning officer, the indispensable W.F. O'Connor, set aside the more fraudulent ballots. Liberals (and some historians) preferred to believe that the scandal had proceeded unimpeded.

Born in a mixture of opportunism and idealism, the new Union government had all the authority it needed to run a deeply divided Canada. Recognition was not its goal. For a generation, prominent English-speaking Canadians had called for an end to party politics. Others had condemned the compromises and concessions needed to conciliate the French-Canadian minority. Still others had pledged that a Canada in which women could vote and no one could drink would enter a new age of social justice and moral purity.

On December 17, 1917, their wishes had come true. Now they could live with the consequences.

STAGGERING LOSSES

Haig had been right in October in believing that the Allies desperately needed a victory. Morale among Allied leaders and followers was bad. Ironically, if Haig had ended Passchendaele in August, he might have delivered the necessary triumph.

Since the spring, British generals had planned an assault opposite Cambrai. In October, Haig finally authorized Sir Julian Byng to revive the plans for his Third Army. That was where Currie wanted his Canadians to be in November and he was right. Cambrai was a leap into the war of the future. At 6:20 A.M. on November 20, virtually without warning, hundreds of British aircraft roared over the German line, blasting trenches with bombs; 378 tanks thundered forward, flattening barbed wire; and the infantry of five divisions followed on a five-mile front. A thousand hidden guns opened fire for the first time, inundating preregistered targets with shells and poison gas. Tanks dropped fascines (huge bundles of wood) into trenches and craters, and crunched across. Six thousand Germans, many of them shell-shocked survivors of Passchendaele, surrendered without resistance. By evening, the British had advanced three to four miles.

But some of the Germans fought back. A single field gun knocked out sixteen British tanks. By nightfall, half the British tank force was broken down, ditched, or smashed. German machine guns ended the hope that the Cavalry Corps would finally break out into open country. A single squadron of the Fort Garry Horse filed across a lock gate at Masnières, cantered into the fields beyond, and came back hours later with 40 survivors and 16 prisoners. The surviving officer, Lieutenant Harcus Strachan, got a VC. In Britain, church bells rang for victory but, by November 23, the advance was over. Byng's eight divisions were exhausted and he had no more to send when the Germans took back Bourlon Wood on the 27th. Passchendaele had devoured Haig's army. He could send no help. On December 1, led by low-flying planes under an ace named Manfred von Richthofen, the Germans counter-attacked. It was the German turn to deluge British defences with shells and to harry them with aerial strafing. It was the British who surrendered or died. In three days, most of the gains were lost. Cambrai was not great as battles had gone — the British lost 44,000 men to the Germans' 41,000. Hopes had been raised too high on the 23rd and now they were dashed too low. Cambrai devastated British morale like no other setback of the war.

There was another reason why Byng had no more men. That fall, von Ludendorff had sent six German divisions to Italy. On October 24, they and the Austrians struck. The Italian line crumpled, steadied at the Tagliamento, and collapsed again. Foch, the French chief of staff, had foreseen the disaster and made plans. Six British and seven French divisions were rushed south, though it was Italian courage and pride and a new general, Armando Diaz, that finally stabilized the line on the Piave. Lloyd George's persistent dream of winning by way of Italy now had an ironic ring.

Lloyd George had tamed the Admiralty, so he boasted, when he marched across Whitehall ón April 30 and forced Jellicoe to adopt the convoy system. In fact, the awful statistics were argument enough. So was experience when, in May, merchant ships left Gibraltar in a convoy and arrived intact and two days faster than if they had travelled separately. By the end of 1917, half of the shipping to Britain moved in convoy and losses had fallen dramatically. Fears of collision at sea and jam-ups in port proved groundless. Lloyd George's self-confidence grew while Haig's reputation fell. Perhaps the field marshal had too many powerful friends but there was no such backing for Haig's loyal ally, the ex-ranker, Sir William Robertson. As a devout "Westerner" and the sole source of military advice to the government, Robertson was the stubborn obstacle to Lloyd George's strategic insight. To each of the prime minister's arguments, "Wully" replied that "he'd 'eard different". The Italian disaster provided the occasion to break his grip.

On November 5, Allied leaders met at Rapallo in the midst of the Italian crisis. Now was the time, Lloyd George insisted, to co-ordinate Allied strategy. The French, Italian, and British prime ministers — and Colonel House for the United States if President Wilson let him — would form a Supreme War Council, with military advisers who must not, Lloyd George insisted, be chiefs of staff. All agreed.

Sir Henry Wilson, hopeless as a fighting soldier but a consummate conspirator, with a fascinating resemblance to a praying mantis, became Lloyd George's general. The faithful Robertson resigned when Haig made it clear that he would not risk his position to save him. Divine guidance told the field marshal that his own position in the field was more important. He may have been right.

It took faith to believe in the Allied cause that winter. In September, the Germans took Riga on the Baltic, with a mixture of devastating artillery and infantry tactics devised by Colonel Max Hoffmann. They would use the techniques again. When a Russian general tried to seize Petrograd, Alexander Kerensky, leader of the Provisional Government, armed the workers as a Red Guard. The general gave up. On November 6, Kerensky tried to crush the Bolsheviks. Instead, Lenin and Trotsky turned the Red Guard on the Winter Palace, seat of the Provisional Government. Six guards died. Kerensky fled. The futile liberal era in Russia was over. Vladimir Lenin and Leon Trotsky were in power. On November 8, they announced an armistice, and released all the embarrassing secret treaties the Allies had signed to bind themselves into the war effort. All over Europe, war-weary soldiers and workers realized that, somewhere, peace was breaking out. Lord Lansdowne finally revealed his own fear for civilization in the *Daily Telegraph*, organ of the British conservative middle class. Peace, he insisted, was the only way to preserve the old order. In the War Cabinet, Lord Milner suggested Germany be bribed out of her western conquests by being given a free hand in Russia. In France, the socialists quit the government to be free to consider peace. Ex-premier Caillaux at last had a following. This was the crisis that helped send the Canadians to Passchendaele.

In Paris, it was peace or war. President Poincaré made his decision: he turned to his old enemy, Georges Clemenceau, a man of seventy-seven who had never forgotten 1870. "You ask what are my war aims?" Clemenceau told the Assembly. "They are very simple: Victory." The compromisers and defeatists, Caillaux and Malvy, were seized, charged with treason, and locked away. Democracy, compromise, idealism were put away for the duration. When Woodrow Wilson, on January 8, 1918, sought to rally idealism with war aims summed up in Fourteen Points, Clemenceau scoffed; "Why fourteen? The Good Lord only had ten." The French would fight.

So would Lloyd George but not, if he could help it, in France. By now, Britain was conscripting eighteen-year-olds and "combing out" war industries. The manpower crisis was desperate. No belligerent found more jobs for women, but almost half of Britain's vast army was tied up in the "side-shows" Haig and Robertson had deplored. The victory Haig had failed to provide came on December 11 in Palestine, when Allenby's army, reinforced with men Haig wanted in France, out-manoeuvred the Turks and marched into Jerusalem. This belated restaging of the Crusades was complicated by a pledge from Lloyd George's foreign secretary, Arthur Balfour, that the Holy Land would be returned to the Jews. It was just as well that the vast Arab revolt, engineered for Allenby by the handsome, romantic T.E. Lawrence, was not kept fully informed.

Somewhere, somehow, Lloyd George believed, "knocking the props" would bring down Germany. Sir Douglas Haig would continue in command but he would have no more men. British divisions, depleted of men, were simply cut from twelve to nine battalions of infantry. With a Lewis gun in each platoon for added firepower, it was mathematically possible to prove they could fight as well as ever. Gough's Fifth Army, restored to the southern flank, took over another twenty-five miles of French trenches. Pétain and Haig, though not on good terms, agreed to share their reserves. With Russia out of the war, they knew that the initiative belonged to Germany.

Germany could look back on 1917 with more satisfaction than her enemies. The nightmare of a two-front war ended with a Russian armistice in December and, after unsuccessful Bolshevik grandstanding, a triumphant peace at Brest-Litovsk in March. In theory the vast farmlands and resources of Poland, the Ukraine, and the Balkans would support the German war effort for ever. Victorious armies were already streaming westward in late December, though hundreds of thousands of troops remained as a *cordon sanitaire* against the Bolshevik bacillus. Even if the Americans arrived — and the creation of their army was slower than anyone had expected — Germany could hold on indefinitely in the West until peace movements forced Paris and London to seek terms. Wilson's Fourteen Points already suggested that the Americans themselves wanted a negotiated settlement.

That was not exactly how Germany's leaders saw matters. The German generals were as appalled as Haig at the prospect of a war ending short of a palpable victory. Riots, labour unrest, even a small naval mutiny suggested serious internal strains in Germany. The agricultural potential of Germany's eastern conquests lay strictly in the future. Regions that had fed most of Europe were now ruined and starving in the wake of marauding Russian, German, and Habsburg armies. Half the cattle in the Austrian Empire were gone by 1918; the swine population had fallen from 7.7 million in 1914 to 214,000 by the summer of 1918. In Germany 800,000 people would die prematurely from malnutrition during the war. Britain's blockade, barely noticed in accounts of battles and battleships, was in fact among the most effective Allied weapons of the war. The German generals knew they could not wait; they must win.

On November 11, von Ludendorff met his key generals at Mons. The war, he declared, would be won in a single, decisive blow, as early in 1918 as possible. Other German leaders, even von Hindenburg, were not consulted. It was still the General Staff's war. The weapons would be mass and surprise, the tactics tested at Riga. The best men in the army, elite storm-troopers — *Stosstruppen* — were concentrated in assault divisions. Lesser soldiers would suffice elsewhere. Under a storm of high explosive and poison gas, storm-troopers would bypass defences, heading for headquarters and gun positions. Operation "Michael" would fall on the British. So would a second assault, when "Michael" had succeeded. The French, a German staff officer predicted, would not "run themselves off their legs" to help the British.

While the Germans massed their troops for the coming 1918 offensive, Haig was forced to extend his line southward to relieve the exhausted French. As their own response to the German u-boat blockade, British (and Canadian) soldiers spent February clearing and planting vegetable gardens and grumbling at reduced rations.

That winter everyone knew that the Germans would attack, but when the blow fell on March 21, it caught the British by surprise. The generals claimed that they had planned defence in depth on the German model but too many troops were in the forward positions, caught under a hurricane of fire from 2,500 guns. German artillery searched out headquarters, gun positions, and crossroads, shattering command communications before a last, savage pummelling of the front lines. Gough's Fifth Army, still weary and under-strength from Passchendaele, was the victim. Dense late-winter mists, as well as smoke, artillery fire, and poison gas, masked the assaulting Germans. Stormtroopers ignored strong points and pushed deep into British territory. Bewildered defenders simply surrendered or fell back, looking for the familiar line of defence. In three days, Germans had recaptured all their losses at the Somme. British battalions disappeared; divisions dissolved. Elated, von Ludendorff poured in more troops. Now he was convinced that he could split the British from the French and roll up Haig's army against the English Channel. On his side, General Pétain seemed ready to co-operate with the German design. As he cautiously fed his reserves to the British, Pétain made it clear to Haig that the French army would swing back to defend Paris.

Sir Douglas Haig, as unshaken by this disaster as he had been by the tragedy of Passchendaele, knew that co-ordination was no longer enough. He took the initiative. At Doullens, on March 26, French and British leaders met and settled the issue. General Ferdinand Foch, the original co-conspirator of the Anglo-French alliance, emerged from the meeting as the effective Allied generalissimo and commander-in-chief. The title and the details followed in days.

A conference would not stop the Germans. On March 28, six British divisions astride the Scarpe halted thirteen German divisions on their drive to Arras. To the west and south, Germans pushed through towns British soldiers had known for years — Péronne, Albert, Noyon, Montdidier — to the edge of Villers-Bretonneux. Then, exhaustion, hunger, and the terrible casualties the storm-troopers had suffered from a shattered but unbeaten British army took their toll. Supporting battalions stopped to loot British supplies. Like the British at Cambrai, the Germans found that an enemy with railways could still move faster than attackers on foot. On April 5, Operation "Michael" petered out. The Allies had not been split but united. They had lost 77,000 French and 163,500 British troops but the German losses were staggering too — 239,000 *Stosstruppen*, the very best of their fighting men. Had von Ludendorff finally thrown and lost?

VIII
THE WEARIEST YEAR

In the winter of 1917–18, the war came home to Canadians in ways more tangible than the deceitful official communiqués or the long lists of casualties, with their tiny half-column photographs of sons and husbands who would never return. In Canada war now meant shortages of fuel and food, shrill exhortations to save, and endless regulations enforced by patriotism and the fear of snooping neighbours. There was a sour vengefulness in the air as Canadians looked on profiteers, "slackers", foreigners, Bolsheviks — or all of them together — as a source of their misery.

Halifax, garrisoned, fortified, and the seaport from which most soldiers departed, had always been closer to the war than the rest of Canada. Nothing could have prepared its 50,000 people for December 6, 1917. At 8:00 A.M., in mid-harbour, two battered cargo ships collided in a screech of metal and sparks. The crew of the *Mont Blanc* saw smoke rising from a hold and raced for their lifeboats and the Dartmouth shore. They could only imagine what a cargo of 3,000 tons of TNT would do. So could the British and Canadian sailors who raced against time to put out the fire. They never found out. At 9:00 A.M., the *Mont Blanc* blew up. Halifax experienced the biggest man-made explosion to that time. The blast levelled the working-class end of Halifax. Wooden clapboard houses collapsed. Farther away, as people rushed to their windows, the back-blast shattered the glass. Hundreds were blinded. Survivors, horribly maimed and bleeding, struggled away from the devastation in fear of fire. That night, a savage blizzard blanketed the city in snow drifts. Freezing rain followed. Rescuers found 1,630 dead and thousands of injured. Help poured in. Boston sent a hospital ship, Ottawa created a Relief Commission, the British sent a million pounds. The U.S. Congress promised $5 million — but forgot to vote on it.

Halifax struggled back to life. It had to. The city was at war. Convoys sailed for Europe every eight days. The Admiralty had belatedly demanded Canadian help in protecting coasts and sea lanes. Long-range u-boats were on their way. Ottawa had sent Captain Walter Hose to Halifax with the crew and guns from the *Rainbow*, commandeered yachts, and built tiny trawlers at a score of shipyards. By the summer of 1918, Hose's Halifax Patrol boasted two thousand men and a hundred small vessels, most of them able to carry a 6-pounder gun and a couple of depth charges. None of them encountered the two German submarines that surfaced that summer, destroyed a few schooners, and vanished. The U.S. Navy despatched a squadron of flying boats to Dartmouth under the command of Lieutenant Richard Byrd, a future Antarctic explorer. An infant Royal Canadian Naval Air Service sent its would-be pilots to train at the Massachusetts Institute of Technology in Boston.

For most Canadians, 1918 meant hardship, resentment, and a special anxiety for those who might receive the cold official death notices from Ottawa. Across Canada that winter, lack of fuel forced schools and factories to close. In February and March, Ontario homeowners observed "Heatless Mondays". Westerners grumbled when the government-appointed fuel controller, C.A. Magrath, tried to force them to use their own brown lignite instead of scarce imported anthracite. W.J. Hanna, the food controller, had tried exhortation and the licensing of grocers and restaurants to stop hoarding and cut consumption. It was, said the political scientist J.A. Corry, like trying to turn off a garden hose by sitting on the sprinkler. A new Canada Food Board replaced Hanna in 1918 and focused on production as well as consumers, but with no better luck. Prices kept rising; bad harvests and a lack of labour cut farm output. An "anti-loafing law" — a regulation under the War Measures Act compelling all men and boys over the age of sixteen to prove they were usefully employed — was a Food Board inspiration. Borden and others were delighted by it — a good law in war, he called it, and perhaps a good law in peacetime — but the effect was insignificant. By the autumn of 1918 Canadian shoppers bought "war bread" with 20 per cent flour substitutes and limited themselves by "honour rationing" to a pound and a half of butter and two pounds of sugar a month. Sir George Foster sourly noted that none of the ladies of his acquaintance in Ottawa seemed to be stinting.

As in most elections, voters had backed Borden on December 17 with contradictory and unspecific expectations. Most wanted to win the war; many expected reforms; a few expected to abolish politics. The new ministers certainly were busy. Within a week of the election, a new Canadian government railway system was announced, incorporating the Canadian Northern. Large increases in freight rates came too late for even the Grand Trunk. Liberals in the government boasted that patronage was dead: hiring for all forty thousand jobs in the public service was handed to the Civil Service Commission, and the War Purchasing Commission took over all government buying. C.C. Ballantyne, the Montreal industrialist who became Minister of Marine, announced plans to build forty-three ships in Canadian yards. He did not mention that they would cost twice as much as British-built ships. An advisory committee on scientific and industrial research busied itself on projects as varied as salmon-spawning to feed the hungry and flax-production to provide linen for British aircraft fuselages. By early January, the War Measures Act abolished even the mail-order traffic in liquor in the name of food conservation. Only a doctor's prescription could authorize the purchase of alcohol. Hardened drinkers had to pursue a sympathetic physician for a "per".

Sir Robert Borden spent a post-election holiday in Georgia and called on the White House on his return. The Americans, he proudly reported, "expressed the view that the resources of the two countries should be pooled in the most effective co-operation and that the boundary line had little or no significance in considering or dealing with these vital questions." It was a change for a man elected in 1911 on the slogan: "No truck nor trade with the Yankees". Lloyd Harris, a vigorous Brantford businessman, went to Washington to head a Canadian War Mission and to support the Imperial Munitions Board search for contracts. A War Trade Board was created to work with the U.S. War Industries Board.

On March 18, the new House of Commons met in the Victoria Museum, as parliaments had since the Parliament Buildings were destroyed by fire on February 3, 1916. There were the usual stale jokes about fossils and dinosaurs but much was new. Unionists could rejoice over prohibition, civil-service reform, and the railway reorganization. Soon, Canadians would experience Daylight Saving Time, an electricity-conservation measure urged by a new power controller. Free-traders took what comfort they could from a budget that removed the tariff from tractors. Though Quebec Liberals raged that the laws of history, religion, and biology would be undone, on May 24 the Unionist majority extended votes to all Canadian women. The reservations of Unionist misogynists were buried in the caucus.

Reforms were one thing, the war was another. Every Unionist supporter had expected the new government to make conscription work, especially in Quebec. In May 1917, Borden had pleaded the desperate need for men but, until January 3, 1918, thanks to his promise to await the election, not a single man was compelled to serve. An "engine of tyranny" had so many apparent safeguards that it was unworkable. In October, the government had called on Class I — single men and widowers aged 20–32 — to register: of 401,882 who appeared, 93.7 per cent sought exemption. Their cases passed through 1,253 local tribunals and 195 appeal courts to a single central appeal judge, Mr. Justice Lyman Duff of the Supreme Court. Duff was strict. Most farmers and their sons were exempted because the government had promised it. Catholic novices were in holy orders and exempt; Protestant divinity students were not. Pacifism was integral to the faith of Mennonites and Doukhobors; for Jehovah's Witnesses and Plymouth Brethren, it was incidental and they could serve without being expelled from their faith. No judge could have worked faster but how many judges faced 42,000 cases in five months?

Quebec was a special case. French Canadians had lost the election but they could try passive resistance. By the end of February, Quebec tribunals had settled only 2,000 of 32,000 appeals. French-speaking applicants were given blanket exemption but, claimed Duff, "they applied conscription against the English-speaking minority with a rigour unparalleled". Few of the men ordered to appear turned up; local Quebec police were unhelpful. The tiny Dominion Police, normally used to guard public buildings in Ottawa, did its best. At Quebec City on March 28, a riot exploded when federal police tried to arrest defaulters. A mob burned the Military Service Registry office, including its records, and pillaged English-Canadian businesses. Municipal officials stood by. General Lessard, summoned by Ottawa, used troops to restore order. On April 1, soldiers from Toronto, trapped by an angry crowd, opened fire. Four civilians were killed. The coroner's jury blamed Ottawa for tactless enforcement of the Military Service Act but the violence had shocked the province. Clergy ordered the faithful to obey the law; politicians cooled their language.

A week before the Quebec riots, on March 21, the long-awaited German offensive had struck. Not even official communiqués could conceal the disaster. The Canadian Corps would soon be in the desperate struggle. From London, Perley's successor, Sir Edward Kemp, cabled for 15,000 infantry reinforcements. Mewburn had only 4,800 available. For Borden the time had come to end the exemptions farce. On April 12, a divided Cabinet reluctantly agreed. A week later, in the drama of a secret session, MPs endorsed the decision by a margin of forty-nine votes, including four Liberals. Single men, aged 20 to 22, perhaps even men 19 to 23, would be taken without exemptions.

There was an explosion of anger. Quebec and Ontario farmers made common cause in demonstrations in Ottawa. They exploded again when journalists sneered at "hayseed profiteers". Western farmers were more restrained but an Alberta appeal court ruled four to one that the government had no right to alter a parliamentary statute. For two weeks in July the Alberta judges tried to enforce *habeas corpus* for the benefit of a conscript while the Supreme

Court in Ottawa shuffled its docket to settle a comparable Ontario case. On July 20, the Court ruled, four to two, that the War Measures Act took priority over the Military Service Act with its exceptions and that Parliament, after all, had given its consent.

The decision may not have been great law but Supreme Court justices reflected a national mood that, outside Quebec, no longer had much patience with dissent. Egged on by local Protestant clergy, military police raided the Jesuit Novitiate at Guelph. Edward Grey, whose case the Supreme Court had decided, was sentenced with nine other conscientious objectors to life in prison. Another man, J.E. Plant, was sentenced to be shot. The sentences were commuted to ten and fifteen years. In Winnipeg, Jehovah's Witnesses were beaten and soaked in icy water to make them submit. One went insane. By the war's end, 117 conscientious objectors were serving prison terms.

When it could, the government resisted the pressure to oppress. "When are the hangings going to start in Quebec?" demanded a prairie voter. "Shooting is too good for them." Of 24,139 defaulters under the Act by November 1918, 18,827 were in Quebec but the government made no serious effort to find them. To reassure farmers, MSA officials were directed to take city dwellers. In the West, 23.3 per cent of eligible farmers were conscripted and 39.3 per cent of non-farmers. The government had promised to find 100,000 soldiers under the MSA; by the end of 1918, 99,561 "MSA men" were in uniform, more than half were overseas, and 24,132 had joined CEF battalions in France.

CANADA'S VOICE AND STRENGTH

By 1918, Borden and his key ministers were as war-weary as any Canadians. The prime minister's closest friend, Sir Thomas White, insisted that he must resign or die. Instead, Borden sent him to California for a rest. Borden would have gladly followed. Once, he had dreamed that a coalition would end the personal and political squabbling he detested. Patriotic ministers would get on with the war. Instead, his ministers jockeyed for post-war advantages. Rowell and Carvell publicly contrasted the morality of the new regime with the evils of the old. New ministers fumbled their responsibilities; ex-ministers took malicious delight. Bob Rogers, excluded by Borden, sniped from the sidelines. So did Sam Hughes. In every Cabinet dispute, Borden alone was the trusted arbiter.

Borden also had to patch up a divided Canada. On January 19, a Liberal member of the Quebec assembly, J.N. Francoeur, proposed that Quebec leave Confederation if "in the view of the other provinces, it is believed that she is an obstacle to the union, progress, and development of Canada". For all the resentment over conscription, imperialism, and Regulation 17, not a single member spoke for separation and no one spoke more eloquently for Canada than Quebec's premier, Sir Lomer Gouin. Borden had his own olive branch: when he cancelled exemptions in April, he emphasized that single men must go so that married men could stay home. In no province did men marry earlier. In May, Gouin and Borden met for dinner. The conversation was easy. Henceforth, Borden suggested, Gouin would be consulted on contracts and appointments in his province. There was no need to spell out Gouin's side of the bargain: he would keep Quebec quiet for the rest of the war.

To Borden, that was necessary but minor political work. The prime minister's real task was to give Canada a voice in the Empire's policies on war and peace. On June 8, he reached London on his third wartime visit. Borden had much to learn.

When the Allies somehow stopped the German advance at Amiens, von Ludendorff had switched his offensive to the north. On April 9, a fresh tornado of artillery had dissolved an already demoralized Portuguese division. Some of them fled on bicycles left by a Canadian cyclist-battalion sent to plug the hole. In a day, all the gains of the Passchendaele offensive were lost. German troops penetrated almost to Hazebrouck and Ypres before they were held. On May 27, it was the turn of the French on the Chemin des Dames. Fifteen German divisions stormed across the Aisne. Pétain formed his line at the Marne and, for the first time, two U.S. divisions joined a major battle at Château Thierry. A huge German gun, nicknamed "Big Bertha", began lobbing shells at Paris. Allied losses were enormous.

Yet there was good news for Borden, too. He might not believe the perennial claim from generals that the enemy was exhausting himself, but it was true. It was certainly true that the Allies had somehow managed to hold their line and that Canadians had helped. Brigadier-General Raymond Brutinel's Motor Machine Gun Brigade, so far a mildly embarrassing element in the Corps, had found a major role in shoring up the crumbling Fifth British Army. One of its batteries had held off a German division for a day until only one gun and five men remained. At Moreuil Wood, all three regiments of the Canadian Cavalry Brigade had helped drive back the German advance on Amiens. A squadron commander, Lieutenant G.M. Flowerdew, had won a posthumous vc for leading his men in a glorious, if hopeless, charge. Battalions of Canadian railway troops, caught in the German offensives, had fought and died as infantry.

Best of all, the Canadian Corps had escaped the devastating impact of the German assaults. When he met Borden, Sir Arthur Currie had an explanation for Canadian immunity: during the winter, his men had worked hard to improve defences and strengthen the wire entanglements while British generals had built tennis courts. That was not fair. It ignored the exhaustion of British manpower, Lloyd George's deliberate policy of starving Haig of troops, and the extended line the British had accepted from the French. It also reflected Currie's growing nationalism and the mood of the Corps. On March 23, struggling to stem the German tide, Sir Douglas Haig had removed the 1st and 2nd divisions from the Canadian Corps. On the 26th, he called for the 3rd and 4th divisions as well, leaving Currie's headquarters with nothing to command. For a normal army corps, with no fixed complement of divisions, this was routine. In the March crisis, the Australian Corps accepted the arrangement but not Currie. Canadian divisions, he insisted, fought best under a headquarters that knew them. Not only did Currie let Haig know, he also warned Kemp in London. The plump and pompous new Overseas Minister took his concerns to the War Office. In the midst of the battle, Haig was directed to restore the Canadian Corps. By April 8, all but the 2nd Division were back under Currie's command. The British commander was furious. Currie, Haig grumbled, suffered from a swollen head.

Perhaps he did. Currie had earlier won an even more difficult struggle with his Canadian political superiors. When the British cut their divisions to nine infantry battalions, they assumed that the Canadians would follow suit. So did Canadians. Since conscription would soon relieve the CEF of the kind of desperate manpower shortage faced by Britain, a dozen extra battalions from the Corps and six from the 5th Division in England would allow two extra Canadian divisions in France, one more than the Australians. In turn, that would mean two Corps headquarters and perhaps a small Canadian army headquarters too: ten new headquarters in all, counting the new brigades — a boost to national pride and more than enough jobs for ambitious generals and surplus colonels. In December, Garnet Hughes offered to bet Currie any money he wanted that he would soon be in France. The British would be delighted to add a couple of new divisions when their real strength was shrinking, and Sir Edward Kemp could rejoice at Canada's enlarged status in the conflict.

Currie absolutely disagreed. The Corps, he claimed, was already a balanced, experienced team, which no one should break up. Where were the extra artillery and the supporting arms the new divisions would need? Well aware of Garnet Hughes and the surplus officers in England, Currie explained that many of the new staff positions would have to be filled by seasoned British officers. First General Turner and then Kemp heard the arguments. From Ottawa, Borden added his own warning. If the British insisted, the expansion could go ahead but, by September, Canada might not have enough men for the new organization. The British generals did not insist: they had no enthusiasm for weaker divisions. Currie's officers gave him an extra argument: adding six battalions would increase fighting strength by about 3,600 rifles but if a hundred men were added to each of the existing forty-eight battalions, fighting strength would rise by 1,400. If reinforcements grew scarce, it would be easier to cut back the extra men than to eliminate whole battalions and divisions.

Kemp was persuaded. When Garnet Hughes made a last bid, getting Lord Beaverbrook to involve Lloyd George, the answer was blunt: "Our cock won't fight." Instead of going to France, Garnet was out of a job. The 20,000 men of the 5th Division, held in England throughout the manpower crisis of 1917, became the manpower reserve that carried the Canadian Corps into the autumn of 1918.

Early in May, Haig pulled the Canadian Corps out of the line to rebuild for the coming battles. Sir Arthur Currie had ambitious plans for Canada's role in the war. He wanted Canadian squadrons in the Royal Flying Corps. "I am a good enough Canadian to believe, and my experience justifies me in believing, that Canadians are best served by Canadians," he had told Turner in November 1917. The government balked at the cost and complications, but in March 1918 it agreed to form a Canadian tank battalion. In April, Currie expanded the new machine-gun battalions in each division from sixty-four to ninety-six guns. At Passchendaele, he remembered, weary infantry had been forced to labour as road menders. That was wrong, and in May Currie used his pioneer battalions and men from the 5th Division to give each division a brigade of three battalions of engineers and a bridging company. Engineers, he foresaw, would be essential if the Corps was to keep mobile in the new conditions of open warfare. Infantry men built up their strength with route marches and practised the new German tactics of infiltration. "Maps to section leaders" had been a Currie slogan; now he had time to make sure that corporals and even privates would know what to do when their leaders were gone.

Currie, as his most recent biographer admits, was not loved by his men. His ponderous figure, stuffed in a general's uniform, looked ridiculous. When he inspected troops, he was pompous and fussy — "a regular Paul Pry", complained one gunner. Currie had an unfortunate gift for the ill-chosen phrase. "That's the way I like to see you," he told survivors of a battered unit, "all mud and blood." During the 1918 retreats, he had tried his hand at an inspiring message: "to those who will fall I say 'You will not die, but step into immortality'". The words brought jeers in dug-outs and billets. Canadians liked colourful, sympathetic officers: the fearless, friendly General Lipsett, the outspoken Archie Macdonell, and the cocky Dave Watson..Only generals themselves and the staff were aware of Currie's genuine openness to ideas and his patient pursuit of cheap routes to victory. What even privates could appreciate was Currie's remarkable technical competence and his determination to be liberal with materiel and conservative with lives.

In France, Currie was creating a Canadian army. In London, Kemp was determined to bring that army under Canadian control. Fresh from a Militia Department in which a politician was in charge, Kemp found that his predecessor had left matters to Sir Richard Turner and the generals. Kemp created an Overseas Council and presided over it. All the generals answered to him. So long as he served under Haig, Currie would be an exception but he did not command the small army of Canadians in France, ranging from tunnelling companies to field hospitals, which served outside the Corps. Canadian Railway Troops, 19,000 strong, played a major role in building and operating the British army's railways; 12,000 members of the Canadian Forestry Corps worked in French forests. By June 1918, Kemp had persuaded the War Office, Haig, and a very reluctant Currie that a Canadian Section at GHQ would oversee these troops and serve as the link between the Corps and the Overseas Ministry. The choice of Brigadier-General J.F.L. Embury, a former brigade commander, Saskatchewan Tory, and judge, won the confidence of both Kemp and Currie. "For matters of military operations," a War Office memo explained, "the Canadian Forces in the Field have been placed by the Canadian government under the Commander-in-Chief, British Armies in France...." Canada was now an ally, not a colony. Lord Derby had warned Haig about his troublesome subordinates late in 1917: "we must look upon them in the light in which they wish to be looked upon rather than in the light in which we would wish to do so".

AMIENS

From May until mid-July, the Canadian Corps enjoyed its longest respite from fighting. It did more than train and reorganize. On July 1, Dominion Day, fifty thousand Canadians gathered at Tincques, west of Arras, for the Corps sports championships. Engineers built a stadium and a platform for Borden, the Duke of Connaught, and the U.S. commander, General J.J. Pershing. On July 6, the 3rd Brigade's kilted battalions welcomed the entire British army to participate in Highland games. It was a time for pipes and drums, massed bands, twinkling brass, and polished boots. Then, on July 15, the Canadians went back to the line. They were part of a plan.

As Allied commander-in-chief, Marshal Foch had lost none of his old enthusiasm for the offensive. The British, he insisted, must attack near Festubert.

For once, Haig rejected Flanders. He had another idea. On July 4, the Australians and sixty tanks had easily captured Hamel in a replay of the Cambrai tactics. Sir John Monash, the Australian Corps commander, was eager to try again on a bigger scale. The German salient at Amiens was the obvious place. The terrain was dry, unscarred, and ideal for tanks. German defences were ill-developed and the defenders were battle-weary and understrength. They could be shoved back from Amiens and perhaps farther. Foch was delighted. The French First Army would join in and, with Rawlinson's Fourth Army, the Boche could be shoved all the way to Roye.

Monash made a condition: his Australians deserved dependable troops on their flank. Canadians and Australians had not been friendly behind the lines but Monash respected Currie and the Canadian Corps was fresh, well trained, and backed by ten thousand reinforcements. The trouble was that the Canadians were thirty miles to the north and their sudden appearance at Amiens would warn the Germans of impending attack. Could a hundred thousand men, their guns and transport, be moved in secrecy? Currie hoped so. He continued the planning and rehearsals for the attack along the Scarpe that had been his original mission. Fresh orders about security were pasted in each soldier's paybook: "Keep your mouth shut!" they began. Two battalions, some medical units, and all the Corps wireless were sent north to Flanders. Currie kept his secret from his divisional commanders until July 31; the troops were told on August 6, two days before the battle.

Secrecy affected everyone. From August 1, GHQ ordered, all movement around Amiens would be at night. Dense columns of guns, wagons, trucks, and buses jammed the narrow roads. Canadian infantry were collected and delivered by buses to secret destinations in dense forests. In the damp undergrowth they slept or played poker. Overhead, planes of the new Royal Air Force tried to spot breaches of secrecy. A thousand guns and a hundred thousand tons of ammunition were hauled into place. As each Canadian field gun opened fire to test the range, an Australian gun fell silent. RAF bombers buzzed up and down the line to hide the sound of hundreds of tanks rolling into position. Assault troops were reminded, in their briefing, of the fate of the *Llandovery Castle*, a Canadian hospital ship torpedoed on June 27. Survivors had been machine-gunned in the water: only 24 of the 244 men and none of the 14 nursing sisters aboard were saved.

Currie had no time for elaborate plans or rehearsals. Secrecy dictated no barrage before zero hour but tanks would crush uncut wire on his front. The French corps on his right, however, had few tanks and depended on its guns to clear a path. That should take an hour; it could take for ever. Lipsett's 3rd Division would have to watch its flank. A tiny "international force" — a platoon each of Canadians and French — would move along the border. Across the Canadian front meandered the Luce, a river infantry could cross. What about tanks and guns? Could Currie's new engineer organization cope? Otherwise, the infantry would be all alone tackling the hundreds of hidden machine guns that formed the real German defences. Above all, had the Germans really been fooled? Were they planning to unleash a storm of fire on the waiting Canadians, packed in their thousands under the trees? At 3:30 A.M. on August 8, there was an explosion of German gunfire. Then it passed away. Soldiers slept, rolled in ground sheets. A few scribbled letters by hooded lanterns. "What I miss most about these months," Captain Fred Adams wrote to his wife, "is you and the sense that I am not seeing Charlotte or Betty grow up...all the babyish talk and the feeling that these are years none of us can live again."

At 4:20 A.M., in the eerie half-light of dawn, thick fog shrouded the ground. Suddenly, an inferno of sound made the ground shudder. The bombardment had begun. Smiling and joking at the power of it, infantry hoisted on their equipment and walked into the mist. It suddenly seemed easy. The German defences dissolved. Infantry threw duck-boards across the Luce and crossed dry-shod. Tanks were blinded and stopped by the fog but so were German machine-gunners. Many Germans simply surrendered. A few fought to a merciless end. Canadian platoons and sections were cut down. Survivors practised the tactics they had learned in the fields behind Arras. As usual, the officers and sergeants fell first but corporals and privates took the lead, pushing around or past resistance. A Black Watch corporal, Herman Good, rushed a German battery with only three comrades. For taking three guns and their shaken crews, he won the VC. So did two other Canadians that day. Both others died of their wounds. As the mist burned off, the tanks came forward to help — "one of the finest features of the day," the 18th Battalion diary remembered. Australians helped too, as their advance kept pace with the Canadians. On the right, as Currie had feared, the French lagged and Lipsett's division had a much harder time. The Royal Canadian Regiment took Mézières in the French sector so it could reach its own objectives.

Currie had expected the trouble, and the 3rd Division had the closest objective. The British 3rd Cavalry Division — including the Canadian Cavalry Brigade — came up behind Lipsett's men and passed through in hope that, finally, the horses would have their heads. Canadian horsemen took Beaucourt and Fresnoy but Germans drove them back from Beaucourt Wood. At 12:40 P.M. the 4th Canadian Division followed, two hours behind the cavalry. Watson had loaded his tanks with machine guns and infantry, with orders to rush four miles to the division objective and hold it. The experiment failed. Heat and fumes overcame the soldiers crammed into the rocking, noisy monsters. German guns in the French sector blasted ten of the tanks into smoking wreckage. Eleven surviving tanks reached their goal under such intense fire that most of them backed away. Troops who saw the carnage preferred to walk. Germans retook Fresnoy and, from the flank, mowed down the men of the 75th and 87th battalions in an open field as they headed for Le Quesnel.

It was the only real setback of the day. By dusk, the Canadians had swept forward eight miles and the Australians seven. The Corps had taken 5,033 prisoners and 161 guns at a cost of 1,036 dead, 2,803 wounded, and 29 prisoners. The French, at much higher cost, had covered five miles; the British corps on Monash's left flank had failed to go a mile. Across the front, the Germans had lost 27,000 men — half of them prisoners — and 400 guns. The Germans had not been entirely fooled: they had expected the attack but not so soon. Tanks and infantry might have done even better if they had known more about the ground and, as Brigadier-General George Tuxford of the 3rd Brigade complained, officers who could not keep a secret were unfit for command.

Both sides reacted to August 8 by instinct. The German Second Army sent in five new divisions; Rawlinson ordered the attack to continue, this time beyond the trench lines of 1916. No one in front pretended it would be easy. The new-style tactics sacrificed the aggressive risk-takers and wore down battalions even faster than the old. Rawlinson promised Currie a fresh British division, the 32nd. Then his staff countermanded the order, forcing Currie at the last moment to change plans, summon back the weary 3rd Division, and shuffle frontages for the 1st and 2nd divisions. Before dawn, the 4th Division took Le Quesnel but the rest of the Corps waited through the day as battalions took up position and batteries worked out fresh fire plans. Finally, between 11:00 and 2:00 P.M., brigades attacked piecemeal.

On August 9, the fighting got mean. Few tanks remained in action and they were sacrificed to German guns as the price of destroying machine-gunners. More than ever, courage and self-sacrifice made the difference. Battalions advanced behind the few men willing to tackle machine guns single-handed: Sergeant R.L. Zengel of the 7th Battalion and Corporal F.C. Coppins and Lance-Corporal Alexander Brereton of the 8th won vcs. Lieutenant Jean Brillant of the 22nd had been wounded on the 8th and he was wounded again when he led two platoons into Vrély to capture fifteen machine guns. Somehow he and the remnant struggled on to Méharicourt where he died capturing a German five-inch gun. He, too, was a posthumous vc. On the right, the 8th Brigade — the Canadian Mounted Rifles — fell victim to enfilade fire because the

French had barely moved. Somehow, by 5:00 P.M., they took Bouchoir and then Arvillers in the French sector.

August 9 took the Canadians to the edge of the old trench systems, an advance of four miles and often more, but there was little sense of triumph and the price was 2,574 dead and wounded — Captain Adams would never see his daughters again. The defence had been as disorganized as the Canadian attack but by evening thirteen German divisions faced Rawlinson's thirteen divisions and the fighting had moved into the rotted sandbags and rusty wire of the old trench line. That night Currie was finally given the 32nd British Division. He matched it with the 4th Canadian Division and ordered both to attack on August 10 to clear the old trench lines.

For Canadians exhilarated by open warfare, there was no pleasure in reviving the evil memory of uncut wire, sagging dug-outs, and collapsing traverses. German defenders no longer gave up; they counter-attacked. By now, the Canadian Corps was far ahead of the Australians and the French and its men could wonder what purpose their sacrifice served. As soldiers, of course, they had no choice. By the evening of August 10, the British and Canadian battalions had pushed their way past the old British trenches and into the German lines, but only at a heavy cost. On August 12, the 3rd Division replaced the British 32nd, and for three days it painfully pushed on, with platoons battling almost independently. One of them, led by a Danish immigrant, Thomas Dinesen, worked its way deep into the German line, adding about a mile of trenches. Dinesen, a private in the 42nd Battalion, earned his VC and a commission. On the same day, Sergeant Robert Spell of the PPCLI calmly sacrificed his life so that his platoon could escape a strong German counter-attack. His VC was posthumous.

Independently, Currie, Rawlinson, and Haig recognized that the battle was losing its point. The sweeping victory of August 8 would soon be forgotten as casualties mounted. In four days, Currie had lost 9,074 men to advance fourteen miles but the cost of each additional yard was soaring. Soldiers could be replaced but not leaders like Jean Brillant. Artillery, too, needed to be repaired and replenished. The tanks had been almost wiped out in two days of fighting; the surviving crews were utterly exhausted. It made no sense to continue. Rawlinson agreed. On August 11, he warned Currie not to drive the 32nd Division into heavy casualties and the Canadian took the hint: the general advance was cancelled. Only Foch was obdurate but he found that Haig, too, could be stubborn. "I spoke to Foch quite straightly," he recorded, "and let him know that I was responsible to my Government and fellow citizens for the handling of the British forces."

Soldiers attend mass in a ruined French church; most have their gas masks to hand. The CEF provided Protestant and Catholic chaplains and enforced attendance at church parades, but most soldiers professed a cautious fatalism. Some senior officers tried to improve morality by enforcing a ban on swearing; others set a roaring example.

The front near Ypres in the summer of 1916, with a shell exploding. This shows the desolate flatness of the landscape after a year and a half of fighting. A year later, this would be the setting for Sir Douglas Haig's Passchendaele offensive.

The Somme battlefield in early October. Dead bodies are rare in wartime photographs and these, from the appearance of their boots, are probably Germans. The scene reflects the grim devastation in what, two years earlier, had been a green and pleasant landscape.

Winter came early in 1916, and brought the coldest weather in generations. By the time the 4th Canadian Division had its last attacks in November, the ground was frozen and snow had settled in.

Canadians on the march in December 1917. In the absence of conscription, their professional fatalism took on a hard edge: even if they were wounded, they would still be sent back to the front again and again until army doctors agreed that they were too badly mutilated to be cannon fodder any longer.

David Lloyd George and Winston Churchill. Both men sought to bring an energy and imagination to the empire's war effort that neither Asquith's Liberal government nor Britain's generals and admirals seemed capable of generating by 1916.

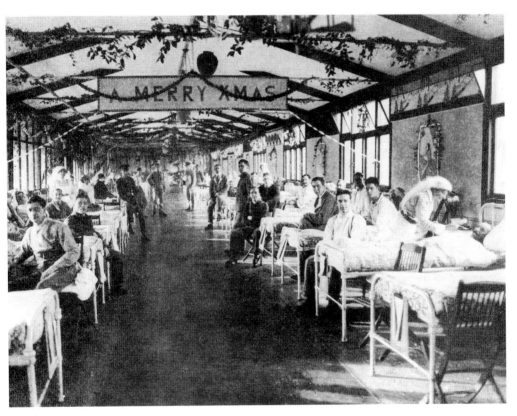

A Canadian hospital ward in France. Soldiers with serious wounds or sickness were evacuated to base hospitals. Without antibiotics, recovery could be a very slow process, but hospital death rates in the two world wars were surprisingly similar. One reason was that soldiers in the Great War were usually much closer to professional medical care.

Soldiers in the second or third wave advance on Vimy Ridge under puffs of German shellfire. Men carry duckboards, extra ammunition, and tools, as well as their own arms and equipment. Humans were the only dependable means of carrying supplies across the ruined expanse of captured ground.

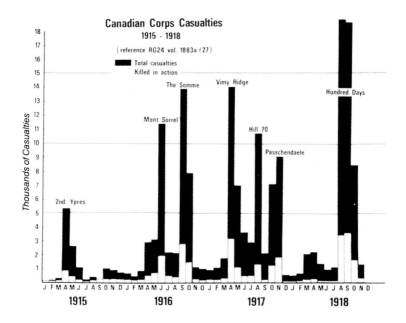

Canadian casualties occurred continuously but they soared to peaks during major battles, particularly in 1917. There was a relative lull during the first half of 1918, but the heaviest losses of the war came during the "Last Hundred Days."

The battlefield at Passchendaele. A light railway track ends in a shellhole. A shattered tank provides a rare landmark in the sea of mud and a shell throws up mud and water. The Canadian Corps carried a dreadful battle to its conclusion over Currie's objections, and at a cost he had grimly predicted.

A Mark IV tank waits during the Amiens offensive on August 8, 1918. Canadians were delighted by the tracked monsters—but by the end of the day many had fallen victim to the enemy or to their own mechanical weakness. Never, until the end of the war, would as many tanks be available again.

On August 15, the Amiens battle ended. On the night of the 19th–20th, Canadians began moving north again, to rejoin the First Army at Arras. They had won a victory but, like Ypres, Amiens was beginning to have unpleasant memories.

VICTORY IN 1920?

It might well have surprised Lloyd George, to say nothing of posterity, to discover Sir Douglas Haig defending the lives of his men from the Allies' new generalissimo, but 1918 was to be full of surprises and Canada was to share in them.

Borden had come to England in June to assert his claims as an Allied leader. He had kept his side of the 1917 bargain; had the British? Had they told him that Australians, New Zealanders, and Canadians would be dragged through the mud of Flanders? Currie's version of his grim experience had raised Borden close to the boiling point. "Mr. Prime Minister," he told Lloyd George, "I want to tell you that if there is a repetition of the battle of Passchendaele, not a Canadian soldier will leave the shores of Canada so long as the Canadian people entrust the government of their country to my hands."

Lloyd George was so pleased by the message that he persuaded Borden to repeat himself to the British generals. On June 20, he announced that the dominion prime ministers would begin meeting with him to review Britain's past and future military plans. At noon the next day, the new committee agreed that the dominions would have "a direct voice in the conduct of the war, and in the plans of campaign, so far as the War Cabinet had power to determine them." This was certainly progress from 1917, though the wily Lloyd George judged that he had created a forum of like-minded advisers to reinforce him against the folly of the generals or their political allies.

The war, by common consent, would not be over soon. Indeed, if the Russians could not be brought back into the struggle, the dominion prime ministers were soon persuaded, it might not end before 1920. Even more than the Germans, the Allies had been persuaded that a two-front war was prerequisite for German defeat. Getting the Russians to fight was an invitation to optimism and opportunism.

"Dunsterforce", a contingent of officers and other ranks (including forty-one Canadians) sent to Baku in the spring of 1918, was an example of both. Major-General L.C. Dunsterville had the task of recruiting Armenian levies, defending the local oil wells, and fending off Germans, Turks, Bolsheviks, and Jangali tribesmen. In September the enterprise collapsed when the Turks advanced, the Armenians fled, and the British escaped under Bolshevik guns.

Landings at Archangel and Murmansk were hardly more successful. Having welcomed the apparent British protection against a German advance, the Bolsheviks rapidly realized that their former allies were bent on renewing the war, or supporting counter-revolution or both.

A more substantial Allied hope was the Czech Legion, formed by Kerensky's government from Austro-Hungarian prisoners and deserters. By the spring of 1918, with its ranks swollen to sixty thousand, the Czech force was the most effective military organization in Russia and the only one eager to fight Germans and Austrians. The Bolsheviks grew alarmed. On May 14, they tried to disarm the Legion at Chelyabinsk. Instead, the Czechs seized the Trans-Siberian Railway from Samara to Irkutsk and set out across Siberia for Vladivostok to join the Allied cause. It was very convenient. So long as the Czechs disrupted the Russian railways, food and liberated prisoners could not get back to Germany. The Japanese, with an appropriate sense of self-interest, proposed to invade Siberia to rescue the embattled Czechs. President Wilson, alarmed at Tokyo's ill-concealed ambitions, insisted on an Allied presence. In July, Britain and the United States decided to send seven thousand men each; the Japanese, with no distractions, sent seventy thousand.

As Borden discovered, there was a price to be paid for belonging to the prime minister's committee. Having favoured every effort being made to revive the Eastern Front, Canada found itself invited to provide most of the British Siberian contingent. There might be other benefits too. Canadians also considered their interests. "Intimate relations with that rapidly developing country," Borden assured his colleagues in Ottawa, "will be a great advantage to Canada in the future." Trade with Siberia might follow the flag. On July 12, Militia Headquarters was ordered to create a force of five thousand. The CEF generated its last two battalions and, after a brief hunt for volunteers, Military Service Act men filled the ranks. A cavalry squadron from the Royal North West Mounted Police, a battery of artillery, machine-gunners, and supporting units left Vancouver in October, long after the Czechs had emerged from Siberia and barely a month before the war ended. A hundred more Canadians went to Murmansk to help organize and train local Russian levies and two Canadian field-artillery batteries, organized in England, left for Archangel in September to join a British, American, and French force under Major-General W.E. Ironside, formerly one of the British staff officers in the Canadian Corps. Canadian flyers with the RAF provided most of the air support for a largely French expedition to the Black Sea.

One may wonder why a country weary enough with fighting Germans would add Russian revolutionaries to their enemies. For Borden and many like him, the answer was simple: Bolshevism was a disease that had sapped

Russia's will to fight. With a little help, the patient would throw off the illness and rejoin the struggle. It was also an infectious disease. By leaving the war, even under the brutal conditions imposed by Germany at Brest-Litovsk, the Bolsheviks had encouraged the war-weary everywhere, including Canada. Bolshevism, with the savage atrocities committed in its name, might also be a warning to those who argued that Canada should emerge from the war into its own social revolution. In 1917, so conservative a thinker as Stephen Leacock had argued that "the government of every country ought to supply work and pay for the unemployed, maintenance of the infirm and aged, and education and opportunity for the children". Bolshevism showed the danger of such radical notions as the welfare state, pacifism, and social equality.

There were those, of course, who would brave such dangers. "If our masters force us to fight," declared Joe Naylor, president of the B.C. Federation of Labour, "let us fight for our own liberty and cast from our limbs the chains of slavery." Radicals, socialists, even liberals had welcomed Lenin's victory and argued for an end to war. Thousands of pre-war immigrants, fugitives from Tsarist oppression, had strong sympathy with Bolsheviks. They had little influence in Canada but they terrified or enraged those who had.

In 1918, there were more strikes in Canada than in the rest of the war years combined, and militancy spread from miners and machinists to municipal workers and even police. Inflation was the real reason, and the stubborn refusal of private and public employers to raise wages. It was "unpatriotic" to raise municipal taxes. Bolshevism was a more congenial explanation, particularly when labour leaders themselves talked of creating "soviets" and the irresistible power of the general strike.

Bolshevism became the excuse for a wave of repression that fed equally on conservatism and anti-alien feeling. C.H. Cahan, a Montreal Conservative, forced his services on the government on the strength of his claims that the country was riddled with sedition. The Dominion Police and the RNWMP, assigned to their respective ends of the country, found very little supporting evidence but orders-in-council in September banned a list of allegedly subversive organizations ranging from the Industrial Workers of the World to the Ukrainian Social Democratic Party. Months of pressure from veterans and patriotic organizations led to a ban on all publications in "enemy" languages. On the argument that minorities would be left with no information the ban was modified to require parallel translations into English. In October, the government simultaneously banned strikes and promised workers decent wages, the right to organize, and equal pay for equal work by women. None of these provisions was enforced.

Bolshevism, like war-weariness, was relative. In Canada, there was no comparison with the mood in Europe, where death and hunger had gone on too long. The German army had outlasted both its allies and its enemies. The Austrians had cracked in 1915; the Russians in 1916; the French, Italians, and even the British in 1917; but von Ludendorff had still found and trained the divisions for three great offensives in the spring of 1918. On July 15, he launched the greatest at Reims, the old cathedral town of France. West of Reims, the German guns crushed French defenders. To the east, the French had mastered German defence tactics. They kept back from the bombardment and smashed the assaulting storm-troopers when they were out of range of their own guns. With massed Renault tanks and no bombardment, Pétain ordered his divisions forward on August 7. French troops forced the Germans back to the Vesle.

A day later, on August 8, von Ludendorff learned of the battle at Amiens. What appalled him was the helpless crumbling of German resistance. Whole battalions had surrendered. Troops hurrying to plug the line had been met with cries of "War Prolongers", "Blacklegs", "Scab", by soldiers retreating from the line. It was, von Ludendorff wrote, *Die Katastrophe*, the Black Day of the German army. "Everything I had feared and of which I had so often given warning, had here in one place become a reality."

Germany was not beaten. Her army had 2.5 million men. Her conquests were intact. Her most powerful enemies were exhausted, as Canadians and Australians had painfully discovered at Amiens. What was gone was von Ludendorff's will to fight. That, like Bolshevism, was a communicable disease.

IX
ROAD TO VICTORY

DROCOURT-QUEANT

On August 17, when Sir Robert Borden left for Canada, he still believed that the war might last until 1920. He had not consulted Haig or Foch. The Allied generalissimo had a simple message for his armies: "Tout le monde à la bataille." Haig agreed. "If we allow the enemy a period of quiet," he warned Winston Churchill after the Amiens drive, "he will recover and the 'wear-out' process must be recommenced." Politicians had heard the message too often to believe it but generals, including Sir Arthur Currie, still had faith. Co-ordinated attacks along the Western Front would also keep the Germans from concentrating their strength.

Foch wanted to attack everywhere and continuously. Like Pétain, Haig had learned moderation. All but his worn-out Fifth Army would have tasks. In the north, King Albert's Belgians and Plumer's Second Army would recover losses in Flanders. With the Australians as spearhead, Rawlinson's Fourth Army would drive the Germans back to the Hindenburg Line while Byng's Third Army would push for Bapaume and Cambrai. The Canadians would lead Sir Henry Horne's First Army in a drive up the Scarpe, through the Drocourt-Quéant Line and into the rolling country behind Cambrai. If they succeeded, the Hindenburg Line would be outflanked and useless.

The point had not escaped the Germans. In 1917, the British had lost 158,000 men trying to force their way up the Scarpe from Arras and it would be no easier in 1918. The hilly, wooded country was ideal for defence and the Germans had done their ingenious best to improve it. Attackers would have to fight their way through the old British and German trenches, past Monchy-le-Preux, where the Newfoundland battalion had been destroyed a second time in 1917, and two miles on to the Fresnes-Rouvroy Line. A mile farther was the formidable defence line the Germans christened *Woton-I-Stellung* and the

British D-Q, for Drocourt-Quéant. Down the slope was another line based on the unfinished Canal du Nord and beyond it, dominating the skyline, was the dark mass of Bourlon Wood. This was not Amiens, with worn-out divisions waiting in shallow trenches. It was the route Canadians would have to take to Cambrai.

There would be no surprises for either side. Currie had preferred the Arras front to the growing hopelessness of Amiens because the Corps had spent most of July preparing to take Monchy. The Germans were waiting too and they let the 31st Battalion take Neuville-Vitasse on August 24 because they wanted their strength where it mattered. Sir Henry Horne gave the Canadians two days to get ready; Currie demanded a third. Only two of his divisions were ready, the 2nd and 3rd. Horne lent him another, the renowned 51st Highland Division. The basic plan was simple. Each division would use up a brigade a day getting to the Fresnes-Rouvroy Line. On the fourth day, the 1st and 4th divisions would take over for the drive through the Drocourt-Quéant Line and, if possible, across the Canal du Nord. Guns were plentiful though many of them would be out of range by the second and third day if they could not be hauled forward. Tanks were scarce — only fifty were available — and experience warned the Canadians that, valuable as they were, there would be few in action by the second day.

That was the dilemma of trench warfare. Twenty years later, armies would have the mechanized equipment to get across the battlefield and support the infantry, but not in 1918. Generals could draw objectives on maps and historians later would draw arrows to show how troops attacked, but the reality was tiny clumps of exhausted, frightened men going forward amid bursting shells and machine-gun bullets. The advance depended on a few men who found a way through the wire or who wormed their way within grenade-throwing range of a German machine gun. If they had the luck to survive and the courage to go on, they and the handful of men who followed them were why battalions reached the goals marked out by staff officers' chinagraph pencils. There was nothing special about Canadians except, perhaps, something in their culture that told ex-clerks or farm boys not to wait for an officer to tell them what to do. Many of those officers were now ex-privates and corporals, picked out because a cool courage had made them natural leaders. When such men were dead or wounded, battalions faltered and the strain of going ahead became more than flesh and minds could endure. Then, if they could be found, fresh battalions took over or sometimes pride would push weary remnants of humanity just a little further beyond their limits.

That was the reality that waited for Canadians on August 26. Once the plan was made and the artillery barrages were planned, there was little more Currie or his generals could do to help, beyond adding a little surprise. The British always attacked at dawn, when first light from the east profiled the German defences; Currie's attack began at 3:00 A.M., in hopes that the night would be clear and the Germans would be dozing. In fact, that Monday, it was drizzling and dark but most of the Germans were asleep. Burstall's battalions found little to stop them until dawn when they and their tanks were blasted in the side from Monchy. Lipsett's 8th Brigade, the CMRs, found a concealed approach to the German stronghold and took it from a flank as field gunners switched their barrage in an hour of hurried calculations — a feat impossible a year earlier. Lieutenant Charles Rutherford, a big, cheerful officer from Colborne, Ontario, was far ahead of his troops when he boldly persuaded a German officer to surrender the remnant of his company. By day's end, he had collected eighty prisoners and a vc. Beyond Monchy, the front widened and both divisions needed two brigades against a German resistance that was even tougher than Currie had foreseen.

Next day, Tuesday, Currie had planned to reach the Fresnes-Rouvroy Line. It was easier ordered than done. Fresh German divisions had rushed into position overnight. Special companies of machine-gunners came with them, and the terrain was full of hiding places for their deadly weapons. Canadians faced a morning of pouring rain and slippery mud. The 5th Brigade waited for its tanks and arrived late. The Quebeckers and New Brunswickers started at 10:00 A.M. and ran into the 26th Reserve Division, tough Württembergers. By the time they got through Chérisy, the 22nd and 24th battalions combined had only a few officers and a couple of hundred men. General Burstall settled for a line just beyond the Sensée. His 4th Brigade and men of the 3rd Division fought a murderous battle for Vis-en-Artois, a fortified village on the Cambrai road. The rest of the 3rd Division did little better than push past the old German trenches.

Currie might have pulled out the skeleton battalions that remained but he stuck with his plan. On the 28th, they must again face the German line. Lipsett spent the night reorganizing his units, concentrating those that remained in the front line and organizing a barrage from all the heavy guns he could muster. Burstall depended on the two brigades still in line. "Oh, it'll be all right," Lieutenant-Colonel William Clark-Kennedy of the 24th reassured Major Georges Vanier, the ex-lawyer who had just taken over the 22nd. The two men knew the grim truth.

On Lipsett's front, the barrage crushed the German machine-gunners; from Rémy to the Scarpe, battalions broke through. On the right, the barrage was feeble, and weary soldiers, some of them eight days without sleep, made little progress. Clark-Kennedy led his men into the German trenches but a counter-attack drove them out. As he lay with a shattered leg, Clark-Kennedy inspired the survivors to another, more successful assault. He won the VC. Vanier also lost his leg, and Lieutenant-Colonel A.E.G. Mackenzie of the 26th New Brunswick Battalion was killed. So were most of the officers, including the Vandoo's medical officer, who rounded up men for a final attack. In all, the two divisions lost 5,801 men. On August 29, the German war communiqué gave special mention to the hard-fighting Württembergers.

Currie had extracted the ultimate sacrifice from Burstall's and Lipsett's men because taking the actual Drocourt-Quéant Line might be an even worse struggle. By dawn on August 29, three fresh divisions were in place, the 1st, 4th, and, on the left, the 4th British, a regular army formation. Brutinel's mobile force moved to the middle, ready to race down the Arras-Cambrai highway to seize bridges on the Canal du Nord. Currie insisted on three days' preparation. The 1st Division used the time to finish Burstall's work. Brigadier-General Griesbach's 1st Brigade worked out an ingenious artillery barrage, slipped two battalions through a British bridgehead in the Fresnes-Rouvroy Line, and took the key German strong point in Upton Wood by attacking from three sides. Of the two battalions of Württembergers, German accounts recorded, only fifty men escaped. The German 26th Reserve Division was pulled out the next night. On the 4th Division front, it was Germans who kept up the pressure, attacking at dawn on September 2, coinciding with Currie's assault.

The D-Q Line lived up to its reputation. So did the Corps. On the right, the 1st Division suffered because the adjoining 57th British Division lagged behind. Hardest hit was the 3rd Brigade and its 16th Canadian Scottish. When a company faltered, Lance-Corporal Bill Metcalf, an American, jumped to his feet and led a tank towards a menacing German machine-gun post. No one knew how he survived. Lieutenant-Colonel Cy Peck, of the 16th, a huge man, walked through the bullets and exploding shells, prodding his men, raging at a tank that lumbered off to safety, and personally bringing up reserves. Both men earned VCs. So did three other Canadians...and many others who would never see them. The Division's objective was two miles beyond the D-Q Line, a stretch of reserve trench called the Buissy Switch. Despite terrible losses, the Canadians made it through though it took until 11:00 P.M.

The 4th Division faced a shorter, tougher route. Beyond the D-Q Line lay Dury and, beside it, a bald knob of ground called Mont Dury. The 47th and 50th battalions got through the line to find the wire in front of Dury uncut. Brave men grabbed cutters to snip open a gap and the 46th Battalion went through. The 38th and 72nd went over Mont Dury and fell in swathes when machine guns caught them. Unaccountably there was no artillery support.

The survivors struggled through without it. Later they learned the reason: the guns had stopped firing to let Brutinel's cavalry and machine-gun trucks go through. The 10th Hussars, a British regiment, saw the carnage and took its horses home. A few fallen trees stopped the trucks. Brutinel's bright idea of driving across the battlefield — with Currie's endorsement — had cost a lot of Canadian lives.

On Monday, September 3, exhausted Canadian and British survivors got up and resumed the attack. It turned out to be easy. The Germans had retreated behind the Canal du Nord — one of the "disagreeable decisions", von Hindenburg recalled. In three days of waiting and fighting, the 1st and 4th divisions and Brutinel's units had lost 5,622 dead and wounded, near-annihilation for the ten battalions that bore the brunt of the attack. Yet they had finished a fight that General Watson for one, and even the over-optimistic Haig, had thought impossible. Canadian infantry had taken on the toughest of defence lines and some of the toughest German troops and they had prevailed.

CANAL DU NORD

The politicians were more worried about losses than gains that month. From London, Sir Henry Wilson passed a blunt warning to Haig that heavy casualties would cost him his command. Lord Milner passed by Currie's headquarters on September 14 to hint that if the war lasted to 1919, the Canadian might have Haig's job. In fact, Currie's men would help make sure that never happened.

By mid-September, there was fighting up and down the Western Front. On September 12, Americans began driving in the St. Mihiel salient. On the same day, Byng's men cleared Germans from Havrincourt. Six days later, Rawlinson launched a fresh attack. Horne got his orders on the 15th: he would take Bourlon Wood and cover Byng as far as Cambrai. The Canadians again would lead the way.

Currie had expected it. Far in the rear, Horne's chief of staff had already sneered that, with a little more energy and leadership, the Canadians could have seized the Canal du Nord. That was absurd. On the 4th, Currie had climbed a hill to make his own assessment of the problem. It was formidable. Opposite the Canadian positions, the canal overflowed its banks, creating a vast, impassable marsh. Farther along, though, a thousand-yard stretch of the ditch was dry. With ladders, infantry could get down one side and up the other, but they would then face a line of German machine guns and, a mile back, a solid defence system called the Marcoing Line. Above it, on a slope covered by old trenches and excavations, was Bourlon Wood, a vast stand of prime oak that could hide a division. To the left the ground was open and bare of cover except for a handful of fortified villages and the Marcoing Line.

On September 18, three days after his orders, Currie submitted his plan. It broke most of the rules of sound generalship. A horrified Horne consulted Haig and even Byng. What the Canadian proposed was to shift his front south to the dry part of the canal, seize a narrow bridgehead, and then expand outward, getting behind the German defences on the canal. It was so easy to see what could go wrong. Three divisions jammed in a narrow defile would be a German gunner's dream. If the advance stalled, troops behind would be slaughtered. For Canadian artillery, the planning would be incredibly complicated, with barrages moving forward, back, and sideways. Failure would hurt the chances of three British armies and possibly destroy the Canadian Corps. Surely Currie should try something simpler. He was adamant. The only alternative — a frontal attack — would be far more costly. Sir Julian Byng was asked to review the plan. Currie was confident. His staff, his gunners, and his infantry would, in his favourite phrase, "deliver the goods". If they didn't, Byng reminded him, "it means home for you".

Of course the Canadians needed time, and they had most of September to get ready. Thousands of reinforcements filled the gaps left along the Scarpe; many of them were now MSA men. There was little discrimination, though colonels complained that the conscripts were poorly trained. Germans gave them a baptism of fire: the weeks along the canal cost an average of one hundred casualties a day. General Odlum was hit; so was Colonel Pearkes, so badly that his intestines were exposed; tough as ever, he lived. On September 13, General Lipsett left, full of regrets, to take over the 4th British Division. Currie might have insisted on keeping his old mentor — unquestionably his best division commander — but another of the Ypres colonels, Major-General F.O.W. Loomis, took over. Canadians now commanded all the divisions of their corps.

At dusk on September 27, platoons shuffled out of bunkers on the D-Q Line, shivered in the cold, damp darkness, and set off down slopes that seemed alive with troops. By midnight, clusters of men waited in the open, huddled for warmth and reassurance. Harness squeaked and chains rattled as field guns moved into position for the dawn rush. Engineers manhandled bridges as close to the canal as they dared. Surely the Germans must know the huge, helpless target in front of them. A few shells fell and there were losses, but not many.

At 5:20, a dreary, overcast dawn, the barrage began. Smoke and high explosive edged the canal as infantry with ladders raced forward. The 14th Battalion, unaccountably unprovided, found it did not need them. The 10th Brigade cleared the bridgehead and rushed the Marcoing Line. The 1st Brigade pushed north to Sains-lez-Marquion and Marquion. Brigadier-General Tuxford stolidly stumped along with his men, pausing to take some prisoners. As Canadians cleared the canal the 11th British Division crossed and pushed through open country to Oisy-le-Verger and Epinoy. The rest of the 1st Division flanked them, battling through Haynecourt and to the edge of the Marcoing Line, where barbed wire and deadly machine-gun fire stopped them at dusk. The 4th Division faced a tougher fight as the 12th Brigade struggled up the slope to the village of Bourlon and the 11th Brigade attempted to surround Bourlon Wood. The 54th Battalion did more than its job, penetrating almost as far as Fontaine-Notre-Dame east of the forest, but on the south side, the 102nd Battalion was isolated by a lagging British attack and dug in for its own survival. Two officers, lieutenants S.L. Honey and Graham Lyall, won VCs for their leadership, their battalions won the right to oak-leaf badges for their heroism amid the trees of Bourlon Wood. Lyall lived; Honey died.

Except on the right, where a tired, understrength British division had failed, the day was a complete victory. Currie had gambled on the professionalism and courage in his corps and won. Those who had condemned his massive engineer organization could reckon with its success in starting the flow of guns, tanks, and supplies within three hours of the first assault, despite German snipers and artillery. Tuxford's brigade had been helped by barrages moving in every direction, including backwards. At nightfall, the Germans abandoned Bourlon and fell back to the Marcoing Line. The diarist of the 188th Regiment, the Bourlon garrison, recalled the 27th of September: "on this day we buried all our hopes for victory".

After the impossible, anything else should be easy. Cambrai, the first real city the Canadians had seen behind German lines, seemed an easy prize. Loomis's rested 3rd Division was brought into line between the British XVII Corps and the 4th Division, with the city a bare two miles away. A continuous, relentless drive seemed the only sensible tactics. Success seemed certain.

Yet experience repeated itself: the second day at Amiens, the second day on the Scarpe. Being victorious was no compensation for exhaustion, the loss of key leaders, the lack of tanks, and the impossible task of dragging guns and ammunition across the battlefield to set up effective fire support. The Canadians could not keep advancing at night into unknown obstacles but the Germans could bring up fresh divisions and supply them from shortened supply lines. Cambrai was too vital to be sacrificed.

At dawn on September 8, the 9th Brigade took Fontaine-Notre-Dame for the British but when it moved east it found the RCR and the PPCLI pinned down by the same tough Württembergers who had stopped the 4th Division almost a month earlier. Captain George Little, filling in for his dead colonel, pulled the remnants of the PPCLI back to a dip in the ground to face his brigadier. "What we have, we hold," said the general. "We didn't have any," replied the captain. On the left, Lieutenant Milton Gregg of the RCR found a tiny gap in the wire and crawled through with a few men. Twice he was wounded, once he went back for grenades but Gregg and dozens like him broke the Marcoing Line. The 10th Brigade, which had led the Corps across the Canal du Nord the day before, struggled through the German line at Raillencourt with men "mowed down like grass". The 46th Battalion, men from south Saskatchewan, got through to the road; the 44th — now from New Brunswick — had 112 men left next day after a night of counter-attacks in front of Sailly. The 1st Division and the British 11th made almost no progress. The 10th Battalion, already trapped in a salient of dense barbed wire, reluctantly obeyed orders for a hopeless attack and lost 100 men, half of them when the Canadian artillery barrage landed in its own positions.

September 29 was hardly better. Brigades attacked at intervals, in hope that this time their guns could offer better support. The Germans were waiting. The 116th — the once-raw Umpty-Umps from Ontario — left two companies dead in swathes; the two others took Ste. Olle. Behind it the 2nd CMR fought its way into the suburb of Neuville St. Rémy. Survivors remembered it as their cruellest fight of the war. The 42nd and 49th battalions got to the Douai-Cambrai road. The Highlanders cut their way by hand through dense thickets of wire. The Germans waited patiently until the Canadians were fully entangled and then opened fire. Most of the 42nd were killed or wounded. Bodies hung from the wire, twitching as bullets struck them. The remnant grimly kept on cutting; when they were done, they avenged their comrades.

In contrast, the 72nd Highlanders of the 4th Division broke through easily, took Sancourt, and sent a six-man patrol to Blécourt to collect 80 prisoners. Then the Canadians found they had been led into a trap: the shallow valley was a German killing ground. The survivors ended up back where they had started. In turn, that contributed to a disaster for the 8th Battalion. Sent into an attack without flank support, the Winnipeggers were decimated. A corporal brought back one company. The day cost the Corps 2,089 men, including the 1st Division's beloved senior chaplain, Canon Frederick Scott, painfully wounded as he tended casualties near the front.

By now, Currie was worried. The fighting was far tougher than he had expected and casualties were heavy. On September 30, the PPCLI got over a defended railway embankment and took Tilloy but that was the day's only real success. Farther along the embankment, Germans crushed an attack by the 11th Brigade. The 75th Mississaugas took 467 into action; 78 walked back.

Next day, October 1, Currie planned a co-ordinated attack by all three divisions in the line. The 11th British Division promised three battalions; as worn out as the Canadians, they sent three companies. Currie described it as an "absolute betrayal". So it proved for the 3rd Brigade, which forced a way up the valley from Sancourt to Blécourt and to Bantigny and Cuvillers only to be isolated from north and south when a 4th Division attack also bogged down. The Canadians fought their way out, using German rifles when their own ammunition ran out. By nightfall, the 14th Royal Montrealers had 92 men left; the 16th Canadian Scottish had 78. It was after dark when the 102nd Battalion reached Cuvillers, at a cost of 177 men. Hardest hit was the 9th Brigade, which took the high ground east of Tilloy only to run into a storm of fire on the forward slope. Dazed survivors simply dug in amidst their own dead and wounded.

That afternoon, Horne sent word to Currie to hold his ground. The Corps could do little more. The 2nd Division had yet to fight but Currie knew that Burstall's shaken battalions were far from ready for serious battle. Instead, they replaced the 1st and 4th divisions and dug in from Tilloy to Cuvillers. Cambrai remained just out of reach. Staff officers counted 7,000 prisoners and reassured Currie that the death rate for casualties since Amiens was unusually low — one in seven compared to one in two or three at the Somme or Passchendaele. Machine-gun bullets left clean wounds. The carnage in the 75th Battalion was a little more tolerable since only 25 of the 389 casualties were killed.

Men who had lost friends in hopeless, unsupported attacks were not consoled. If victory was now imminent, it was all the worse to die. Soldiers grumbled that Currie was a glory-seeker, demanding the bloodiest tasks for his corps. Australians in Rawlinson's army made the same bitter charges against Sir John Monash. Currie's anger at the 11th Division on October 1 was his own version of inter-Allied friction. So were complaints by British generals that dominion troops got too much credit for the progress all along the British front. Beaverbrook, now in charge of Lloyd George's propaganda, took care of his own, and both Currie and Monash needed victorious reputations if Lloyd George was to give them command of the British armies in 1919. Around Cambrai, as the cold October rain pelted down, there was anything but a mood of triumph.

PURSUIT TO MONS

If the Canadians felt exhausted and resentful of their thirty thousand casualties since August 8, that was exactly what von Ludendorff had intended by his hard-fought withdrawal to the Hindenburg Line. Without conscription to fill its ranks and with minor mutinies erupting in exhausted battalions, the Australian Corps was pulled out of the line on October 5. British divisions, cut to nine battalions, lacked fighting endurance, as the Canadians had learned to their cost, but, taken as a whole, Haig's armies were in far better shape than Pétain's. The American drive into the Argonne forest in October turned into a near-disaster because of staff inexperience and logistic breakdown.

That was not how it looked to the Germans. All along the front, their gains from the spring offensives had vanished. In the Argonne, the Americans and French had moved seven miles in seven days. British and Belgian troops took Passchendaele and the Messines ridge in two days. On September 27, Byng's army broke the Hindenburg Line south of Cambrai. After Amiens, von Ludendorff had urged that Germany negotiate an immediate armistice — preferably on the basis of Wilson's Fourteen Points. On September 28, he found to his fury that nothing serious had been done. Next day at Spa, he and an unhappy Field Marshal von Hindenburg demanded an immediate armistice. That night von Ludendorff learned that Rawlinson's Fourth Army, with a couple of American divisions, had again broken the line and pushed three miles beyond it. The German army seemed to be collapsing.

Nor was there comfort from anywhere else. General Louis Franchet d'Esperey, relieved of his army during the German offensives, arrived at Salonika with Clemenceau's permission to restore his reputation. On September 15, he sent his French, British, and Serbian troops up the Vardar and the Bulgarian army, ragged and starving, collapsed. By the 29th, King Ferdinand had asked for an armistice and "the gardeners of Salonika" were free to threaten both Vienna and Constantinople. Turkey was lost. A British army advanced from Baghdad to the oil wells of Mosul. In Palestine on September 19, Sir Edmund Allenby began the envelopment and destruction of three Turkish armies in the battle of Megidoo — the biblical Armageddon. By the end of the month, he had 70,000 Turkish and 3,700 German prisoners and the road to Damascus was clear.

Everywhere, an unexpected actor played a part: a pandemic of acute influenza which the French blamed on Spain but which seems to have had its origins in India. Such pandemics were not new: doctors remembered the mass outbreak of 1890 when the old and middle-aged had sickened and died; this time it was young adults who seemed to be most susceptible, an ironic yet appalling ally to war as a killer of the young. Both virology and antibiotics were unknown in 1918. The disease swept through Europe in the spring and summer and returned, with even more virulence, in the autumn, adding to the exhaustion, bereavement, and despair of four long years of war.

Influenza could not be allowed a role in diplomacy or strategy. Haig was winning his war and, albeit with little gratitude, the politicans had to let him do it. The Germans, too, had to fight because, as von Hindenburg warned his generals, the armistice terms would depend on how well their armies held together and what damage they could inflict. Behind the Hindenburg Line, prisoners and deportee labour struggled to build a *Hermann-Stellung* from the Dutch border through the old fortress town of Valenciennes to the Oise River. Air reconnaissance told the Allied generals what to expect. The more time they gave the Germans, the tougher the next fight would be. The Canadian respite was over.

On October 6, Currie got his orders. The Corps would take Cambrai and link up with the Third Army. Burstall's battalions would seize crossings over the Canal de l'Escaut. For the operation he called "Peace Proposal", Burstall chose a night attack. Canadians were not fond of them but they made sense after the 3rd Division's experience of attacking down the same forward slope from Tilloy on October 1. Poison gas, dumped in the valley between Blécourt and Batigny, discouraged any German flank attack. At 1:30 A.M. on the 9th, the barrage began. Men of the 6th Brigade started forward. They caught the Germans getting ready to withdraw. By mid-morning, the 5th Brigade was fighting for the canal crossings, as teams of engineers hunted feverishly for demolition charges to defuse. At Pont d'Aire, Captain Charles Mitchell of the Canadian Engineers had to stop dismantling German explosives and fight off German defenders. He won his corps's first VC. The 25th Battalion took Escaudoeuvres; the canal was crossed.

In Cambrai, men of the 4th and 5th CMRs crossed the canal on partly demolished bridges and made their way gingerly through a city undefended except by German snipers and occasional shells. Engineers followed to repair bridges, clear streets, and fight the fires deliberately set by the retreating enemy to destroy the old city. As General Loomis entered at 11:00 A.M., his men encountered the first British troops entering the far suburbs. That afternoon the Corps's cavalry regiment, the Canadian Light Horse, tried its hand at chasing a retreating enemy; German machine guns hit a dozen men and forty-seven horses, and the pursuit ended. The Germans were not in flight. Burstall's men faced hard fighting on the 10th and 11th as they battled their way north-east along the canal. The 20th Battalion, sent past Iwuy with the 21st Battalion to seize high ground, lost three hundred men from enfilade fire. One of them was Lieutenant Wallace Algie, who had earned a VC by rushing two machine guns. As the Canadians moved down the far slope a soldier cried: "My God, look at them houses moving". They were German tanks. The Canadian infantry and nearby British troops fled back up the slope until a battery of Canadian field guns galloped up and disposed of the threat. The shaken infantry were content to hold their ground.

The capture of Cambrai changed the Canadian mood. Now they felt victorious and, when they saw what German occupation had meant for the French, they were angry too. Civilians were hungry; their homes and cities had been pillaged, and mines and factories had been systematically destroyed. They were also cautious; who wants to die on the eve of victory? General Lipsett, scouting in front as usual, was killed on October 14, after only a few days in his new command. Currie and men of Lipsett's old battalion, the 8th, went to Quéant on the 15th for the funeral. It seemed a waste but men might also wonder what place a good general would have in a post-war world. Horne shuffled his army, putting the Canadians in the middle, between the VII and XXII corps, along the Canal de la Sensée. Beyond a morning barrage and a few patrols, the front was quiet. On the 17th, there was no reply; the Germans had gone. The pursuit was on.

Some Canadians had already joined in. On October 8, near Le Cateau, the Canadian Cavalry Brigade helped advancing infantry from the Fourth Army. While dismounted men from the Fort Garry Horse held the front, the Strathconas and Royal Canadian Dragoons swept around on horseback in successful flanking attacks while the Royal Canadian Horse Artillery provided support. At a cost of 168 men and 171 horses, the cavalry finally showed the little that was left to them by 1918. Haig and his fellow cavalry generals were delighted.

For the most part, the war of movement advanced at an infantry pace of three miles an hour. Thanks to their engineer brigades, the Canadians outmarched their neighbouring corps, but everything seemed to conspire to hold them up. The Germans had emptied the country of food, demolished every bridge, ripped up every railway, and mined every road. The crowds of civilians who cheered the Canadian infantry and gunners desperately needed food and medical care. The Corps's trucks, worn out from months of hauling heavy shells, faced a sixty-mile turnaround on roads that, at their best, usually were limited to one-way traffic. Soldiers, footsore and weary from forced marches, cursed the staff for late and inadequate supplies; Currie, in turn, raged at "Higher Authorities" who had failed to plan.

Four days on the road brought the Canadians to Valenciennes, an industrial city of 36,000 people that was the key to the new German defence line. Five divisions, admittedly understrength, guarded the city. Two of them faced the Canadians across acres of flooded land, the Canal de l'Escaut, and a well-fortified city. Three of them defended Mont Houy, a 150-foot hill that dominated the southern approach. Horne ordered the 51st Highland Division to take Mont Houy. Currie's 4th Division would move through it to the high ground east of Valenciennes and the rest of the Corps would then cross the Escaut, avoiding the city and its population as much as possible. Currie sent Brigadier-General Andrew McNaughton, now commanding the Corps heavy artillery, to offer the British his help. He was rudely rebuffed. On October 28, the 51st Division sent a single battalion to take Mont Houy: it took the hill only to be thrown off with heavy losses.

First Army staff were upset: the defeat might interfere with the general advance Haig had ordered for November 3. The Canadians must take over and do the job. Currie refused. He remembered St. Eloi in 1916, when Canadians had also inherited a mess. Either the 51st Division would take the hill or he would do it his way. On the 29th, the Army headquarters grudgingly agreed. Then they told McNaughton to economize on shells. The Canadians refused. This might well be their last barrage of the war and they would do it well. McNaughton sent officers to beg, borrow, and salvage all the shells they could. At dawn on November 1, he had 108 heavy guns and the field artillery of three divisions. With the aid of old French maps and new air photos, gunnery staffs prepared an elaborate fire plan: box barrages, rolling barrages, even a reverse barrage to give German defenders the illusion they were being hit by their own guns.

At 5:15 A.M., Mont Houy exploded in a deluge of fire. A single battalion, the 44th, walked up the hill behind a wall of fire. Other battalions passed through on the other side. Not until they reached the suburb of Marly and a demolished steel plant did they meet tough resistance: the remnants of the German 8th Division. Sergeant Hugh Cairns, an ex-apprentice of twenty-one from Saskatoon, led his men through three machine-gun nests. He was arranging for sixty Germans to surrender when their officer shot him. Few of the Germans survived. Canadians that day were in an ugly mood. Too many Germans surrendered, complained the diarist of the 50th Battalion, but "some very useful killing was also achieved".

That night patrols of the 3rd Division crossed into the city and by dawn the Germans had left. On the 2nd, the British had taken the steel works and the Hermann Line was history. Including Cairns, the last Canadian vc winner of the war, 80 men had died and 300 were wounded. Burial parties counted 800 German dead. McNaughton boasted that his guns had fired 2,149 tons of shells, not much less than both sides had used in the South African War.

From Valenciennes, the Canadian route lay to the Belgian border and Mons. It was a country of hills, rapid streams, hedges, and dense forests, ideal for tough rearguard fighting. Rain poured down on marching troops on every day but one. As transport lagged behind, weary infantry had to carry all they needed, from spare ammunition and grenades to extra rations. Engineers concentrated on keeping three brigades of heavy artillery up with the Corps as back-up for any rearguard battle. On November 5, at the Aunelle River on the Belgian frontier, Watson's division ran into a stiff rearguard fight. After a brief set-back, the 85th Battalion forced a passage. On the 6th, the 2nd Division took over the advance. On the left, the 3rd Division ran into the German rearguard at Vicq on November 4. Soon, its men were in Belgium too, noticing, like all Canadians, that there were young men in the crowds, goods in the stores, and no devastation. Belgians had fared a lot better under the Germans than the French.

By November 9, the 7th Brigade reached Jemappes, outside Mons. To the south, Burstall's battalions had to fight their way through the densely clustered villages and coal tips of Belgium's best mining district. Air observers and deserters warned of a real battle at Mons. On the 10th, both Canadian divisions found hardening German resistance. Fighting through the coalfields south of Mons, with German machine-gunners hidden at every tip, cost 350 Canadian casualties, only a few of them killed. The 3rd Division, in the approaches to Mons, spent the day cautiously probing its way around the west side of the city, losing 116 men to machine guns and a few shells. Late that night, companies of the RCR and the 42nd Highlanders moved cautiously into the city. The Germans were gone. Excited soldiers woke the residents by clattering their bayonets along the grilled windows. The 5th Lancers, a British regiment that had retreated from Mons in 1914, rode through the streets and out towards Nimy. To the south, the 2nd Division advanced as far as St. Symphorien, and battalions of the 6th Brigade sent patrols as far as the Canal du Centre. At 10:55 A.M., a German sniper spotted Private George Price of the 28th Northwest Battalion and shot him in the chest. By 11:00 A.M. on November 11, he was dead, the sole Canadian killed that day.

THE ARMISTICE

Von Ludendorff's anger had worked. At the suggestion of the high command, a new chancellor with a liberal reputation, Prince Max of Baden, was appointed, a few social democrats were invited into the government, and, on October 4, President Wilson was invited to offer an armistice based on his Fourteen Points. Wilson was taken aback. Were the Germans serious? Would they evacuate all conquered territory? They must do so before he would act. On October 12, Prince Max eagerly agreed. On the same day, a German U-boat torpedoed the s.s. *Leinster* in the Irish Sea and 450 passengers, some of them

American, drowned. Wilson and the Americans were indignant. The deal was off. Military commanders would have to settle any armistice.

Prince Max tried again. So did Wilson. On October 23, the American president told the Allied commanders to arrange the cease-fire. The commanders were not equally pleased. Pershing wanted more battles to give his soldiers victories. The French wanted a lot more than the Fourteen Points; they wanted the Rhineland. Admiral Sir Rosslyn Wemyss, Foch's British deputy, wanted the German battle fleet. Haig was the moderate. A badly weakened German army should survive, if only as bulwark against the Bolsheviks. American voters had an influence too. In the November mid-term elections, Republicans won a commanding lead. Their policy was simple: win the war, bring the boys home, and let Europe settle its own affairs.

The war was certainly being won. On October 30, Turkish delegates signed an armistice with a British admiral and his fleet sailed through the Dardanelles, four years too late. Allenby had reached Damascus. Franchet d'Esperey reached the Danube. From Vienna, Emperor Karl also asked Wilson for a peace based on the Fourteen Points but the American president had already promised self-determination to Czechs, Poles, South Slavs, and even Romanians. Most of the Habsburg Empire could switch from vanquished to victors by proclaiming independence. Only Hungary and the Austrians were too late. On November 2, Hungary recalled its troops from Italy. The Italian armies advanced in the glorious and nearly bloodless battle of Vittoria Veneto and took 300,000 unresisting prisoners.

On October 26, the Kaiser dismissed von Ludendorff, who prudently withdrew to Sweden. His successor, General Wilhelm Groener, had managed Germany's industrial mobilization and worked closely enough with union leaders and social democrats to have their confidence. Otherwise, the hapless Kaiser and his commanders hardly knew what to do. On the 29th, the Kaiser went to army headquarters and refused to leave. The admirals decided that they would wreck the armistice talks by sending the High Seas Fleet to sea. Their sailors mutinied. By November 3, they had taken over the dockyards. By November 9 revolution had reached Berlin. Groener, the son of a Swabian sergeant, was given the unpleasant task of telling the Kaiser that the army would not fight for him. Von Hindenburg and the more aristocratic generals had spared themselves such embarrassment. On the 10th, the Kaiser crossed the Dutch border after tiresome haggling, and never returned.

There were no generals on the German armistice commission, chiefly because they might have made trouble. Matthias Erzberger, leader of the Catholic Center Party, had that dirty job. Foch and Admiral Wemyss met him in a railway carriage in the Forest of Compiègne on November 8. The Germans, Foch announced, must hand over their war materiel, fleet, and submarines. They must withdraw from all invaded territory and Alsace-Lorraine. The treaties Berlin had signed with a defeated Romania and Russia were annulled. The Allies would occupy the west bank and bridgeheads for fifty miles beyond. Erzberger was appalled but, by the time he could report, the Kaiser was gone and an ex-saddlemaker and socialist, Friedrich Ebert, had replaced Prince Max. He must sign. Erzberger returned on the 10th, pleaded in vain for the Allies to lift their blockade on Germany, and at 5:00 A.M. on November 11, he signed. "A nation of seventy millions of people suffers," said Erzberger, "but it does not die." "Très bien," said Foch, and left without shaking hands.

Around the world, people had watched the collapse of the Central Powers with astonishment and a realization that other problems were already pushing for attention: Bolshevism, starvation, and the killer influenza. In Canada, the disease had arrived in mid-September, at a Polish army training camp at Niagara-on-the-Lake. Other cases spread up the St. Lawrence from ships docking at Quebec and Montreal. Troopships, loaded with conscripts, carried it back across the Atlantic. The *City of Cairo* lost 32 of its 1,057 soldiers and crew, the *Victoria* lost 40 of 1,549. Across Canada, one in six fell ill and 30,000 to 50,000 died. A third of the people of Labrador died, including half the Inuit. There was no treatment or cure, or even an understanding of the cause, until 1933. By October, schools and theatres were closed, coal production fell, and railways were disrupted. Alberta made gauze masks compulsory. Since people of military age were often the hardest hit, military hospitals in Canada overflowed, only months after the Army Medical Corps had taken them over from the civilian-run Hospitals Commission. A public indoctrinated in the legend of Florence Nightingale knew whom to blame.

A country that was prone to sickness, shortages, and displays of wartime wealth could fear Bolsheviks and foreigners — and the two were easily linked. Government responded with fresh regulations and restrictions. The only escape would be peace and, for a moment on November 7, it seemed to have arrived. Reports of an armistice spread from New York, bringing joyful crowds into the streets. Within hours, the people learned that it was all a rumour.

On November 11, the armistice was no rumour. The timing let Canadian newspapers lay out their biggest headline type for the early editions. Canadians awoke to the news and went out on a cold grey morning to celebrate. In small towns, they decorated carts and trucks and fire engines and staged impromptu processions. In the cities, people thronged the main streets, jamming traffic. On Parliament Hill, the sober Methodist Newton

Rowell sought to lead Canadians in solemn thanksgiving. Elsewhere, Canadians broke into whatever stock of liquor prohibition had left them, to celebrate the peace.

In London and Paris and Rome, there were cheering crowds, too. In Trafalgar Square, Canadian soldiers lit a bonfire by Nelson's Monument that left marks that are still visible. At Canadian bases at Witley and Bramshott, celebrations boiled into attacks on the neighbouring "tin towns", the shops on the edge of camp where merchants had spent a profitable war, separating Canadian soldiers from their pay. At Mons and along the front, no one remembered cheering. News of the armistice reached the Canadian Corps at 7:00 A.M. but it took two hours to spread the order that all shooting would stop at 11:00 A.M.

In Mons, the 42nd Battalion sent its pipe band to play through the city at 7:00 A.M. and General Loomis invited Currie to stage a triumphant entry at 11:00 A.M. He had a reason. A week earlier, the mayor of Valenciennes had invited the Canadians to celebrate its liberation. Sir Henry Horne had intervened to insist that British troops also be honoured and that he would take the salute. Currie was even angrier when the British troops took precedence over Canadians in the parade. Currie rode into Mons with an escort of the British 5th Lancers but the 1,500 troops drawn up in the Grand Place were all Canadians. General Horne bore no grudge. "The Capture of Mons at the last moment," he wrote to Currie, "is a splendid crowning achievement on the part of the Canadian Corps. It is, I think, just about the best thing that could have happened."

The Canadians had ended their war where a younger Brigadier-General Henry Horne had begun it in August 1914.

X
COUNTING THE COSTS

An armistice only interrupted the conflict. Neither the war nor the fighting was over. Two of Currie's divisions, the 1st and 2nd, rested a few days and then set out on a long, wet march through Belgium and Germany to the occupied bridgeheads at Bonn and Cologne. Far away, at Tulgas, south of Archangel, the infant Red Army had chosen November 11 to attack Canadian gunners and American infantry. By the spring, twenty-four Canadians would be dead or wounded in north Russia. Four thousand more Canadians waited at Vladivostok. In Belgium, there were some Canadians who would have fought on. "We have them on the run," wrote General Andrew McNaughton. "That means we have to do it over again in another twenty-five years."

Borden was on the *Mauretania*, a day out of New York on November 11. "The world has drifted far from its anchorage," he noted a little sadly, "and no man can with certainty prophesy what the outcome will be." For Canada, he intended that outcome to include international status and recognition. When Lloyd George had summoned the dominion prime ministers on October 27, to develop a British Empire position for the peace conference, Borden made his point firmly: "The press and people of this country take it for granted that Canada will be represented at the Peace Conference." That did not mean, he repeated in London, sharing one of the five British seats with one of the other dominions or India. He had other views too. Putting the Kaiser on trial — a popular theme in the British election campaign in December — Borden found repugnant. So was the grab for German colonies by Australia and South Africa. Such behaviour, he warned, would anger Americans. An Anglo-American accord, he insisted was "the best asset we could bring home from the war".

President Wilson, Borden soon discovered, was just as offended at Lloyd George's efforts to get seats for the dominions; it seemed to the Americans just another scheme to enhance British influence. Besides, the conference would be crowded enough. A score of nations had hopped on the winning side in the last months of the war. Perhaps one seat each would suffice. Borden was furious. Canada would not settle for less representation than Belgium or Portugal; she had "lost more men killed in France than Portugal had put into the field". In the end, after a reminder that seats carried no votes, Wilson gave way. India, Canada, Australia, and South Africa would each have two seats, like Belgium and Portugal; New Zealand would have one; and Newfoundland would have none at all.

In January, Borden and the remaining premiers and their delegations moved to Paris. It was soon apparent that seats made no difference; the issues were settled in a Council of Five (or Ten, when foreign ministers attended) with only the United States, France, Britain, Italy, and Japan represented. In practice Wilson, Clemenceau, and Lloyd George decided most things. The results were imperfect but, given their exhaustion, their personal differences, and their incessant domestic interruptions, it is a marvel that there were any results at all.

Of the three, the U.S. president had come farthest. The first president to leave the United States during his term, Wilson left a hostile Congress and restive citizens. To the throngs gathered to cheer him, the tall, bespectacled Wilson seemed to promise a fresh idealism and a respect for small nations. In fact, Americans had ended their involvement in the financial and transportation problems of the Allies on November 11, and most of them wanted to go home. Wilson believed he would have to fight for his dream of a League of Nations. To his surprise, he found his allies eager to embrace it. The British had even worked out a detailed scheme, which Wilson, lacking his own, largely adopted. Indeed, Wilson found that his allies wanted to do more than he did. The Japanese proposed to make racial equality part of the covenant. The French wanted a league militant enough to protect it from German vengeance. Australia, South Africa, and New Zealand found that a league "mandate" gave respectability to their seizure of German colonies.

With the league and mandates settled and the German fleet safely under guard in Scapa Flow, the British, French, and Americans could settle down to decide the terms of peace. The Germans now felt confident of a reasonable settlement: the Kaiser and his ministers were gone, socialists were in power, and there could be no victors or vanquished in President Wilson's world. They were wrong. Allied propaganda had insisted that there were no "good" Germans. In a triumphant election campaign, Lloyd George and his followers had talked of squeezing Germany "til the pips squeaked". At the end of the Napoleonic wars a century earlier, aristocratic leaders from all sides had met at Vienna and, amidst balls and receptions, easily become reconciled. Democracies were less forgiving, and their leaders knew it. They also knew that their democratic armies had largely melted away with demobilization. What remained to pressure Germany was a blockade that reduced the enemy to such a state of hunger that thousands died prematurely.

France dictated the terms, with minor modifications imposed by her major allies. Germany would be disarmed — no air force, tanks, submarines, or dreadnoughts. France proposed a peacetime German army of only two hundred thousand conscripts; Wilson and Lloyd George insisted that a small professional army like their own was less militaristic and Germany was allowed a hundred thousand professionals. France wanted the Rhineland; Lloyd George insisted instead on demilitarization and a fifteen-year occupation of the Saar as compensation for German sabotage of French coal mines. France, of course, got Alsace and Lorraine and the Belgians got a few villages. In the East, the Poles and Czechs got most of what they wanted from Germany, with warm French support. The biggest issue was reparations. In 1871, Germany had imposed a five-billion–franc indemnity, confident that it would cripple the French economy for generations. France remembered. Leaders, if not their voters, might admit that Germany could hardly bear the whole cost of the war but she had been wholly immune from damage while large regions of France, Belgium, and Italy had been devastated. South Africa's Jan Smuts reminded delegates that war pensions might also be financed from reparations. The details would be complicated. The solution, Allied leaders agreed, was to force Germany to accept her full guilt for starting the war and leave the specifics to a commission of experts.

The German delegates first saw the Allied terms in May. They were appalled. They were permitted to object in writing. As a modest concession to self-determination, the people of Silesia were allowed a plebiscite on their fate. Nothing else would be altered. Germany would be disarmed in the middle of its enemies. Millions of Germans would live under Polish, Czech, or French rule. The war-guilt clause was a national humiliation few Germans felt they deserved. The German national assembly, meeting at Weimar to debate a constitution for the new republic, paused to consider renewing the war. President Ebert asked von Hindenburg for an opinion. Once again, the low-born General Groener was left to tell politicians the truth: Germany was defenceless. There could be no more war. Ebert accepted the facts as he heard them. He did not have to be reminded of the starvation and the disorder.

On June 28, 1919, Paris society followed the Allied delegations to the Hall of Mirrors at Versailles where, in 1871, the German Empire had been proclaimed. Now the delegates of the German republic were escorted in to sign, as their triumphant conquerors waited. Then it was the turn of the conquerors. Under Great Britain, but slightly indented at the insistence of James T. Shotwell, one of Wilson's aides, the dominions were listed. Then the guns fired salutes, the fountains danced, and the Germans withdrew to reflect on their own special bitterness.

Borden was not at Versailles; nor was Sir George Foster, though his face appears in Sir William Orpen's painting of the occasion. A.L. Sifton, the former Alberta premier, and C.J. Doherty, the Minister of Justice, signed for Canada. Canadians took little interest in the other treaties that, in the following months, ended wars with Bulgaria, Austria, Hungary, and Turkey. Most wrote themselves, with exchanges of territory and reparations that were never paid. Only Versailles really mattered. In the end, Borden and his colleagues had had little to do with the tone or the details. They were more concerned with the League Covenant and its Article X, requiring that the "High Contracting Parties undertake to respect and preserve against external aggression the territorial integrity and existing political independence of all State members of the League". Such a clause, warned Doherty, meant that Canada, though no longer willing to be involved automatically in Britain's war, would be forced to defend France, Italy, and someday even Germany. The Canadians could protest but discreetly, because for Borden it was even more important to belong to the league and its first subordinate body, the International Labour Organization, than to fuss about details.

Did Canadians agree? Borden insisted that Canada's Parliament would ratify the treaty even if the British had to wait. A day after the special session opened, on September 2, Borden presented the treaty. It was, for him, the climax of a five-year ordeal and he sought, in his own fashion, to instruct Canadians on the importance of his diplomatic role:

On behalf of my country I stood firmly upon this solid ground: that in the greatest of all wars, in which the world's liberty, the world's justice, in short, the world's future destiny were at stake, Canada had led the democracies of both the American continents. Her resolve had given inspiration, her sacrifices had been conspicuous, her effort was unabated to the end. The same indomitable spirit which made her capable of that effort and sacrifice made her equally incapable of accepting at the Peace Conference, in the League of Nations or elsewhere, a status inferior to that accorded to nations less advanced in their development, less amply endowed in wealth, resources, population, no more complete in their sovereignty and far less conspicuous in their sacrifice.

As so often on such occasions, party rancour clouded the significance of the occasion. Liberals split on whether Borden had wickedly separated Canada from the Empire or whether he had surrendered her sovereignty to a new league. Bringing the peace treaty to Parliament, claimed William Fielding, Laurier's old finance minister, was "a colossal humbug, designed to impose upon an innocent Parliament and to bamboozle a too-credulous people". Quebec Liberals deplored Article X. So, privately, did Borden, but a nation newly emerged in the world had to accept worldly imperfection. Without division but with far less enthusiasm than Borden would have hoped, Parliament ratified the treaty on September 12.

The U.S. Senate did not. Three times it refused. Among the arguments hurled at President Wilson was the provision that allowed votes to Britain's colonies. To Washington, at least, Canada remained a British dependency. The war itself dragged on in law, if not in practice, until midnight on August 21, 1920, a fact trivial to all but pension claimants.

DEMOBILIZATION

Like her allies, Canada did not wait for the peace treaty to demobilize. Within days of the armistice the Imperial Munitions Board cancelled its contracts, put its factories up for sale, and laid off 289,000 workers. By death or discharge, more than a third of the 619,636 members of the CEF had left before November 11; at the end of July, another 321,188 officers and other ranks of the CEF had been released.

Many, of course, would not return. In all, 59,544 members of the CEF had died during their service, 51,748 by enemy action, 51,346 of them in France or Belgium. The tiny Canadian navy recorded 150 deaths from all causes but there was no count of the Canadians who died with the Royal Navy, as reservists or volunteers with the British army, or in the Allied forces. A painstaking search of Royal Air Force records allowed the Canadian official historian to report that 1,388 Canadians died as aircrew with the British flying services out of a British total of 6,166. At the war's end, 43,000 patients lay in British or Canadian hospitals overseas. During the war, 154,361 men reported wounds, though many soldiers were wounded several times and there was no record of those whose mental or emotional damage went undiagnosed. In all, 3,846 Canadians were taken prisoner, of whom 3,478 returned from German camps. Many of them had survived appalling brutality and exploitation in German mines and labour camps; most had little to report but boredom and malnutrition.

Planning for returned soldiers had begun in the summer of 1915 with the formation of the Military Hospitals Commission. Its secretary, Ernest Scammell, devised his own policy in the absence of better guidance and no one altered its fundamentals. The state, he insisted, owed disabled soldiers more than a pension; they must also be restored and, if necessary, retrained for a suitable job. "There must be a minimum of sentiment and a maximum of hard business sense," Scammell warned. A Toronto engineer, Walter Segsworth, created a no-nonsense vocational-training organization that began with female ward aides teaching occupational therapy to the bedridden and culminated in "scouts" who found job placements for retrained veterans. Courses were limited to men who could not go back to former occupations. Retraining, insisted Segsworth, was a need, not a right.

Scammell's policies also meshed with a military-pension system specifically designed to spare Canada the bloated pension burden of the post–Civil War United States. Widows' pensions depended on good behaviour; their offspring were expected to support themselves at age sixteen for boys and seventeen for girls. The disabilities of sick or wounded veterans were examined by a medical board and assessed in Ottawa by a pension examiner, using a French-inspired "Table of Disabilities". Loss of both legs, both arms, or both eyes was 100 per cent disability; a missing eye or lower leg was 40 per cent. Though reproductive organs hardly affected earning power, a burst of Gallic sentiment valued them at 60 per cent. The scheme made generosity cheap. No more than 5 per cent of Canadian pensioners ever earned the rate for total disability.

By 1918, the Hospitals Commission and an independent Board of Pension Commissioners could boast that Canada had the most logical, efficient, and generous repatriation program of any of the Allies. Pressure from the Great War Veterans' Association (GWVA), formed at Winnipeg in 1917, helped persuade Parliament to keep Canadian pension rates even higher than in the United States, mainly by levelling up the rates for lower ranks until by 1920 a totally disabled private received as much as a lieutenant, $900 a year. Hospitals, training programs, tuberculosis sanatoria beds, even a government-run prosthetics factory in Toronto, bespoke a country eager to do its duty by disabled veterans and their families.

Like most veterans, the disabled defied stereotype. Most suffered from illness, not wounds. By the end of 1919, military hospitals had treated 8,508 cases of tuberculosis or referred them to sanatoria. Grants and building by the MHC doubled sanatorium accommodation during the war and introduced x-ray and other modern equipment. The CEF also recorded 2,000 insane, many of them victims of tertiary syphilis. Among the wounded, 127 men had been blinded and 3,461 men and one woman had suffered amputation of a limb. A black soldier, Curly Christian, was the lone quadrilateral amputee to survive; three others had lost three limbs. Shell shock, in the opinion of the official medical historian, was "a manifestation of childishness and femininity" and, as such, best cured by offering no pension, no encouragement, and no medical record. No count of psychological victims was kept until long after the war.

Planning to bring soldiers home began in 1917. Staff prepared forms, devised procedures, and explored a British plan to release soldiers in occupations specially necessary to restart a peacetime economy. A questionnaire administered in October 1918 revealed an unexpected enthusiasm for taking up farming. Unfortunately, the November armistice interfered with the official plans. So did the soldiers. The imminent winter meant slumping employment, ice-bound ports, and bad weather on the Atlantic. Worn-out railways more than shipping shortages limited Canadian ports to thirty thousand men a month. Business, unions, even the GWVA urged the government to postpone demobilization until spring. Sending two Canadian divisions to help occupy Germany was an added complication.

The government wanted early repatriation: it wanted to cut its costs. Soldiers, too, wanted to come home. If they could not do so at once, "first over, first back" was the only fair way. Mutinies by British soldiers ended schemes to release "pivotal men" and "demobilizers". Sir Arthur Currie also had his ideas: he wanted his battalions returned intact, to be welcomed by the cities and towns that had sponsored them. To politicians terrified that war had turned soldiers into homicidal barbarians, he had a powerful argument: only in cohesive units, under their own officers, would soldiers observe discipline. The Overseas Ministry compromised. Men outside the Corps would return in drafts, with married men having priority. Disgruntled soldiers disembarking from one of the first troopships to reach Halifax brought another directive from Ottawa: only the best ships would do for returning heroes.

In an England afflicted by cold weather, shortages, strikes, and influenza, the Overseas minister, Sir Edward Kemp, and his officials did their best. "You cannot blame the soldiers for kicking and complaining," he reported to Borden. "You are living in paradise in Canada as compared with this place." At Kinmel Park, a Canadian transit camp near Liverpool, "kicking" took the form of a riot on March 4–5 when soldiers learned that MSA conscripts in 3rd Division units were already headed for Canada while one of their ships had been cancelled as being unfit. Five soldiers died in various affrays. Canadian authorities blamed "Bolshevism" but the British provided more ships. In April and May, there were more riots at Witley and Bramshott, and again more ships were provided. Clashes between the British and their reluctant guests climaxed at Epsom in June with the death of an elderly policeman.

By September, the Overseas Ministry had despatched 267,813 Canadian soldiers and 37,748 wives and children. Despite dire warnings and Kemp's disapproval, 15,182 soldiers took their release in England, though they were outnumbered by 24,753 "Imperials" who went to Canada. Among those left behind were 34 Canadians, including 2 murderers, serving sentences in British prisons. A remnant of Kemp's officials stayed to oversee shipping of weapons and equipment and a British gift of $5 millions' worth of aircraft and spare parts to launch a Canadian air force. The brave promise in 1914 that Canada would bear the full cost of her contingent had degenerated by 1917 into haggling over the cost of the vast quantities of artillery ammunition consumed by the Corps. Arguments about dead horses, barrack damages, and mysterious Serbian soldiers ended in a Canadian agreement in April 1920 to pay $252,567,942.03 for the cost of her overseas army. The Overseas Ministry could at last be dissolved.

The delays in England and Belgium allowed soldiers to complete elaborate documentation and medical examinations before they embarked for Canada. Despite worn-out railways and damage in Halifax, demobilization in Canada proceeded with impressive speed. Men with families disembarked at Saint John, hospital ships docked at Portland, Maine, and most soldiers landed at Halifax's Pier II. A Repatriation Committee, headed by Herbert J. Daly, president of the ill-fated Home Bank, helped organize civic welcomes, reception committees, and volunteers. The Red Cross distributed comforts, boy scouts carried family baggage, and Rotary Clubs organized cars and drivers. CEF battalions formed up, marched through cheering crowds, endured the speeches of municipal dignitaries, and waited for the last command most of them ever wanted to hear from the army: "Dismiss!" Next day, men handed in their rifles and equipment, collected a discharge pin, a transport warrant, $35 for civilian clothing, and a War Service Gratuity that averaged $240. "I was in Civies," Claude Craig recorded in his diary. "It was great."

What happened next? In the 1917 election, soldiers had been promised "full re-establishment", a phrase that left much to the imagination and seemingly a great deal of responsibility to the new Department of Soldiers' Civil Re-establishment, created in February 1918. In practice, it was the old Hospital Commission, with Scammell's doctrine intact. If the disabled could work, so must the able-bodied. Full re-establishment for them meant the right to earn a living, raise a family, and pay taxes — and the sooner the better. Even before the armistice, returning soldiers seemed afflicted by such a lassitude and dependence that some doctors wondered if the Germans had a secret weapon. Perhaps the disease was army life. "Most of the men come back with sluggish mental action," a Hospitals Commission pamphlet explained. "They have been under military discipline so long, clothed, fed and ordered about that they have lost independence." A new Employment Service of Canada, created to help munition workers, was available to help soldiers find a job. To do more was to risk permanent psychological damage.

The one exception to official *laissez-faire* was more apparent than real. Free land for ex-soldiers was an old Canadian tradition. It had also become impossible: the last available public land had been distributed to South African War veterans in 1907. However, both soldiers and the public expected a settlement program, and a series of half-hearted measures culminated in the Soldier Settlement Act of 1918. As presented by Arthur Meighen, it was strictly a business proposition. Soldiers who proved their strength and experience — nurses were excluded — could borrow up to $7,500 at 5 per cent for land, livestock, and buildings. A Soldiers Settlement Board held the title, supervised the settlers, and protected the public's money. When returning soldiers discovered wartime farm prices, whole battalions applied for loans, though only about twenty-five thousand became settlers. Within a few years, when prices had collapsed but the debts remained, the difference between old-fashioned military bounty and the new businesslike soldier settlement became painfully clear.

Apart from soldier settlement and government employment bureaux, most returned men were on their own. Veterans could claim a year's free medical care at military hospitals, and government-sponsored Returned Soldiers Insurance offered them a life policy with no medical examination. Manitoba offered property-tax relief. Ontario, New Brunswick, Saskatchewan, and British Columbia offered otherwise unsaleable land for soldiers' colonies. When universities sought federal help in educating veterans they were rebuffed: it would be "class legislation".

Most veterans accepted their situation, found work, and tried to rebuild their lives. Others carried such crippling burdens of emotional or psychological disability that normal life was impossible. Few ex-soldiers escaped a sense of grievance. It was too easy to see that those who stayed home had done better. Medical officers and lawyers came home to find their practices had been dissolved. So had innumerable businesses. Farmers had lost the profitable wartime years. Even when workers' wages had lagged behind inflation, they had increased but a private's $1.10 a day and $20.00 a month for his family was unchanged from 1914.

The war did not radicalize veterans; it gave them a special stake in the nation they had defended. That underpinned the ethnocentrism of the GWVA and the occasional violence of its members against Greeks in Toronto, Ukrainians in Winnipeg, labour radicals in Vancouver, and the Chinese in a score of small communities. Veterans' conservatism had an egalitarian edge. The GWVA urged members to address each other as "comrade". Preferences for officers rankled. "That an officer with an arm off should get twice as much pension as a private with an arm off," raged Harris Turner, a blinded veteran and Saskatchewan MLA, "is unfair, unjust, unsound, undemocratic, unreasonable, unBritish, unacceptable, outrageous and rotten." (The government got the message.) Naturally, few senior officers felt welcome in veterans' organizations.

In 1917, the GWVA had called itself "the advanced guard" of a returning army, but its priority, like its membership, was the disabled. Grant MacNeil, the GWVA secretary-treasurer after 1918, made himself an expert and a major force in the evolution of veterans' benefits in Canada but he could not speak for the frustrations of the able-bodied veterans. On February 23, 1919, returned men, meeting in a Calgary theatre to escape boredom and the icy cold, persuaded themselves that "full re-establishment" for them was a bonus of $2,000 for each man who had served overseas, to be paid by slackers, profiteers, and, perhaps, by German reparations. Politicians, editors, the Liberal party, found the bonus easy to endorse. GWVA leaders, torn between responsibility and a grass-roots cause, found it a nightmare. The Borden government found the courage to say no: the "Calgary Resolution" would cost a billion dollars, almost half the national debt, and no one could promise that the veterans would not come back for more. With a single dissenting vote — Colonel J.A. Currie — the Unionist caucus stood firm. The Liberals ignored their convention resolution four months earlier. The bonus was dead. During the bonus campaign, GWVA membership soared from twenty thousand to two hundred thousand. It then drained away to rival organizations or, most often, to the more private concern of re-establishment. Grant MacNeil was left with the increasingly lonely fight for pensioners against the Pension Commissioners and their allies in the Senate. In 1925, a fading and penniless GWVA gave way to the generals and the colonels, and the newly formed Canadian Legion took over the veterans' cause.

By 1920, demobilization was over. Canada's wartime army vanished faster than anyone had predicted. Canadians, if they cared, could take pride in generous pensions and innovative programs for the war-disabled. There was no crisis of unemployment in 1919 and four-fifths of the money set aside to help veterans and their families through the winter of 1919–20 went unspent.

RECONSTRUCTION

"Very quickly," Herbert Daly had warned Canadians in 1918, "will the world realize how much easier it was to make the war than to make peace." The Union government had adopted "Reconstruction" as its phrase for planning the post-war world. Like "re-establishment", it was a carefully ambiguous word, at once progressive and conservative. Most Canadians, like their prime minister, yearned for an old, familiar anchorage but knew that it did not exist. Others had dreams of a new society, emerging from the pain of war. Norman James was welcomed home by the mayor of his small Alberta town with the hope that he and other veterans would create a "New Order in Canada". "To be frank with you," James replied, "we were hoping that you would do something about that while we were away."

In fact, governments had been busy. By the end of the war, Ottawa controlled most of the railways, wheat marketing, and coal distribution. In June 1918, it had enforced national registration on women as well as men. The government mildly taxed incomes and profits and, with a war debt approaching $2 billion, it could not stop. The habit of authority grew with feeding. In 1919, Unionist ministers distributed grants to build homes and highways, to control the spread of venereal disease, and to promote technical education — among the first federal-provincial cost-sharing programs. Soldier settlement, at an outlay of $100 million, was the largest land-development operation in Canadian history. Veterans' hospitals, sanatoria, and training schools took Ottawa deep into provincial, private, and charitable domains. So did a Department of Health, created in 1919 because of the influenza epidemic and the fear that returned soldiers would spread a new epidemic of syphilis. By the end of the year, Ottawa controlled the Grand Trunk and its Pacific extension.

By ordinary standards, the government in 1919 had marched at a revolutionary pace but the times were not ordinary. J.W. Dafoe of the *Manitoba Free Press* had warned that anyone in government after the war would face a thankless task: "It is going to be demanded of him that he do things which are mutually contradictory and destructive, and whatever he does will have more critics than friends." Reformers had imagined that the consensus that made a government powerful in wartime would somehow continue into the peace. "During reorganization after the war," Dr. J.L. Todd, the architect of Canada's military pension system, told an American audience, "it will be unbelievably easy to achieve social ideas which, before the war, seemed impracticable and impossible of attainment." Todd was wrong.

Ideas there certainly were. Physicians, anxious to make work for colleagues home from the war, argued for a national health-insurance plan. Thomas Adams, a British urban planner summoned to Ottawa in 1914 to design a national capital, had spent a frustrating war. Now, he announced, was the time for his vision of a city beautiful: veterans would be the major beneficiaries. The Military Hospitals Commission in 1916 proposed a trans-Canada highway as a war memorial, a massive public work for veterans and a recognition of the new automotive age. The West, in particular, seethed with radical ideas. Farm leaders debated the single tax, the benefits of government-managed grain marketing, and the early abolition of political "party-ism". Having spawned the veterans' bonus campaign in February, Calgary was the meeting place in March for the Western Labour Conference. Delegates demanded a six-hour day, praised the Bolshevik Revolution, and promised themselves a One Big Union for all workers.

Two months later, thirty thousand Winnipeggers walked out in a six-week general strike, ostensibly to support two local unions, in fact to protest low wages, high prices, and the failure of the post-war world to repay their wartime sacrifices. From Nanaimo to Sydney, workers responded to Winnipeg with sympathetic strikes of their own. By the end of 1919, Canada had lost a greater share of working time to labour disputes than in any year before or since. A Royal Commission on Industrial Relations, headed by Mr. Justice T.G. Mathers, concluded that economic conditions, not foreigners, had caused the unrest and recommended a minimum wage, an eight-hour day, unemployment and health insurance, and the right of free collective-bargaining.

Nothing happened. A National Industrial Conference in September dissolved in wrangling. Doctors forgot about national health insurance until the Depression when, again, they needed patients. The One Big Union came and went, speeded on its way by veterans who attacked organizers and bundled them out of small western towns. The Commission of Conservation, which had employed Adams, was wound up in 1921. The Board of Commerce, created in April 1919 to control cost increases, was gone by the end of the year when its two leading members, Mr. Justice Mathers and W.F. O'Connor, had fought each other to a standstill. The Wheat Board wound up in 1920; the Grain Exchange returned as world prices fell. Prohibition of liquor faltered when the Senate allowed regulations under the War Measures Act to lapse. All provinces but Quebec promptly reinstated it, but "Moderation Leagues", spearheaded by veterans and reinforced by the obvious unenforceability of temperance legislation, gradually won back the bottle if not the bar. Women had won the vote in all provinces but Quebec by 1922 but their feminism was still maternal. The economist Margaret MacMurchy reminded Canadians that "the great employments of women, in comparison with which all other employments appear insignificant, are homemaking and the care of children". Women's share of the Canadian workforce was hardly greater in 1921 than in 1911. Post-war feminist politics focused on motherhood, morality, and the new crypto-science of eugenics.

The real decisions about reconstruction had already been made by banks and businesses and by a government alarmed at its burden of $2 billion in debt. For a moment near the end of the war, business had glimpsed the potential power of government and its frail progressive idealism promptly shrivelled. "Legislation has its function," admitted *Industrial Canada,* the organ of the Canadian Manufacturers' Association, "but legislation which attempts to limit or pervert great natural laws will defeat its own ends...." For industrialists, the tariff was a great natural law and a Canadian Reconstruction Association ensured that governments would hear a firm and persuasive message from free enterprisers. A discreet subsidy to the Trades and Labor Congress added most union leaders to the cause of the tariff and moderate reform, in opposition to the free-trade Progressives. Acting on their own natural laws, the chartered banks celebrated peace by calling in exposed loans, raising interest rates, and curbing inflation with such success that prices, by 1921, had dropped back to 1917 levels. Unfortunately the economy had also collapsed, throwing a quarter of all veterans and most of their disabled comrades out of work. A proper concern for economy prevented the Department of Soldiers' Civil Re-establishment from making a second attempt at training and placement. Other depression victims included thousands of soldier settlers and the humble depositors in Herbert Daly's Home Bank.

In retrospect, Borden and his government should have sought a renewed mandate early in 1919. Instead, the prime minister had crossed the Atlantic and his weary colleagues had soldiered on, encountering all the misery Dafoe had predicted. "I should be happy to return to Canada," Borden wrote from Paris in May, "were it not for politics." That summer, he made an attempt to win over Sir Lomer Gouin. He beat the Quebec premier at golf but he could not bring him to Ottawa. Laurier had died in February and Liberals met in August to choose a new leader. Lady Laurier preferred the elderly and dignified Sir William Fielding. Quebec delegates insisted on William Lyon Mackenzie King because, unlike Fielding, he had been loyal to Sir Wilfrid in 1917. None of them knew how close King had come, in that summer of torn loyalties, to declaring for Unionism.

Doctors persuaded Borden to quit at the end of 1919; desperate Unionists pleaded with him to stay on. Months of recuperation in the southern states and New York left the government without its leader. Finally, on July 1, 1920, Borden resigned. He wanted Sir Thomas White as his successor but the finance minister was as worn out as his leader. Instead, Unionists chose Arthur Meighen, the architect of conscription and of most other policies that demanded a hard-edged mind and debating skill. Meighen knew the odds. Quebec had forgotten nothing and wealthy Montreal would never forgive him for refusing to hand over Canada's railways to the CPR. Agrarian reform and free trade swept rural Canada. The new prime minister returned to the old party, and to the old issue of 1911, the tariff. Mackenzie King refused to be pinned. The sweeping reform policies of the 1919 Liberal convention, he insisted, were "a chart"; the Liberals believed in a tariff that would help farmers, manufacturers, workers — everyone but multi-millionaires. On December 6, 1921, Canadians were too divided to give anyone a majority. A solid Quebec and seats in Ontario and the Maritimes gave King 116 members. Thomas Crerar's new Progressives swept the west and rural Ontario, 65 MPs in all. Meighen salvaged only 50 seats. North Winnipeg remembered the 1919 strike, forgot the war, and elected J.S. Woodsworth, the frail pacifist who had stood by the workers in 1919.

Reconstruction was over. The great conciliator, William Lyon Mackenzie King, could help Canada find peace with her divided selves.

CONCLUSIONS

The Great War of 1914–19 lies like a great angry scar across the history of Western civilization. At least thirteen million people died in the war, most of them young men. So did four old empires. A dozen newly sovereign states emerged, among them Canada. Those who lived through the 1914–19 war recalled it as the great divide in their lives. A golden glow of nostalgia suffused the pre-1914 years, blotting out the reality of poverty, violence, and cruelty. Never again would life be so assured for the middle class or so comfortable for the well born and they, of course, are the people who write history. "Before the war" evoked a romantic magic that somehow died in the mud of Verdun, the Somme, or the Ypres salient. Not for generations and perhaps never again could war be portrayed as romantic or heroic.

Modern historians have sometimes been harsh about this image. If influenza killed fifteen million people in a few months of 1918 was it a greater or a lesser event than the war? Was it European arrogance to claim world status for a conflict that essentially engaged the white nations and their colonies?

Was the Europe of 1914, with its slums and suffering, a haven of civilization or a jewelled corpse? Were the war dead a "lost generation" whose brilliance might have saved the world from future folly or was A.J.P. Taylor correct in his brutal conclusion: "Young males could be more easily spared than at any other time in the world's history"? Why was there no comparable myth after the 1939–45 war, when far more people had perished?

The war transformed much of daily life. Automobiles, cigarette-smoking, and the wristwatch became commonplace. Women abandoned heavy, constricting clothing and, in the 1920s, wore less than at any time in modern history. Would these changes have occurred without war? Wartime saw rapid progress in orthopaedics and rehabilitation medicine. For the first time in any major war, death from disease was far outweighed by death from enemy action, at least on the Western Front, and despite conditions that invited epidemic sickness. Never had the power of immunization and hygienic practices been more clearly demonstrated or in worse conditions.

Probably these changes would have come without a war. Other changes depended on the savage competition of belligerents. The air war forced Germany, France, and Britain to transform aircraft from fragile toys in 1914 to the tough, durable vehicles that, by 1919, were capable of crossing the Atlantic. The United States, birthplace of aeronautical technology in 1903, was left far behind in the war years. Tanks, however, which certainly invited technological innovation, remained vulnerable and undependable until major improvements in suspension and armament in the unmilitary 1920s. Canadians have been acutely conscious of the innovative influence of creating a munitions industry in wartime but, as the historian Michael Bliss has pointed out, most of the IMB's products were technically unsophisticated and its aircraft factory and shipbuilding activities proved utterly uneconomic. Canada's chief wartime success story was the automotive industry but the dramatic growth in car production, a by-product of the sudden wealth of farmers and industrialists, was not widely celebrated. It reflected profiteering.

History would have gone on without a war. Three of the four dead empires were in visible decay before 1914. If Britain was spared a civil war in Ireland in 1914, it resumed in 1916 and again in 1919 and persists, with intermittent savagery, to the present day. Canada would have discovered her sense of nationality without capturing Vimy Ridge and it hardly required a war to reveal the frustrations of "imperial federation".

Yet the war had happened and its consequences remained in broken dreams, broken bodies, and broken families. By 1935, Canada paid its hundred thousand dependent and disabled pensioners $41 million a year, an item second in the national accounts only to servicing a national debt that was $2 billion larger than it might have been without the war. These were the vulgar valuations of loss and suffering that no one could ever measure in a more satisfactory way. For the rest of their lives, the war-disabled would never escape the awkwardness of a missing limb, the shame of disfigurement, or the pain and breathlessness of being gassed. No one could ever count the tens of thousands who bore permanent psychological scars from the war, made all the deeper by public rejection and family friction. Canada's cost in lives and outlay was almost identical to that of the far larger United States, but across Germany, France, Russia, Britain, and the successor states of the Habsburg Empire, the toll could be multiplied a hundredfold.

From mourning, it was easy to move to disillusionment. The pre-war pacifists had denounced the "merchants of death" as manufacturers of war but now their theories explained a terrible reality of profitable devastation. Krupp, Vickers, Schneider, and other vast armament firms had profited from the war. Generals, too, emerged with little credit from a war that they had seemingly prolonged. The same electorates that had accepted their genius in wartime now felt savagely disillusioned at bemedalled commanders who lived in safety while their orders sent hundreds of thousands of uniformed civilians to their deaths. A host of voices insisted that victory could have come swiftly and cheaply if Joffre, von Ludendorff, and, above all, Sir Douglas Haig had not been so blindly stupid. Surely aircraft, more tanks, or a real effort in the Mediterranean would have spared Europe the remorseless savagery of attrition. It would take another war to justify that cruel doctrine. The Second World War would be won only after the Soviet Army, at horrifying cost, had worn down Hitler's *Wehrmacht*. Only then could Stalin's allies win in Italy or Normandy. It took four years of brutal attrition before the Australians and Canadians could win their victories in the autumn of 1918 and, even then, at heavy cost.

Such a horrible calculus had no meaning for the post-war generation. In Canada, autonomy was an argument for turning away from Europe. Having joined the League of Nations, Canada did what she could to undermine its frail provision for collective security. Nor was Ottawa much moved by the shrinking Imperial shadow. In 1922, when British troops faced a resurgent Turkish army at Chanak, the Conservative leader, Arthur Meighen, instinctively repeated Laurier's words of 1914: "Ready, Aye, Ready". A more politically sensitive Mackenzie King understood what had happened to Canadians and said nothing — beyond an assurance that "Parliament would decide."

Veterans of the war showed little enthusiasm for new conflicts. Many CEF officers insisted that their battalions survive in the post-war militia and a committee headed by the venerable Major-General Sir William Otter surrendered far enough to create a vast paper organization in which new units like the 3rd Toronto's or the 10th Calgary Highlanders figured with the Royal Highlanders and the Winnipeg Rifles. It made little difference. Men who had served in the ranks of the CEF were in no hurry for another dose of drill and order-taking and their officers, after a first flush of enthusiasm, found themselves too busy trying to earn a living. By 1936, Otter's militia organization had to be drastically pruned. In Parliament, Canada's first woman MP, Agnes Macphail, made an annual ritual of her demand that military spending be cut to a dollar a year and there were sympathetic echoes. In 1922 a Quebec Liberal and CEF veteran, Major C.G. Power, demanded a $300,000 cut in the militia estimates. By the time his fellow back-benchers had finished, they had slashed $700,000.

Power's Canadien and Irish constituents found nothing in his isolationism to criticize. It is easy to exaggerate the depth and durability of the wound conscription left in Quebec. By 1930, Quebec had sufficiently forgiven the Conservatives to give them seats, but the Liberals would do their best to keep evil memories alive. So would an array of movements and institutions, from Abbé Groulx's Action Nationale to the new Catholic trade-union organization, created at Hull in 1921. There were no more illusions about a Bonne Entente between Quebec and Ontario, although, in 1926, an Ontario Conservative government discreetly buried Regulation 17 and, by retaining a Royal 22e Régiment in its post-war permanent force, the Militia Department set out to remedy its pre-1914 neglect of French Canada.

Even Canadians who wanted the 1914–19 war to be the last in human history wanted it commemorated. The reconstruction of the burned-out Parliament Buildings allowed the Borden government to designate its crowning central structure as a "Peace Tower". For a time, that was all. Dreams of a National Memorial Gallery, with Lord Beaverbrook's magnificent collection of war art, withered and the works of Nash, Varley, and Augustus John remained half-forgotten in storage. The government could alternately plead cost-cutting and opposition to the glorification of war. Across Canada, communities debated the construction of war memorials and pestered their politicians for German war trophies to decorate their parks and vacant intersections. An American firm, complained the GWVA, was peddling its mass-produced sculptures to gullible officials and committees. Winnipeg launched a war-memorial competition and then made itself ridiculous by rejecting a series of winning entries because the successful artists had German-sounding names.

Canadian veterans had toyed with adopting St. Julien's Day, April 22, as a reminder of sacrificial struggles but the martyred son of St. Symphorosa was easily supplanted by Armistice Day, November 11. A bleak day fostered bleak memories. Poppies, introduced in 1921 as a fund-raising device for the benefit of French and Belgian war orphans, were seized on by the impoverished GWVA to finance its work for pension claimants. In turn, a hostile Senate turned the Poppy Fund into a political scandal that helped discredit the Great War Veterans and bring on the Canadian Legion in 1925. The red paper flowers survived as both a reminder of John McCrae's poem and a source of employment for disabled veterans.

In 1922, France handed over to Canada in perpetuity 250 acres at Hill 145, the crest of Vimy Ridge. Walter Allward designed the memorial: two soaring pillars of marble for the duality of French and English Canada, mounted on a vast concrete plinth. By the 1930s, veterans' organizations everywhere had turned from the barren struggles for compensation and employment to the concern for commemoration. In Canada, the Legion took almost four years to prepare for the unveiling of the Vimy memorial. On July 26, 1936, six thousand ex-soldiers had assembled on the slopes the Canadians had climbed more than nineteen years before. Now, instead of snow and sleet, the sun broke through, uncertainly at first and then with full force. Edward VIII, no longer the boyish prince and not much longer to be king, shared the dais with the French president and lesser Canadian cabinet ministers. Veterans stood, a little self-consciously, enduring the official speeches. Then, swooping low and racing across the memorial and the crowd, came flights of modern fighter planes.

They were unwitting precursors of another war.

XI
To War Once More

Ottawa, September 3, 1939. The Minister of National Defence urgently summoned a staff officer to the Privy Council offices, where the Cabinet had just learned of Britain and France's declaration of war on Germany. Ian Mackenzie, the minister, told the chiefs of staff to put all defence measures into effect. The Canadian armed forces, he later recalled, could "fire on any blinking German who came within range of our guns...." But, he added, "we were not at war." The minister was absolutely correct, however puzzling his words may have sounded, for Canada was still neutral and would remain so for another week. Not until Parliament met and formally decided to participate in this war was Canada a belligerent.

A quarter-century before, when Canada had been brought into the conflict immediately on Britain's declaration of war, people had turned out by the thousands to shout and to cheer the prospect of war, to hail militia men in uniform, to sing "God Save the King" and "Rule, Britannia" with a fervour as great in Montreal as in Toronto. But that was before the boys went overseas to the horror of the trenches. That was before the casualty lists swelled to fill pages in the daily newspapers. And that was before the survivors of the carnage in France and Flanders came home with their terrible wounds in body and mind. Canadians remembered all this, and this time there were no cheering crowds in Halifax, Montreal, Toronto, or Vancouver. There were few Canadians who gloried in the coming of the second German war.

The Rise of the Dictators

If the mood on the streets was sombre, there were many who believed that the job had to be finished this time, as the British Empire, France, Italy, and the United States had not completed it in 1918. The battles of the First World War had left Germany's territory physically unravaged, although the 1919 Treaty of Versailles had imposed heavy and humiliating burdens on the defeated nation, giving German territory to Poland and Czechoslovakia and even obliging the Germans to admit guilt for starting the war. The treaty's punitive clauses soon began to seem almost "unfair", however, as the British, French, Americans, and others tried to forget the long, hard struggle in a search for amusement and profit.

But the Germans did not forget their humiliation. The government that came into existence after the 1918 abdication of Kaiser Wilhelm was a shaky creation. The great inflation of the early 1920s wiped out the savings of the middle classes, and the Depression that began in the fall of 1929 caused the same widespread unemployment in Germany as elsewhere. And the Germans — much like the Italians, Spaniards, and others — saw the economic crisis lead to burgeoning growth on the left wing of the political spectrum. Everywhere, socialists and Communists argued that capitalism had broken down and that only they had the answers. Workers flocked to march under their party banners.

Not all German workers went to leftist parties, however. Tens of thousands joined parties that called for a rebirth of German pride and strength and for an end to the rearmament limitations the Treaty of Versailles had imposed on Germany. Ominously, many among the middle class and the industrialists — frightened of Communism for economic reasons — also turned to the right-wing parties. The great beneficiary was the National Socialist German Workers' Party, led by a mesmerizing orator named Adolf Hitler. Hitler's speeches played on people's fears, pointed to scapegoats, and promised every true German a place in the sun.

The Führer, as Hitler was adoringly called by his followers, was thought to be radical on social questions, but the sober right-wing industrialists were sure that he could be controlled by sensible men like themselves. Early in 1933, as the result of backroom political manoeuvring, the Nazi party took power, with Hitler being made chancellor but with conservatives holding some of the key portfolios. The new chancellor, however, quickly demonstrated that he was not a politician like the others. He began to consolidate his party's domestic power by officially sanctioning a policy of anti-Semitism and by crushing the political opposition of the Communists and socialists. Opponents were murdered or jailed in concentration camps, and the free discussion of ideas was frozen into fearful silence. At the same time, the Nazis began to test the restrictions the Versailles treaty had placed on rearmament. Hitler, it was becoming clear, sought total control in Germany. His followers, marching in their disciplined and goose-stepping ranks, sang "Today Germany, tomorrow the world", and throughout Europe the fear was that the Nazi stormtroopers meant exactly what they said.

Worse, the victorious Allies of 1918 were far from united. They had split asunder under the strain of imperial rivalry and economic competition in the 1920s, and the divisions between them increased in the next decade as the Great Depression savaged their industries and trade. In the dog-eat-dog world of the depressed 1930s, there seemed no will to act for peace. The United States professed little interest in Europe's affairs, and in 1935 President Franklin Roosevelt signed the American Neutrality Act, banning shipments of war materiel to nations at war; a 1936 amendment also prohibited loans to such nations. The boneless League of Nations, so ineffectual that Joseph Stalin's tyrannical Soviet Union often appeared as the staunchest supporter of collective security and freedom, certainly could do little to rally the democracies. Among the dominions only the smallest, New Zealand, was staunch for collective security. It was easily ignored. The seizure of Manchuria by Japan's militarist government early in the decade had drawn only the lightest of slaps on the wrist from the League. In the fall of 1935, Italy — under its fascist leader, Benito Mussolini — invaded and annexed the African nation of Ethiopia; the League responded with mild, ineffective economic sanctions, and further attempts to help Ethiopia were aborted by Britain and France. Clearly the League, and the collective will it was meant to embody, were faltering. Had there been unity Hitler might have been stopped early in his career: perhaps in 1936, when he sent his troops into the demilitarized Rhineland from which they had been barred by the Versailles treaty; or in 1938, when he marched his army into Austria and united it with Germany.

Canada had played its small, discreditable part in all this. Its representative to the League had actually congratulated Japan for bringing stability to Manchuria, and in 1935 the government had disavowed the oil sanctions against Italy proposed by its permanent representative in Geneva. Successive governments had argued against any attempt to bind League members to act against aggressors. Entry to the League of Nations in 1919 had been one of the steps on the road to national autonomy, but the Canadian record there and in the world had shown more attention to symbolic steps towards nationhood than willingness to work to keep the peace or to put teeth into collective security.

Through the mid-1930s, domestic issues continued to attract more interest in Parliament and press than foreign squabbles. In the First World War there had been bitter divisions over conscription, and the memory of that rankled still, especially in Quebec. Now politicians argued that Canada was "a fireproof house far from inflammable materials", as Senator Raoul Dandurand had told the League in the 1920s — delicately implying that the rest of the world should put its house in order and leave North America to get on with the business of making money.

Canada, in other words, had turned its back on the world's problems. The 1920s had not been a boom time for the whole country. There had been terrible drought in Alberta and widespread unemployment in much of the country. There was interest in international trade, and those in political circles worried about events that affected the British Empire, but there was very little ambition, among either politicians or populace, to play a world role. Mackenzie King, the Liberal prime minister from 1921 to 1926 and 1926 to 1930, had taken that view, and so too had R.B. Bennett, the Tory prime minister from 1930 until his defeat by King in October 1935. But by the late 1930s outside events at last began to force themselves into the Canadian consciousness. Hitler, Mussolini, Stalin, and the generals who exercised enormous influence in Japan compelled attention. The drumbeats of war were beginning to resound in many quarters.

There was conflict in the Far East, where since 1937 Japan had been busily engaged in swallowing as much of China as it could grab. There were bloody purges in the Soviet Union in the last years of the decade, as Stalin slaughtered generals, politicians, intellectuals, and ordinary citizens wholesale; those who did not die were sentenced to the Gulag. And there was civil war in Spain, where the social-democratic government, supported by the Soviet Union and by volunteers from around the world, was under assault by fascistic army officers led by General Francisco Franco and backed by the fascist regimes in Italy and Germany.

The Spanish war stirred many Canadians. Roman Catholics in Quebec and throughout English Canada overwhelmingly supported Franco, the man who would rescue the Church from the attacks of the left. But others saw the Loyalists as a democratic government under attack and Spain as the first real test of democracy against fascism. Thousands of Canadians — most, but not all, Communists — overcame the roadblocks placed in their way by Ottawa and joined the International Brigades formed to resist Franco. The Canadian Mackenzie–Papineau battalion (named after the rebel leaders of 1837) fought long and hard in the losing effort to save Spain, while a Montreal doctor, Norman Bethune, pioneered techniques to give the wounded blood transfusions right on the battlefield. (In 1938 Bethune turned his attention from Spain to China, and went to work with Mao Zedong's Red Army in its fight against Chiang Kai-shek and the Imperial Japanese Army; he died of septicemia in 1939.)

But it was Hitler's Germany that attracted most attention. There the Nazis were launching increasingly violent pogroms against Jews and imposing ever tougher restrictions to make their lives impossible. And always, Herr Hitler made his shrill demands for the return of territories and peoples that had been lost in the 1919 treaty — demands that focused on Czechoslovakia and Poland. A superbly efficient and completely mendacious propaganda machine, skilfully directed by Joseph Goebbels, turned the Führer's demands into psychological weapons. If repeated often enough, "the big lie" became something to be believed, however ludicrous it may have been. At the same time, Field Marshal Hermann Goering's air force was expanding, the army was growing, and the navy was building submarines and pocket battleships as fast as the North Sea shipyards could turn them out. Germany had rearmed its militant population with a powerful ideology and modern weapons, while the world watched and worried.

The dictatorships had their supporters in Canada. Home-grown fascists, stirred by visions of themselves as Aryan supermen, dressed up in black shirts and denounced Jews and foreigners. Parades and occasional riots disrupted Toronto and Montreal. Fascist leader Adrien Arcand in Quebec was even given financial assistance by R.B. Bennett's Conservative Party. The Communists, following orders issued by Moscow, had their members working in the trade unions and in the Depression's relief camps, and Communist Party leader Tim Buck almost won a martyr's halo when he narrowly escaped assassination in Kingston Penitentiary. The Japanese consulate in Vancouver spread propaganda about Japan's "civilizing mission" in its war against China, and many old-timers in the Japanese community listened. Italo-Canadians felt much the same about Mussolini's war in Ethiopia. At last Canada was caught up in the political ferment. Radio, still less than twenty years old, brought direct reportage on the events of the day to Canadian living-rooms. The world out there was at the boil, and everyone knew it.

All the same, some people tried to hide their heads in the sand. After 1935 the Mackenzie King government made tentative efforts to begin military preparations for the war that many could see coming, but these were bitterly resisted. The Québécois remembered all too well the way Anglo-Canadians had pressured them during the 1914 war; Liberal politicians had won election after election by promising that never again would anyone be conscripted for a British war. There was a small pacifist movement whose supporters believed that any war for any cause was insane. There were advocates of collective security and the League of Nations. There were imperial loyalists, ready to follow Britain wherever she led, whether to war or to appeasement. And a great many people were simply isolationists, convinced that Canada was as safe as any place on earth if only the sentimental links to London and the European vortex could be cut.

In this whirl of argument about war and peace, one fact was clear: the Canadian armed forces scarcely existed. Defence appropriations for 1937–38 were $36 million (up $10 million from three years before), and for 1939–40 the budget forecast for the three services was $64.6 million, sums that allowed only the tiniest of forces. The Royal Canadian Navy in 1939 had a regular-force strength of under 2,000, ludicrously small but almost double its size three years before. The fleet consisted of four modern destroyers, two older ones, and four minesweepers. The Royal Canadian Air Force was equally weak, despite its role in survey work and mercy missions in the inter-war period. In 1939, regular-force strength was 298 officers and 2,750 airmen, and there were eight squadrons. The RCAF had 270 aircraft of 23 different types, but only 37 were even remotely combat-worthy.

The Canadian Army was no better off. Up-to-date equipment was woefully lacking: in 1939, for example, the army had four anti-aircraft guns, five mortars, eighty-two Vickers machine guns, ten Bren guns, and two light tanks. Even trucks were in short supply. The Permanent Force had only 4,261 all ranks in mid-1939, every unit being under strength.

If the regular forces were pathetically weak, so too were the reserves — the Saturday-night soldiers, airmen, and sailors. The militia had a strength of 51,000 in armouries in countless small towns from Prince Edward Island to Vancouver Island, where units were often the focus of social life. Officers used their pay to help their units attract and hold volunteers. In many regiments, even men in the ranks gave their pay to unit funds. This was patriotic but it did not make the militia more warlike. With equipment in short supply, the militia was ill prepared for anything like modern war, but its members had the rudiments of military training. The figures were equally depressing for the air reserve, with its total strength of 1,000 organized into seven auxiliary squadrons. The Royal Canadian Navy Volunteer Reserve had a strength roughly equal to that of the Air Force auxiliary. That the men of the regular and reserve forces were game, no one doubted; that they would not survive two minutes (assuming their ammunition lasted that long) against a first-class foe was equally certain.

As the situation in Europe grew blacker, Canadians still hoped against hope that war could be avoided. Canada's influence on the issues was limited, but that influence, such as it was, was exercised in support of peace and appeasement. When Britain, France, Italy, and Germany met in Munich in September 1938 to discuss Hitler's demands for the return of the Sudetenland to Germany, and when the Great Powers pressured Czechoslovakia into acquiescence, there was relief all across the country — and the world. Instead of war there would be "peace in our time", the dessicated British prime minister, Neville Chamberlain, said after he returned from Munich. Meet Germany's "just" demands, in other words, and Herr Hitler would prove a reasonable man. Mackenzie King had met the Führer in 1937, and he shared Chamberlain's views, adding his own gloss to them by noting Hitler's deeply spiritual nature and desire for peace. Like Mackenzie King, Hitler had loved his mother.

In April 1939, with the ink on the Munich document scarcely dry, Hitler's army, the *Wehrmacht*, invaded the rest of Czechoslovakia. The full force of the Nazi propaganda machine was then turned on Poland, and the "Corridor" that gave the Poles an outlet to the sea at Danzig and divided Germany in two. Appalled at this turn of events, Britain quickly offered guarantees of military support to Warsaw, without consulting Canada and the other dominions. Chamberlain's abandonment of appeasement horrified the Canadian prime minister, who was informed of the guarantee only after it had been made. But King knew that his options were limited.

AN AUTONOMOUS NATION?

The Statute of Westminster of 1931 had made Canada autonomous in foreign policy, an independent nation within the British Commonwealth. But without sources of diplomatic information, and with only a tiny foreign service, Canada could scarcely be expected to create an external policy of its own. The Statute of Westminster, in other words, was only a paper statement of independence, and psychologically Canada remained the colony it had legally been in 1914, when the British declaration of war against Germany had committed Canada as well.

Moreover, Mackenzie King *wanted* Canada to go to war if Britain did. Usually seen as an isolationist, the strange, dumpy little man who ruled Canada was a sentimental Anglophile, an imperialist and a monarchist, one who believed fervently that Britain stood for the ideals of democracy and godliness that he cherished. It was Mackenzie King who brought George VI and Queen Elizabeth to Canada in the spring of 1939 to be cheered by loyal subjects from the Atlantic to the Pacific, and it was King who gushed in his diaries about the great qualities of Canada's monarchs. How could Canada let down such splendid people if it came to war?

What of Quebec? Although the royal couple had been hailed in Quebec City and Montreal, there was no desire in *la belle province* to send troops overseas again, to go into another war that would see the conscriptionists demanding their tithe of blood from French Canada. Here King was helped by his great colleague Ernest Lapointe, the Minister of Justice. A big man, Lapointe was trusted as was no other Quebec political figure. In the months after Munich, he and King performed a delicate ballet to calm public opinion and to satisfy those who still hoped Canada might be able to stay neutral in a European war. One day the prime minister would declare that it was "madness" to assume that Canada would send troops to Europe every twenty years to rescue a continent that could not govern itself. The next day Lapointe would maintain just as strongly that there could be no doubt of the Canadian response if there was a prospect of an aggressor raining bombs on London. And the day after, the prime minister would subject the British high commissioner in Ottawa to a tirade against London's policy, which aimed at dragging Canada into a war over Eastern European issues. What did it all mean?

It meant that King and Lapointe were manoeuvring, however reluctantly, to bring a united Canada into war through a decision of Canada's Parliament. "Parliament will decide" had been the prime minister's invariable answer to questions about his foreign policy, and King actually intended this. That only one decision would be possible was another matter. For Quebec it was essential that Canada actually have a choice — but the province's concerns about conscription also had to be satisfied.

And they were. At the end of March 1939, the prime minister pledged that if war should come, there would be no conscription for overseas military service. The leader of the Conservative Party, Dr. R.J. Manion, echoed that promise. The sigh of relief in French Canada was almost audible. The Liberal Party, dependent on Quebec, surely could not betray its promises, particularly so long as Ernest Lapointe was there.

King had thus laid the groundwork to take Canada into war. And by August 1939 war was fast approaching. As German pressure on Poland mounted, and as the Poles prepared to send their cavalry squadrons against the Nazi tanks, Germany and the Soviet Union — hitherto bitter enemies — signed a pact on August 23. The public clauses talked of friendship; the secret ones divided Poland between the Nazis and the Soviets. With one of his enemies bought off, Hitler hoped that Britain and France would draw back.

By this time, however, it had become all too clear that appeasement was a failure. Sooner or later, the Germans would have to be stopped. And so, when the Panzer divisions of the *Wehrmacht* crossed the border into Poland on September 1, the British and French issued an ultimatum. On September 3, they declared war.

Technically, Canada was still at peace. The Statute of Westminster had given the King of Canada the right to declare war on behalf of his dominion, but Parliament had not yet decided. A special session called for September 7 heard the prime minister say that "We stand for the defence of Canada; we stand for the co-operation of this country at the side of Great Britain; and if this house will not support us in that policy, it will have to find some other government to assume the responsibilities of the present." And Mackenzie King justified his tortuous course on foreign policy by noting that he had made it "the supreme endeavour" of his leadership "to let no hasty or premature threat or pronouncement create mistrust and divisions between the different elements that compose the population of our vast dominion, so that when the moment of decision came all should so see the issue itself that our national effort might be marked by unity of purpose, of heart and of endeavour."

The prime minister also repeated his pledge against conscription for overseas service: "No such measure will be introduced by the present administration." That reference to "the present administration" was a delicate reminder that other parties, whatever they said now, might not be as trustworthy. As four years had elapsed since the last general election, a contest at the polls could not be far off.

The special war session lasted only three days. J.S. Woodsworth, the leader of the Co-operative Commonwealth Federation and a genuine pacifist, was heckled when he spoke out against the war, and one or two Quebec MPs, voicing the real concerns of French Canada, called on Canada not to participate in this British war. Those lonely voices aside, Parliament voted $100 million for war expenditures (double the amount voted twenty-five years before) and decided to enter the war at Britain's side. George VI signed the proclamation on September 10, and Canada was at war with Germany — one week after Britain.

Why? Did Canada go to war because Hitler represented an unspeakably evil regime or because Poland was a democracy worth the saving? Hitler *was* evil, but in 1939 few had heard of concentration camps, and the "final solution" of the "Jewish problem" was not yet Nazi policy. There was some talk of atrocities, but after the popular exposés that had debunked most Great War claims of Germans cutting the hands off Belgian priests or crucifying Canadian soldiers, people were skeptical. And the Poles themselves ran a tyrannical regime marked by authoritarianism and anti-Semitism. A few months before, in fact, Warsaw had insisted on its territorial share of Czechoslovakia. Poland was no democracy. Czechoslovakia had been one, but the British and French had abandoned it (and its efficient army and armaments factories) to Hitler a year earlier.

Halifax after the explosion. The devastation flattened much of the working-class section of the city. The British cruiser *Highflyer* suffered only minor damage in the harbour, but clapboard houses ashore collapsed like cardboard.

A Canadian howitzer is readied to fire as dawn mist rises from the gunpit. The target is the German line east of Arras as the Canadian Corps launches the second phase of its "Last Hundred Days." Infantry carried the brunt of the fighting, but effective artillery support made their advances possible.

With food shortages a reality by the summer of 1918, the Canada Food Board did its best to inspire and then to frighten Canadians into buying only what they needed. But it was left to municipal authorities to enforce the regulations, and there is little evidence that many of them took a nearly impossible task seriously.

A Canadian gunner attempts to feed and comfort a Belgian orphan whose mother was killed at the end of the war by a stray German shell. Contemporary accounts suggest little of the live-and-let-live spirit between Germans and Canadians, and none at all when Canadians saw for themselves the effect of German occupation on civilian populations.

The burning ruins of Cambrai. The fight to capture Cambrai was the bitterest and most costly part of the long autumn struggle by the Canadian Corps. Here, a Canadian patrol pauses to find its direction in the rubble-clogged streets.

Crowds celebrating the Armistice in Vancouver on November 9. Unfortunately they were two days early, misled by a rumour that may have originated in New York.

Men of a Canadian battalion march past Sir Arthur Currie over the Rhine to Bonn. Canada initially committed two divisions to an Allied occupation force in Germany. The Canadians occupied bridgeheads at Bonn and Cologne.

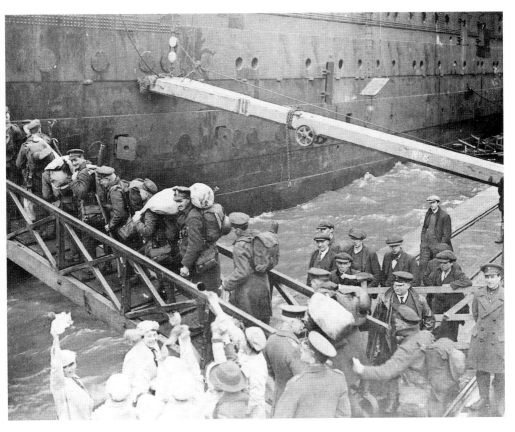

Canadian soldiers board the *Olympic*. The Kinmel riots helped persuade the British authorities that it was better to risk one of their few remaining luxury liners in Halifax's inadequate port facilities than to face further disorder. A "monster ship," the *Olympic* could carry 5,000 troops.

Disabled soldiers at work on their handicrafts. Part of their "re-establishment" was a systematic revival of the work ethic and the acquisition of suitable skills. "Ward Occupations" were the first stage in demonstrating that even the most disabled soldiers could become at least partially self-supporting.

Returned men, out of work during the 1921 depression, ask a question many war veterans have asked over the centuries. By pressing for better pensions, unemployment insurance, and special aid for the "burned-out" cases, veterans became an important force in creating Canada's social support system—but veterans of a later war would be the main beneficiaries.

While Canadian leaders wrestled fruitlessly with the Depression, the dictators of Europe had greater success. Here Hitler and Mussolini (foreground right and left) are clearly in step. While Hitler put Germans back to work (or in the army) and drew the frenzied adulation of his countrymen, Mussolini gave the Italians a policy of foreign aggression and imperial grandeur which for a time satisfied most. Behind and between the two is Rudolf Hess, who would parachute into Scotland in 1941 in a bizarre personal "peace mission;" the smiling figure left of Mussolini is Hermann Goering.

As headlines blared out the news, the *London Free Press*—a Conservative paper convinced that when Britain went to war, Canada was automatically included—was one week early in its proclamation.

The Great Depression was the central fact of most Canadians' existence in the 1930s. This young unemployed worker is "tin-canning" to raise pennies for food and shelter in Vancouver; in a few years he would be expected to enlist and risk his life for a system that, in the eyes of many, had failed.

Although rationing was limited to a few foodstuffs—like butter, sugar, and meat—there was pressure to conserve everything.

Winter weather conditions in the North Atlantic varied from dreadful to appalling. Waves washing over the deck deposited ice faster than the crew could hack it off, making vessels almost unmanageable; if the weight of ice became too great, the ship could capsize. Here, the corvette *Wetaskiwin* comes into St. John's harbour in December 1942.

The Canadian army in Britain received its baptism of fire on August 19, 1942, when the 2nd Division staged a raid on the French port of Dieppe. The result was a slaughter, with two-thirds of the attacking force being killed, wounded, or captured.

The peaceful appearance of this convoy, formed up in Halifax's
Bedford Basin, is deceptive. The thousands of cargo ships that kept
Britain supplied with munitions, food, and other vital war materials
had to be co-ordinated, not just with each other, but with trucks
and trains for loading and unloading. Factory schedules, troop
movements, and even the strategy of the war were timed around the
arrival of convoys—and the intricate system was at the mercy of
weather and U-boat wolf packs.

On the frigate *St. Catharines* some men resorted to sleeping in the open, while the fresh air and exercise of the cruiser *Uganda*'s "physical jerks" were a welcome break.

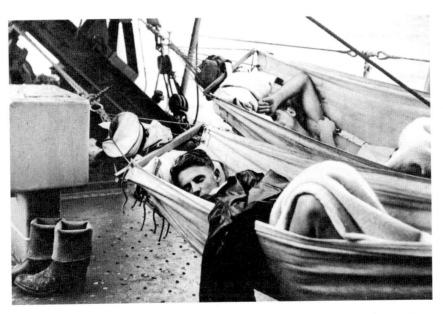

Living conditions at sea could be horribly cramped. On corvettes like *Kamsack* (above), hammocks were slung everywhere, and those who could not find slinging space slept on seat cushions or on the deck. Since washwater had to be distilled from the sea, little washing was allowed. One sailor remembered trying to sleep "while below me someone put sardines on toast, and the smells from the paint-locker and the heads fought the other smells, and the motion went on, and everything creaked and groaned and rattled."

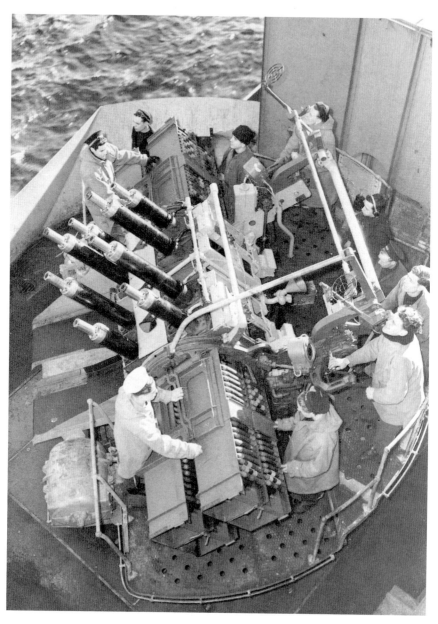

U-boats were not the only menace; the *Luftwaffe* also posed a threat to RCN ships venturing into the English Channel or the Mediterranean. One effective means of defence, mounted on such armed merchant cruisers as HMCS *Prince Robert* and *Prince Henry*, was the 20mm "pom-pom" gun, which could throw up a stream of 2-pound shells from its eight barrels.

In other words, Canada went to war in September 1939 primarily for the same reason as in 1914: because Britain went to war. Not for democracy, though that was crucial. Not to stop Hitler, though that mattered. Not to save Poland, though that was the ostensible reason. Canada went to war only because Neville Chamberlain felt unable to break the pledges he had made to Poland in March 1939. Had he slipped free, as he tried to do, Canada would have sat by and watched the Reich devour Poland without feeling compelled to fight. Some Canadians knew that Hitler had to be fought; in 1939, however, that motive was not as powerful as the old loyalties.

The much-trumpeted autonomy that Canada had won was, therefore, irrelevant in the face of a war involving Britain. Ties of sentiment, blood, and culture had foreclosed every option but one. The simple truth is that the English-Canadian majority wanted Canada to fight because of the link to the mother country, not because of any understanding of the issues at stake. Ethnic Canadians were generally cooler, but acquiescent. French Canadians were willing to allow English Canadians to volunteer, so long as the threat of conscription no longer existed. The decision to go to war may have been the only possible one, but large numbers of Canadians were not enthusiastic about the prospect.

MARCHING AS TO WAR

Enthusiastic or not, Canada was now in the war. Plans had to be made for the volunteers who were starting to queue up at militia armouries and naval stations. The prime minister, fearful of casualties and of the impact of another conscription crisis on his country and party, was hoping that Canada could wage a war of "limited liability" — like a cautious insurance company protecting itself against undue risk. He was delighted to be told by London twice in the first week of September that the defence of Canada was the first and major charge on his government. Once Canada was at war, however, London began pressing the Canadian government to send troops overseas.

Cabinet met on September 15 to prepare the war program. The ministers were horrified when the chiefs of staff presented plans for the first year that would cost $491 million, almost as much as the country's entire peacetime budget. That sum, they decided, had to be cut back to $314 million. The army's plan for three divisions was reduced by one — a saving of approximately 20,000 men. But there was to be an expeditionary force, despite Mackenzie King's reluctance. One of the infantry divisions was to go overseas as soon as possible, and the second was to be recruited and trained in Canada for dispatch if necessary. In command of the First Division was Major-General

Andrew G.L. McNaughton, a very successful artillery officer in the Great War, a respected scientist, and the head of the National Research Council. Mackenzie King liked Andy McNaughton because he thought the general was against conscription; moreover, because the general had been close to Prime Minister Bennett, some thought he was a Tory, so no one could claim that the Liberal government was playing patronage games with the army!

While those decisions were being implemented, London proposed the establishment of a giant air training plan, as well. The British had been trying for some years to persuade Canada to allow the training of Royal Air Force pilots in its great open spaces. Although a small project had been agreed on in April 1939, the war had intervened before the first trainees had reached Canada. Now the idea was to train some 20,000 pilots and 30,000 air crew in Canada each year. The British Commonwealth Air Training Plan (BCATP), as it came to be called, had been suggested by the Australian high commissioner in London and by Vincent Massey, the Canadian high commissioner, and had been seized upon by the Air Ministry.

King initially liked the idea, but the more he thought about it, the angrier he became. If the British had produced this scheme at the outset, it could have been Canada's major contribution and might have made an expeditionary force unnecessary. He and his ministers were worried about the financial costs, as well as the political complications. The war program decided upon in mid-September had been based on their assessment of the maximum Canada could do.

In the end — after difficult, often bitter negotiations with a British mission and dominion representatives — the BCATP was created. The total cost was set at $607 million, with the Canadian share being $353 million, a vast increase on the original budget fixed for the first year of war. The RCAF was to administer the BCATP, and some Canadian graduates were to be placed in RCAF squadrons. The agreement, signed in the early morning hours of December 17, 1939, was announced in a national radio address by Mackenzie King. That day, not coincidentally, was his sixty-fifth birthday.

The military side of the war effort was beginning to take shape, but there was opposition in the country. In Quebec, Premier Maurice Duplessis, whose Union Nationale party had been in power since 1936, looked on the unease created by the war as an opportunity to seek re-election. Duplessis's government had not been a notable success, and the province's creditors were unhappy about the worth of provincial bonds, but his snap election call on September 25 caused near panic in Ottawa. The premier was "a little Hitler", King wrote, and his election announcement a "diabolical act". The concern was genuine: Ottawa's carefully constructed national unity could be jeopardized by the acrimony certain to be created by a provincial election, and if

Duplessis won, his government would be a thorn in the federal government's side.

The solution came when King's Quebec ministers decided, over his initial opposition, to enter the provincial contest. "They took the view," King wrote in his diary, "that if Duplessis carried the province, it would be equivalent to a want of confidence in themselves as Federal ministers, and that they would feel it necessary to withdraw from the Cabinet as having lost all influence...." Moreover, the ministers campaigned on the issue of conscription: if Duplessis won and they resigned, then French Canada would have no voice in Ottawa, making conscription a certainty. That argument had force. By calling for provincial autonomy in the face of Ottawa's wartime centralization, Duplessis put himself on the defensive. The election saw the Liberals take 53 per cent of the popular vote and 69 seats in the Legislature.

Duplessis had argued implicitly that Canada was doing too much, but the reaction in parts of Ontario was precisely the opposite. The Liberal premier, Mitchell Hepburn, had been fighting with his federal cousins for years, and King's half-hearted support for the war intensified Hepburn's distaste for the prime minister. In the Ontario Legislature on January 18, 1940, Hepburn moved and easily carried a resolution "regretting that the Federal Government at Ottawa has made so little effort to prosecute Canada's duty in the war in the vigorous manner the people of Canada desire to see." Mackenzie King was appalled at this challenge from the most populous province, but he quickly saw the potential advantages. Parliament was due to reassemble for a partisan and bitter pre-election session. Hepburn's accusation offered the perfect excuse for a sudden election.

The MPs and senators gathered to hear the Speech from the Throne on January 25 sat stunned when the governor general announced the dissolution of Parliament. It was trickery to force a sudden election because of Hepburn's move, to be sure, but — aside from the outrage on the Opposition benches — few in the country seemed to object. The election campaign that followed, taking place during the "Phony War" that left the European front uneasily calm for seven months, was quiet. The Conservatives promised to form a government of the "best brains" in the land and unwisely dubbed themselves the "National Government" party, a name that stirred recollections in Quebec and elsewhere of the Union Government that had been created in 1917 to enforce conscription. The CCF, torn by the pacifism of its leader and many of his followers, was ineffective. Only the Liberals, pledging no conscription and promising a sound war effort, had the experienced men Canada needed in wartime, or so Grit propaganda claimed. The people believed them, and on March 26 they gave the Liberals 51.5 per cent of the popular vote and 181 seats, a huge majority in a House of 245. The Tories were slaughtered wholesale, even Manion losing his seat. The CCF's Woodsworth was barely re-elected. Social Credit dropped from 17 seats to 10. It was a Liberal triumph, and Mackenzie King was again firmly in command.

BUILDING THE FORCES

With politics temporarily out of the way, the business of preparing for war continued slowly. War production, eagerly sought by the government as a way of putting the still-large numbers of unemployed men and women back to work after ten years of Depression, began at a glacial pace. The British firms that held the patents on modern machines of war were reluctant to give the rights to produce guns, tanks, and bombs to Canada. The strictly limited federal budget did not allow for many new factories to be built or for industry to convert from peace to war production. In Ottawa's war of limited liability, not many businessmen or politicians wanted to take risks either.

Some Canadians stepped forward, though, and put more than their money or careers on the line. On September 1 — the day Hitler invaded Poland — Father Mike Dalton, a Roman Catholic priest in Windsor, Ontario, telegraphed Ottawa to volunteer: "If you are called upon to furnish Chaplains for the Service, I shall be ready on land or sea or air." There were more like him, too. In September 1939, 58,337 men and a few nursing sisters enlisted as volunteers in the army's active service force for the duration of the war. That was just about the same number that had enlisted in the first five months of the Great War. In fact, there were more men lining up outside the headquarters of militia units than the authorities could handle, and many "old sweats" from the previous war tried in vain to re-enlist. Farley Mowat recounts the story of the veteran who had his son drive him to the nearest headquarters of the Hastings and Prince Edward Regiment:

> he could not drive himself, having lost most of his sight and most of his lungs to mustard gas in 1918. He wept when they turned him away. But the Regiment did not forget him, for the son enlisted before the two returned to their farm that night.

There were many like that veteran. But there were also those parents who dreaded the thought of their sons enlisting. One father wrote the RCMP to try to stop his boy from joining up:

> My son Noah Summers has volunteered to go overseas and I feel I need him here. I lost one leg in the last war and had another one come back disabled.... Now I am not as young as I used to be and I need my boy each

fall to help me, I have farm lands which I have to go back and look after each fall.... You will do me a great favour if you turn him down I feel I've done my duty for my country and you know those boys have to be fed over there I am a Sask wheat farmer and have had plenty grief the last few years.

Still, there were thousands who had been unemployed for so long during the Great Depression that the prospect of a private's pay of $1.30 a day (and dependants' allowance of $60 a month plus $12 for each child), three squares a day, and a warm greatcoat looked pretty good, particularly with winter only two months away. Patriotism was the motive force for many; for some, the war offered a chance to escape from a life of relief, bread lines, skimpy food, and no money; for others, it was a simple desire for adventure or a chance to flee an unhappy marriage.

But after the imposition of stern fitness standards ("Men perfectly fit, mentally and physically, for all active service conditions of actual warfare in any climate, who are able to march, can see to shoot, and hear well") and admonitions from Ottawa to go slowly in recruiting those with dependants, the flood of volunteers turned into a trickle. There was no equipment and little barrack space. One Winnipegger who enlisted in the artillery in September remembered being issued a Great War uniform of "breeches, long puttees, brass-buttoned tunics, bandoliers — and boots that we dyed ourselves with thick, black army issue coloring. We had no barracks and lived out." Only 64,902 had been enrolled by the end of 1939 and just 20,000 more were taken on strength in the first four months of 1940. There were not enough uniforms even for those.

Recruiting for the navy was slower yet, only a few handfuls being enrolled. By the end of the first month of the war, only 3,000 sailors were in uniform all told, and waiting lists swelled across the country. Small as it was, however, the RCN quickly got its destroyers ready for war service. HMCS *Fraser* and *St. Laurent* steamed out of Esquimalt immediately after fighting broke out on August 31 and arrived via the Panama Canal to join the other ships at their war station at Halifax on September 15. Already, harbour defences were in place at the great port from which the convoys were starting to go forth.

The Royal Canadian Air Force too struggled to get ready. Thirty-five modern aircraft from the United States barely managed to get over the border in the week after September 3, before Canada declared war and the American Neutrality Act came into effect. The regular and auxiliary squadrons went on full-time service on September 3, their ancient Wapiti aircraft and their few modern Hurricanes cranking up for action. Over the next two weeks, the reserves mobilized and recruiting began.

But it was the army that attracted the press coverage in the first months of war. The 1st Canadian Division, including such famous infantry units as the Royal Canadian Regiment, Princess Patricia's Canadian Light Infantry, the Royal 22e Regiment (the "Van Doos"), and the Seaforth Highlanders, began its move overseas in December 1939. In contrast to the situation in 1914, this time the division's officers and men were wholly Canadian. Almost 7,500 officers and men left Halifax on five great liners on December 10. One soldier remembered that these ships that eventually carried thousands of troops at a time "now carried only hundreds. It was a classy way to travel.... State rooms were allotted on a first-come, first-served basis....the ships still had their peacetime crews, and...they wouldn't let us do anything." Other ships were less grand. Robert Fulton of the Army Service Corps sailed on an old liner, the ss *Armonda*, and lived in the hold. "Top tier was in hammocks, second tier slept on top of the mess tables and third tier slept under the mess tables. And you prayed that the guy above you didn't get seasick."

Two additional convoys brought Canadian army strength in Britain to 23,000 by February 1940. The division was largely untrained, about half of its men never having served even in the militia before the outbreak of war. Training before embarkation had concentrated on foot and rifle drill, and only the most rudimentary tactics had been practised. The coldest winter of the century hampered training in England ("sniffles, coughs, frozen winter pipes, plugged toilets, largely unheated barrack rooms," one soldier remembered it), and not until April could more advanced training take place. Each infantry battalion spent time in a model trench system learning the patrolling and raiding techniques with which the Canadian Corps had won the Great War, and although vehicles were in short supply, units could pool their transport for mobile exercises.

One private in the Royal Canadian Army Service Corps, Jack Ainsworth of Calgary, wrote to his parents on May 6 about the monotony of training: "We're going for marches and doing rifle drills same as we did when we first joined up and all in all we aren't doing a thing new but just seeming to stand still." Worst of all, Ainsworth said, "I've finally found out what's missing over here. There's no place we can get a hamburger...." Still, as one British woman remembered, "all the girls were on Cloud 9 if they could go out with a 1st Div. Canadian."

Herr Hitler was unwilling to let the division get ready for Great War–style trench warfare at its own pace. In April, the Phony War suddenly came to an end. Germany invaded Denmark and Norway, and most of the 2nd Brigade of the 1st Canadian Division left for Scotland on April 18 to await embarkation for northern Norway. Those orders were changed the next day: British units were sent into the cauldron, and the disappointed Canadians returned to their camp at Aldershot. They had been spared a hopeless campaign, as Denmark fell at once and Norway held out only into May.

The one bright spot in this increasingly serious military situation was that Neville Chamberlain was out of power in London on May 10. Toppled by revolt on the Tory backbenches, caused by the poor planning and disastrous results of the Norwegian campaign, Chamberlain had been replaced by a different sort of leader. Winston Churchill was a fighter, an innovator, and a man to inspire a nation at war. Mackenzie King had little confidence in the new prime minister, noting in his diary that Churchill was "tight most of the time". Perhaps it was true, but better Churchill drunk than Chamberlain sober. Britain soon was to need all the inspiration it could find.

On May 10, the same day Churchill took power, Hitler let loose his Panzer divisions in a *Blitzkrieg*, or "lightning war", against the Low Countries and France. The Germans used their tanks and mechanized infantry in a revolutionary way, large units bypassing pockets of French resistance and sweeping into the lightly manned rear areas. The *Luftwaffe* added to the panic and confusion caused by the Panzers with carefully co-ordinated dive-bombing attacks on enemy units; their Stukas were equipped with sirens to increase the terror, and the combined effect was to create chaos and spread despondency. The Dutch were overrun in a few days, and when the British and French forces left their prepared positions along the Franco-Belgian border to move forward to assist the Belgians, they and the Belgian army were cut off by a German thrust through the Ardennes forest and across the Meuse River. By May 20 the Germans were at Amiens and by the next day the Panzers, incredibly, had reached the English Channel near Abbeville, trapping the retreating British Expeditionary Force in a pocket. Only the miracle of Dunkirk — when a great flotilla made up of ships of the Royal Navy and hundreds of small civilian craft evacuated 338,000 British and French soldiers, while the *Wehrmacht* inexplicably sat by — would prevent the war from being lost completely before the end of May.

The situation in France had turned critical in less than two weeks. A desperate War Office called on General McNaughton and his Canadian division to support the beleaguered troops. McNaughton went to France on May 23 to study the battlefield, and while he was there his troops moved to Dover — but then he advised London that there was no prospect of his division rescuing the situation, and the men were sent back to Aldershot. Anxious to get into the fight, the Canadians sat discouraged and unhappy in their barracks while great events transpired at Dunkirk. "The Great Retreat from Dover" or "the Plymouth Panic", the troops called their abortive mission. The miraculous rescue of most of the British Expeditionary Force (but not its equipment) could not hide the magnitude of the disaster. Yet — despite the critical situation in France, and the collapse of the once-mighty French army — there was still wishful thinking in Churchill's London about the possibility of constructing a fortified Anglo-French redoubt in the Breton peninsula.

The Canadians were fated to be key players in this scheme, and on June 12 and 13 one brigade of infantry and a regiment of artillery — or about 5,000 men all told — landed at Brest, on the western tip of France. When Mackenzie King learned of the plans to send the division to France, he wrote in his diary that "it was like sending our men into a fiery furnace to be devoured in whole, almost in their first encounter." Fortunately, the fires were postponed this time. On the 14th, the Germans marched into undefended Paris, and although most of the Canadians had already moved inland by truck and by train, wiser heads concluded that there was little point in seeing the division thrown away for no prospect of gain. The troops were ordered to return to the coast and to abandon their vehicles and guns. The commanding officer of the Royal Canadian Horse Artillery, Lieutenant-Colonel J.H. Roberts, flatly refused to destroy his precious guns and brought them back to England. His war diary bitterly noted, "Although there was evidently no enemy within 200 miles, the withdrawal was conducted as a rout." The guns were more than welcome in an almost undefended England; the trucks, 216 of which were run off a cliff or set on fire, might also have been rescued had there been less panic.

The grumbling over the fiasco was very pronounced, the soldiers bitching that CASF, the initials of the Canadian Active Service Force, really meant Canadians Almost Saw France. In fact, the providential order to withdraw had saved thousands from death or capture; with the French capitulation, nothing was going to stop the *Wehrmacht*, certainly not the Canadians scattered across France. Six men were left behind in the rush to disembark: one was mortally injured in a road accident, four were interned but subsequently made their way back to England, and one became a prisoner of war. Given the chaos, the losses were remarkably small. Inevitably, the returning soldiers told tall tales about the French girls they had met, and one (probably apocryphal) story persisted of a Canadian who had managed to contract venereal disease during his brief excursion on the Continent.

But no one could see anything funny in Britain's situation in the summer of 1940. Hitler now controlled western Europe and the French shore of the English Channel and, although most of the British forces in France had been rescued at Dunkirk, there was only one division in England that was reasonably well equipped: McNaughton's Canadians. From being a slightly reluctant partner in a war of limited liability, Canada had suddenly become Britain's ranking ally in a war for survival.

XII
War at Home and Abroad, 1940–42

The calamitous events in France stunned Canada. The six-million–strong French army had been thought to be the most powerful in the world, and the pride of its vaunted generals had collapsed like a pricked balloon. The confusion and muddle that had bedevilled the British Expeditionary Force were apparent despite the press censorship, but there was a curious kind of relief in Britain and Canada. The untrustworthy French (for so the British had always seen them) were gone, and now Britain and the Commonwealth could carry on all the better for being alone. "Chin up, there'll always be an England," said one lapel button sported by Canadians in the summer of 1940. Most Canadians agreed that, so long as the Royal Navy remained intact, Britain would survive and ultimately prevail.

That was a slim chance at best, and Ottawa realized it. A limited-liability war was no longer possible for Canada, and the only question now was what could be done. In April 1940, even before the *Blitzkrieg*, the government had agreed to the formation of an overseas Canadian Corps of two divisions. The prime minister persuaded his cost-conscious colleagues that this was owed to General McNaughton for his work in creating the 1st Division.

That seemed a feeble response after the middle of May. Under increasing public pressure, the government announced a series of measures to accelerate the war effort, including the early despatch of the 2nd Division overseas, the stationing of infantry in the West Indies and Iceland, and a greater financial commitment to the war and to Britain. King admitted to his caucus on May 23 that he almost feared to tell the country that the war effort would cost more than a billion dollars a year. The entire pre-war federal budget had amounted to about half a billion dollars; after less than a year of war, defence expenditure was already twice that much. "We had to consider whether that would not occasion a run on the banks...."

Some provinces thought Ottawa was weak and half-hearted. In Saskatchewan, where pro-Nazi organizations had been active before the war, Attorney-General J.W. Estey created the Saskatchewan Veterans Civil Security Corps in early June. The corps was to help the police by acting as a deterrent against defeatism and subversive talk, and to bring "comfort and assurance to our people in isolated areas, especially where Anglo Saxon settlers are in the minority." Immigrants might well become a fifth column — or so the attorney-general believed. Estey was not alone in the panicky summer of 1940. His corps soon had 7,500 men mobilized to watch for troublemakers and to check out rumours of Nazi sympathizers. In September, for example, a man at Nipawin was reported to have served the Kaiser in the Great War and to be an "open admirer of Nazi progress". Checking, however, demonstrated that the suspect was "loyal to Canada and very thankful to be living in a free country."

For many people, the sign of a serious war effort was conscription. The Canadian Legion, the biggest veterans' organization, began deluging Ottawa with telegrams calling for the complete mobilization of the manpower, financial, and industrial resources of the country, and the newspapers were beating the drums. Aware that many thought him completely unacceptable as prime minister during a total war, King was sensitive to the demands. On the other hand, as a realist, he had to consider what might happen if Britain was knocked out of the war. Canada had to keep "our own defences strong; possible danger arising later on," he wrote in his diary. "... up to a few weeks ago, our thoughts were all with respect to cooperation overseas. Today we would have to turn them to possibilities of internal troubles to be dealt with in Canada."

The answer might be conscription for home defence only. And by the middle of June, King had persuaded himself that this was the right course. On June 18, he himself drafted a bill, subsequently known as the National Resources Mobilization Act, and presented it to Parliament that day. The bill conferred "upon the government special emergency powers to mobilize all our human and material resources for the defence of Canada". To calm Quebec, still nervous about conscription, the prime minister affirmed that the NRMA related "solely and exclusively to the defence of Canada on our own soil and in our own territorial waters." As a first stage, a national registration was ordered, but King stated that "no measure for the conscription of men for overseas service will be introduced..."

In Quebec the NRMA drew worried looks. The bill seemed only the first bite at the cherry of conscription. After all, had not registration in 1916 preceded conscription in 1917? But the three leading Quebeckers in the Cabinet — Ernest Lapointe, Charles G. "Chubby" Power, the Minister of National Defence (Air), and P.J.A. Cardin, the Minister of Public Works — spoke strongly for the bill, and it passed into law on June 21. Even so, before the registration took place on August 19, 20, and 21 the populist mayor of Montreal, Camillien Houde, urged his people not to register. Ottawa moved with swiftness and Houde was interned for his foolish comments, a deliberate step to *encourager les autres*. The registration took place without further difficulty, and Houde remained behind barbed wire for four years.

The results showed that there were almost 8,000,000 men and women over the age of sixteen, and 800,000 civilian men who were single or childless widowers between the ages of twenty-one and forty-five — a number that had been reduced slightly by the race to the altar following the government's announcement that only those wed before July 15 would count as married. As of August 27, single men became liable for military service.

The first home defence conscripts called up under the NRMA reported for training at camps across the country on October 9, 1940. There were 30,000 new trainees in the group, all between the ages of twenty-one and twenty-four, and the plan was to train 240,000 men a year. But the term of service was only thirty days, which could have little military value; at most, the drill and sports might help get the conscripts into better physical shape. "Trainees reporting Friday are urged to bring along any basketball or badminton equipment they have available," one press notice in Toronto actually said. Officers commanding the camps thought the discipline of the NRMA scheme would help overcome the effects of "twenty years of pacifist debauchery." But if the government's purpose in creating the NRMA was to persuade men to go on to volunteer for active service, it got off to a slow start; the army initially forgot to create any system of enrolment.

In fact, the army was short of equipment and instructors, and had all it could do to handle the home defence soldiers. Even so, General Harry Crerar — the Chief of the General Staff and, like many senior officers, a graduate of the Royal Military College and a veteran of the trenches — soon was pressing the government to extend the training period to a more useful four months. The Cabinet eventually agreed, and announced its decision in February 1941. Now, the "R" recruits called up under the NRMA would take their basic and advanced training with the "A" recruits, who had enlisted voluntarily. Two months later, when unemployment had disappeared across the country and the pool of twenty-one–year–olds was starting to dry up, the King government moved to keep NRMA men on service for the war's duration, thus freeing volunteers serving in home defence units for overseas. For the first time in the war, manpower pressures were starting to pinch just a little. Moreover, Canada now had two armies: one of volunteers willing to serve anywhere, and one of conscripts limited to service in Canada.

To its credit, the government resisted substantial public opposition and permitted conscientious objectors to refrain from military service. Ottawa established various forms of alternative service that "conshies" could do, including working in national parks for fifty cents a day. Jehovah's Witnesses in particular refused to recognize the authority of the state and almost 200 Witnesses were prosecuted. In all 10,851 men opted for alternative service during the war.

MR. KING AND MR. ROOSEVELT

By late 1940, the threat Hitler posed to the survival of freedom was all-consuming. If Britain fell, Canada's physical security would be threatened as never before, and only the United States would be able to guarantee it. Striking an alliance with the United States was essential. President Franklin Roosevelt was as supportive as he could be, given the necessities of American election-year politics, his quest for an unprecedented third term, and the strong current of isolationism that ran through the United States. The patrician Roosevelt, a shrewd political tactician and an inspiring leader, had won sweeping election victories in 1932 and 1936, and he had given hope to a nation that had been shattered by the Depression. He and Mackenzie King, both Harvard graduates, were friendly, and their governments had co-operated in 1935 and 1938 to negotiate and sign trade agreements that lowered tariffs and greatly increased the movement of goods across the border. And Roosevelt had been helpful in persuading his officials to get aircraft to Canada in that crucial week before Canada officially joined the war.

Even so, the United States had hung back while France went through its death agonies in May and June 1940. The Americans were beginning to fear that the Western hemisphere might have to become self-sufficient in a world in which Europe was under German sway while Japan increasingly controlled the Pacific. What would Canada's place be in such a world? What would happen to the remnants of the British Empire if Britain itself was swallowed by Nazi tyranny? In particular, what would happen to the Royal Navy? With the great fleet in German hands, in addition to the smaller but powerful German navy, North America would be in grave jeopardy.

Much to his discomfort, Mackenzie King found himself having to convey Roosevelt's thinking on the world situation to the new British prime minister. Churchill was tough, combative, and aggressive, and King "felt something of a sinking feeling" when he realized what message Roosevelt wanted delivered: the fleet had to be kept in action as long as possible and then dispersed to the Empire — even if that meant the occupation of Britain and destruction comparable to that visited upon Poland or France. Otherwise Japan was sure to have a virtual free hand in the Pacific to build its captive "Greater East Asia Co-Prosperity Sphere" while Germany and Italy would swallow all of Britain's colonies. Mackenzie King blanched at the thought of delivering this message. It seemed to him, he recorded in his diary, "that the United States was seeking to save itself at the expense of Britain.... That the British themselves might have to go down. I instinctively revolted against such a thought. My reaction was that I would rather die than do aught to save ourselves or any part of this continent at the expense of Britain."

Nonetheless, King delivered the message. His reward came when Churchill told the Westminster Parliament that

> We shall never surrender, and even if...this island or a large part of it were subjugated and starving, then our Empire beyond the seas, armed and guarded by the British fleet, would carry on the struggle, until, in God's good time, the New World, with all its power and might, steps forth to the rescue and liberation of the old.

Even though some of the telegrams from London struck a less forthright note, it was one of Churchill's greatest orations in a summer of magnificent speeches. Oratory was almost the only weapon Britain had.

Meanwhile Mackenzie King was looking to Canada's own defences. The one effective RCAF squadron and the tiny resources of the RCN had been sent to England in late May 1940, and Canada's coasts were now more or less naked. There was some prospect that Roosevelt might be able to get around the confines of the Neutrality Act by swapping surplus American destroyers for British bases in Newfoundland and the West Indies; that would ease the strains on the hard-pressed Royal Navy. But it would do little to defend Canada directly. Moreover, studies by the Bank of Canada showed that the defeat of Britain would cripple the Canadian economy, creating massive unemployment as much of Canada's overseas trade disappeared at a stroke. In the face of such dangers, Canada had to look to Washington for help. It had only one card to play: the necessity for the United States to plan a continental defence of which Canada was an integral part.

Roosevelt took the initiative on August 16, 1940, inviting Mackenzie King to meet him at Ogdensburg, New York, the next day. King accepted at once and the conversations between the president and the prime minister altered Canada's history. The two leaders agreed to establish a Permanent Joint Board on Defence to study defence problems and recommend ways the two governments could resolve them.

The PJBD agreement guaranteed that Canada was safe from invasion so long as the United States remained a great power. The Ogdensburg Agreement — the first the United States had signed with a belligerent — was a major gain for the Allied cause because it tied Washington and Canada closer together and meant that Canada could continue to send men and material overseas.

Those were entries on the asset side of the ledger. On the other side, the Ogdensburg Agreement was a clear demonstration that the world had changed and that Ottawa realized it. Britain could no longer guarantee Canadian security, and Canada had been forced to turn to the south. No Canadian government could have done otherwise. Churchill, however, was unamused at what he saw as Canada's scuttling to save itself and telegraphed King that "there may be two opinions" about Ogdensburg. "Supposing Mr. Hitler cannot invade us...all these transactions will be judged in a mood different to that prevailing while the issue still hangs in the balance." Convinced that he had done his bit for the Empire, King was shattered at Churchill's carping. Not until the old British lion (prompted by his high commissioner in Ottawa) sent him a telegram congratulating him for "all you have done for the common cause and especially in promoting a harmony of sentiment throughout the New World" did King recover.

A few Canadians could not accept the new defence relationship. Arthur Meighen, the former Conservative prime minister, was furious at King and Roosevelt. "Really I lost my breakfast," he wrote a friend, "when I read the account this morning...and gazed on the disgusting picture of these potentates posing like monkeys in the middle of the very blackest crisis of this Empire." And Frank Underhill, a noted Canadian historian, was almost fired by the University of Toronto when he told a conference at Lake Couchiching that the Ogdensburg Agreement showed that "we can no longer put all our eggs in the British basket." The historian was saved, in part, by Ottawa's efforts to persuade the university that the Americans might misunderstand his firing for such statements. The new world reality took time to sink in.

Canada's physical defences were secured by the new alliance, but its economy was in danger because of its efforts to assist Britain. Every ship or truck or airplane that was made in Saint John or Windsor or Montreal and sent to Great Britain contained parts imported from the United States. There was nothing wrong with that; indeed, it had been true in peacetime. The difference was that the war had forced Britain to put controls on its currency, ending the easy convertibility of pounds into dollars. Canada's exports of war materiel built up huge reserves of pounds sterling in London which could not be converted into the American dollars needed to cover its trade deficit with the U.S. At the same time, the extra imports required to meet the demands of war production had to be paid for in full. Canada was caught in a double bind: every effort to help Britain forced the nation deeper into a hole with the United States.

This problem was minor compared to Britain's. As early as December 1940, the British ambassador to Washington had told the press, "Boys, Britain's broke. It's your money we want." And it was true. The costs of fighting a second world war in a single generation had quickly swallowed up Britain's currency reserves. The necessity of paying for purchases in the United States forced London to sell off most of Britain's remaining American holdings. But while Roosevelt was a tough bargainer with an eye on post-war commercial advantage, he was also committed heart and soul to the Allied cause, and he came up with the brilliant idea of lending or leasing munitions and supplies to the Allies; "repayment" could be "in kind or property, and any other direct or indirect benefit which the President deems satisfactory." At a stroke, Britain's financial crisis disappeared.

But at the same time, lend-lease increased Canada's financial problems. While it had extended generous assistance to Britain, Ottawa had not been handing over supplies without charge. Instead, British-held Canadian stocks and bonds had been taken in payment for the wheat, flour, bacon, cheese, and munitions shipped overseas. If Britain could now get everything it needed on lend-lease from the U.S., why should it pay for goods from Canada? Then what would happen to the Canadian economy and to the full employment the war had brought? The answers were all too clear.

Canada could have sought lend-lease aid itself from the Americans as a way out of its difficulties. Led by James Ilsley, whose transparent integrity made him one of the few popular ministers of finance in Canadian history, the finance department wisely decided not to do so — especially after it learned that one American demand was for Canada to sell its holdings in the U.S. It was one thing for Britain, separated from the Americans by an ocean, to take lend-lease, whatever the conditions. It was another for Canada, with its common border and with the already large American stake in the Canadian economy. Who knew what concessions the Americans might demand after the war in return for their largesse?

Even with lend-lease ruled out, Mackenzie King and his officials were equal to the challenge. In mid-April 1941, the prime minister travelled to Hyde Park, New York, Roosevelt's family home, to talk about Canada's financial problems with his friend. Meeting on what Roosevelt called a "grand Sunday", the two struck a deal that resolved Canada's difficulties.

The president agreed that the components Canada had to import for munitions intended for Britain could be charged to the British lend-lease account.

In addition, Roosevelt undertook that the United States would purchase more raw materials and supplies from Canada to offset Canada's increased wartime purchases in the U.S. The Hyde Park Declaration signed by the two men anticipated that Canada could "supply the United States with between $200 million and $300 million worth" of defence articles such as ships and aluminum. It was a triumph for King, one that ended his country's financial difficulties for the duration of the war. And once freed of the problem posed by the shortage of American dollars, Canada was able to do far more for Britain. In January 1942, the government announced a gift of a billion dollars' worth of materiel, an indication of the country's burgeoning strength — and an effort to keep employment and production up in Canada. There would be further gifts as the war wore on.

Meanwhile, King's government had launched a series of fund-raising campaigns at home. Beginning in January 1940 and running through the duration of the war, nine War Loan and Victory Loan campaigns produced an astonishing $8.8 billion for the war effort. Every device of publicity was employed, from celebrities buying bonds (the five-year–old Dionne Quints took $20,000 in January 1940) to entertainments, speeches, and magazine advertising. All the stops were pulled. One advertisement for the Second Victory Loan in 1942 showed two tiny blond tots asleep with their teddy bear. "Let's Keep Our Canada a Happy Land for Them," the headline read.

> Pinky-white Dimples; a button of a nose; wee, slender fingers clutching at your coverlet — what kind of world is this to which you will awake?
>
> Your life, we hope, will be rich in love and laughter. God forbid that your Canada should ever come under the heel of ruthless barbarism, where babies are born to be the future shock troops, or the mothers of a brutal military race.
>
> We promise that you shall inherit a Canada blessed with the promise our fathers bequeathed to us....We will buy Victory Bonds to the very limit....

The advertisements worked.

THE WAR ECONOMY

The Victory Bond results were but one sign of Canadian war prosperity. Workers had money because every factory in the country was going full blast. C.D. Howe, the hard-charging Minister of Munitions and Supply who had made his fortune building grain elevators, co-ordinated the production effort. Soon, Canadian plants and workers were producing the goods in completely unparalleled fashion. From a standing start in 1939 (war orders to the end of December amounted to only $60 million), production accelerated year by year. In 1941 it passed the billion-dollar mark, and the next year the total reached $2.5 billion. Considering that the gross national product in 1939 had been just over $5 billion, the growth in war industry was phenomenal.

By sector the gains were equally impressive. Before the war Canadian shipbuilding had been insignificant, but between 1939 and 1945, 391 cargo vessels, 487 escorts and minesweepers, and 3,600 specialized craft came down the ways. The story was the same for military vehicles: at the peak of production in 1944, 4,000 trucks and 450 armoured vehicles a *week* were built. In the aircraft industry, production went from near zero to 4,000 military airplanes a year, including huge four-engined Lancaster bombers. The same kind of increases were visible in every area of war production, from ammunition to guns to radar sets, and much of the money to help build the new war plants — $750 million between 1939 and 1944 — was put up by the government. Howe's department itself created at least twenty-eight crown corporations to produce everything from rifles (Small Arms Limited) to synthetic rubber (Polymer Corporation) to wood for aircraft (Veneer Log Supply Limited).

To staff the factories, hundreds of thousands of new workers were needed, a serious problem when the army, navy, and air force took most fit men from the labour force. The result was jobs for everyone. Families that had had no one gainfully employed during the 1930s now had father overseas, mother working in a munitions plant, and grown children, male and female, bringing home good wage packets each week from aircraft factories or shipyards. There was all the overtime work anyone could want, and Canadians suddenly had plenty of money. In the first week of January 1942, the Unemployment Insurance Commission offices in Halifax announced that not a single claim had been filed.

Moreover, the war created new opportunities for women — even if those opportunities only lasted for the duration. Beginning in 1941 women were enlisted into the army and air force; the next year, the navy followed suit. CWACS (Canadian Women's Army Corps) and Wrens (Women's Royal Canadian Naval Service) and WDS (Women's Division, RCAF) enlisted in large numbers. Over 17,400 served in the RCAF in Canada and overseas, as parachute riggers, wireless operators, clerks, and photographers. In addition to nursing sisters, the army enlisted over 21,600 women — and grudgingly opened up mechanics' jobs, among others, to them. The RCN signed up over 7,100 Wrens. No women in any of the services performed combatant duties, though some came under enemy fire.

In an era when the double standard was very strong, rumours about loose morals among CWACS, Wrens, and WDS spread widely and wildly. There were even stories of troopships returning from England to North America full of pregnant CWACS. While there were single CWACS who became pregnant (about thirty-five per thousand per year), such exaggerated stories were lies, apparently fostered by soldiers who resented women encroaching on the traditional masculine preserve of the armed forces, or by scandalmongers at home. The whispering campaigns in no way diminished the value of the services performed by women in the military, although they likely hurt recruiting and caused pain to families in Canada.

Traditional male jobs opened up at home, as well. Women drove buses, taxis, and streetcars in the streets of Halifax, Toronto, and Vancouver for the first time (they had only been allowed to collect streetcar tickets during the Great War), and found work in factories. "Roll Up Your Sleeves for Victory!", one advertisement seeking women for war work called, and in September 1942 the government registered all women born between 1918 and 1922, a clear sign of the growing scarcity of labour. At the peak of wartime employment in 1943–44, some 439,000 women worked in the service sector and 373,000 in manufacturing. In the aircraft plants, 30 per cent of the workforce was female; in factories manufacturing artillery pieces, almost half were women. In October 1943, for example, 261,000 women — usually dubbed "Rosie the Riveter" by the press — were working in munitions industries, garbed in overalls or jumpsuits and with their heads swathed in the mandatory bandanas or turbans to keep long hair from getting caught in the machinery. There were even 4,000 women construction workers. Women's wages rose more in wartime than did men's, perhaps in an early and tentative recognition of the principle of equal pay for work of equal value.

Women without war work helped the national effort as much as they could. Many worked in servicemen's canteens, making sandwiches or pouring coffee. Others rolled bandages for the Red Cross or donated blood ("Make a Date with a Wounded Soldier...and KEEP IT!", the ads said). Still more knit socks, sweaters, and scarves for servicemen. Mothers, sisters, and wives wrote letters to loved ones overseas — sometimes putting their emotions and fears into words, more often hiding them in a forced cheerfulness. Letters from servicemen were read by military censors, and sometimes arrived with whole sections snipped out or blacked over. "Careless talk costs lives," the posters warned, and careless letters were dangerous too. Whole families tended Victory gardens to produce vegetables and fruit for canning. Women ran salvage campaigns, gathering metal scrap, tin cans, and bones and fats. They tried to cook supper with the minimum use of scarce electric power, and scrambled to produce nourishing meals in the face of shortages.

For the first time, the woman worker was important enough that the governments of Canada, Ontario, Quebec, and Alberta agreed to co-operate to set up a few day-care centres in the factories, thus freeing young mothers from the house. Social workers worried about older children "who wander about the streets" creating "a sudden upward leap in the statistics of juvenile delinquency." *Canadian Forum*, a left-wing monthly, called for action to "prevent the indiscriminate employment of young mothers where other labour is available." But where was that other labour to be found?

Some was on the farms. Farm daughters and sons, tired of milking cows at 5 A.M., were powerfully attracted to better-paying jobs in the cities. Since large numbers also enlisted, the burden of farming then fell on the farmer and his wife. But somehow they did the job and harvested bumper crops during the war. The climate co-operated. Canadian wheat, hard-hit by drought, dust storms, and grasshoppers during the Depression, now poured forth in huge quantities from prairie farms, and prices were good. Butter, eggs, cheese, bacon — everything that could be produced could be sold overseas to hungry Britons lining up for their pitifully small rations. As the U-boat gauntlet reached its peak of deadly efficiency over the winter of 1942–43, delaying and destroying precious supply ships, Britain's travails made boom times for Canadians.

Boom time or not, there was little that Canadians could do with their dollars. They could save them. They could buy Victory Bonds. But there was not much else to buy. Factories that had produced automobiles, radios, or refrigerators before the war now made army trucks, wireless sets, and field kitchens. Consumer goods dried up, and imports from Europe or Asia disappeared completely. A black market flourished in such things as tires and whisky, and Canadians were urged to report profiteers and speculators. The police used these tips to crack down on the black marketeers, sending 253 to jail, prosecuting 23,416, and collecting $1.7 million in fines. Still, everyone "knew someone who knew someone" who was getting rich illegally, and the rumours rippled through society, making the problem seem worse than it was.

The Wartime Prices and Trade Board, created at the beginning of the war to monitor prices and shortages, had played a minimal and largely advisory role until late 1941. Then inflation began spiralling as too many people with too much money chased too few goods. The government responded by slapping a freeze on prices and wages. After December 1, 1941, no one was allowed to sell "any goods or supply any services at a price or rate higher than that charged...during the four weeks from September 15 to October 11...." Donald Gordon, the hard-drinking Scottish-Canadian banker who headed the WPTB, became one of the most powerful figures in wartime Canada.

Gordon's agency also controlled wages, despite the objections of organized labour. Unions had looked to the war as a heaven-sent chance to recover ground lost in the 1930s. "No employer in Canadian industry or commerce may, without permission, increase his present basic wage rates," the WPTB decreed. To ensure that no one suffered unduly, Ottawa created a cost-of-living bonus to ensure that wages kept pace with prices. The bonus was eventually fixed at 25 cents a week for each one-point rise in the cost of living index, for those earning more than $25 a week. At the end of 1941 most workers still earned less than $25 a week, but by 1946 — the WPTB notwithstanding — the average wage for production workers had increased from $975 a year in 1939 to $1,516; for office and supervisory employees, it had gone from $1,746 to $2,305.

Labour made other major gains during the war. In June 1940, the government had recognized labour's right to organize and bargain collectively in industries subject to federal jurisdiction, though it did almost nothing to enforce those rights. Even so, union membership rose substantially, 200,000 new workers being added to the rolls in 1941 and 1942 alone. Manufacturers in established industries such as steel continued to take a tough line against union recognition, however, and the tension in these industries grew apace. There were major strikes in some critical wartime industries, most notably in the steel mills in Sydney and Sault Ste. Marie at the beginning of 1943. When politicians glumly concluded that locking up strikers would not produce steel, the government had to recognize the need for change.

By late 1943 the government had begun to consider the problems of postwar reconstruction — and King and his ministers had also started to consider their own political survival. One product of this contemplation of the future came in February 1944, when the King government passed an Order in Council, PC1003, that recognized the right of all employees to organize, bargain collectively, and strike, rights earned a decade earlier by American workers. Most of the provinces that had not already given unions their rights duly followed Ottawa's lead. Even the Steel Company of Canada, the hardest of hard-line anti-union bosses, was forced to the bargaining table once the company's steelworkers' local was certified. PC1003 was Canadian labour's Magna Carta. The wage controls took some of the gloss off the measure until after the war, but for the first time Canadian labour unions had their rights in place.

From Ottawa's point of view, if not that of every businessman or worker, the freeze on wages and prices was completely successful. The cost of living had risen by 17.8 per cent from September 1939 to October 1941, but from October 1941 to April 1945 the increase was a mere 2.8 per cent. The cost of fuel and light actually fell by about 5 per cent, while the cost of clothing and home furnishings was stable. Only food rose modestly in price.

Unquestionably, however, the quality of goods produced under the price controls for the domestic market grew shoddy. Leather shoes fell apart if they got wet. Clothing manufacturers used cheaper fabrics as a way around the price freeze. And to save cloth, the government declared the two-pant suit illegal and forbade cuffs on men's trousers. (By 1943, zoot suits — with wide lapels, overlong jackets, and draped pants — somehow began to appear on tough teenagers flaunting their defiance of wartime regulations.) No woman's dress could have more than nine buttons — and bloomers were forbidden for the duration! There was no elastic to hold them up, in any case.

Food rationing began in 1942, when the government introduced coupons for sugar, coffee, tea, butter, and gasoline, and ration books became an essential part of weekly shopping. It became illegal to trade rationed goods — housewives could not swap a pound of butter for a pound of coffee, nor could a rationed commodity, such as sugar, be given away. Even at its most draconian, rationing never pinched very tightly. Still, housewives had to learn to manage with less sugar than before the war, and some foodstuffs became very scarce on the shelf. Clark's Soups told shoppers that "When the Japs give in, we'll get more tin...supplies are low, short of tin, you know." The butter ration allowed six ounces per person per week, and housewives stretched that by mixing butter with gelatine and evaporated milk. Still, the weekly meat ration (secured from butchers by presenting small blue tokens) was never smaller than one to two and a half pounds (depending on cut) per person.

After April 1943 non-essential automobile users were entitled to 120 gallons of gasoline a year, enough for some 2,000 miles of pleasure driving. "A gallon a day keeps Hitler away," the slogan went, and drivers were urged to slow down and ease up on the brakes to conserve scarce rubber. The Garden Taxi Company in Halifax got around the shortage by putting tires made of birchwood on one of its cars. The noise "is something awful", people complained. "You can tell the car is coming by the squeaks and groans." But the truth is that, thanks to relatively good wages and full employment, almost all Canadians ate and dressed far better than during the dreadful decade of the 1930s.

Even children were pressed into the service of the state. Schoolkids brought their nickels and dimes to class to exchange for War Savings Stamps which they stuck in special booklets for post-war redemption. They collected bottles, cans, fats, and bones. They sang "God Save the King" every day and "O Canada" less frequently, watched National Film Board shorts from the *Canada Carries On* series, and studied war poetry and the events at the front.

They gathered metal scrap and picked milkweed pods for processing into oil in an abortive National Research Council project. They read "Canadian whites", comic books printed in black and white, instead of full-colour American ones, which were barred to save scarce U.S. dollars. These comics featured super-heroes like "Johnny Canuck", who was "Canada's answer to Nazi oppression", "devoting his time to the destruction of Hitler's war material factories in the Berlin area." They and their parents went to the movies to be thrilled by Jimmy Cagney in *Captains of the Clouds* because it was set in Canada and featured the RCAF, to laugh at *Abbott and Costello in the Navy*, and to weep with Irene Dunne in *The White Cliffs of Dover*. They listened to the CBC news read in the doom-laden voice of Lorne Greene. Boy Scouts, Girl Guides, Brownies, and Cubs thought of themselves as junior soldiers on the home front, memorizing airplane silhouettes or building airplane and ship models. Boys still followed the National Hockey League, though the older ones complained knowingly that the war had diluted the League's quality, so many hockey players having enlisted.

Children were also seen as a potential national resource, in part as a reaction to the relatively low state of general fitness that armed forces recruiting examinations had uncovered. Vitamins were deemed critical to health, and children began each day with a spoonful of vile-tasting cod liver oil, swallowed down with gasps of outrage and a firmly pinched nose. Dinnertime had its admonitions to "eat your carrots", supposedly to improve night vision and build better fighter pilots. High-schoolers tried to master arms drill in cadet corps commanded by teachers who had served in the 1914 war. At the universities, officer training corps prepared men for their future obligations. For the only time in Canadian history, the whole nation was organized, involved, and mobilized in a grand effort.

DISASTER IN HONG KONG

The national mobilization that marked the later years of the war was no sentimental response: the stupendous demands posed by the war required nothing less. After installing his puppet Vichy regime in France in June 1940, Hitler had turned his attention across the English Channel and unleashed the savage air war of the Battle of Britain. At the same time the Italians, who had joined the German cause in June, attacked British possessions in North Africa; control of the Mediterranean and the Suez Canal hung in the balance. By the end of 1940 Hungary, Romania, and Bulgaria had all cast their lots with the Axis. Germany seemed unstoppable.

For a time it appeared that Yugoslavia might manage to maintain neutrality. In the spring of 1941, however, the *Wehrmacht* turned to Yugoslavia and easily conquered it, although the brutality of the Nazis spurred Serb nationalists, and a guerrilla war led there by a Communist named Tito would turn into the war's most successful people's struggle. Next Hitler sent his legions into Greece to rescue his Italian allies — who had invaded the country in October 1940 — from their own military ineptitude. Churchill ordered British and ANZAC (Australian and New Zealand) troops to leave their North African bases to assist Greece, but once again the Germans' skill and daring swept them aside.

Then Hitler, his ambition unbounded, made the greatest mistake of the war: on June 22, 1941, he sent the *Wehrmacht* into the Soviet Union. The non-aggression treaty of August 1939 was just another scrap of paper now, and the Russians were instantly embraced by Great Britain as they reeled under the massive Panzer assault. By late fall, as the weather turned cold, the Nazis were at the outskirts of Moscow. There, to the surprise of almost everyone in the West except die-hard Communists, the Soviets held — greatly assisted by "General Winter", an old Russian ally.

Supplies for Marshal Stalin's Red Army went by convoy to Murmansk, or by air from Canada through Alaska to Siberia. The casualties in the Russo–German war were enormous, so much so that some Canadians actually felt guilty that Russia was suffering while Canada, thus far, had faced little fighting. Still, Canada did its bit for the Soviets. Pre-war outrage at Stalin's purges and chagrin at Russia's invasion of Finland in 1939 were forgotten as the Canadian Aid to Russia Fund mobilized business and society leaders to raise money and to collect food and clothing. Canada-Soviet Friendship Societies sprang up, with patrons including premiers and bishops. The war made strange bedfellows; as Winston Churchill said, if Hitler had invaded hell, he would at least make a favourable reference to the devil!

While all these great events occurred in North Africa, the Mediterranean, and Russia, the Canadian army was still training in England. There was a lot to learn about modern war, as one armoured regiment commander noted. Major Bill Murphy, placed in command of the British Columbia Dragoons, wrote to his parents about his regiment:

...my command consists of something like 600 all ranks.... Naturally with temperamental monsters such as tanks you must have very skilled men to run them and their equipment, and it takes lots of work to train men for these jobs. The driver must not only know how to drive, where to drive, and how to get there without being knocked out, but he must also be able to do a great deal of repair work.... In short he must be a skilled soldier and also a skilled mechanic. Then in each tank we have a driver operator. He is the man who operates the radio set in each tank, and also acts as loader of our guns.... Then you have a certain number of gunners.... Ruling the roost you have a crew commander who commands the tank. In the regiment also are experts from the signal regiment to assist with the sets and a Light Aid Detachment from Ordnance — skilled mechanics who also help to keep vehicles on the road and repair them.

Add to that the administrative side, and the trucks carrying food, gasoline, and ammunition, and the complexity of the task of readying a regiment of under 1,000 men for combat becomes apparent. A division of 20,000 involved much more, of course — and all this was to be commanded by officers who in peacetime had never even seen a full-strength battalion.

The Royal Canadian Air Force also trained in Britain, but once its pilots were deemed fit to fight, they saw action almost every day in RAF or RCAF squadrons. The fighter pilots took their toll of *Luftwaffe* raiders while bomber crews perfected the night-bombing techniques that would eventually reduce Germany to rubble. By the end of 1941, the RCAF had had 1,199 members killed; while that was a heavy loss, compared to the carnage of 1917 it seemed tolerable. At sea, the U-boats were sinking merchant ships by the score, while occasionally the RCN's corvettes and destroyers depth-charged a Nazi submarine into submission — often in co-operation with the RCAF's long-range aircraft. Again, the losses of merchantmen, escort vessels, and officers and ratings — 439 by late 1941 — were heavy but sustainable. There was no comparison with the toll after two years of fighting in the Great War; at the 1916 battle of the Somme alone, for example, Canadians had suffered over 24,000 casualties.

Soon there was action enough to satisfy all but the most bloodthirsty, as the war became truly world-wide. On December 7, 1941, Japan capped its years of aggressive expansionism in China by attacking Dutch, British, and American possessions in the Pacific. The United States Navy suffered huge losses as much of its Pacific Fleet was caught at anchor at Pearl Harbor in Hawaii. American aircraft in the Philippine Islands were destroyed on the ground, leaving that great archipelago almost defenceless. And the Japanese struck at the British possessions of Malaya and Hong Kong. The only bright spot after a day of unparalleled disaster was that the United States Congress declared war against Japan and, responding to Hitler's declaration of war on Washington, against Germany and Italy.

Among the defenders of the crown colony of Hong Kong were two battalions of Canadian infantry. The Pacific theatre was not a natural one for

Canadians, Eurocentric as they had always been. But British generals in London, convinced that the Japanese army was inefficient and weak and might be deterred by even a small show of strength, had persuaded themselves that a Canadian reinforcement for the colony's British and Indian troops would have "a very great moral effect in the whole of the Far East". No one in London believed that Hong Kong could be defended against a serious attack, but the Minister of National Defence in Ottawa did not know this, and it was difficult to turn the War Office down. The units sent to the Far East in October 1941 were the Royal Rifles of Canada, a bilingual unit originally from the Quebec City area, and the Winnipeg Grenadiers, a battalion that had served on garrison duties in Newfoundland and Jamaica. The Chief of the General Staff apparently considered that Hong Kong service would be similar. Neither battalion was among the best trained in Canada at the time.

Under the command of Brigadier J.K. Lawson, a Permanent Force officer, the Canadians arrived in Hong Kong on November 16. They had scarcely had time to acclimatize themselves when Japan's powerful 38th Division left its staging area near Canton in occupied China and fell upon them on December 8. The 14,000-man British garrison had no air cover, and insufficient artillery and motor transport, and the Canadians' vehicles had been diverted to the Philippines. Soon there were shortages of food, water, and medicine. The British planners' notion that Japanese soldiers had difficulty operating at night was overturned when the ferociously effective Japanese overran the mainland defences called the Gin Drinkers' Line. The morale of the population and the military never recovered.

On December 18, the Japanese launched an amphibious assault on Hong Kong island, rapidly establishing themselves ashore in force with the aid of fifth columnists who cut the barbed-wire entanglements on the beaches. The Canadian troops, split up among their own commanders and British officers, found themselves engaged in hand-to-hand combat against heavy odds. For a dreadful week, they shared in a succession of hopeless counter-attacks against superior forces and grim defensive actions in the face of well equipped and heavily supported enemy units.

One of the many casualties was Company Sergeant-Major John Osborne of the Grenadiers, who led the survivors of his company in an attempt to retake Mount Butler. Osborne directed the attack, picking up and throwing back enemy grenades. There were only a handful of his men left when a grenade landed just out of his reach. Osborne shouted a warning and threw himself on top of the explosion. He was posthumously awarded the first Victoria Cross won by a Canadian in the Second World War. Another of the dead was Brigadier Lawson, whose headquarters were overrun at 10:00 A.M. on December

19. Lawson told General Maltby, the Hong Kong commander, by telephone that he was "going outside to fight it out" with a pistol in each hand. A Japanese colonel later said, "We wrapped up the body in the blanket of Lieutenant Okada, o.c. No. 9 Company, which had captured the position. I ordered the temporary burial of the officer on the battleground on which he had died so heroically."

That was almost the only chivalry shown by the Japanese. When the defenders, their position completely hopeless, finally surrendered on Christmas Day, the victors engaged in an orgy of brutality. The wounded in hospital were murdered, nurses were raped and slaughtered, and soldiers attempting to surrender were maltreated and sometimes butchered. "They took us," one private later wrote, "ripped off our insignia, took our shoes, belts, pictures, and wristwatches. We walked with our hands up and they nicked us in the back with bayonets. They took out DeLaurier and two or three others and used them for bayonet practice all night long. We could hear them."

The last message to reach Canada from Hong Kong arrived after the surrender: "Situation critical. Canadian troops part prisoners residue engaged casualties heavy.... Troops have done magnificent work spirit excellent." It was all true. The Canadians had suffered terrible losses in the fighting — 23 officers and 267 other ranks killed and 28 officers and 465 other ranks wounded, or 40 per cent of the 1,975 Canadians on the island. Survivors faced harrowing experiences in the brutal North Point and Sham Shui Po prisoner of war camps (where Canadian POWs suffered the special attentions of Kanao Inouye, a Canadian-born Japanese known as "The Kamloops Kid"). Later, many were moved to Japan to work twelve-hour days in the mines and on the docks at Niigata, on a ration of 800 calories a day. Many of the soldiers who returned to Canada after the Japanese surrender in August 1945 were so broken physically that they never recovered. The government's policies, otherwise generous in monetary and rehabilitation terms, failed to meet the special needs of the Hong Kong veterans.

The events in the Pacific had major repercussions at home. About 22,000 Canadians of Japanese origin lived in Canada, most in British Columbia, where they were largely fishermen, loggers, and market gardeners, with a smattering of young professionals. Racism against Orientals had been endemic in British Columbia for decades. Japanese-Canadian support for Japan's war with China, the coming of war in the Pacific, and reports (sometimes very exaggerated) of Japanese espionage and fifth-column activities in Pearl Harbor, Malaya, and elsewhere all combined to bring panic to the surface.

Egged on by municipal and provincial politicians, the public and press demanded action, and the federal government acquiesced. Male Japanese citizens were ordered off the B.C. coast on January 14, 1942. On February 26, days after the Japanese army had captured the supposedly impregnable British fortress of Singapore, the order was extended to cover everyone of Japanese origin — male or female, Canadian citizen or not — living in designated "security areas" along the coast. "It is the government's plan," Ian Mackenzie, the Minister of Pensions and National Health and B.C.'s representative in the Cabinet, assured his province,

> to get these people out of B.C. as fast as possible. Every single man, woman and child will be removed from the defence areas of this province and it is my personal intention, as long as I remain in public life, to see they never come back here.

The government moved the Japanese Canadians inland to rudimentary housing, often in former ghost towns, and put men to work on road gangs or cutting trees. Later, Ottawa confiscated the property of the evacuees and sold it at sacrifice prices. The military necessity behind the decision to move the Japanese Canadians inland was at least arguable; there could, however, be no justification for judicial theft of property. Yet almost no one protested.

The disaster of Hong Kong set off a storm of political fury in Ottawa. George Drew, the Ontario Conservative Party leader, urged Canadians to "face the shameful truth" that untrained men had been sent to Hong Kong. The disaster was all the proof necessary for Drew and others who believed Canada was short of trained men. It was also proof positive that the voluntary system of recruitment had failed and that conscription for overseas service was needed immediately. Mackenzie King soon established a royal commission under the Chief Justice of Canada, Sir Lyman Duff, to examine the Hong Kong affair. Duff's report, released in June 1942, concluded that the expedition was neither ill conceived nor mismanaged. But, he said, there had been inefficiencies that had resulted in the Hong Kong force being separated from its transport; and he conceded that some of the men had not been completely trained.

CONSCRIPTION AGAIN

What was most significant about the Drew charges was less what they said about Hong Kong than what they signified about the resurgence of conscriptionist sentiment. Complaints were heard all across the country about the NRMA soldiers sitting safely in Canada. The "R" recruits, training with their "A" comrades, bore the brunt. In his novel *Home Made Banners*, journalist and editor Ralph Allen talked about the pressure at "Camp Salute", where camp badges and arm patches differentiated conscripts and volunteers. Subtle efforts were often used to persuade "R" men to go "active", but sometimes more open means were employed. Allen has his training company commander deliver the message:

> If good old Number Nine platoon can show a one hundred percent active service roster by Wednesday morneen, the whole platoon will leave on forty-eight hour passes at noon and I'm confident. It just means all pulleen together and talkeen it over among yourselves.... I know that no man in Number Nine would want to deprive his entire platoon of the last leave they'll be getteen for a long time....

As Allen described it, the platoon verbally and physically beat up the "R" recruits until all finally agreed to volunteer. The platoon got its leave.

In truth, there was no shortage of volunteers as yet — there scarcely could be, given the light casualties the Canadian army had suffered. But the government had caved in early in 1942 to demands from the generals for a "big-army" plan of five overseas divisions, organized into two corps and grouped in the First Canadian Army. To get the necessary men for that size of organization, better suited to a great power than to a nation of just eleven million, as well as the men for the RCAF and the RCN, and to sustain the vast industrial and agricultural effort at home, was bound to put severe strains on the country's human resources. But the public insisted that Canada do its bit in the war — and in early 1942 that war looked as if it was going to be lost. Japanese forces spread irresistibly across South-East Asia and the Pacific. Germans pounded at the gates of Moscow and at Britain's only major fighting front, Egypt, where the Eighth Army was being routed by General Rommel's Afrika Korps.

The critics of government policy, however, scarcely thought of the strain on Canada's human resources. To them, the fact that Canadian soldiers had not yet gone into action against Germany was just further evidence that men were lacking. To them, the fact that recruiting in Quebec lagged behind that in English Canada (although much less so than in the Great War) was proof that only conscription could make French Canada fight.

The leader of the campaign for conscription — or total war, as it was now called — was Arthur Meighen. The architect of the Military Service Act of 1917, Meighen had been brought back to lead the Conservative Party in November 1941. Bolstered by an extensive press campaign organized in Toronto, Meighen and his supporters bombarded the country with arguments for conscription. And with some in his Cabinet, most notably defence minister Colonel J. Layton Ralston, making similar arguments, the prime minister had to listen.

Yet those promises against conscription for overseas service had been made and repeated endlessly since March 1939. How could they be overridden? The answer came easily to King's fertile mind. A non-binding plebiscite would allow the government to decide to impose conscription — or not — at its discretion. The decision to ask the people to release the government from its pledges against compulsory overseas service was announced in the Speech from the Throne on January 22, 1942, and the ballot was scheduled for April 27.

In the intervening few months, Meighen's attempt to win a by-election in the Toronto constituency of York South was scuppered by the victory of a CCF schoolteacher, Joe Noseworthy. That was a body blow to the Tories and to conscriptionists, a relief for King, who now would not have to face his relentless and sharp-tongued opponent in the House, and a boost for the CCF. The defeated Meighen, still the nominal Tory leader, now could only rail at King from his Toronto home.

More important, French Canada quickly demonstrated that it did not choose to forget the promises King and Lapointe had made. Lapointe had died of cancer in November 1941, but his shade was mobilized to serve the Ligue pour la Défense du Canada, an anti-conscriptionist umbrella organization that captured the province with its campaign for a "Non" vote in the plebiscite. "Jamais, Jamais...a dit M. Lapointe," the posters said, and the result was an overwhelming vote of 72.9 per cent against conscription in Quebec. Six heavily French-speaking constituencies outside Quebec and such Ukrainian- or German-speaking constituencies as Rosthern, Saskatchewan, and Vegreville, Alberta, also voted no. But throughout the rest of the country, the vote was heavily in favour of giving the government the power it sought: in Prince Edward Island 82.4 per cent voted yes, in Ontario 82.3, in Alberta 70.4, and in partly French-speaking New Brunswick 69.1 per cent. The overall result showed 2.95 million voters in favour of conscription, 1.64 million opposed.

The strong rejection in Quebec shook Mackenzie King and confirmed him in his views against compulsion for overseas service. But what could his policy be after the plebiscite had settled matters? As King put it, his position was "Not necessarily conscription but conscription if necessary," a confusing but exact statement of his intent. If conscription became necessary to win the war, it would be imposed; but if conscription was not needed, it would not be. To the outrage of some in his Cabinet and many in the country, all King agreed to do was to delete Section 3 of the National Resources Mobilization Act, forbidding the use of conscripts overseas. P.J.A. Cardin resigned, claiming that

Quebec had been betrayed, and the defence minister, Ralston, threatened to leave the Cabinet because of the breach of faith with English Canada. He was dissuaded with difficulty, though King providently filed his letter of resignation. Quebec was angry but hoped against hope that conscription might not be necessary. English Canadians were convinced they had been gulled by the plebiscite. King was unmoved by the complaints from both sides. If he was in the middle under attack from both extremes, he must be right. In fact, for a time, the issue died.

DEBACLE AT DIEPPE

What helped weaken conscription's force as an emotional issue in the summer of 1942 was the national grief over the disaster at Dieppe. The little French resort town on the English Channel, with its stony beaches and its popular casino, had been a favourite summer vacation spot for Parisian bourgeoisie for decades. For the planners at Admiral Lord Louis Mountbatten's Combined Operations Headquarters in Britain, however, Dieppe seemed an ideal place to test out theories and equipment for amphibious warfare (the last major amphibious landing had been at Gallipoli in 1915) and to establish whether a fortified port could be captured.

At the top political levels, there were additional motives. The Americans wanted the earliest possible opening of a second front in Europe, but Churchill and his General Staff worried about the logistical difficulties and feared the horrible casualties that might result. An assault on Dieppe might demonstrate the feasibility or otherwise of a great cross-Channel invasion. Moreover, the Soviet Union needed all the support it could get; a major raid on the French coast would show Stalin that the western allies were in the war and would divert Nazi resources away from Russia. As well, people in the Allied nations were demanding help for the Russians. Finally, the Canadian generals — and some politicians — wanted action for their boys in England, who were bored and frustrated after training for almost three years.

At the end of April 1942, the British had suggested that Canadians make up the attacking force, and General McNaughton, commanding the First Canadian Army, and General Crerar, commanding I Canadian Corps, had agreed. Crerar designated the 2nd Canadian Division, under Major-General J.H. Roberts (the officer who had saved his guns in the chaos of France two years earlier), to provide the men. The assault on Dieppe was first scheduled for early July; this attempt had to be abandoned because of rough weather, and the troops returned to their bases, understandably disappointed and talking freely. That breach of secrecy should have ended the Dieppe project. But because Mountbatten's planners argued that the Germans, even if they had heard of the raid, would not now anticipate it falling on the same town, the amphibious assault was rescheduled for August 19.

The plan called for six squadrons of fighter-bombers overhead and eight destroyers and one gunboat offshore to provide covering fire while infantry from the Essex Scottish and the Royal Hamilton Light Infantry, accompanied by tanks from the Calgary Regiment, hit the beach in front of the town from landing craft. To the east, at Puys, the Royal Regiment of Canada and three platoons of the Black Watch were to land. On the western flank, the South Saskatchewan Regiment and the Queen's Own Cameron Highlanders were to go ashore at Pourville. British commando units numbering just over 1,000 men were to take out coastal batteries farther east and west of the main landings. The infantry of the Fusiliers Mont-Royal would form a floating reserve. The object of the raid was to capture and hold Dieppe just long enough to establish a perimeter so that dry docks, harbour installations, and "any other suitable objective" could be blown up. About 6,000 men, 5,000 of them Canadians, constituted the "Jubilee" force. The raid's celebratory code-name soon was to seem grotesquely inappropriate.

The complex plan went awry even before the Canadians began to go ashore. By chance, the raiders' ships encountered a German coastal convoy in the early morning, and the firing alerted coastal defences. Surprise may have been lost as a result. In any case, the German shore defences were at readiness, and almost no Canadians that August 19 found getting ashore a simple chore.

The assault at Puys saw the Royal Regiment and the Black Watch destroyed by withering fire from two platoons of Germans located in a fortified house and on a cliff to one flank of the beach. "At the instant of touchdown," about 5:10 A.M., one Canadian officer later wrote, "small arms fire was striking the [landing craft], and here there was a not unnatural split-second hesitation in the bow in leaping out onto the beach. But only a split second. The troops got out...and got across the beach to the [sea]wall; and under the cliff." There most stayed and died in "ten hours of unadulterated hell", unfortunately joined by their comrades of the second and third waves, who reinforced failure and landed despite the slaughter of the first wave. Gunner Joseph Dessureault, his fingers blown off, asked a friend to take his false teeth out of his pocket and put them in his mouth. "He said he didn't want to die without his teeth being in," the friend remembered. Though Lieutenant-Colonel Catto and a few men managed to scale the cliffs, most survivors clung to the beach. The surrender at Puys occurred before 8:30 A.M. One captured Canadian, Bob Prouse, remembered that "There wasn't one Jerry whose lips weren't trembling" when the victors rounded up the survivors. "Maybe, like us, it was their first time to meet the enemy face to face."

At Pourville, Colonel Cecil Merritt's South Saskatchewan Regiment and the Cameron Highlanders got ashore against relatively light opposition, but Merritt's force ran into heavy fire at the River Scie. The colonel repeatedly led his men across a bridge swept by fire — "Come on over, there's nothing to it" — earning a Victoria Cross, but the infantry, hooking to the left in an attempt to take Dieppe from the rear, were stopped short. Merritt's bridge and Merritt's courage were glorious events on a black day. "It wasn't human, what he did," one officer said. The Camerons advanced about 2,000 yards inland before the withdrawal orders came.

On the main front, where the assaulting force touched down half an hour after the Puys and Pourville landings, the disaster began at once. The well-placed Germans dominated the beaches with fire from a sheer cliff at the left of the landing beaches, destroying landing craft loaded with men and equipment before they grounded, and slaughtering those few organized platoons that managed to make their way up the beach. Because General Roberts had only faulty information on these events, the Fusiliers Mont-Royal went ashore at 7:00 A.M., its men adding to the toll. The Calgary Regiment's brand new Churchill tanks, intended to land with the first wave, arrived late. The first tank off the ramp sank in deep water. Those that got ashore provided little help, their treads failing to find purchase on the baseball-sized pebbles that made up the beach. Any that did manage to move found their way blocked by the seawall. Bogged down, the tanks became sitting ducks, while their light guns made little impression on the defenders.

There was much heroism at the charnel-house of Dieppe. The Royal Hamilton Light Infantry's padre, Captain John Foote, repeatedly dragged wounded men to an aid post set up in the lee of a landing craft, miraculously surviving amid the hail of fire. When the evacuation order finally came, Foote deliberately stayed ashore to look after those who were captured; he was a prisoner until 1945 and was awarded the Victoria Cross. Billy Field, an RHLI dispatch rider, remembered that the Germans seemed to be able to spot assault engineers, their packs loaded with high explosives. "Each one went off like a bomb. I tried to keep my distance." A few Canadians fought their way off the beaches and into the casino, where they battled the defenders from room to room. Others got into the town, shooting up Germans heading towards the beaches. It was magnificent but entirely futile. By 9:00 A.M. the raid was seen to be a disaster, but the evacuation did not begin until 11:00 A.M. Using assault landing craft, the Royal Navy took the survivors off, a few at a time. That operation, which finally ceased about 2:00 P.M., was an extraordinary feat.

The cost of the raid was high. Of the 4,963 Canadians who had set off from England, 2,211 returned, almost half of whom had never gone ashore. Only

300 to 400 men were evacuated from the main beaches in front of the town, about 600 from Pourville, and half a dozen at best from Puys. The fate of the remainder was death, wounding, or capture. First reports on the Essex Scottish were that only 44 of 550 had made it back; all the officers were lost. The invading Canadians had 1,946 captured in the raid (more than in the whole campaign in north-west Europe from June 6, 1944 to the German surrender in May 1945). So fierce was the fighting that only the Fusiliers Mont-Royal brought their commanding officer back to England.

One German after-action appraisal noted that the "Canadians on the whole fought badly and surrendered afterwards in swarms." That was too harsh. Another observed that the Canadian soldier "fought — so far as he was able to fight at all — well and bravely." One lesson was that an amphibious assault was not the best way to give infantry or armour its first taste of battle.

Overhead, the Royal Air Force and the Royal Canadian Air Force had ensured local air superiority, and only the strong air cover had allowed the evacuation to proceed. In all, 74 squadrons of fighters, day bombers, and reconnaissance aircraft had taken part. Missing had been the heavy bombers that might have neutralized the German defences. But even in the air the Germans had won the day, destroying 106 aircraft against a loss of 48. Total *Wehrmacht* and *Luftwaffe* losses amounted to 591 killed and wounded.

The Canadians taken prisoner at Dieppe suffered a further indignity after the raid. The enemy had found orders that called for captured Germans' hands to be tied to prevent destruction of documents. In retaliation, the *Wehrmacht* ordered Canadian POWs to be shackled. Inevitably, the Allies responded by chaining German prisoners in Canadian camps. At the POW camp in Bowmanville, Ontario, Canadian troops had to be called on to enforce the order; the result was 82 casualties, almost evenly divided between Canadians and Germans. At the camp at Gravenhurst, Ontario, 86 Germans easily removed their handcuffs and hid them, greatly embarrassing their captors. Soon, face became involved for both sides, and only sustained efforts by Swiss intermediaries finally ended the whole discreditable affair.

Dieppe was a costly lesson for the Allied high command. The idea of assaulting a fortified port now seemed mad, and the necessity for massive fire support became clear. Better training, communications, equipment, planning — all were now seen to be essential. Why no one realized the necessity for these sooner remains inexplicable, just one more example of the human inability to foresee the obvious. Nor is it clear why the planners failed to realize that every Dieppe beach was commanded by almost unassailable cliffs, and that tanks could not operate effectively on pebbled beaches. It was as if Dieppe were ten thousand miles from England, not a few miles across the

Channel. Yet planners needed Dieppe to learn the necessity for painstaking preparations, and for a huge diversion of resources into landing craft, radios, and supporting weapons. Dieppe's losses were part of the price of the Normandy landings almost two years later.

The day after the débâcle, as the Canadian army's official historian, Colonel Charles Stacey, wrote in his memoirs, Admiral Mountbatten turned up at American army headquarters "with a bushel basket of decorations for the small detachment of U.S. Rangers" who had gone to Dieppe. "I, in my simplicity, asked why Lord Louis should be so interested in sucking up to the Yanks." The reply was that "He wants to be a Supreme Commander." A year later, Mountbatten was just that, in India.

In countless towns across Canada — in Windsor, where the Essex Scottish had been raised, or in Weyburn, Estevan, and Bienfait, whose men had filled the ranks of the South Saskatchewans — the casualty lists with their grim tale of suffering and death shook everyone. The Germans seemed more formidable than ever.

The beautiful Canadian military cemetery at Hautot-sur-Mer, a few miles inland from the Dieppe beaches, holds the remains of 656 victims of the abortive raid. Of them, 121 could not be identified, one testimony to the ferocity of the fighting; their headstones say only "A Soldier of the Second World War — A Canadian Regiment — 19 August 1942." For the others, cut down in their prime, the headstones — marked with crosses and the occasional Star of David — stretch on, row after row.

XIII
ACTION STATIONS: THE WAVY NAVY AT WAR

S he was short and stout, the corvette. Under 1,200 tons fully loaded, about 205 feet in length, the "Patrol Vessel, Whaler Type" could cover a range of 4,000 miles at twelve knots. Her maximum speed was only sixteen knots, but she was manoeuvrable. Her main armament was depth charges, dropped off the stern or fired over the side, although there was one 4-inch gun, a two-pounder "pom-pom", one or two 20mm Oerlikon guns, and a few machine guns. The standard crew for this little vessel, first proposed in 1938 by William Reed of Smith's Dock Company in England, was forty-seven officers and men, and the estimated cost of building and equipping one was £90,000. The corvettes were, in Winston Churchill's words, "cheap, but Nasties". Exactly.

The corvette was the main fighting component of the Royal Canadian Navy, the ship in which most of Canada's war at sea was to be fought. Food, munitions, aircraft, and tanks — almost all the materiel that North America produced for the European war had to cross the sea in convoys — vast arrangements of tankers, freighters, troopships, and other supply and escort vessels that could occupy as much as thirty square miles of ocean and could travel no faster than their slowest ship. The convoys were vital to the Allied cause, but they were desperately vulnerable to attack, and their defence would depend mainly on Canadian corvettes.

BUILDING A FLEET

The Royal Canadian Navy, like the army and the air force, had survived the inter-war years in penury. The RCN had in fact had to fight against being disbanded in 1933 as an unnecessary luxury. It had survived but in a strictly attenuated form.

Just thirteen ships. That was the fleet when the Second World War began. There were *Saguenay, Skeena, Fraser, St. Laurent, Restigouche,* and *Ottawa,*

211

six destroyers, the oldest being eight years old. (Arrangements for acquisition of a seventh had been under way some months before the outbreak of war, and in October 1939 *Assiniboine* was added to the navy.) There were four modern minesweepers, all built in Canada in 1938, a training schooner and a training ship, and a trawler. Even that roster was a marked improvement over 1922, when the navy had been able to put only one destroyer and two trawlers to sea on each ocean. In January 1939, Mackenzie King's Liberal government had announced an expansion plan intended to produce eighteen destroyers, sixteen minesweepers, and eight anti-submarine vessels — enough to defend the Atlantic and Pacific coasts — but that plan was effectively scrapped in May.

Just 2,673 officers and ratings. That was the RCN's manpower after the outbreak of war, once the regulars and reserves had been called to duty. There were 1,990 officers and ratings of the regular navy, 145 of the RCN Reserve — made up of officers and men who made their living from the sea, largely as merchant sailors — and 132 officers and 406 ratings of the RCN Volunteer Reserve, the Wavy Navy, so called from the thin wavy stripes RCNVR officers sported on their sleeves. It was the RCNVR officers — lawyers, accountants, recent college graduates — who ultimately commanded most of the RCN's wartime vessels. There was no shortage of hyperbole, even if men were scarce. The *Victoria Daily Times* in November 1939 hailed Canada's "jolly, well-behaved sailor boys...splendid young blue jackets...[who] face the world and its troubles with a grin." Unfortunately, it would take more than a grin to win the Battle of the Atlantic.

The pre-war fleet was completely insufficient for the demands of wartime. Ports had to be defended, and to do this the RCN "persuaded" other government departments to turn over auxiliary vessels, sixty of which, along with most of their crews, were incorporated into the navy by the end of 1939. In late 1939 and early 1940 the government also purchased a number of rich men's yachts for conversion into escorts, and three liners from Canadian National Steamships were turned into "armed merchant cruisers". Later in 1940 the RCN received six old American four-stack destroyers. This was part of the "destroyers-for-bases" deal made between President Roosevelt and Prime Minister Churchill in the summer of 1940, in which fifty destroyers were exchanged for 99-year leases to bases in Newfoundland and the West Indies, a bad deal at any time — except in the desperate days of summer 1940. The RCN christened these new ships *Annapolis, Columbia, Niagara, St. Clair, St. Croix,* and *St. Francis.* These obsolete, spartanly equipped destroyers rolled fiercely in rough weather, especially when low on fuel, and were hated by their crews.

A major burst of wartime construction got under way in February 1940 when the government placed contracts for sixty-four corvettes with Canadian shipyards, intending to take twenty-four — and possibly an additional ten — into the RCN; the remainder were being built for the Royal Navy. Contracts were similarly let for twenty-four Bangor-class minesweepers. Further contracts followed in a flood as the war went against the Allies after June 1940.

Building ships for war was a major challenge for Canadian shipyards, which had little experience of naval construction. Most yards had never been required to supply machinery, fittings, and materials of naval standard. Now fifteen tiny shipyards on the east and west coasts and on the St. Lawrence and the Great Lakes set out to build corvettes, each of which required 700 tons of steel plate, 1,500 valves, and 39 tons of copper wiring. There was not enough yard space, too few skilled workers, and insufficient equipment. Soon there would be shortages of steel, copper, rubber, and guns to contend with. Factories somehow had to produce ship and engine parts to specification, and all the parts had to be put together in the yards. Over the course of the war naval ship-building expanded to ninety yards employing 126,000 men and women.

The first corvettes slowly took shape, and before 1940 was over, 14 of them had made their way to Halifax. They were late, not completely equipped, undermanned, and had no armaments; but they could move through the water, though they "rolled in a heavy dew". The first few set off for England in December 1940, armed with wooden dummy 4-inch guns, there being none of the real thing available in Canada. One story, probably apocryphal, has it that a Royal Navy admiral saw the drooping wooden weapons on *Windflower* and *Mayflower*, the first two corvettes to reach the British Isles, and expostulated, "My God! Since when are we clubbing the enemy to death?" But however unprepared the first corvettes may have been, they and their successors — and in all, 122 corvettes came off the ways in Canada — eventually packed a wallop.

So too did the volunteers who were slowly joining the navy. Slowly, not for lack of interest or enthusiasm, but because both the government and naval headquarters were cautious about expansion. By the end of 1939, RCN regulars had increased by only 60 since the onset of war, RCNR by 719, and RCNVR by 1,590. The rate of growth remained glacial: in January 1941, total strength was only 15,000 — most of it among those who enlisted in the RCNVR for "hostilities only", or until the defeat of Germany.

Initially, and for some time afterwards, medical qualifications were very high. Peter Dankowich, a naval recruit at the Lakehead, remembered, "I joined with three other fellows, and one had something wrong with his eye, one didn't have enough education, one passed his medical with me and joined the Air Force." Good eyesight was deemed the most important attribute for officers and ratings, and the largest number of rejections were for imperfect vision. The basic educational standard was Grade 8; after March 1942 intelligence tests were employed to screen out those with deficient capacities to learn. Later in the war, all three services would be less scrupulous in accepting volunteers.

In fact, the RCN never had much difficulty in recruitment, and it was by far the most popular of the services; it enlisted over 100,000 men and women during the war. The force was at its peak in January 1945, when 87,141 men and 5,300 women were carried on strength — a number approximately equal to Britain's Royal Navy in 1939.

One widespread myth was that the RCN drew especially heavily on prairie farmboys who had never seen the sea. It was said that many desperately wanted to join the navy — like Earle Johnson, who "had never seen sea water before" and said the war provided an opportunity. Moreover, Johnson claimed, "prairie boys made good sailors because it seemed like hardly any of them were seasick!" In fact, most naval recruits were from the twenty cities that had naval reserve divisions. HMCS *Discovery* in Vancouver, referred to as a "ship" like all RCN shore stations, drew more than three-quarters of its 7,221 recruits from that city, and *Donnacona* in Montreal found 70 per cent of its 8,125 there. The three prairie provinces produced just over 20 per cent of the recruits for the RCN, almost exactly their share of the male population from eighteen to forty-five years of age.

Early in the war, new entry training took place at the naval reserve divisions. Its object was to help a novice sailor adapt to living and working with a large group of men. Training aimed to begin the process of instilling discipline, to adapt civilians to an authoritarian military system. Training also aimed to make men fit and to teach some of the basic skills of the sailor, including seamanship, knot-tying, and the proper way to wear the arcane uniform of jumper and bell-bottom trousers. None of this was very sophisticated. Norm Lilly, who enlisted at HMCS *Griffon* at the Lakehead in 1940, remembered that the training there was "*basic*...more or less to get [recruits] so that they knew how to march, so you could march them down to the station and put them on the train" to the coast — that is, to *Stadacona* and, after 1942, to *Cornwallis* in the east or *Naden* in the west for further training.

By 1941, the training curriculum had expanded and become more relevant to the actual duties sailors had to carry out. The basic training, however, remained much as it had always been. Cliff Webber, a new naval recruit from Brantford, Ontario, wrote to his friends at home in July 1942 of his daily routine at *Cornwallis*:

Get up at six have P.T. By eight we are marching on the training field. Stay there till about half past eleven and come back for dinner. At one we start marching again until half past four and have our supper and that finishes the day.

Webber added that there was nothing to do in Nova Scotia, "only go to a show. There's nice girls down here but you don't know what you're going around with. If you get what I mean." That was unfair. Halifax was a good-sized city. The dance floor of the Silver Slipper attracted many servicemen; so did the good food at Norman's. If young sailors wanted to swap tales with old salts, they could always try the Allied Merchant Seamen's Club on Hollis Street, and after 1942 beds could be found cheaply at the Navy League's Hollis Street hostel.

In 1942, women were at last allowed to join the newly established Women's Royal Canadian Naval Service. Training of the Wrens, as they were universally known, took place at *Conestoga* in Galt, Ontario, a shore station called — like every Wren barracks — the Wrennery. Mary Kraiger, who enlisted at Port Arthur, Ontario, joined up when she was seventeen. It was an exciting time. "It made women out of us. It was fantastic, the discipline and everything that went with it. Especially in basic [training]. That's where they either made you or broke you. So I guess most of us were made." In all, over 7,000 women signed on with the RCN; they did most kinds of work at shore establishments, notably in offices and as wireless operators, and served in Canada, Britain, and the U.S.

THE WAR FOR THE CONVOYS

The RCN's operations in the first days of the war were ruled by the government's order to "cooperate to the fullest possible extent" with the Royal Navy. But that proved less than satisfactory, and early in 1940 the Cabinet War Committee approved a recommendation from Naval Service Headquarters in Ottawa to put all the RCN's destroyers under the operational control of the Admiralty. Only the British had the capacity to see the global naval situation and to ensure that each ship was used to best advantage. Thus in late May 1940, as the situation at the front in France turned towards disaster and as naval losses mounted rapidly, the Admiralty urgently requested that RCN destroyers be sent to help protect the British Isles against invasion.

To its credit, the King government abandoned its rigid insistence on autonomy. The Cabinet saw the situation as one of "extreme emergency", and the RCN put all its resources, except for the bare minimum needed to carry out duties on the coasts, at the disposal of the Royal Navy.

Immediately, three destroyers set out for Britain. Two more were in refit and would not be ready until mid-June; another was due for refit; and yet another was en route to Bermuda but was instead diverted to England. By June 3, four RCN destroyers were at Plymouth, and soon they were fighting E-boats (torpedo boats) and U-boats (submarines) and assisting in the evacuation of Allied soldiers from parts of France not yet under German control. HMCS *Fraser* picked up the Canadian minister to France, Lieutenant-Colonel Georges Vanier, from *Le Cygne*, a sardine boat, off Arcachon on June 21 as the French capitulated at Compiègne. (Never, said Vanier later of the tub from which he was rescued, "never have I seen a boat which looked less like a swan in line or in colour.") Four days later, *Fraser*, whose captain had had one night's sleep in the last ten, was rammed by the British cruiser HMS *Calcutta*. So crushing was the impact that the whole forepart of the Canadian destroyer was ripped off, leaving the bridge — and the *Fraser*'s captain — on the cruiser's bow. *Fraser* was lost, along with forty-seven of her crew and nineteen British sailors.

As the Germans took over French ports and airfields on the Bay of Biscay, the cruising range of the U-boats and the *Luftwaffe* increased. The convoys from Halifax, hitherto largely unmolested except in the near vicinity of the British Isles, now were exposed to attack for a much longer period of time. With France out of the war, and Britain in desperate straits and fighting with only the Commonwealth at its side, those convoys now were all the more important.

Inevitably, as the British Isles came under threat of invasion, the Royal Navy had to concentrate in home waters. Escort vessels were taken from the convoys, and the merchant ships, to a terrible extent, were left to their fate. For the U-boats, the summer of 1940 was the first "happy time", with months of fat pickings from the almost unprotected convoys. But the Royal Air Force's victory in the Battle of Britain halted Hitler's invasion plans. The RN still had to keep strong forces in British waters, but as the fear of invasion lessened, escort vessels again became available for the convoys.

In the North Atlantic, the worst was yet to come. Admiral Karl Dönitz, Commander-in-Chief U-boats, had been developing the idea of the "wolf pack" since 1935. He had tested out the concept in pre-war exercises and had even published a book about mass submarine attacks on convoys, in January 1939. The theory was simple: a line of U-boats was stationed at right angles to the usual convoy routes. The first U-boat to spot a convoy radioed its location to Dönitz's headquarters and shadowed the supply ships. Headquarters then directed all U-boats in the vicinity onto the convoy, each submarine captain attacking independently. There were potential problems in this method, not least the number of wireless transmissions required to operate the system and the potential target offered to the defenders.

But in September 1940, when the first wolf-pack attacks began, the odds were in favour of the Germans. The u-boat commanders and their crews were professionals who had absorbed the lessons of the Great War, and they were backed by a first-rate intelligence and cipher system that could read many British naval codes. Their boats were equipped to remain at sea for an amazing three months or more, and they carried up to twenty-one torpedoes, which could be fired on or below the surface at ranges up to nine miles. Their one vulnerable point was the necessity to surface to recharge batteries or to send signals. Even so, under air or naval attack the German submarines could "crash dive" in thirty seconds, and within a minute the u-boat could be as much as 700 feet from where it had dived.

The RN and RCN were operating at a severe disadvantage. Both were desperately short of convoy escorts, air cover was strictly limited — and impossible over much of the North Atlantic, thanks to inadequate aircraft range — and anti-submarine expertise had yet to be gained. Moreover, the asdic used to locate u-boats under water was still primitive and subject to a variety of confusions that could result from water temperature, shipwrecks, and schools of fish; radar to find u-boats on the surface was in its infancy; and anti-submarine weaponry to sink them was primitive. (Asdic was named for the Allied Submarine Detection Investigation Committee that had been formed in 1918 to devise sound-locating devices; the American term, "sonar", has since become the NATO standard.) The Royal Navy's intelligence resources also were limited. Ultra, the great secret operation by which codebreakers operating from Bletchley Park in England worked to decipher German Enigma-coded messages, could not be used unless the encoding machine's key was known. Not until a u-boat's Enigma machine was captured intact along with the papers detailing its settings — on May 8, 1941, by a boarding party from the Royal Navy destroyer *Bulldog* — could the British predict German submarine deployment. In the terrible winter of 1942–43 that advantage was lost for a time when the key was changed. The German navy, on the other hand, had cracked the British convoy code and used this knowledge with success until the ciphers were changed in June 1943.

Fortunately, the Germans had relatively few u-boats in the beginning — their construction program only began to produce them in quantity in 1942. Even so, in March 1941 alone the Nazis sent more than 200,000 tons of shipping to the bottom.

The defenders tried desperately to redress matters. British and Canadian troops occupied Iceland in May and June 1940; at that time the North Atlantic island was still closely tied to Denmark, which the Germans had overrun in April. Air bases soon went into operation there to extend the range of air cover. Allied scientists worked feverishly to upgrade the effectiveness of asdic and radar. And the captains and crews of escort vessels slowly learned how to defend their charges more effectively.

The Canadians were learning too. In May 1941, the RCN accepted an Admiralty request to assume responsibility for convoy escort in the area of the British colony of Newfoundland and, as much as possible, to use its own resources for this purpose. St. John's, located well along the great circle route from North America to Britain, was the logical site for the Newfoundland Force to be located. Under Commodore L.W. Murray, RCN, seven corvettes arrived in St. John's on May 25. They were soon joined by two Royal Navy destroyers and the RCN destroyers that had been serving in British waters. Murray, a Nova Scotian who had joined up in 1911 as a fifteen-year-old and had served in the Royal Navy until he returned to the RCN in the Depression, set up headquarters on the top floor of the Newfoundland Hotel, and St. John's, or "Newfyjohn" as it was universally known, was to become a huge base and a more popular posting than Halifax. The number of RCN officers and ratings stationed in the city rose from 900 in 1941 to 5,000 three years later.

The Newfoundlanders, Signaller Don McEwen remembered, were "great people, wonderful people", a common reaction to the way ordinary Newfoundlanders pitched in to look after the RCN, inviting sailors home for dinner and organizing dances and parties. The Caribou Club catered to the ratings while the Crowsnest, an old loft reached by a high staircase (lethal after too many drinks), looked after officers. The ties forged during the war, and wartime prosperity brought by servicemen's spending, likely helped lead to support for Confederation once peace came.

St. John's was a long way from Ottawa, however, and simple administrative messages, let alone intelligence, seemed to take a long time to arrive. Moreover, the naval stations and air bases were widely separated, hampering co-ordination, and the bad weather in the area made matters worse. From the beginning of Murray's command, communications, climate, and distance conspired against the effective achievement of his task.

Nonetheless, convoys leaving Halifax now were accompanied by escort ships based there or in Sydney to a rendezvous point where the Newfoundland Escort Force took over. Murray's ships had sole responsibility to 35° west, where ships of the Iceland Escort joined them. At 18° west, British-based ships assumed responsibility for the final leg. This system, in effect by July 1941, meant that convoys had continuous naval escort; air cover, provided by RAF Coastal Command and the RCAF, was also complete except for the "black hole", a 300-mile gap in the middle of the North Atlantic, the RCN's sector.

The RCAF's air strength on the Atlantic coast was strictly limited — five obsolete and slow Douglas Digbys in Newfoundland; in Nova Scotia, ten Dig-bys, nine relatively new but completely inadequate Stranraer flying boats with a speed of 105 mph and an effective range of only 300 miles, and fifteen more modern two-engine Hudson bombers with a range of 350 miles. More-over, the RCAF had almost no experience in conducting far-ranging ocean operations and absolutely none in anti-submarine operations. Not until the spring of 1941 were long-range Catalina flying boats devoted to patrols in the western Atlantic, and they were so few in number that they were insufficient to help the struggling, straggling convoys much.

In August 1941 President Roosevelt and Prime Minister Churchill held their first wartime meeting, off Argentia, Newfoundland. The resulting Atlantic Charter propounded a series of international aims, such as self-government and freedom from fear. That had an impact on morale, especially in Britain. Of more immediate import was the way the summit affected the anti-submarine campaign. Although the United States was still neutral, and would be so until the Japanese attack on Pearl Harbor that December, U-boats had been attacking American cargo vessels sporadically since 1940, and the pres-ident had decided that this could no longer be tolerated. Under his direction the U.S. Navy secretly agreed to assume responsibility for the western Atlan-tic in September 1941. A United States Navy officer at Argentia, one of the leased Newfoundland bases, now took control of the northern part of the western Atlantic. The Newfoundland Escort Force thus fell under command of the USN. These changes, instituted by Britain and the U.S. without any con-sultation with Canada, naturally produced some hurt feelings.

The new command structure was window dressing, however, to the real war that was fought at sea between the lumbering merchant ships and their escorts and the U-boats. Under command of its commodore, usually a retired naval officer, a convoy moved in columns a thousand yards apart, each ship some six hundred yards from the ones ahead and behind. There might be ten or more columns, each of five or more ships. Thus a convoy filled a substan-tial block of ocean — a ten-column convoy would have a frontage of roughly six miles.

In 1941 alone, over 5,000 ships were convoyed east across the Atlantic. The ocean space covered by each convoy was enormous because the loads carried by the freighters were huge. One convoy in July 1944 would carry a million tons of cargo — 85,000 tons of grain, 85,000 of sugar, 38,000 of molasses, 50,000 of other food, 35,000 of lumber, 37,000 of iron and steel, 310,000 of oil, 80,000 of tanks and other military vehicles, and 250,000 of other military sup-plies. All Britain — and all the Allied armies training there — ran on the goods transported by the convoys.

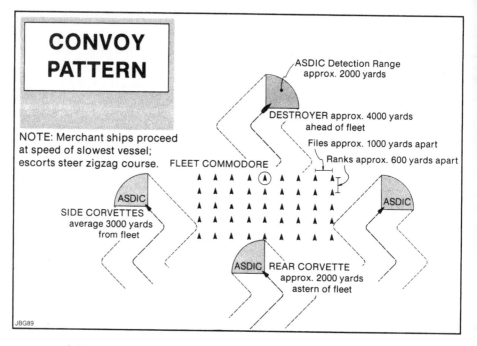

CONVOY PATTERN

NOTE: Merchant ships proceed at speed of slowest vessel; escorts steer zigzag course.

ASDIC Detection Range approx. 2000 yards

DESTROYER approx. 4000 yards ahead of fleet

Files approx. 1000 yards apart

Ranks approx. 600 yards apart

FLEET COMMODORE

ASDIC

SIDE CORVETTES average 3000 yards from fleet

ASDIC

ASDIC REAR CORVETTE approx. 2000 yards astern of fleet

JBG89

Around the convoy were the naval escorts, ordinarily corvettes or destroyers. While the merchantmen ploughed straight ahead, the escorts took up station on each side of the block, zigzagging back and forth to cover as much ocean as possible with their asdic sweeps, trying to pick up the tell-tale "ping" that would indicate the presence of a U-boat.

In winter the waves washed over the deck and the escorts iced up. Spud Graham of Thunder Bay, Ontario, remembered that a ⅜-inch stay could measure five inches around as it iced up. "You had to get rid of that, because there was a lot of weight up there. Lots of times, we went chop, chop, chop. If you didn't, you'd be liable to turn over."

That work was tremendously tiring. So too was the perennial seasickness, the shortage of sleep, the overwork, the pounding the body took from the constant rolling and pitching, and the lack of privacy in crowded conditions. Corvette crews had increased in number as new equipment was squeezed into the tiny hulls. From the original forty-seven, crews grew to fifty-eight, then to eighty and ninety-three. Some corvettes late in the war had more than a hundred men aboard. That crowding meant acute shortage of "slinging space", places to hang hammocks. New seamen on corvettes simply didn't get space and were obliged to wait until crew members left and they moved up in the "hammocking order". The unlucky just slept where they could, most often on the deck.

The food supply was frequently a problem; Vic Cousins remembered one crossing when Christmas was celebrated with dehydrated cabbage and potato, and the crew resorted to eating the lifeboat rations. In *A Bloody War*, Hal Lawrence remembered how awful it could be on a corvette in a gale:

> ...it is impossible to keep food on the galley stove. The bread grows green mould. The cockroaches pit-pat around the decks and bulkheads energetically. The rats grow bolder as they become hungrier. Dry clothes are forgotten. In the foetid, crowded messdecks exhausted men sleep where they can.... Wretchedly sick men...lie in their vomit until the bosun's-mate hauls them up to push them on watch again.

All that held the crews together in such circumstances was their youth. The average age of RCN sailors was around twenty-two years, and most of the corvette captains were no more than five years older. The daily rum ration also helped ward off the North Atlantic's chill, even if it had to be tossed down as soon as it was dished out. Abstainers received six cents a day in lieu of the tot of grog to keep them warm. Cigarettes were also cheap at ten cents a pack — and in England they could be picked up free. "Welcome to Canadian Overseas Forces", cards tucked into cartons said. "These cigarettes have been sent to you with the compliments of the Ontario government.... George A. Drew, Prime Minister of Ontario." Humour helped too. The ship's badges painted on the gunshields became exercises in ingenuity and word play. HMCS *Wetaskiwin's*, for example, showed a queen sitting in a puddle — a wet-assed queen.

The logistics of riding herd on a convoy were also wearing, however neat the theory. In practice, the convoy blocks were often less than symmetrical. Ships straggled. Skippers accustomed to keeping their distance from other vessels in peacetime found it hard to keep station in calm seas and almost impossible in storms. In the North Atlantic, especially in winter, it was far from uncommon for seas to be so rough that waves swept right over the deck, even on large ships. Vessels broke down and had to be abandoned to make their way when and if repairs were effected. There were language difficulties, since the merchant crews were often Norwegian, Dutch, Greek, or any of twenty other nationalities. English was the common language, but understanding varied.

The "black hole" in air cover in the mid-Atlantic also helped the Germans. Various devices to remedy this problem were tried. One was Catapult-Armed Merchant ships (CAMS), equipped with Hurricane fighters that could be hurled into the air by catapults, to fend off long-range *Luftwaffe* bombers. Flying one of those Hurricanes was like playing Russian roulette; if the bomber didn't get the pilot, chances were that a crash landing in the ice-cold ocean would. There was no way of landing the aircraft back on the ship; ditching or escape by parachute were the pilot's only options.

Another self-defence measure was the gun mounted on some merchantmen. One RCN naval gunner wrote a friend in July 1941 that he was aboard a 1,500-ton Norwegian freighter which was a DEMS — Defensively Equipped Merchant Ship — to direct the operations of its single gun. "I am the only rating aboard and have quite a lot of equipment besides the big gun. I had a really smart crew coming over," he added. "I lead a good life aboard as I am my own boss with my cabin to myself and my meals with the officers. Of course, in the danger zone I have to stand watch from 9 a.m. to 10 p.m., but I don't mind as I can't sleep much anyhow. I had less sleep in Toronto." The gunnery rating concluded by noting that the submarines were "bothersome, but we came through unscathed." He was not so lucky on his next trip. That letter was his last.

The merchant sailors on the 456 Canadian merchantmen also suffered enormously in the North Atlantic struggle. Working for $75 or so a month and a war risk bonus of $44.50, Canadian merchant seamen, some making crossing after crossing, had 68 Canadian ships sunk from underneath them; 1,148 men died, blown up by torpedoes, burned by exploding fuel, or drowned in the icy waters. It was a small fraction of the total loss of seafarers.

THE FATE OF SC-42

The fate of convoy SC-42 in September 1941 illustrated the dangers faced by merchant seaman and their naval escorts. SC-42 (the initials stood for "slow convoy") had sixty-four vessels arranged in twelve columns, and its escort consisted of the destroyer *Skeena* and the corvettes *Orillia*, *Alberni*, and *Kenogami*. None of the ships had radar; the *Kenogami*, commissioned in Montreal on June 29, 1941, was on its first tour of sea duty. The cargo ships, wallowing ahead at little more than five knots, were south-east of Greenland on the evening of September 9 when a wolf pack of at least eight U-boats fell upon them.

The first sign of attack was the "whump" of the explosion produced by a torpedo hitting the fourth ship in the outside port column, the SS *Muneric*, which sank immediately without survivors. The corvette on that side of the block, *Kenogami*, commanded by Lieutenant "Cowboy" Jackson, RCNVR, launched its asdic sweep without significant success, but then saw a U-boat on the surface. An attack with its 4-inch gun was unsuccessful, the U-boat getting away. *Skeena* came to assist, but was called away by word of a submarine near the front of the block. By this time, merchantmen were reporting numerous U-boat sightings, and the convoy commodore was ordering emergency course changes. Two more ships were hit by torpedoes, this time throwing survivors into the water as they went down. The last ships in the columns, although designated as rescue ships, were reluctant to linger very long to pick up survivors; the corvettes did what they could, but their task was to protect the surviving cargo ships. As a result, many survivors of the initial attacks had to wait a long time for rescue — if rescue came at all.

Two hours later the U-boats struck again, hitting two ships; one of them sank. *Kenogami* and *Skeena* moved out and searched in vain for the attacker, though a few depth charges were dropped on suspected contacts. *Orillia* now began to take a disabled tanker in tow, effectively removing it from the rest of the struggle. *Alberni* was the only corvette remaining with the convoy, and as the convoy commodore changed course, it found itself surrounded by merchantmen and unable to check out U-boat sightings. For some hours the convoy proceeded unprotected, before the escort pattern was resumed, but fortunately no attacks came in this period.

A merchant ship loaded with grain was torpedoed near dawn, the escorts again failing to find the enemy. Attacks continued during the daylight hours, another merchant being hit, and the defending destroyer and two corvettes staged an attack at a sighted periscope. "Charge after charge rained down on the U-boat, held now by asdic," Hal Lawrence wrote. "A large bubble of air rose to the surface, along with some oil. Asdic contact faded. A probable hit? A possible, anyway." *Skeena*'s captain, Lieutenant-Commander Jimmy Hibbard, RCN, declared the U-boat sunk.

That night, after two more ships had been hit by torpedoes, the convoy escort received reinforcement when the corvettes *Chambly* and *Moose Jaw* arrived. The two came in from the dark side, hoping to catch surfaced U-boats silhouetted against the southern sky. *Chambly*, under Commander J.D. Prentice, RCN, soon picked up a definite contact, closed with it, and dropped depth charges. *Moose Jaw* was close behind when the wounded U-501 surfaced. "Stand by to ram," *Moose Jaw*'s captain, Lieutenant Frederick Grubb, RCN, ordered. The corvette fired at the submarine with its guns, preventing the submariners from manning their deck gun. At this point, as the U-boat and the corvette were a few yards from each other, the German captain leapt from his bridge onto the fo'c'sle of the *Moose Jaw*. "See what he wants" Grubb said. The U-boat captain identified himself, and surrendered. The *Chambly* came alongside as the U-boat crew gathered on deck and put a boarding party aboard to search for code books. But the sub began to sink, and the boarding party withdrew — except for one Canadian, Stoker W.I. Brown, who was trapped inside along with eleven Germans. U-501 was the first confirmed kill of the war for the RCN.

That was the navy's only success that night. Five more vessels of SC-42 were sunk before the convoy was reinforced by nine ships on September 11 and came under effective air cover from Iceland. All in all, SC-42 lost sixteen of its sixty-four ships to the wolf pack.

That convoy disaster was one of the war's worst. Subsequent evaluations of the battle agreed that a four-ship escort was simply inadequate to protect a large convoy from a wolf pack. Another lesson was that the escort groups had to be better trained to operate as a group, and that escorts could not be detached to shepherd crippled ships to safety or search for survivors in the midst of an action. Hard lessons, those, and paid for in lives. In November 1941, after another convoy received a thrashing from U-boats, the RCN concluded regretfully that most corvette captains knew very little of the fundamentals of anti-submarine warfare. Better training could be given, and time would give experience. Radar would also help, and it soon made its appearance on the escorts — by the end of the winter of 1941–42 every escort had some form of radar. Often those sets, produced in Canada to Canadian design, were almost useless in the rigorous conditions of the North Atlantic, but they improved as the war went on. More effective weaponry was also needed, and it became available in 1943; the forward-throwing "hedgehog" that launched an intricate circular pattern of 65-pound bombs 230 yards ahead of the corvette would be the most effective anti-submarine weapon. That helped mightily, as did HF/DF, the "Huff-Duff" High Frequency Direction Finding sets that pinpointed nearby U-boats by triangulation.

New weapons and equipment seemed to reach the RCN long after Royal Navy ships had them. There was a natural tendency for the British to fit their own ships first with the newest equipment, but sometimes the very conservative Naval Service Headquarters in Ottawa was to blame. Officers there considered some types of equipment — HF/DF and hedgehog were only two examples — "unproven" and refused to press for their installation on RCN ships. Scientists, engineers, and politicians all played their roles in a serious technological failure. Since the main victims, as in SC-42, were foreign merchant seamen, Canadians have been blessedly indifferent to their naval failure.

WAR IN HOME WATERS

Although the attack on Pearl Harbor on December 7, 1941, brought the U.S. into the war, that did not relieve the pressure in the North Atlantic. The USN

Although the initial expectation was that Britain would supply most BCATP aircraft, the defeats of 1940 forced the British to keep every plane they could produce for their own defence. As a result, Canadian plants were converted to produce aircraft, such as these Avro Anson trainers on the production line at the Canadian Car and Foundry plant in Amherst, Nova Scotia, in 1942.

This striking photograph shows a Halifax bomber from the RCAF's No. 6 Group over France. The Halifax first flew in action in 1941, and had the reputation of being able to absorb tremendous punishment and still get its crew home.

One of the best all-round aircraft of the war—and the most glamorous—was the Supermarine Spitfire. Its design had originated in the 1920s but was so fundamentally sound that, with ceaseless improvements, the plane maintained a margin of superiority over *Luftwaffe* aircraft throughout the war. This painting of a Spitfire IX is by wartime pilot R.W. Bradford, now director of the National Aviation Museum in Ottawa.

Germany and its people suffered terribly under the rain of high explosives. This photograph of the north German city of Bremen demonstrates how little of the city remained habitable by war's end.

The Allies returned to Europe to stay in the summer of 1943.
American, British, and Canadian forces invaded Sicily on July 10,
and landed in Italy on September 3.

Regalbuto was a tougher nut to crack, for the Hermann Goering
Division was firmly entrenched on the heights overlooking the town.
But a careful, well-planned flank attack forced a German withdrawal
and the town fell on August 2. Sherman tanks of the Three Rivers
Regiment are seen moving through the ruins after the battle.

Ortona—an ancient town perched on cliffs above the Adriatic—had a valuable modern port, and in December 1943 the Canadians were ordered to take the town without damaging the port's facilities. The desperate struggle involved the most vicious fighting I Canadian Corps faced in Italy. Here, Canadians move an antitank gun into position.

This *Luftwaffe* sergeant from the Hermann Goering Division seems no more than a boy, like so many of the soldiers on both sides. The photographs, two of himself and one of the Führer, suggest either that the corpse was rifled for papers and valuables or that the photographer tried too hard to make a point.

Despite the carnage, a traditional Christmas dinner was served in Ortona's Church of Santa Maria. These officers and men of the 2nd Infantry Brigade headquarters seem well scrubbed and cheerful—but very little *vino* is in evidence, a reminder that a few hundred yards away the killing continued.

had to move much of its strength to the Pacific to make up for the losses caused by the surprise Japanese attack and the disasters that followed. That left the Atlantic defences much under strength, and the U-boats extended their operations westward. Also, the United States Navy unaccountably failed to impose a convoy system along the Eastern seaboard; with the great cities along the coast still lit up at night and silhouetting passing ships, American waters provided a perfect hunting ground for the U-boats. Heavily laden oil tankers, travelling alone up the coast, were slaughtered wholesale. In the first six months of the year, 3 million tons of Allied shipping were lost. Eventually, the Americans put a convoy system into effect and the losses eased.

That changed the anti-submarine role of many RCN ships. Now they went on "the triangle run", sailing eastward from Halifax and Sydney until they handed over the convoys in mid-ocean. They refueled at St. John's before picking up a westbound convoy for Boston or New York; then it was another convoy to escort to Halifax. The triangle run — with its pleasant spells of leave on Broadway and in the fleshpots of Manhattan, mixed in with too frequent spells of horror at sea — became the war for a large part of the RCN.

The U-boat war had also come to Canada in the spring of 1942. The Gulf of St. Lawrence, hitherto an area of safety where convoys were thought unnecessary, suddenly became a theatre of war. The first sinkings in the gulf occurred on the night of May 11, when two cargo ships were destroyed by torpedoes. The RCN quickly put convoys into operation and formed a scratch St. Lawrence Escort Force from minesweepers, armed yachts, and motor launches. This undermanned anti-submarine navy had special difficulties as the peculiar qualities of the gulf and river distorted asdic signals, something the U-boat skippers quickly realized. The submariners found air attack more frightening and deadly; the RCAF mounted bomber patrols that repeatedly forced U-boats to submerge in unnerving crash dives that often made it difficult to recharge batteries. Nonetheless, by the end of 1942 two escorts and fourteen merchant ships had been lost in the St. Lawrence. More were to follow, and there was such panic among the politicians in Ottawa that the government closed the St. Lawrence to merchant vessels for much of the remainder of the war and moved substantial numbers of troops into the area. The experience that many Gaspé communities had of helping oil-soaked survivors ashore brought the war home to Quebec — in a spring when Bill 80, to authorize the use of conscripts overseas if necessary, was being debated.

Another disaster occurred farther afield when U-69 sank the ss *Caribou*, the passenger ferry plying its regular way from Sydney, Nova Scotia, to Port-aux-Basques, Newfoundland, on October 13, 1942. The submarine fired one torpedo, scored a direct hit, and dived to evade the attack of the minesweeper

Grandmère. On the *Caribou*, there was chaos as mothers scrambled to find their children. One woman, witnesses said, was so frenzied that she threw her baby over the side and jumped after it; both died. Another baby, fifteen-month–old Leonard Shiers of Halifax, was lost in the sea three times that night but was saved each time by a different rescuer. An RCN Nursing Sister, Margaret Brooke of Ardath, Saskatchewan, struggled all night to keep Nursing Sister Agnes Wilkie on the overturned lifeboat to which they clung; Wilkie was washed away just after daybreak. In all, 137 died in that disaster, many of them women and children. Angus L. Macdonald, Minister of National Defence (Naval Services), said that if "there were any Canadians who did not realize that we were up against a ruthless and remorseless enemy, there can be no such Canadians now." It seemed small compensation that between July and November 1942 the RCAF had sunk three U-boats and the RCN four.

The Battle of the Atlantic, of which the St. Lawrence war was only a small subsidiary, was now intensifying. In the fall of 1942, New York City outstripped Halifax as the main convoy port, and the U-boats concentrated in the Greenland air cover gap for a massive effort to stop the steady flow of men and supplies to Britain. The German submarine fleet had suffered considerable losses of boats and crews, but thus far their extraordinarily efficient production lines still turned out U-boats faster than the Allies could sink them. During 1942, for example, strength rose from 91 operational U-boats to 212. That led to heavy merchant losses — in November 1942 the U-boats sank 119 ships, in February 1943 they sank 63, and the next month 108. The loss of merchant ships was staggering, almost unsustainable, and Canadian ships were part of the problem. For a time RCN escorts were pulled out of the fight in the North Atlantic for retraining and re-equipping on the easier Gibraltar–United Kingdom run, after the Royal Navy observed that four-fifths of the merchantmen recently sunk had been lost while being escorted by RCN ships.

But the tide of the battle slowly began to turn. In March 1943, the RCN, RN, and USN held the Atlantic Convoy Conference in Washington to decide how best to combat the U-boats. One decision, much desired by the Canadians, was to put the RCN and RN in complete charge of convoys on the northern route. As a result of the forceful arguments of the Canadian representative, Rear-Admiral Victor Brodeur — a sturdy nationalist — Canada got its own operational sector. Admiral Murray took over as Commander-in-Chief Canadian Northwest Atlantic, responsible for the Atlantic from 47° west and south to 29° north. To be out from under the command of the Americans was enormously gratifying to RCN officers. One senior officer, the magnificently named Captain Horatio Nelson Lay, had earlier noted that the USN's "general attitude appears to be that they consider the R.C.N. as purely a small part of their own fleet...." That had rankled, as had the USN's doubts — probably justified — about Canadian efficiency and effectiveness. The new command arrangement was just one sign of the stature the RCN had begun to earn in the war. A further sign came in 1944 when the RCN assumed responsibility for *all* North Atlantic convoys. In four years, the tiny Royal Canadian Navy had somehow become the third-largest Allied fleet.

Far more important than this shuffling of command, however, were the steady modifications in equipment — corvettes were improved enormously through structural alterations, rewiring, and new weapons — and an exponential growth in the number of ships. Canada alone produced 70 frigates — twin-screw super-corvettes especially designed for anti-submarine work, with better speed and armaments — over the course of the war; the United States launched 379 destroyer escorts in 1943. This meant that convoys had more protection from the moment they set sail; it also meant that support groups, unattached to particular convoys, could be called on for assistance. The 300-mile gap in air cover was closed by the entry into service of long-range Liberator bombers, and thanks to the Convoy Conference even the RCAF managed to get its hands on some. By November 1942, the RCAF had four anti-submarine squadrons based in Newfoundland and five in the Maritime provinces, and bore the responsibility for all air cover north and east of Newfoundland.

Moreover, small escort carriers, their flight decks built on merchant ship hulls, now sailed with support groups, bringing heavy concentrations of air support to convoys under attack. And newly developed MACs — Merchant Aircraft Carriers, tankers or grain carriers equipped with a flight deck and three or four aircraft — also began to sail with the convoys.

The Germans countered these measures with the "Gnat" — a new acoustic torpedo that homed in on the noise made by ships' screws. An early victim was HMCS *St. Croix*, a destroyer. The survivors, picked up by two British ships, fell victim again to another acoustic torpedo and a sole Canadian survived. Among those lost was Mackenzie King's nephew, a naval surgeon. Acoustic torpedoes were in turn defeated — within seventeen days, so responsive were Allied scientists — by the development of "Cat gear", a simple noise-making device towed behind each vessel to deflect the torpedo harmlessly. Later the Germans developed the snorkel and equipped their bigger and faster new submarines with it. This breathing device let U-boats stay submerged for as long as ten days, and charge their batteries during that time, a great advantage given the Allies' air superiority and advanced radar. Hitler's navy was also moving rapidly towards putting very effective hydrogen peroxide–fueled submarines to sea — boats that could dive deeper, stay submerged longer, and attack from a submerged position with an array of sophisticated weaponry. These would be true submarines, instead of diving boats. Happily, the war ended before significant numbers of them saw action.

The sinkings continued right up to May 1945 in this increasingly scientific war. By war's end the u-boats had sunk a total of 12 million tons of shipping. But now they paid a heavy price in return. In May 1943 alone, 41 submarines went to the bottom — and stayed there. Even so, in March 1945 the Germans had an impressive 463 u-boats in service.

The RCN's escorts played their full part in the struggle for the sea lanes. Canadian ships provided half the escorts for the North Atlantic convoys, and the RCN, often aided by the RCAF, destroyed or shared in the sinking of twenty-seven German or Italian submarines; seventeen of those sinkings took place after November 1944, a testimony to the length of time needed to make Canadian sailors into truly effective specialists. But they finally mastered the necessary anti-submarine arts and they came to excel at them. And now, when the RCAF and RCN sang the unofficial anthem of the anti-submarine war, they did so knowing that they had the upper hand. "The North Atlantic Squadron" had many verses, almost all unprintable except for the chorus:

> Away, away, with fife and drum,
> Here we come, full of rum,
> Looking for women to peddle their bum,
> In the North Atlantic Squadron.

As Admiral Murray said, "The Canadian Navy did not win the Battle of the Atlantic by itself, but without it the battle could not have been won."

THE BIG SHIP NAVY

By late 1943 the Royal Canadian Navy had turned into more than just an anti-submarine force. In the middle of that year Canada and Britain agreed that the RCN would take over a variety of ships from the Royal Navy, including escort and light fleet carriers, cruisers, frigates, landing craft, and destroy-ers. That greatly pleased the navy's senior officers, who, in truth, had never really considered that anti-submarine warfare was what a "real" navy did. Sometimes that attitude had had serious effects. When Naval Service Head-quarters insisted on building big Tribal-class destroyers in Halifax in 1942, the impact on yard space and scarce resources of skilled manpower was such that repairs and modifications to corvettes had to be slowed. Ultimately, that probably meant that merchant ships went to the bottom for want of escorts, and men and supplies were lost.

At the end of 1943 the RCN had 306 operational warships, 71,549 officers and ratings, and 4,553 Wrens. The six destroyers with which it had begun the war had been joined by the six received from the USN in 1940 (and two received subsequently) and four new Tribal-class destroyers acquired in 1942–43, as well as eight more turned over by the Royal Navy. There were losses too, of course. The *Ottawa* and the *St. Croix* were torpedoed in the North Atlantic and the *Margaree* sank after colliding with a freighter.

Some ships, like the *Haida*, under Commander Harry DeWolf, earned a fearsome reputation; this Tribal destroyer (now moored in Toronto harbour as a memorial to the men and women of the RCN) participated in the sinking of two German destroyers, a minesweeper, a submarine, and fourteen other ships of war. The *Haida* and the *Athabaskan* were chasing three enemy destroyers off the French coast on April 28, 1944, when the *Athabaskan*, hit by a torpedo fired by one of the German ships, sank. Commander DeWolf kept his ship picking up survivors as long as he could. The *Haida*'s historian, William Sclater, described the scene as the destroyer came alongside a raft.

"Take the wounded first," said the men on the raft, and the wounded were helped out.

It was slow work for they could not help themselves. Many were burned. The last of them were just coming up when the ship started gently ahead. She went very slowly at first, and the men on the nets worked desperately to get the survivors inboard.

From somewhere at the back of the raft a voice was heard to call, "Get away, *Haida*, get clear." A sailor said it was the voice of the young Captain of the *Athabaskan*. Other survivors said he had swum to a raft and rested his arms on it, as if they were burned, and had encouraged them to sing.

Haida rescued 44 of her sister ship's crew; another 83 were captured by the Germans; 129 officers and men, including Lieutenant-Commander John Stubbs, the young captain, were lost.

The new navy operated all over the world. It ran motor torpedo boats out of England, and minesweepers that served from Canadian and British ports and helped clear the Normandy approaches for the D-Day landing. Flotillas of Canadian landing craft took part in the invasions of North Africa, Sicily, Italy, and Normandy, where they carried Canadian infantry ashore in all but the first of those landings.

But it was the big ships that most sharply differentiated the new RCN from the old. The very idea that a navy which had begun the war with a handful of men in a tiny fleet of ships would have the capacity four or five years later to man two aircraft carriers engaged in the complex task of air operations at sea was almost unbelievable. But true it was, and Canadians manned the *Nabob* and the *Puncher* (except for their air crews), though both carriers remained on the rolls of the Royal Navy. The *Nabob*, commanded by Captain Lay, RCN, was on only her second operation when she was hit by a torpedo in the Barents Sea in August 1944. The Germans had transferred most of their U-boat operations to the Norwegian fjords, and there they based their one remaining pocket battleship, the *Tirpitz*. Thanks to luck and sound seamanship, *Nabob* made her way the 1,100 miles to the Royal Navy base at Scapa Flow in northern Scotland under her own power, despite a hole in her side 50 feet by 20 feet, but the carrier was considered so badly damaged as not to be worth repair. *Puncher* saw a few months of action, sending her Barracuda and Wildcat aircraft against German shore installations in Norway, then was converted to a troop carrier to return Canadian servicemen home from Europe.

The RCN also acquired the cruisers *Uganda* and *Ontario*, in 1944 and 1945 respectively. As part of its commitment to the Pacific war, the government agreed to contribute two light fleet carriers, two cruisers, the armed merchant cruiser *Prince Robert*, rearmed as an anti-aircraft ship, ten destroyers, and fifty frigates and corvettes. As it turned out, however, only one cruiser and the *Prince Robert* reached the Asian theatre before the Pacific war's end.

On the west coast, the RCN had to protect communications off British Columbia, an important task after Japan entered the war. By January 1942, the navy had two armed merchant cruisers, three corvettes, five minesweepers, and a number of smaller ships on patrol. One freighter, SS *Fort Camosun*, was torpedoed and shelled by a Japanese submarine on July 19–20, 1942. The next night, the same submarine shelled the lighthouse at Estevan Point, B.C., helping greatly to increase the alarm and fear of invasion in that province. Fortunately no Japanese invasion attempts occurred, though the British and American Joint Chiefs of Staff and Canadian planners did not discount the threat for another year.

The growth of the Royal Canadian Navy during the war was extraordinary by any standard. It played a vital role in a critical area of the war and acquitted itself well. Its teething troubles, complicated by sometimes weak command arrangements and vicious fighting between admirals and politicians, were inevitable. There were technical problems aplenty in learning how to fight the U-boats, especially in the early years. But the RCN's record was highly creditable, all the more so for being accomplished by volunteers who learned their tasks from scratch. The "Wavy Navy" won Canada's war at sea, though the price of naval inexperience and unpreparedness was enormous.

XIV
PER ARDUA AD ASTRA: THE RCAF AT WAR

S ir Gerald Campbell, Great Britain's high commissioner in Ottawa, was angry. Mackenzie King, he informed London on December 19, 1939, was the "narrowest of narrow Canadian nationalists", a man full of "mystical and idealistic talk of a crusade or holy war against the enemies of civilization and democracy," and at the same time interested primarily in "what the common cause can be made to do to help Canada."

Campbell was furious at the Canadian role in the negotiation of the British Commonwealth Air Training Plan (BCATP), concluded just two days before. In the high commissioner's view, King's government initially had reacted positively to the proposed training scheme

> because if they played their cards right, they could employ the essential features of the scheme for the greater honour and glory of Canada. It would, incidentally, be an effective weapon against the enemy, and this fact had its own value, since the Canadian people were pressing for effective measures on the part of their Government. But first things come first, and here was a plan which promised a far better return in the way of political capital than the despatch of a mere division or two to the Western Front.

That scathing telegram demonstrated all too clearly that the BCATP, quite possibly Canada's major contribution to the war against the Axis powers, was conceived in bitterness and anger.

CREATING THE AIR TRAINING PLAN

The Canadian people had never doubted that their country would play a major role in the air in the Second World War. After all, pilots such as Bishop, Barker, Collishaw, and hundreds of others had distinguished themselves in the air combat of the Great War. But the condition of the RCAF at the beginning of September 1939 was not such as to inspire much confidence. The one squadron of the Permanent Active Air Force that was equipped with modern Hurricane fighters had only two of them. The Auxiliary Active Air Force had twelve squadrons, most dependent on the Tiger Moth. The reserves, pilots and air crew with flying experience, were soon called up, and men were slowly enlisted in the Special Reserve for wartime service. Canada had a flying heritage — but few up-to-date aircraft and only a tiny number of trained personnel.

There had been pre-war schemes to train pilots for the Royal Air Force in Canada's wide-open spaces, but they had never been implemented. In the days immediately after the war against Hitler had begun, however, Vincent Massey and Stanley Bruce — the Canadian and Australian high commissioners to London — put a proposal for an empire-wide air-training plan to the British government. London was delighted to accept and, on September 26, asked Canada to participate. What London wanted was a plan to train "not less than 20,000 pilots and 30,000 personnel of air crews annually." The British estimated that at least ninety flying schools would be necessary to produce that many air crew, and they said, selling the idea as hard as possible, that the "immense influence" such a plan could have on the war "might even prove decisive".

For Prime Minister Mackenzie King, this proposal came days too late. Had the telegram from London come before the Cabinet decided to send the 1st Canadian Division overseas, he would have been much happier. But London's request was on the table, and won a favourable response from his Cabinet, and King had to let matters proceed. Proceed they did, and a British delegation headed by Lord Riverdale, a blustering industrialist, arrived in Ottawa in mid-October for discussions. London had sent no forecasts of cost with Riverdale, and when these were produced in Canada, the Cabinet was stunned. The estimate for the plan's total cost over three and a half years was $888.5 million, of which the British proposed to make a "free contribution" of $140 million and hoped that Ottawa would pay half the remainder. Other dominions were to pick up the rest of the tab. But $370 million was a staggering sum for a country that had had a pre-war gross national product of $5 billion and a 1939 federal budget of $500 million. Mackenzie King said quickly that "it was not Canada's war in the same sense it was Great Britain's", a comment that infuriated the British team, adding that "he was afraid there could be no question of taking on responsibility for the scheme in the [suggested] proportion...."

That set the tone for the rest of the negotiations, as the Canadians and British argued bitterly with each other, using every economic lever to manoeuvre for advantage. At last, on November 13, the negotiators struck a deal: Britain was to pay $218 million, Canada $313 million, Australia $97 million, and New Zealand $21 million. Later changes raised the proposed Canadian share an additional $40 million. (In fact, the plan ultimately was extended into 1945, and the costs escalated far beyond the 1939 estimates. In the end, Canada paid $1.6 billion of a total cost of $2.2 billion.) We had gone further than intended, King said, but it was right "so that the British Government might feel that we had acted generously." But because King had insisted that the BCATP be recognized as taking priority over all other Canadian contributions to the war, London was furious at Ottawa.

There was more quarrelling to come between the great partners in the training plan. The question was what was to happen to the Canadian graduates — would they be organized in RCAF squadrons or would they be merged into the RAF? Mackenzie King, naturally enough, wanted RCAF pilots, observers, bombardiers, and wireless operators to be under Canadian control, just as the army's divisions and RCN's ships were. The British were troubled by this. In the first place, Canada expected London to pay the costs of RCAF squadrons overseas in return for its share of the BCATP's costs. Also, if Canadians were "segregated", the Australians and New Zealanders might demand the same. As both sides raced to reach a final accord that Mackenzie King could announce on December 17, the solution was to fudge the issue. The unresolved issue of "Canadianization" was to cause major problems down the road.

The plan agreed to in Ottawa called for Canada to become, in President Roosevelt's later phrase, "the aerodrome of democracy". There were to be three Initial Training Schools, thirteen Elementary Flying Training Schools, sixteen Service Flying Training Schools, ten Air Observer Schools, ten Bombing and Gunnery Schools, two Air Navigation Schools, and four Wireless Schools. Other administrative and training units brought the total to seventy-four schools or depots, and each *month* the BCATP was expected to graduate 520 pilots with elementary training, 544 with service training, 340 air observers, and 580 wireless operator–air gunners. The RCAF had the administrative responsibility for the plan, estimated to require 3,540 aircraft — or more than twelve times the number of military aircraft in Canada in September 1939. To staff the plan's schools, 33,000 air force personnel and 6,000 civilians would be needed. This was a gigantic plan, all the more so when the pre-war RCAF's tiny 4,000-man strength was considered.

THE BATTLE OF BRITAIN

While the RCAF scrambled to locate, construct, and man the airfields necessary to get the British Commonwealth Air Training Plan operating by the spring of 1940, the first RCAF squadrons were already proceeding overseas. In February 1940, 110 Squadron arrived in England to train for "army co-operation" duties. Intended to accompany the 1st Canadian Division to France, the squadron was supposed to provide combat ground support for the infantry and to carry out observation duties. No. 1 Squadron (later renumbered as No. 401) arrived in June 1940.

The summer of 1940 was to be the Battle of Britain — when the German air force set out to destroy the fighters of the RAF, clearing the way so *Luftwaffe* bombers could bring Britain to its knees by wreaking havoc on the cities. Huge air armadas of bombers and their escorting fighters would leave French bases each day, and each day the outnumbered pilots of the RAF would rise from their stations to meet them, with British radar guiding the interceptors to their targets, and providing that crucial extra minute or two of warning time.

Equipped with Hurricane fighters, No. 1 Squadron became the first RCAF unit to fly in combat when its pilots sortied on August 26. Three Dornier 215 bombers were shot down, but Flying Officer R.L. Edwards died when a Dornier downed his fighter. Five days later, the still untried Canadian pilots ran into experienced Messerschmitt pilots, and three RCAF aircraft were lost. By the end of October, when 1 Squadron flew to Scotland for a rest, its pilots had claimed thirty-one "kills" and forty-three "probables". But the squadron had lost sixteen of its eighteen Hurricanes in action; three of its pilots had been killed and ten more wounded.

Another squadron of Canadians was also flying, in the RAF. So many Canadians had gone to Britain before and just after the outbreak of war to join the RAF that the Air Ministry had created 242 Squadron entirely from Canadian pilots. Soon it was under command of Squadron Leader Douglas Bader, a famous RAF officer who flew with two artificial legs after losing his own in a flying accident in 1931. Flying Hurricanes from the Biggin Hill airfield south of London, the Canadians of 242 Squadron flew air cover over the Dunkirk evacuation and then played a distinguished role in the Battle of Britain.

On August 30, for example, nine Hurricanes of 242 Squadron met head on with a huge force of the attacking *Luftwaffe*. After one flight of three fighters had tackled the covering German fighters — a dangerous task as the Hurricanes (unlike the faster, more manoeuvrable Spitfires) were markedly inferior to the Messerschmitt 109s — the remaining two flights of 242 Hurricanes claimed twelve victories without loss to themselves.

Those numbers may have been inflated by the pilots — at 400 mph it was difficult to tell if a plane had been shot down or simply damaged — and then redoubled by the Air Ministry, which was desperate to keep up British morale in that dark summer. What is certain, however, is that more German than British and Canadian aircraft were destroyed; equally certain, every *Luftwaffe* pilot shot down over Britain was taken prisoner or killed, while RAF and RCAF pilots, if they bailed out successfully, could fly again. By the end of September, as the *Luftwaffe* slowed the tempo of the daylight attacks that had cost Field Marshal Hermann Goering's air force so heavily, it was becoming clear that the Battle of Britain had been won.

TRAINING AIR CREW

None of the pilots who flew in the Battle of Britain had been trained under the British Commonwealth Air Training Plan. Before long, however, the BCATP's graduates were arriving in Britain and North Africa and the Far East in large numbers, so large that in retrospect the great training scheme seemed to have sprung up full-blown after the signing ceremony in December 1939. In fact, the birth-pangs were long, the labour enormous.

The BCATP had to begin by building the necessary bases. The Department of Transport took on the task of organizing airfield construction, first inspecting the country's 153 airports (some little more than dirt strips with a tumbledown shack or two) and deciding which could be employed for training. The DOT decided that 24 existing airfields could be used if additional buildings were provided. Dozens of other sites for airfields, gunnery ranges, and supply depots were chosen, depending on climate, ground conditions, and water supply. Political considerations occasionally entered in as well — Mackenzie King's constituency of Prince Albert, Saskatchewan, was the site of an air observer school; other politicians also tried to press their ridings' claims. Even so, every province had an array of BCATP installations. Saskatchewan, flat and open, trained a fifth of the pilots and up to a third of some categories of air crew. To have so many Canadians from all across the country in the province, as well as thousands of British, Australian, and New Zealand airmen, undoubtedly made a mark.

Air crew recruits had to be physically fit and, initially, between 18 and 28 years of age. As the war went on, standards eased and the age range became 17½ to 33 for pilots and 17½ to 39 for air gunners. Medical standards were also lowered.

Recruits joined the RCAF as "Aircraftsmen 2nd Class" (usually called Acey-Deucey after the abbreviation AC2) and withstood the lengthy rigours of the manning depot. These included parade square training, spit and polish, lessons in military courtesy, and other measures to turn civilians into "uniformed raw material suitable for further training", as one BCATP graduate,

Murray Peden, put it. Another recruit, Syd Wise from Toronto — who was just eighteen in 1943 — remembered his surprise at "how totally your life was controlled by the junior NCOs." Hardest for some was accepting the complete lack of privacy. In his memoirs, Robert Collins wrote of his first day at the manning depot at Brandon, Manitoba:

> I am surrounded by 750 naked and half-naked men. Skinny men, plump men, Greek gods. Men in boxer shorts, dirty shorts, and no shorts. Men with body odor that would fell an ox. Men brooding silently on their bunks. Men shouting, laughing, punching biceps, breaking wind, cursing.... I know none of these people.

After basic training, air crew trainees received their white cap flashes. That mattered, said Wise: "one little distinctive symbol can make you feel first part of a group and then something special." Then they went to Initial Training School for a ground school lengthened, by 1943, to ten weeks, and so intensive that, as Peden was warned, "If you stop for a leak — you'll fall a week behind." The best and fittest ITS graduates then proceeded to an Elementary Flying Training School for an eight-week course. The less fit were routed to Observer or Wireless School.

In the first days of the BCATP, when pilot instructors were in scarce supply, elementary flying was taught by commercially organized and civilian-managed flying clubs. The RCAF watched over the instruction and provided the discipline, but civilian pilots did the teaching — under the maxim "There Are Old Pilots, and Bold Pilots; There Are No Old, Bold Pilots." Eventually, the RCAF took over the training as well. The pilot trainees, now AC1s, learned to fly on De Havilland Tiger Moth biplanes, and later on Fairchild Cornells (built by Fleet Aircraft Ltd. at Fort Erie, Ontario) which, despite their 122mph top speed, had flying characteristics closer to the military aircraft then in use. All Training Command aircraft were painted bright yellow for easy spotting. Trainees learned navigation and something about armaments; they worked on engines, airmanship, and the theory of flight.

A substantial proportion of trainees failed to qualify. One pilot recalled that nineteen out of forty-one in his class "washed out" in six weeks, including the apprentice pilot who couldn't land. "Thirty or more times he executed a beautiful approach, then climbed just before touchdown." An instructor flew up alongside to try to lead him to earth, but nothing worked. "Finally, just at dusk, the frightened boy dropped to the grass in a perfect three-point landing. Next day he was on his way to gunner's school."

The survivors — 856 trainees died in crashes during the BCATP's operation, and in 1943–44 the rate of fatalities was one for every 20,580 hours of flying time — then proceeded to Service Flying Training School, where the RCAF provided the instructors, and where students flew tricky, unforgiving Harvards or multi-engined Cessna Cranes or Anson IIs. There they began to master night flying, formation flying, and radio work, in a course that eventually was extended to twenty-one weeks. Those who passed received their wings. About a third were commissioned as pilot officers; the others became sergeant pilots. Training was not yet over, however. Pilots proceeded to Advanced Flying Units and then to Operational Training Units before being posted to squadrons, overseas or in Canada. Smart ones going overseas stocked up on the things, as Robert Collins remembered, "that wise men said would win the everlasting gratitude of British girls, all allegedly starved for North American sex and consumer goods...crimson nail polish, silk stockings, and two dozen malted milk chocolate bars."

The air crew trainees included a substantial number of Americans who crossed the border to get into the war both before and after their country did. At the time of Pearl Harbor, the RCAF had 6,129 Americans on strength. Trainees from abroad — 42,000 from the RAF, 9,600 from the Royal Australian Air Force, and 7,000 from the Royal New Zealand Air Force — lived and trained with the 72,835 Canadians. Like them, they made friends in small-town Saskatchewan, went to dances in Quebec, or sailed in the Maritimes. One air gunner training at Mont Joli, Quebec, remembered that his group of trainees included "a New Zealander, a Cockney, a Welshman, and a Yorkshireman whom no one could understand without an interpreter. A Jew from Cambridge University, two Scotchmen, a full-blooded Chippewa Indian, and an odd assortment of Canadians, including a schoolteacher and two ministers' sons, completed the list." In a curious yet heartwarming way, the war brought the Commonwealth together. Many of the friendships formed in Canada carried over to bomber crews in England.

The BCATP initially produced only pilots, air observers, and wireless operator–air gunners. But as the war went on and new and larger aircraft came into service, the training changed as well. By the wrap-up of the plan, eight air crew categories were being produced: pilot, navigator, navigator B (with bombing training), navigator W (with wireless training), air bomber, wireless operator–air gunner, air gunner, and flight engineer. In all, 131,553 graduated, more than 50,000 of whom were pilots. Canadians accounted for 55 per cent of the graduates.

There were far more Canadian air crew, in fact, than there were RCAF positions to absorb them. In January 1941, Ottawa announced that as a result of an agreement with London up to twenty-five additional RCAF squadrons overseas would be formed from BCATP graduates. Other RCAF graduates were to wear Canadian uniforms even if serving in RAF squadrons.

That 1941 agreement resolved some of the problems of Canadianization, though there were recurring difficulties between Ottawa and London. The Minister of National Defence (Air) was Charles G. Power, known as Chubby to everyone. Power was a decorated infantry officer of the Great War, a Quebec Catholic, and a professional politician — tough, hard-drinking, and very able — and he wanted his senior RCAF officers to get experience of command overseas instead of being fully engaged in running the BCATP. The British policy interfered with this. But over time Power got his way, and there was soon a Canadian bomber group, as well as fighter wings. Power also won agreement for all suitable Canadian graduates of the BCATP to get commissions, thus eliminating the arbitrary distinction between pilot officers and sergeant pilots. By the end of the war, the RCAF had forty-eight squadrons overseas, flying bombers, fighters, transports, and U-boat hunters.

Other administrative problems were harder to resolve. Power told the prime minister about a Montreal father whose son was shot down in 1941 while flying with the RAF.

> In May he received a notification from the R.A.F. that the boy was missing. Then followed a cable from the R.A.F. giving some of the circumstances of the tragedy, then a formal notice, the first to be received from Canadian sources, addressed to the boy's mother, that the dependants' allowance to which she was entitled was now cut off.

In other words, the furious Power complained, it seemed that "Canada's only interest in a Canadian boy was to save a paltry thirty dollars a month." The air minister worked hard to establish clearer lines of control and communication over Canadian airmen, wherever they served.

What should be added, however, is that most Canadians who served with the RAF and flew in bomber crews that often included Australians, New Zealanders, South Africans, and other men from dominions and colonies felt some reluctance to be remustered into all-Canadian squadrons. Their crews had bonded together and developed a mutual trust, and in wartime that was a critical factor. Moreover, they could get away with murder in British-commanded squadrons. Flight Sergeant Bill Eccles, serving in RAF Coastal Command and Bomber Command squadrons as a radar specialist, remembered being sent on course and subjected to a full kit inspection. Neatly folded on his bed was a pair of bright orange silk boxer shorts, a gift from his mother in Montreal. "What are these, Eccles?" the inspecting officer demanded with great disdain. "Canadian issue, sir," was the reply — and it was accepted, presumably on the grounds that nothing better could be expected of the RCAF.

Some BCATP graduates never did get overseas. Many, especially from the earliest training classes, were fed back into the BCATP to act as instructors. Still more were posted to the Home War Establishment to defend Canada. The first class of pilots, graduating in November 1940, had 7 of its members go to home defence squadrons and 27 join the BCATP. Of the 203 Canadian pilots trained in 1940, only 20 went overseas, while 165 became instructors. That was inevitable, but frustrating.

At the start of the war, the idea that Canada might need direct defence seemed little more than a joke: protected by two oceans, the North American continent was almost invulnerable. Almost, but not quite. Nazi U-boats began picking off fat merchantmen within months, and that meant the RCAF had to develop the skills to attack U-boats from the air. Some pilots learned well. Flight Lieutenant David Hornell, pilot of a twin-engine Canso amphibian operating from Scotland on June 24, 1944, came across a surfaced U-boat north of the Shetland Islands. The submarine's deck gun fired at the lumbering Canso, hitting the starboard engine, but Hornell pressed the attack, dropping four depth charges in a perfect "straddle" that blew the U-boat's bows out of the water and sank it. The Canso landed on the ocean without breaking up, thanks to Hornell's "superhuman efforts at the controls", but it sank shortly after, and it was twenty-one hours before rescue launches reached the eight crew members. "There was only one serviceable dinghy and this could not hold all the crew. So they took turns in the water, holding on to the side...." Two of the crew had already died of exposure, and Hornell, blinded and exhausted, failed to survive the trip back to Scotland. He received the Victoria Cross posthumously.

On the Canadian west coast, there was a great public fear of invasion after Pearl Harbor. Although the military chiefs in Ottawa discounted any risk of attack, being unwilling to divert men and equipment from the European war, the commanders on the coast were far less certain. Their fears, plus the understandable political necessity to protect the homeland first, led in March 1942 to the decision to create a Home War Establishment of forty-nine squadrons, twenty-five of which were to be located in British Columbia. In June 1942, the Japanese occupied Attu and Kiska, American islands in the Aleutian chain off Alaska, and for a time the threat of invasion seemed real enough that RCAF fighter and bomber squadrons went to Alaska to operate with the American forces there. The squadrons launched attacks on the Japanese-held islands on September 25, 1942, and Squadron Leader K.A. Boomer shot down an enemy plane; he would be the only RCAF pilot to score victories over both

Japanese and German aircraft. But in the same month that the Japanese took the islands, the United States Navy won the great naval air battle of Midway and began to take the offensive in the Pacific. The Japanese were driven from the Aleutians by the summer of 1943 and the threat to the west coast gradually receded; so too did RCAF strength on the home front.

WAR AROUND THE WORLD

By the summer of 1941, the RCAF had had five fighter squadrons in Britain. The *Luftwaffe*'s daylight raids had almost ceased, and when air raids had come it had been under cover of darkness. Released from the struggle against Messerschmitts and Dorniers over England, RAF and RCAF fighter squadrons had begun daylight attacks on occupied France, either on their own or as escorts for bombers. Rail and road traffic were targets, as were factories, airfields, enemy shipping, and gun positions. If the *Luftwaffe* rose to meet the attackers, that was an opportunity to tackle them as well. Hugh Godefroy, a pilot in an RCAF fighter squadron based at Biggin Hill, remembered one sweep over France in late October 1941 when the *Luftwaffe* jumped the Spitfires:

> ...suddenly I realized that the sparks were going forward not backward! "TRACER!" I pulled the stick back in a wild break out of the formation. Looking back, I was just in time to see Brian Hodgkinson behind me roll slowly over, flames pouring from his engine, and a Messerschmitt pass below me within yards of my tail, his nose and wings rippling with fire. Ten voices scream on the R/T at once:
> "For God's sake, break, 109s!"
> "I'm hit. I'm on fire."
> "Bail out, you fool."
> "My tail's gone. I'm bailing out."
> It was complete pandemonium, but it lasted only for a minute.

"This was no joust bound by the rules of chivalry," Godefroy said. "I had never witnessed such persistent savagery. They were out to kill us by any means possible."

While they had been bested over England, the enemy continued to be a strong and skilful force. When the Canadian raid went in at Dieppe in August 1942, for example, seventy-four Allied squadrons, including eight from the RCAF, provided air support. But the *Luftwaffe* shot down twice as many aircraft as it lost; it was the worst day of the war for the RAF. The RCAF lost thirteen planes and pilots on that black day.

Canadian pilots were having better success elsewhere. In the air battles over the Western Desert and in the disastrous British intervention in Greece, Flight Lieutenant Vernon Woodward had twenty-two kills against Italian and German pilots. The RCAF's 417 Squadron operated in the desert from the spring of 1942, first patrolling the Suez Canal and then providing air cover over the supply lines of Britain's Eighth Army as it advanced east towards Tunisia after the great victory of El Alamein in November 1942. In May 1943, the squadron moved to Malta to provide fighter support for the invasion of Sicily. Earlier at Malta, Pilot Officer Buck McNair shot down nine enemy aircraft in one three-month tour — two years later he was commanding an RCAF wing. The RCAF also operated three squadrons of radar-equipped night fighters from England after 1941, and provided Intruder squadrons of Mosquitoes and Mustangs.

Canadian airmen served in other theatres of war as well. Hundreds of Canadians served with RAF squadrons throughout the Pacific. Two RCAF transport squadrons, No. 435 and No. 436, flew out of Burma, dealing daily with Japanese interceptors, wholly inadequate facilities, and some of the world's worst flying weather. No. 413 Squadron was based in Ceylon in 1942 when one of its Catalina flying boats, flown by Squadron Leader L.J. Birchall, spotted a Japanese fleet heading for Ceylon on April 4. "We immediately coded a message and started transmission," Birchall said after the war. "We were halfway through our required third transmission when a shell destroyed our wireless equipment." Then the Catalina was shot down. Six of the nine crew members survived; Birchall himself, "the saviour of Ceylon", withstood brutal Japanese interrogation and more than three years in a POW camp. But his warning had given the British time to prepare for the attack, and it was driven off. Birchall won the Distinguished Flying Cross for his exploits.

The Canadian pilot who attracted the most attention for his feats in the air war, however, was George Beurling. Rejected by the RCAF before the war because he had insufficient education, "Buzz" Beurling was finally accepted into the RAF in 1940. Ill-disciplined, unsuited to formation flying, and totally fearless, Beurling was a natural flier and a skilled shot, not unlike Billy Bishop in the Great War. He had two kills before he was posted to Malta in May 1942, and there, flying a Spitfire, he improved his score to seven by July and to twenty-nine by October — the highest total by a Canadian ace. The Spitfire could attain a speed of 404 mph, and with its powerful Rolls-Royce engine it could climb to 20,000 feet in just over six minutes, so it was generally used against enemy fighters while Hurricanes dealt with the lower-flying bombers. In this deadly combat Beurling was a master, combining reckless flying with the uncanny eye of the dead shot. He described shooting down an Italian

Macchi aircraft: "One of my shells caught [the pilot] right in the face and blew his head right off. The body slumped and the slipstream caught the neck, the stub of the neck, and the blood streamed down the side of the cockpit." Although the chivalry that had graced many pilots in the First World War was now replaced by pragmatic ruthlessness, pilots rarely saw their opponents die. "You have to be hard-hearted," Beurling said publicly. "You must blaze away whenever you are in a position to get his oxygen bottles or gas tanks." But to his sister Gladys he said, "I see their faces."

Nonetheless, "These are the best years of my life," Beurling said, and when he was decorated by George VI at Buckingham Palace — he received the Distinguished Service Order, Distinguished Flying Cross, and Distinguished Flying Medal and Bar — he told the king that he had enjoyed every minute in Malta. After being shot down and wounded, Beurling came back to Canada for a publicity tour; then it was back to England for more action, this time with the RCAF, until, in January 1944, he was taken off operations for repeated insubordination. A brilliant lone wolf, Beurling seemingly could not accept the necessity for discipline in the air. He returned home, was again lionized by press and public (something he could not abide), and left the RCAF in August 1944; he died in an unexplained plane crash in Rome four years later, on his way to fight for the infant state of Israel.

Meanwhile, the Allies' preparations for invasion had started by the beginning of 1944. By this time, the *Luftwaffe* had largely withdrawn from French skies; Hitler needed the fighters at home as the Reich attempted to ward off devastating day and night bombing attacks launched by the United States Army Air Force and the RAF and RCAF. That meant that many Spitfires could be converted into fighter-bombers, able to deliver heavy attacks at German air bases, gun positions, or headquarters in France. That activity, in which Typhoon fighter-bombers also participated, increased enormously as the date set for the invasion neared.

By D-Day — June 6, 1944 — the Allies had achieved virtually total air superiority over the Normandy battlefield. The Canadian government, Air Marshal Harold Edwards (the senior RCAF officer overseas), and the senior commanders of the First Canadian Army had all assumed that No. 83 Group of the Second Tactical Air Force would work directly with the Canadian army in France, providing aerial reconnaissance and attacking ground targets. Fifteen of No. 83's twenty-nine squadrons and half its ground establishment of almost 10,000 men were Canadian. Such a powerful force of Mustangs, Spitfires, and Typhoons could respond quickly to calls for air support and roam over the rear areas behind the *Wehrmacht's* lines, shooting up targets at will. But military exigency interfered with this plan; early in 1944 No. 83 Group was assigned to support the Second British Army because it would spearhead the landings. No. 84 Group, with few Canadians and less experience, was designated to provide air support for the First Canadian Army when it came to Normandy later. That caused hurt feelings, but it did not markedly affect the air support offered to either army.

The air forces' mastery of the air did not change for the rest of the war in Europe. American, British, and Canadian soldiers could be almost certain that aircraft overhead were friendly; the *Wehrmacht* had to consider every plane hostile. This edge was crucial in the struggle in Normandy in the summer of 1944. In the first few days after the invasion, Panzer formations suffered delays in reaching the front as their columns were repeatedly attacked by rocket-firing Typhoons, which were very effective in a tank-killing role; the delays helped the Allies secure their beachhead. By August almost all of the tactical squadrons were operating from forward airfields on French soil, which devastated the Germans. RCAF wings alone estimated that they had accounted for 2,600 enemy armoured vehicles and trucks. And when the *Luftwaffe* did take to the air, its pilots, as one RCAF officer noted, were "not the experienced and daring *Luftwaffe* of old, thank goodness!"

The Germans still had tricks up their sleeves, however, as the Allies discovered soon after the invasion of France, when pilotless v-1 flying bombs began falling on British cities. Fortunately, the v-1s, or "buzz bombs", flew slowly enough that fighters could shoot them down. Those that eluded the interceptors and the anti-aircraft weapons flew on noisily until they started their descent — then the interval of silence before the explosion was heart-stopping. That was not the case with the v-2, the first guided missile, which appeared a few months later; it travelled faster than the speed of sound and exploded before those on the ground heard it coming.

The pilots of the RCAF ran up impressive totals of destruction in north-west Europe. No. 126 Fighter Wing claimed 361 enemy aircraft destroyed in more than 22,000 Spitfire sorties. No. 143 Wing, flying the fast, heavily armed Typhoons, dropped almost 6,500 tons of bombs on enemy defences and destroyed 16 bridges, and 3,600 railway cars, vehicles, or barges. The *Luftwaffe* had been driven from the skies and the *Wehrmacht* was virtually paralysed in its tactical movements; in all of this, the RCAF's fighter and fighter-bomber pilots had played their role.

THE BOMBER WAR

Canadians also played a substantial part in the destruction of the German homeland. Undoubtedly, most of the damage inflicted on the enemy by the

RCAF came from bomber crews. Most RCAF casualties were suffered by those same crews.

Although the pre-war strategic planners in the RAF had spent substantial time planning for a bomber war, and although the RAF had bigger and better bombers than the Germans when the war started, the bombing of Germany had begun in an amateurish way. The British bombers at the beginning of the war were slow twin-engined machines capable of carrying only limited bomb loads, and equipped with unsophisticated aiming devices and what would soon be thought to be quaint ideas of morality. Only military and naval targets would be hit, most often without much damage, and the British public was proudly told in such films as *The Lion Has Wings* that no civilians could be hurt in such raids. Yet fighter aircraft could inflict heavy losses on bombers attacking by daylight, as the *Luftwaffe* discovered in August and September 1940. The answer for both sides was night bombing; this made it much easier to get past the enemy's defences, but also meant that any pretence of hitting military targets alone disappeared. Only one in ten of RAF Bomber Command crews in 1941 dropped their payloads within five miles of their targets in the Ruhr.

The RCAF formed its first bomber squadron in June 1941, entirely from Canadians serving in the RAF, and within days the squadron flew its first missions, in twin-engined Wellington bombers (known as "Wimpeys") with a speed of 235 mph. The Wellington was no prize, as this air force song (to the tune of "Bless 'Em All") suggested:

> Worry me, worry me,
> Wellingtons don't worry me,
> Oil-chewing bastards with flaps on their wings,
> Buggered-up pistons, and buggered-up rings,
> The bomb load is so effing small,
> Four-fifths of five-eights of eff-all,
> There'll be such a commotion when we're o'er the ocean,
> So cheer up my lads, eff 'em all.

The next year, seven more RCAF bomber squadrons took to the air, though by this time the technology of the bomber war had begun to alter as scientists raced to improve direction-finding devices. The British now had increasing numbers of four-engined heavy bombers at their disposal. Each new plane could carry up to ten tons of bombs, and target-finding aids like "Oboe", "Gee", "H2s", and improved bombsights were major advances. Oboe used two radar beams, one to direct the bomber towards its target and the other to indicate the point at which the bombs should be dropped. H2s radar bounced an echo off the ground, producing a "map" of the area below on a screen in the bomber. Gee allowed a navigator aboard a bomber to determine his exact position by calculating the difference in travel time between three radio signals transmitted by "master" and "slave" stations on the ground. Pathfinder aircraft now flew ahead of the bomber streams, marking the targets and directing the bomber streams onto them. Pilots like Wing Commander Johnnie Fauquier won fame for their pathfinding work.

The result of these innovations and others was that massive bombing raids became possible by mid-1942. In the space of two years, RAF Bomber Command had gone from virtually undirected single-plane attacks on military targets to co-ordinated thousand-aircraft raids on cities. Moreover, the United States Army Air Force was now in Britain in strength, and its B-17 "Flying Fortresses" flew over Germany by day, their thirteen .50-calibre machine guns taking a toll of the *Luftwaffe* interceptors. The Germans endured the Army Air Force by day and Bomber Command by night.

Against the bombers, the Germans mustered a sophisticated radar network that directed interceptors towards the attackers. *Luftwaffe* fighters soon had effective airborne radar that became more so as the war went on. To counter German radar, the Allies developed "Window", simple strips of aluminum foil that were dropped from the air and appeared as bomber-sized "blips" on the screen. Simple and effective, Window for a time neutralized radar-directed interception. The powerful and accurate radar-controlled anti-aircraft guns that threw up tons of flak at the bombers were also fooled by Window. Only the searchlights raking the skies were unaffected by the aluminum strips, and they provided a terrifying feeling of exposure for night-flying crews.

Air Marshal Arthur Harris, commanding Bomber Command, had become convinced that three hundred bombers were insufficient "to saturate the defences of a major industrial town." By April 1942, the technology existed to direct larger attacking fleets, and on May 30 the first thousand-bomber raid struck Cologne with a monstrous blow that forced the evacuation of 200,000 people and left 6,500 acres of the city in ruins, its cathedral spire rising alone out of the rubble.

Bomber Command then attacked the great city of Hamburg with its population of 1.5 million on July 24, 1943; this was the first raid to use Window. About 10 per cent of the almost eight hundred Lancasters, Halifaxes, Stirlings, and Wellingtons that came at the city in a near-continuous stream were from the RCAF. The first bombers arrived just after 1:00 A.M. to find that the Pathfinders' markers were clearly visible. The German radar, paralysed by

Window, was ineffective; so too were the fighters and the flak, though Hamburg was, next to Berlin, the most heavily defended target in the Reich. The bombers dropped their loads of incendiaries and 4,000- and 8,000-pound blockbusters, and only twelve aircraft were lost. As the Germans would normally have expected to destroy fifty bombers from a force that large, the effect of Window was apparent. Three days later, Bomber Command was back in force, dropping more incendiaries into the still-smouldering ruins. This time a firestorm was created, the flames creating 150-mph winds that fanned the flames further. Howling winds sucked people into the air. Fires devoured the oxygen. People who jumped into rivers and canals for safety boiled to death. At least 50,000 died, 75 per cent of the city lay demolished, and a million survivors fled the ruin and carnage. A week later, Hamburg was hit a third time.

For the bomber crews, the morality or immorality of their task was not something that troubled many. They were under orders, and they had to carry them out. Of course, said Donald Schurman, an RCAF air gunner serving with Bomber Command and later a historian, "every airman who could think had some idea of what we were doing. Nobody was much fooled by talk concerning military targets around which civilian houses 'just happened' to be grouped...." However, he added, "we were very young and we thought it a good idea at the time to kill Germans." Significantly, though a few British clerics and parliamentarians protested the savagery of the bombing, none raised a voice against it in Canada. When Cologne was bombed by a thousand aircraft in 1942, the *Globe and Mail* commented that this was the best way to deal with the "Hunnish hive".

To Hitler, raids such as those on Hamburg were "terror bombing", a not inapt term. German leaders who now complained about area bombing had, of course, all but originated the concept in the Spanish Civil War, and had continued it in their attacks on Warsaw in 1939, Rotterdam in May 1940, and British cities such as Coventry and London in the blitz. But whichever belligerent had started the bombing of civilians, the Allies had brought the technique to perfection, and in the circumstances Hitler had to pull the *Luftwaffe* home to defend the cities and factories, and to urge his scientists to new efforts to counter Window. By 1944 bomber losses were climbing again. On March 30, when 702 aircraft attacked Nuremburg, 94 bombers were downed — an almost insupportable loss.

For bomber crews, the war was terrifyingly dangerous. Casualties were staggering. There was none of the glamour of the fighter pilots for the men in Bomber Command, just long periods of boredom interspersed with moments of sheer terror. Murray Peden, who flew as a pilot with 214 Squadron of RAF

Bomber Command and wrote the very best book on the air war, *A Thousand Shall Fall*, described what a trip or "op" was like:

> Once we hit the enemy coast, the ever-present strain mounted rapidly to the higher level that was the concomitant of being in the enemy's ball park, blindfolded by night. I always waited tensely for the first burst of flak to stab at us, hoping it would not be too close. Once that first burst came up...I breathed a little easier and began the game that every pilot had to play, changing altitude, course, and speed, to throw off the next burst....
>
> At a point about 20 minutes from the target we began to approach an outlying belt of searchlights which stood before us on either side of our intended track in two great cones. I feared and hated those baleful blinding lights more than anything else the Germans used against us.... A pilot trapped in a large cone had little chance of escape....the searchlights' accomplices, the heavy guns, would hurl up shells in streams....

Then there were the *Luftwaffe*'s night fighters, Messerschmitt 110s and, later, jet-powered 410s, firing cannon shells able to riddle the heavy bombers and send them, trailing smoke, to the ground. Some carried upward-pointing guns, and sidled underneath the unknowing bombers to deliver a nasty surprise.

Crews might be able to parachute to safety if their pilot could hold the bomber level long enough for them to jump. If not, they rode their flaming aircraft to almost certain death. If they jumped safely, they were over hostile Germany or occupied Holland or the bitter cold of the North Sea. If they were lucky, they survived the landing and the understandable hostility of German civilians, and made it to a *Stalag Luft*, a POW camp for airmen. If they were even luckier, they might land in Ireland, neutral in the war; though they were interned in the same camp as Germans, these airmen ate splendidly, could leave the camp at will on day passes if they promised to return, and got on well with their guards.

Once in captivity, even in Ireland, it was an officer's duty to try to escape. On March 24–25, 1944, seventy-six Allied airmen participated in the Great Escape from the *Stalag* at Sagan in East Prussia. Three made their way to safety, eighteen were recaptured and returned to Sagan, five ended up at Sachsenhausen concentration camp, and fifty were executed by the ss and Gestapo on Hitler's order. "I can see their faces now," remembered Wally Floody of Toronto, a fighter pilot and an architect of the escape. "The Gestapo and ss took the fifty out, two by two, and under the pretext of allowing them to answer the call of nature, dispatched them with shots in the back of the head." Six of those murdered were RCAF officers: flight lieutenants Pat Langford of Penticton, British Columbia; George McGill of Toronto; Jimmy Wernham of Winnipeg; Gordon Kidder of St. Catharines, Ontario; George Wiley of Windsor; and Hank Birkland of Calgary. After the war, the Allies hunted down and hanged fourteen Nazis for their part in this murder.

The main Canadian share in the bomber war was borne by No. 6 Group, formed January 1, 1943, with eight squadrons. At its peak, No. 6 included fourteen RCAF bomber squadrons. Based in Yorkshire, No. 6 Group's officers and men became part of the community, in between their night-time visits to German airspace. They learned to drink tea and to avoid the NAAFI (Navy, Army, and Air Force Institutes) canteens if they could, they took out local girls, visited pubs, and accepted invitations for Sunday dinners from Yorkshire families. They named their aircraft after girls back home. And they tried to avoid dwelling on the fact that less than one-third of them would survive their 30-ops tours. It was hard to escape that realization. Before takeoff, one crew member said, you looked around at the sun and the trees, and you "think about the folks at home and how they're going to feel if you go missing." For this, sergeant pilots drew $3.70 a day.

No. 6 Group suffered from serious problems in its first year of operations. There were more training accidents than the norm, and more operational losses too. Between March and June 1943, losses amounted to more than a hundred aircraft, a rate that virtually guaranteed that no more than one in eight crews would survive their tours. Part of the reason for the heavy losses was bad luck, part the old machines the group had to fly. A lot was due to the extra distance No. 6 Group's aircraft had to fly to reach Germany from their Yorkshire stations, and the high risk of fog, snow, and sleet in the Vale of York. Too much was due to inexperience at the top. Commanders lacked the skill or the will to motivate their crews to press on to the target and not to abort their ops before German airspace was reached or, as often happened, before takeoff.

When Air Vice-Marshal "Black Mike" McEwen, a Canadian ace of the Great War, took over the group in January 1944, training was stepped up and discipline was reinforced. McEwen enforced dress regulations and, more important, he went on operations — something few senior officers ever did — acquiring the status of a good luck charm. There were further heavy losses after he took over, but gradually his discipline and some good luck reversed the numbers, and morale in No. 6 greatly improved. By this time all the squadrons had acquired Lancasters or Halifaxes in place of Wellingtons, and that helped. The Lanc was a wonder to fly; it could go 272 mph, and was almost as manoeuvrable as a fighter. It carried a seven-man crew and from seven to eleven tons of bombs, and it had nine .303 machine guns for defence. The Halifax, just slightly faster and with the same armament, had a record of being able to absorb punishment and still get its crew home. The confidence produced by those bombers was deserved. Then, as the D-Day invasion grew near and targets were chosen in France rather than in well-defended Germany, losses dropped further.

Raw courage also helped boost morale, and some actions stood out even in those areas where courage was the norm. Pilot Officer Andrew Mynarski, a twenty-seven–year–old air gunner from Winnipeg, was aboard a Lancaster from 419 Squadron when it bombed Cambrai six days after D-Day. Attacked from below by a *Luftwaffe* fighter and set afire, the Lancaster spun out of control. The pilot ordered the crew to bail out. Mynarski left his gun turret and went towards the escape hatch, but saw that the rear gunner was trapped. The citation for Mynarski's Victoria Cross described what happened next:

Without hesitation...Mynarski made his way through the flames in an endeavour to move the turret and release the gunner. Whilst so doing, his parachute and his clothing, up to the waist, were set on fire.... Eventually the rear gunner clearly indicated to him that there was nothing more he could do and that he should try to save his own life. Pilot Officer Mynarski reluctantly went back through the flames to the escape hatch. There, as a last gesture to the trapped gunner, he turned towards him, stood to attention in his flaming clothes and saluted, before he jumped out of the aircraft.... He was found eventually by the French, but was so severely burnt that he died from his injuries.

The rear gunner miraculously survived the crash, and his account of Mynarski's courage led to the posthumous award of the VC.

No. 6 Group played a major share in the bomber offensive. Its aircraft flew 41,000 ops and dropped 126,000 tons of bombs. That was almost one-eighth of the total dropped by all of Bomber Command. Those No. 6 Group bombs accounted for a goodly portion of the 560,000 dead and 675,000 wounded Germans.

In thirty months of action, No. 6 Group lost 3,500 men. Another 4,700 Canadians died while serving with other Bomber Command squadrons. Others were wounded, many suffering disfiguring injuries from burns; plastic surgeons like Dr. A. Ross Tilley of Toronto won fame for their efforts in re-creating faces for men whose ears and noses had been burned away. The victims called themselves "guinea pigs", and Tilley called them "a pretty tough group....there was always someone worse. They never allowed one another to feel sorry for themselves." But in the dark of the night, the horror of their disfigurement must have been all-consuming.

How effective the bombing carried out at such human cost was at winning the war remains unclear, as the United States Strategic Bombing Survey, compiled after the German surrender, showed. Raids on cities such as Cologne, Hamburg, and Dresden wreaked havoc and forced tens of thousands of German survivors to live in great discomfort in the ruins of their homes. Undoubtedly that hurt morale; undoubtedly the loss of sleep hampered workers at their jobs. But there is also no doubt that German war production continued to rise almost to the end of the war. More tanks, for example, were produced in 1944 than in any previous year. How much greater the production would have been without the bombing is uncertain, although the factories would presumably have poured out even more weapons than they did. The German armies also continued to fight with great skill and savagery until May 1945; whether that savagery increased because of the bombing of civilians is a moot point.

The RCAF bomber crews — like the fighter pilots, transport crews, and ground crews — had done dangerous and difficult wartime jobs with increasing professionalism and skill. They believed that they had played a major part in the war's outcome, and their commanders thought the same. When Air Chief Marshal Arthur "Bomber" Harris said farewell to Canadian air crew going home in 1945, he told his boys that "when you come to dandle your children on your knee, and they ask, 'What did you do in the last war, daddy?' you can tell them that you won it, because you did."

In all, a quarter of a million Canadians served in the RCAF and RAF, with 94,000 going overseas. Of these, 17,101 failed to return. Mackenzie King had favoured the idea of the BCATP in 1939 because he believed that air casualties could never be so numerous as to lead to a cry for conscription. But RCAF deaths were almost exactly equal to army battle fatalities in the European theatre. War had changed between 1939 and 1945, and nowhere was this change felt so clearly as in the war in the air.

XV
SICILY AND ITALY

After the Dieppe débâcle in August 1942, the Canadian army in Britain had returned to its exercises, more than a little sobered by the casualties that had befallen the 2nd Division. The *Wehrmacht*'s reputation as near-supermen had been enhanced yet again. But so had the quality of Canadian training. Dieppe had forced a tough new realism, including live ammunition, in exercises for the once-jaded infantrymen.

By November of that year General Bernard Montgomery's Eighth Army had decisively defeated General Erwin Rommel's Afrika Korps at the battle of El Alamein, bringing nearer the end of the see-sawing campaign that had seen British and German-Italian forces alternately advancing and retreating across North Africa for two years. At almost exactly the same time as the victory of El Alamein, the Soviets surrounded the besieging German army at Stalingrad, cutting their supply lines and reducing them to starvation, and British and American forces landed in Algeria and Morocco and began moving east. Supermen or not, the Germans could be beaten.

By January of 1943 the German army at Stalingrad had been demolished, and by May the Germans had also been totally defeated in North Africa, crushed between Montgomery's army and the combined forces of the First British and Seventh U.S. armies led by General Dwight Eisenhower. What was to be next for the Allies? The decision had already been taken. At Casablanca in January 1943, Prime Minister Churchill and President Roosevelt and their military chiefs had agreed that the next operation should take place in the Mediterranean theatre, with the aim of forcing Mussolini's Italy out of the war. There was a range of possibilities: Italy itself could be invaded, or Sicily, Sardinia, or Corsica. Sicily was chosen, primarily because its capture would make the Mediterranean Sea virtually an Allied lake, and the two leaders quickly decided that Eisenhower would once again be in command. Under him would be General Harold Alexander, hitherto the overall commander of Britain's Middle East forces. In February, Montgomery and General George Patton, a successful American tank commander in North Africa, were placed

251

in command of the invading British and American armies. On April 23, after discreet prior negotiations, the Chief of the Imperial General Staff, General Sir Alan Brooke, invited General McNaughton to contribute a Canadian infantry division and tank brigade to the invading force. Two days later, having consulted Ottawa, McNaughton accepted the proposal and named the 1st Canadian Infantry Division and the 1st Army Tank Brigade for the operation.

BLOODING IN SICILY

By April 1943 the First Canadian Army in Britain was a very substantial force. It included army headquarters, two corps headquarters, three infantry and two armoured divisions, and two army tank brigades — in all, almost a quarter of a million Canadian soldiers. These soldiers were for the most part young — about twenty years old on average. Half came from big cities, half from small towns and farms. Most were uneducated; many lacked even Grade 6 education. The army was full of Depression kids, those who had suffered the worst the "Dirty Thirties" had to offer. They might be young and untaught, but they were tough.

Their commander, the General Officer Commanding the First Canadian Army — Andy McNaughton — had vigorously resisted attempts by Whitehall and Ottawa to divide his command and employ the army in bits and pieces. The First Canadian Army was Canada's and his own, and McNaughton intended to lead it into battle as a great national force.

But by 1943, many units of the army had been in England for more than three years without hearing enemy fire. Training was an essential preparation for battle, but too much of it was hard on morale. Moreover, training was not the same as combat, and if the troops didn't get a taste of battle they might suffer grievously when they were finally dumped into large-scale action. There were also considerations of national prestige and self-respect. Was Canada's land force contribution to the war to be limited to Hong Kong and Dieppe?

A few hundred Canadian officers and NCOs had already been sent on a tour of duty in the North African campaign to get battle experience. When the British requested more troops for Sicily, Ottawa was quick to agree. Defence minister J.L. Ralston told the Cabinet War Committee that "he was 100 percent behind the decision. That it would give battle experience without which it was questionable whether the morale of the Army could be maintained."

The invasion of the Italian island, codenamed "Husky", was to be launched by the Seventh U.S. Army and the British Eighth Army in the second week in July. The 1st Canadian Division was to come under British command, and to be led by Major-General H.L.N. Salmon. But the division's first losses came well before it went into action; General Salmon and some of his staff died in an airplane crash on April 29 while en route to Cairo for briefings. Within hours, McNaughton had given the command to Major-General Guy Simonds, an RMC graduate, a former gunner, and at thirty-nine Canada's youngest general. Simonds had been one of the officers in North Africa under General Montgomery, an obvious advantage.

Simonds now had the job of getting his new division and the tank brigade ready for their role in Sicily. That meant training in Scotland for an amphibious landing and for mountain warfare, and issuing and breaking in new equipment including a rocket launcher called the Projector Infantry Anti-Tank (PIAT), and the U.S.-built Sherman tank. It meant that Simonds and his operations staff had to put the new commander's personal stamp on the plans already prepared for the Canadian landing. It meant that the divisional headquarters had to plan how to load each transport and troop carrier in a succession of convoys so that everything needed would be available at the right time and place. To carry the Canadian division, ninety-two ships would have to be organized into a fast assault convoy, a slow assault convoy carrying the bulk of the transport and supplies, and two follow-up convoys carrying the tank brigade — except for one armoured regiment which was to land with the first waves. The first, slow convoy left England on June 19; the last, the fast assault convoy, on June 28. Unluckily, three ships in the slow assault convoy were torpedoed in the Mediterranean with the loss of fifty-eight Canadians, five hundred vehicles, and some guns.

The Allied invasion plan targeted the south and south-west coasts of the island. The Americans were to land on the left from Licata to Scoglitti, the British and Canadians on the right from west of Pachino to Syracuse. Airborne forces would go in before the sea landing. No fortified port would be attacked — a lesson of the Dieppe raid — and heavy naval fire support would precede the assault.

The defenders included large numbers of Italian conscripts organized into weak coastal units, low in morale and poorly trained. The German forces, in strength in Sicily only since May 1943, consisted of two motorized formations, the 15th and 90th Panzer Grenadier divisions, and the Hermann Goering Panzer Division. All three were recently reconstituted divisions, full of untried reinforcements. They would fight and fight well, however, unlike Mussolini's dispirited and badly armed troops, and the rugged topography, traversed by narrow dirt roads and defiles and passes, made Sicily ideal for defence.

Simonds had been advised by intelligence reports that beach defences were fairly light in the Canadian sector, the extreme tip of the Pachino peninsula.

The general's assault plan called for two brigades to hit the beach at 2:45 A.M. on July 10. Belated discovery of a sandbar in front of the Canadian beaches forced some hasty improvisations.

The major objective was Pachino airfield. That, like almost all the invading forces' objectives, was taken at negligible cost in the first hours of invasion, despite a storm that blew up a heavy swell. The sandbar forced some of the troops out of their LCA landing craft and into DUKWs — American-built amphibious trucks, made partially of wood, that could run on land as well as water. (General Montgomery, landing in Sicily aboard a DUKW, was said to have told his driver, "Steer away from the troops; if they recognize me they'll wonder why I'm not walking on water.") The port of Syracuse fell on the first day and three days later Augusta was taken. Patton's men struck out to the west and north-west, faced only by weak Italian opposition. Montgomery's Eighth Army moved northward along the coastal plain, the Canadians moving through mountainous terrain to hold the western edge of the British advance.

If any of the Canadians expected to find spaghetti and meatballs awaiting them in little trattorias, they were to be disappointed. Apart from purloined fruit and "liberated" livestock, food was the ubiquitous and much despised British "compo pack", here described by Lieutenant Farley Mowat of the Hastings and Prince Edward Regiment (Hasty Pees):

> ...the compo pack consisted of a wooden crate containing everything fourteen men were supposed to require for twenty-four hours: hard-tack biscuits in lieu of bread; canned yellow wax, misleadingly labelled margarine; tins of M&V (unidentifiable scraps of fat and gristle mushed up with equally unidentifiable vegetables); canned processed cheese which tasted like, and may well have been, casein glue; powdered tea, milk and sugar, all ready mixed; turnip jam (laughingly labelled strawberry or raspberry); eight (count them) tiny hard candies for each man; seven India-made Victory cigarettes which, it was rumoured, were manufactured from the dung of sacred cattle; six squares of toilet paper per man...; and one further item...a twelve-ounce can of treacle pudding that was an irresistible object of desire...we were starving for sweet stuffs.

British rations never reached a high standard, in England or in the field. But Private Mel Perrin of the 48th Highlanders was soon writing home to Toronto that "We have had quite a few ripe oranges, grapes, lemons, figs and so forth...." Even so, "I would give anything to be back buying those things...."

Others received food parcels from home. One soldier listed the contents of a parcel from his brother and sister-in-law: "One large tin of chicken, one tin of pork & beans, 3 pkgs of lemon, 1 tin of Kam, 1 small fruit cake, 5 bags of fruit drinks, 4 chocolate bars, 4 cubes Oxo, 1 pound cheese, 1 candy roll, 1 tin of lobsters" — and told his wife that three more parcels were on the way. "So, you see, Darling, I have quite a few things to eat."

The Sicilian roads were so bad that mule trains had to be improvised to haul food and ammunition forward over the hills. Private Jack Ainsworth of a Service Corps transport company told his parents how the mules had been rounded up. "We just took them where we saw them, on the road pulling wagons or in a field where we could catch them." One "old boy" had tried to say his beast was lame; "That didn't save his mule for him though." Incidents like that tended to turn the Sicilians, generally happy at the prospect of liberation, into bitter people who felt their fascist overlords had been replaced by equally uncaring foreigners.

By July 15, after a relatively untroubled advance (except for the hills, the dust, and the lack of water), the Canadians finally encountered the German defence — and it was skilful and well planned. The Germans' object was delay. As Brigadier Howard Graham of the 1st Brigade recalled, they would station "a minimum force of mobile troops and guns on half-track vehicles at innumerable strategic points at four- or five-mile intervals. By so doing, they forced us to deploy a force ten times their own numbers." The Allies expended time and energy and suffered casualties, and around the next bend in the road the entire exercise had to be repeated. By July 17 the Canadians had taken Piazza Armerina, in the centre of Sicily, after a stiff fight, but the battle had delayed their advance for a full twenty-four hours.

A few miles farther north lay Valguarnera, held in force by the 15th Panzer Grenadiers. Simonds decided to use two of his three infantry brigades in the attack. The 3rd Brigade led off with the Van Doos in front, riding in trucks. The Van Doos were temporarily stopped by a large crater in the road; they filled it in and continued in the moonlight until stopped again by heavy machine-gun fire from a German patrol. After repelling the patrol, they dug in for the rest of the night. The next morning, Brigadier M.H.S. Penhale sent all his battalions forward, taking the critical road junction en route to Valguarnera. Meanwhile Brigadier Graham's 1st Brigade had sent the Hasty Pees cross-country over rugged terrain to the heights overlooking Valguarnera. While half the regiment shot up German vehicles, the remaining two companies fought off a German counter-attack, then retreated to firmer defensive positions. The Royal Canadian Regiment (RCR) was simultaneously attacking from the front, while the 48th Highlanders descended on the town from the hills to the south.

Valguarnera was a confused struggle, and a costly one. Canadian losses were 40 killed and 105 wounded. The enemy lost 280 captured and at least 200 killed or wounded. Field Marshal Albert Kesselring, the German commander, told Berlin that "troops trained for fighting in the mountains" had been encountered. "They are called Mountain Boys and probably belong to the 1st Cdn Division." That was almost a tribute.

Taking Leonforte and Assoro would also be difficult, thanks again to the terrain and stubborn defence. Assoro fell after the Hasty Pees, led by Major the Lord Tweedsmuir (son of a former governor general of Canada), scaled an astonishing cliff in the dark and, at dawn, found the German defenders below eating breakfast and washing, completely unaware of their enemies' presence. At Agira, Simonds put together a tremendous artillery barrage moving forward a hundred yards at a time; behind the exploding shells came the infantry. As often happened, though, the shelling had missed several enemy strongpoints, and the town was taken only after air attacks and bitter hand-to-hand fighting. Lieutenant John Dougan of the Loyal Edmonton Regiment had led his platoon behind the German lines when a German tank appeared at a bend in the road:

> Time seemed to stand still at that moment. Our PIAT man calmly and resolutely fired his anti-tank projectile — and missed! With the tank's gun now bearing almost directly on us, the PIAT man recocked his weapon and against all recognized procedures stood up and fired the gun from his shoulder. The recoil bowled him over but the projectile this time found its mark....

The PIAT was unwieldly and weighed thirty-two pounds, but was effective against virtually every German tank — if fired from close range.

By the end of July, the Canadians were pressing into Regalbuto, against heavy resistance and in the face of extreme mid-summer heat. The town fell on August 2 and by the 6th the Van Doos were knocking at the gates of Adrano. At that point — after twenty-seven days of hard fighting — the Canadians were pulled out of the line and into army reserve. Sicily would finally be in Allied hands after thirty-eight days.

Early in the Sicilian campaign, General McNaughton had arrived in Malta and had asked General Montgomery for permission to go to Sicily to see his 1st Division in action. Montgomery had refused; as he wrote in his memoirs, the division was just finding its feet and Simonds was "young and inexperienced — it was the first time he had commanded a division in battle." Moreover, Simonds' own response to the proposed visit had been "For God's sake keep him away."

By the time McNaughton paid his visit — after the fighting had ended — the division had marched 130 miles through the dust and heat, and had paid a heavy price: 2,310 officers and men, including 562 dead. All the same, the losses were not unusually high for a division in constant battle, and the division — often nicknamed the "Old Red Patch" for its distinguishing rectangular shoulder-flash — had faced a series of graduated challenges that prepared the Canadian formation for bigger tests to come.

UP THE ITALIAN BOOT TO ORTONA

While the Germans and the Allies battled over Sicily, events in Italy took their own course. Benito Mussolini's policies had brought nothing but disaster, and on July 25 Il Duce was toppled from power. On September 8, 1943, Marshal Pietro Badoglio, Mussolini's successor, announced that Italy had surrendered unconditionally, thus becoming the first Axis power to pull out of the war. Unfortunately, that changed little; the Germans simply took control of the country, put most of the Italian army in prisoner of war camps, and let loose the Gestapo to enforce Hitler's will. In Italy, as in Sicily, the Allies would have to advance against the entrenched and disciplined lines of the *Wehrmacht*.

Just before the assault on Italy, 1st Canadian Division headquarters issued its men a little booklet on Italy, mixing history, commentary, and crude stereotype. The Fascist Party, they were told, "is not in the least like our Conservative, C.C.F. or Liberal parties." The discipline of the Italian people was "generally slack" and they would "take to guns and knives instead of fists to settle a quarrel.... As to the women," the booklet said, more in hope than in expectation, "the less you have to do with them, the better."

The Allied plan called for the Eighth Army to cross the Straits of Messina on September 3 and surge up the toe of the Italian boot. The Fifth U.S. Army would land at Salerno, south of Naples, on September 9 and cut off the enemy's retreat. These landings were carried out as planned. Meanwhile the 1st Canadian Division landed just north of the port of Reggio Calabria and took it without effective resistance. Indeed, the Van Doos invaded a fort near Reggio only to find all its officers eating breakfast in their best uniforms while the fort's guns stood unmanned. "Seen very little of Jerry," a private wrote home to Canada on September 14, "and the Wop isn't worth bothering with." Within a week, in the face of *Wehrmacht* delaying actions, the division had pushed seventy-five miles forward.

After the Salerno landing, the Eighth and Fifth armies had to join up as quickly as possible. Montgomery ordered Simonds to take Potenza, a road junction fifty miles east of Salerno, and this was accomplished on September 20. Two days later, however, Simonds fell ill with jaundice and was replaced temporarily by Brigadier Christopher Vokes, a big, explosive peacetime soldier. On October 1, Naples fell to the Allies, and by that date the Canadian division — some of which had been operating along the east coast towards Taranto — was reunited in the centre of the peninsula, close to Campobasso.

By this time Hitler had ordered that Rome must be held at all cost, not only for its symbolic value but because its airfields were perilously close to Germany. The first sign of the new enemy resolve came at Motta Montecorvino, where the Royal Canadian Regiment and tanks of the Calgary Regiment ran into the 3rd regiment of the 1st Parachute Division, a *Luftwaffe* formation with a well-earned reputation as an elite force. The paras resisted fiercely for as long as possible, then withdrew without notice to the next defensible feature. The tactic was delay; the Germans had decided to move into a winter defence line fifty miles north of Campobasso, and south of Rome.

The delaying actions lasted for another month, and were costly to the advancing Canadians. Farley Mowat later wrote that he went out with the padre and a burial party to recover the bodies of some Hastings and Prince Edward Regiment soldiers killed a few days earlier. The bodies had bloated. "They did not look like men anymore. They had become obscene parodies of men.... For the first time I truly understood that the dead...were dead." At the time he wrote home to say that he wondered why it was Lieutenant Swayle and his men who had died. "Why him? Why them? And when will it be you? That's the sort of question you ask yourself."

Decisions were now being made that would determine the deaths and lives of many more Canadians. The original intent had been that the 1st Division would return to England after Sicily was taken. That, obviously, had not happened. Public opinion had been so positive about the fighting in Sicily that Ottawa was persuaded that Italy was a good place to send troops. Now, after several efforts by the Canadian government, the British agreed to send I Canadian Corps headquarters (some 8,500 men in all, including ancillary units) under General Harry Crerar to Italy, along with the 5th Canadian Armoured Division. The Canadian convoy was attacked by *Luftwaffe* JU-88s and one ship sank, though so slowly that there was no loss of life. Among the rescued were ninety-eight Canadian nursing sisters.

The defence minister, Colonel Ralston, had overridden General McNaughton's desire to keep the army together and had decided that the opportunity for a corps to fight and gain experience — and flattering publicity — was too great to pass up. General Alexander in Italy was unhappy that the decision had been made without consulting him. A raw armoured division was the last thing needed in Italy's steep hills and narrow valleys. McNaughton was furious that his cherished Canadian army would be split. The general's performance on exercises in England had led the British to doubt his ability to command the First Canadian Army in action, and now their concern — and his unhappiness — resulted in his enforced resignation from command by the end of the year. Having proved himself with the infantry division, Simonds took command of the 5th Armoured as of November 1 (although the division was not ready for action until the beginning of 1944). Vokes — whom Montgomery described as "a good rough cook" in comparison to the brilliant Simonds — was confirmed in command of the 1st Division.

The decision to split the army meant that Canada now had to maintain two supply and reinforcement lines — one to Britain and, once the invasion of France had taken place, to north-west Europe, and one through the Mediterranean to Italy. For a small nation this was a heavy burden, absorbing scarce manpower without any of the benefits of economy of scale. From that point of view, McNaughton's desire to keep the army together made eminent sense. But Ralston knew that troops had to see action and commanders had to gain experience. Also, ordinary Canadians felt that, without soldiers fighting, Canada was somehow out of the war. No number of bombers or corvettes could substitute for fighting divisions.

The Allies' advance on Rome was now blocked by the formidable obstacle of the Germans' winter line, which had its Adriatic base on the Moro river, two miles south of the town of Ortona. After stiff fighting on the upper Sangro River, Vokes' division was given the task of taking Ortona. As usual, the geography of the Italian peninsula favoured the defenders. First the division had to cross the Moro, an effort begun on December 6, 1943. The valley of the Moro was deep, cut by gullies and ridges, and, thanks to *Wehrmacht* demolitions, unbridged. The German defenders were the crack 90th Light Panzer Grenadier Division, famous from the desert war.

Initially the attack went well, infantry of the Princess Patricia's Canadian Light Infantry (PPCLI) fording the Moro at midnight without any covering fire. The enemy, surprised in their beds at Villa Rogatti, were driven out of the village. At San Leonardo the Seaforth Highlanders had more difficulty once the lead companies had waded across the Moro. Fifteen to twenty machine guns sprayed the attackers, who had only a small bridgehead after five hours' fighting. The morning brought the inevitable heavy counter-attack on the PPCLI, but that was driven off with the aid of British tanks. So was a second enemy effort, supported this time by Panzers. The German unit's war diarist praised the fire discipline of the Patricias, "who let our tanks approach to within 50 metres and then destroyed them." The Moro bridgeheads survived.

By December 8, the Canadians were ready for another major two-brigade assault across the river, supported by the troops who had won the bridgehead two days before. The soldiers were shivering from tension and cold weather, despite their long johns, wool shirts, khaki sweaters, scarves, and battledress jackets. Each man carried his rifle, several clips of .303 ammunition, an awkward and uncomfortable "tin hat" (worn now over a wool toque or balaclava), a shovel, a can or two of food, cigarettes, lucky charms and a few personal mementos, and extra socks. Most carried a grenade or two, and some unlucky souls were inevitably detailed to lug extra magazines of ammunition for the three Bren guns that each platoon of infantry had. The platoon commander's signaller had a heavy radio with a large aerial whipping back and forth. Soldiers waddled rather than ran; they could hardly do more.

Matthew Halton of the CBC watched the preliminary bombardment of the German lines over the Moro and recorded the scene for broadcast back to Canada:

> It's a terrific shelling. We get one or two enemy shells every minute on this position; the Germans get hundreds every minute on theirs. The valley of the Moro down there, through which our infantry have to attack, is one dense pall of smoke, and we can hardly see the town of Ortona, just a few miles away.

Led by the Royal Canadian Regiment and the 48th Highlanders, the division fought its way towards San Leonardo, greatly assisted by a field company of the Royal Canadian Engineers who built a bridge across the river despite heavy enemy fire. Tanks could now get across the Moro to beat back the enemy's counter-attacks, though mines and the terrain still posed enormous problems for the armour. Meanwhile the Seaforths, with tanks of the Calgary Regiment, were assisting in the battle for the town by pressing out of their bridgehead. One company of infantry riding aboard a squadron of tanks suffered heavily — two tanks rolled off a cliff and another blew up on a mine — but five tanks and the thirty-nine surviving infantry cleared the town. Lieutenant J.F. Maclean of the Seaforths led his platoon so effectively in silencing the German machine-gunners that he won the Distinguished Service Order, an award only rarely given to junior officers. It was "our first real battle on a divisional level with the Germans," the 1st Division's headquarters noted.

The Loyal Edmonton Regiment, who were in the thick of the fighting, had the grimness of the struggle eased by the presence within their lines of sheds full of hogsheads of maturing *vino*. "Most of these casks," the Eddies' padre remembered, "were being breached by 'stray bullets', shrapnel and 'other weapons'. There seemed to be a continuous party (with no cheese) interrupted by much fierce fighting against the enemy, they being only a short distance away."

Further counter-attacks by the *Wehrmacht* were beaten off, and the Germans finally conceded San Leonardo and withdrew to new positions. At the same time Field Marshal Kesselring, still trying to delay the Allies' advance at all cost, had the 2nd Battalion of the 3rd Parachute Regiment reinforce the *Wehrmacht* troops defending Ortona.

The Canadians had yet to reach Ortona. There was a lengthy and gruelling struggle around "The Gully", a long ravine that extended in front of the Ortona–Orsogna road. Here the mud was almost as much of an enemy as the Germans, impeding movement and engulfing the tanks and trucks. The Germans were dug into the forward slope of the ravine, fighting with a ferocity that was, for the Canadians, absolutely unprecedented. Not until December 13, when an attack by Seaforth Highlanders and the West Nova Scotia Regiment made some headway, was the defence breached. Then the Van Doos took up the charge, aiming at Casa Berardi, a grandly named cluster of farm buildings.

Defending the Casa were units of the 1st Parachute Division. At the van of the attack were the eighty-one men of the Van Doos' c Company, led by Captain Paul Triquet and backed by seven tanks of the Ontario Regiment. The Canadians jumped off at 7:00 A.M., after an hour of artillery preparation, and at first made good progress. But after they had gained a few hundred yards, the Germans counter-attacked with four tanks and a company of infantry. The exchange of fire came to an astonishing halt when an Italian woman and two children headed for the Canadian position. It resumed after they were under cover, and once a second Panzer had been destroyed the counter-attack fizzled out.

By this point, c Company had fifty men left. The surviving tanks tackled the machine guns that had caused most of the casualties, and Triquet carried on towards the farmhouses, still a mile and a half away. By noon, Triquet's command had shrunk to thirty men, and the Germans had effectively surrounded the little band. As Triquet told his men, "Never mind them, they can't shoot. There are enemies in front of us, behind us and on our flanks, there is only one safe place, that is on the objective." That seemed true, and by 2:00 P.M. Triquet had finally reached Casa Berardi, with fourteen men and the tanks. Casa Berardi was still occupied by the paratroopers, so Triquet had to clear the buildings while simultaneously beating off enemy attacks. The order of the day was "Ils ne passeront pas," and indeed the Germans did not pass. All through the rest of that day and into the night the Van Doos held their prize, until at 11:00 P.M. reinforcements arrived.

The battle continued all the next day. The reinforcing company of the Royal 22e suffered heavily, and additional reinforcements did not arrive until after midnight on the second day of battle. The Royal Canadian Regiment linked up with the Van Doos and consolidated the breakthrough on December 19. c Company by this point had nine men left including its commander. Triquet, thirty-three years old, was promoted to major and won the Victoria Cross, the first awarded to a Canadian in Italy.

Ortona, the anchor of the German line, now seemed open to the Canadians. But Hitler had put the highest priority on holding the town, and the Germans dutifully obeyed. By December 21, the Seaforth Highlanders and the Loyal Edmonton Regiment were clearing houses in the town, struggling forward house by house and street by street. The more experienced soldiers of the 1st Parachute Division had used demolitions effectively to channel the attackers into the main square, which they had selected as a "killing zone" and surrounded with machine guns and mortars. They also attempted to mousetrap the advancing infantrymen into houses wired with explosives, blowing up the house once the Canadians were inside. A platoon of the Edmonton Regiment was destroyed that way, except for one soldier who was found alive in the rubble after more than eighty hours. But the Canadians could play that game as well: infantry pioneers laid charges under two buildings occupied by the Germans, and an estimated two enemy platoons were buried by the simultaneous explosions.

Most of the struggle for Ortona took place in the row houses of the town. Mouseholing parties blasted through walls with explosives, then advanced with grenades and Sten guns clearing the path. It was brutal fighting, like a little Stalingrad. As General Vokes said, "Everything before Ortona was a nursery tale." Halton of the CBC told his audience, with wartime hyperbole, "The Germans were demons; the Canadians were possessed by demons. The more murderous the battle, the harder both sides fought...." Yet on Christmas Day, in the ruins of the Church of Santa Maria di Constantinopoli, Christmas dinner was somehow put together for the Seaforth Highlanders. "This was really a fantastic thing," Halton told Canada:

> not four hundred yards from the enemy, carol singers, the platoons coming in relays to eat a Christmas dinner — men who hadn't had their clothes off

in thirty days coming in and eating their dinners, and carol singers singing "Silent Night".

"Well," the padre of the regiment said, "at last I've got you all in church." For many of the Seaforths, this Christmas dinner was their last supper.

The 48th Highlanders had no Christmas respite — or dinner. They had worked their way behind the German defences on December 22–23 in an attempt to cut off the retreat of the paratroopers, and they spent forty-eight hours under constant fire. Not until Christmas night did reinforcements from the Saskatoon Light Infantry, a machine-gun regiment, make it to the 48th's lines; tanks of the Ontario Regiment got there the next night.

By December 27, the town was almost entirely in Canadian hands. That night the Germans simply disappeared in a well-managed withdrawal, all the more impressive for being staged when the Canadians were breathing down their throats. Ortona had been taken at last.

The 1st Canadian Division had lost 2,339 officers and men since the first attack on the Moro on December 8. Sickness or battle exhaustion had forced the evacuation of 1,600 more, including Brigadier Graham of the 1st Brigade. While reinforcements had been received, the division was still more than a thousand men below strength. Worse, every infantry battalion had suffered 50 per cent casualties in its rifle companies, the experienced men killed and wounded being virtually irreplaceable. The survivors were shaken and exhausted.

"Without a pause for reorganization," General Vokes said, "the offensive power of an infantry division was bound to become spent, not for lack of offensive spirit, but because the quality of team play within the rifle companies had deteriorated." That was true enough; indeed the entire Allied attack was grinding to a halt. Even so, Ortona had been a victory for the Canadians. "We smashed the 90th Panzer Grenadier Division," Vokes reported, "and we gave the 1st German Parachute Division a mauling which it will long remember." The 1st Canadian Division — and the widows and grieving mothers of its many dead — would remember it too.

NORTH TO THE SENIO

The Canadians got their respite, but the winter of 1944 was no Italian holiday. Although the front was largely static, patrolling and limited attacks continued. One private in the 48th Highlanders wrote on January 27 of "the whistling shells and whirr of bullets.... My nerves are not what they used to be and Jerry is really putting up quite a fight." But there were no major attacks and that allowed I Canadian Corps to go through a number of command changes. Guy Simonds left the 5th Canadian Armoured Division before it had seen much action to return to England and take command of II Canadian Corps for the upcoming invasion of France. He was succeeded by Major-General E.L.M. Burns, an intellectual but uncharismatic soldier who had served in the Permanent Force's signal corps. In March, Lieutenant-General Crerar returned to England to take over the First Canadian Army and Burns became commander of I Canadian Corps. Italy had been the training ground for Simonds and, less so, for Crerar. Montgomery, transferred to command the imminent D-Day invasion, would remember them both.

Despite the advances of the Allies, Rome remained in German hands, protected by heavy defences. The Americans had landed at Anzio, near the Italian capital, in January, but the Germans had quickly sealed off the beachhead. Farther south, the Eighth Army's advance had been blocked by the Gustav Line (and, a few miles behind that, the Adolf Hitler line). Over them all towered the massive bulk of Monte Cassino, impregnable and awesome, topped by the ruins of its great Benedictine monastery. During the early spring the Eighth Army — which, in addition to its Canadian divisions, had Indian, New Zealand, Polish, Greek, and British formations — was transferred secretly to the Monte Cassino area.

The battle for Rome began at 11:00 P.M. on May 11, when a thousand guns opened up on the defences of the Gustav Line. Tanks of the 1st Canadian Armoured Brigade participated in the opening battles in support of the 8th Indian Division. Brigadier Bill Murphy, in command of the brigade, wrote proudly, "My tanks were the first over the river.... Our losses in both tanks and personnel have been astoundingly light thank God and we are still full of fight." The 1st Canadian Division joined in on May 16, its actions helping to clear the way for the Poles who finally captured Monte Cassino on May 18. The Gustav Line had been breached; the Adolf Hitler Line was next.

I Canadian Corps moved into the action on May 23, Canadian soldiers fighting as a corps for the first time during the war. The French Expeditionary Corps had pushed through a lightly fortified part of the Hitler Line on May 17 and threatened the German rear, but the defences in front of the Canadian Corps remained strong. In a day-long and costly battle the Canadian 1st and 5th Armoured divisions cracked the Hitler Line, with its earthworks, pillboxes, bunkers, mines, and huge concentrations of concertina wire that hung up unlucky soldiers just as it had their fathers in the trenches of Flanders. The tanks poured through the gap carved out by the infantry. Lieutenant John Windsor, a troop commander in Lord Strathcona's Horse, remembered his regiment pushing forward up the Liri valley towards the Melfa River. "A mile, two miles, three miles, crashing through tangled woods and trim orchards." Others had been hit, Windsor said, "but I was indestructible." A moment later, a German shell crashed into his Sherman. It promptly burned, or "brewed up", and Windsor was left blind for life. His regiment's tanks crossed the Melfa, however, and with a company from the Westminster Regiment held their ground in the face of fierce counter-attacks. Major J.K. Mahony of the Westminsters led the Canadians' defence and, though twice wounded, held on, his men taking fifty prisoners, killing more Germans, and knocking out a Panther tank and three self-propelled guns. Mahony won the Victoria Cross, and the Strathconas' reconnaissance troop officer, Lieutenant E.J. Perkins, was awarded the Distinguished Service Order.

The same day, the Americans broke out of the Anzio bridgehead, and they soon linked up with General Mark Clark's Fifth U.S. Army (and its attached Brazilian Expeditionary Force) advancing northward. That threatened Rome, and the Allied advance turned into a pursuit of a shaken enemy. Peter Stursberg of the CBC reported on May 26 that "It's becoming a mad chase in blinding dust over bumpy mud roads to keep up with the Canadian advance now." Barry Rowland, the chaplain of the Irish Regiment of Canada (a Toronto unit in the 5th Armoured Division), wrote that "Our lads are doing a splendid job pushing Jerry right out of the war. They have taken a good number of prisoners and they are a poor lot." In fact, the inexperienced 5th and its corps headquarters contributed to a massive traffic jam in the narrow valley, making it easier for the Germans to get away. For General Burns, the ungenial Canadian commander, it was a first black mark. (A private in a 1st Division unit wrote home that "the censor would never let my opinion" of the 5th Armoured be sent in a letter.) On June 4, a few days after the Canadian Corps had been put into army reserve, the Americans liberated Rome, the first Axis capital to be taken.

Two days later, though, the Allies invaded France, and the Italian theatre became secondary in the eyes of the public and press at home. That hurt the soldiers still fighting in Italy; a Canadian killed there was just as dead as one killed in Normandy. Insult was added to injury when American-born Nancy, Lady Astor, the first British woman Member of Parliament, called the Eighth Army "D-Day dodgers", implying that its men were almost deliberately avoiding service in the "real war" in France. As a result, the bitter song "D-Day Dodgers" (sung to the tune of "Lili Marlene") became popular with the troops:

We are the D-Day Dodgers, out in Italy,
Always on the *vino*, always on the spree,
Eighth Army skivers and their tanks,

We go to war, in ties and slacks,
We are the D-Day Dodgers, in sunny Italy.

Lady Astor's contribution to morale did nothing to stop the advance. The Fifth and Eighth armies moved north from Rome, the Americans along the west coast towards Pisa, the Commonwealth forces towards Florence. Again the Germans used skilful rearguard actions and demolitions to buy time, but by August Florence was taken and, on September 2, Pisa. In August, however, three American and four French divisions had been pulled out of the line for an amphibious assault on the south coast of France. The shrunken Allied armies now prepared to assault the Gothic Line — a defensive barricade just north of the Via Flaminia that the Germans had been preparing since before Rome's liberation.

I Canadian Corps had had two months of rest, recuperation, and training. Most units were still below full strength (and there were complaints about the training of reinforcements), but they were ready to tackle the eastern end of the Gothic Line, anchored at the town of Pesaro.

The attack began on August 25. Six rivers lay between the Canadians and their objective of Rimini. Each was a major obstacle defended by a waiting enemy; each was crossed at heavy cost. The West Nova Scotia Regiment got caught in a minefield that the Germans skilfully covered with small-arms fire and turned into a killing ground. Nonetheless, by August 31 Canadians had a small foothold in the Gothic Line, obliging the shaken Germans — who had been surprised by the speed and depth of the Canadian penetration — to pull units from other sectors to check the corps's advance. That helped the Americans' progress, but slowed the Canadians, whose men were badly in need of a breathing spell.

The Germans also brought their 56-ton Tiger tanks into action in Italy for the first time. "We kept hitting it," a major in the 8th Hussars wrote of the first encounter his Shermans had with the Panzer, "but our 75mm shells just bounced off." If the Tiger's 88mm gun hit a Sherman, on the other hand, it was game over. However, as Brigadier Murphy wrote his family — in words that probably came more easily to a brigadier than to a tank commander — the differences in quality between the German and Allied tanks mattered less in Italy's close country than elsewhere. "We can use ground and creep up on him — manoeuvring until we can bring our guns to bear on a weak spot on his tank — all of which are known to us....we invariably heavily outnumber him. So we engage him from hull down positions with some tanks and creep up on him from the side with others."

Sometimes other methods had to be used to destroy the Panzers. In one action on the Savio River, Private Ernest Smith of the Seaforth Highlanders stood up in full view of an approaching Panther to fire his PIAT. The projectile hit the tank, but ten German Panzer-grenadiers dropped off the tank's back and charged at Smith. "Without hesitation," the Canadian official history said, "he moved into the centre of the road, shot down four of them with his tommy gun, and dispersed the remainder." A second tank now opened fire and more of the enemy began closing in on the Canadian, but Smith replenished his ammunition from a wounded Seaforth and fought off the Germans. Smoky Smith's raw courage was honoured with the Victoria Cross.

Not until September 22, after almost a month's heavy fighting that cost 2,511 casualties including 626 killed in action, did I Canadian Corps break through the Apennine barrier. They had savaged eleven German divisions — one German commander called them "right good soldiers" — and before them now stretched the great northern Italian plain.

Progress unfortunately was slow. The rains had come, turning the dust of summer into the mud of October and November. Tanks sank to their bellies in the ooze. The Germans, bruised though they were, remained "right good soldiers" themselves, and the *Wehrmacht* had lost none of its skill in defence. Every river required a major assault, hampered by the difficulty tanks had in operating in the mud. The new Eighth Army Commander, Sir Oliver Leese, had blamed Canadian delays on General Burns, a humourless officer with the ironic nickname "Smiling Sunray", and had removed him. His successor, brought from France, was no better loved by his men but had a shrewder grasp of Allied diplomacy. Lieutenant-General Charles Foulkes, a university-educated Permanent Force officer who had served in the RCR, took over I Canadian Corps on November 5.

The corps took Ravenna on December 4 and reached the Senio River by Christmas. After the new year the corps cleared the Senio area and fighting then largely ceased as both sides hunkered down to wait out an appalling winter.

There were still casualties, however. A major with the Seaforth Highlanders was wounded on January 4, 1945, after "13 months without a scratch — which is a pretty good record nowadays." He wrote a friend that "I rather expected something to happen this time, though — felt my luck was running low — yet I got a terrific shock when it happened. There's something very personal about a machine gun bullet." He added that "It was quite an experience — lying waiting for the stretcher bearers and thinking, the blood, the pain, then the morphine, the evacuation, the operation, the first bed pan, all the things you had watched others go through and never thought that one day you might be doing the same thing. Yet here I am. It all seems so damned natural."

As it turned out, the Senio operations were the last for the Canadians in Italy. In February 1945, after months of pressure from Ottawa, the decision was made to reunite all the Canadian troops under the First Canadian Army in north-west Europe. General McNaughton's dream of a Canadian army pointing the way to Berlin was at last to be realized, in March.

The casualties suffered by Canadian forces in Italy had been heavy. In all, 92,757 Canadians served in the Italian theatre and more than a quarter became casualties. There were 408 officers and 4,991 men killed; 1,218 officers and 18,268 men were wounded; and 62 officers and 942 men became POWs. Another 365 died from other causes, bringing the total to 26,254. As always, most of the losses fell to the "poor bloody infantry" — always in the forefront, always with the worst of tasks.

XVI
CHANGES AT HOME

By 1943, the succession of Allied defeats had ceased, and victory seemed more likely than it had a year earlier. For the first time, Canadians and their government began to think of what their future would — and should — be like.

There were differences of opinion between regions, parties, and individual ministers, but everyone agreed that the post-war world had to be different from the pre-war one. The Depression had put hundreds of thousands out of work and onto relief, destroying families and fostering political repression at home and fascism and Communism abroad. Opinion polls — begun in Canada during the war by the Canadian Institute of Public Opinion and also taken secretly by the Wartime Information Board, the federal government's new propaganda agency — suggested that people feared the return of depressed economic conditions. They wanted security: they wanted to know that there would be jobs for them, and for their children. They wanted the federal government to intervene in the economy to ensure that their wartime economic gains could be protected. The *laissez-faire* attitudes that had been so dominant in the country's pre-war history had been shattered by years of hardship. After all, the controls and rationing that had been imposed during the war had given Canadians a far higher standard of living. Why should controls and planning not work just as well in peacetime?

THE EMERGENCE OF SOCIAL WELFARE

The Co-operative Commonwealth Federation was one of the major creators and beneficiaries of this new mood. Since its formation in 1932, the CCF had failed to make much headway with the electorate. Bad times seemingly did not help a party with radical ideas. Nor had Woodsworth's pacifism helped the party in the 1940 election. But the war got the social democrats moving, particularly after Joe Noseworthy's victory over national Conservative leader Arthur Meighen in the York South by-election of February 9, 1942. That result made the country sit up and take notice of the CCF, and the party's stock began to rise as Canadians digested its message of nationalization, social welfare, and social security. In August 1943 the party captured thirty-four seats in the Ontario provincial election, a dramatic rise from holding no seats to forming the Opposition. That same month, the party won two federal by-elections, one each in Manitoba and Saskatchewan. By September the CCF had 29 per cent of the country's support in the national opinion polls. For the first time ever, it was ahead of the Liberals and Conservatives — by one point. This was an astonishing ascent from oblivion, a tribute to the wartime effectiveness of the party's message.

The Conservatives were the first to react to the changed national mood. Badly battered in the 1940 election, the Tories had dumped Dr. Robert Manion, their leader since 1938, at the first opportunity. From May 1940 until Meighen took over in November 1941 they had been led in Parliament by Richard B. Hanson, a lacklustre New Brunswicker who had served briefly in R.B. Bennett's cabinet. After the York South débâcle, Hanson once more led the party in the House, while Meighen glowered from Toronto and observers speculated that the historic party was on its deathbed, its policies of high tariffs, *laissez-faire*, and the maintenance of the imperial connection all seeming outdated in the midst of the war.

The party put on a new face at a "thinkers' meeting" in Port Hope, Ontario, at the beginning of September 1942, and pushed its way into the twentieth century. The emphasis on tariffs disappeared, to be replaced by "a New National Policy" with social security as its goal. James M. Macdonnell, the businessman who had organized the meeting, argued that the state "had to see that every citizen is provided with employment at a wage which will enable him to live in decency." To colleagues who were dubious about reform, he put the point more bluntly: "Would you rather adopt a policy which will retain the largest amount possible of free enterprise or — hand over to the CCF? Half a loaf is better than no bread." The Tories then staged a national convention in Winnipeg in December and, under the influence of the "Port Hopefuls", selected Manitoba's long-time premier, John Bracken, as party leader. (One of the defeated candidates for leader was a little-known Saskatchewan MP named John Diefenbaker.)

A dour, silent man who had been a professor of field husbandry at the Manitoba Agricultural College before his selection as Progressive premier in 1922, Bracken had eventually turned himself and his provincial party into Liberal-Progressives. His only connection with the Conservative Party, some said, was that his father had attended John A. Macdonald's funeral in 1891. As a condition of taking the leadership, Bracken insisted on changing the party's name to Progressive Conservative, in an attempt to link the Tories to the still-powerful memory of the Progressive Party, the farmers' movement of the 1920s. Although humorists gibed that the "Pro and Con" party was going in two directions at once, the selection of Bracken and the new name demonstrated that the Conservatives, now publicly committed to social security, full employment, collective bargaining, medical insurance, and free enterprise, were in the centre of the political spectrum. The CCF was on the left, and Mackenzie King's Liberals, absorbed in running the war effort, were now the right-wingers.

Not for long. While the prime minister and the key ministers in the Cabinet War Committee reeled under the weight of their responsibilities, other ministers and the bureaucracy had been quietly preparing their plans to deal with the expected post-war slump. One major weapon was already in place. Unemployment insurance had won provincial consent early in 1940 and had passed through Parliament in the summer of that year. There was a certain cruel irony that unemployment insurance came into effect when the war had all but eliminated unemployment, but that was quite deliberate. As an insurance scheme, the plan had to begin in good times so that a healthy balance of funds could be accumulated before the claims began.

The Department of Pensions and National Health, under British Columbia's Ian Mackenzie, was also at work. In March 1941 the minister organized a Committee on Reconstruction to study the effectiveness of wartime controls and their applicability in peacetime and to consider trade problems and the conversion of war industry to civilian uses. The research director of the committee, Leonard Marsh, prepared the committee's major work, the "Report on Social Security for Canada". The Marsh Report analysed Canada's existing social legislation, suggested improvements, and laid down the principles to be followed to make social security work. It called for "provision for unemployment, both economically and socially", which was to include programs to combat unemployment at the end of the war, retraining programs, and a "national reserve program of public employment projects". In other words, Ottawa had to be prepared to create jobs to cushion the shock of the transition to peace.

The Marsh Report also looked at the "universal risks" of sickness and old age and suggested a national health insurance plan — an idea that Ian Mackenzie's department had been working on for years and that the Liberals had ostensibly adopted back in 1919. Marsh called for universal old age pensions of $45 a month for married couples, and for family allowances of approximately $7.50 a month for each child. As the report demonstrated, a couple with three children under twelve needed $122.85 a month to live; two-thirds of the male heads of city families and three-quarters of rural families were below that minimum income level in 1941. It was a shocking situation, the best proof of the necessity for schemes like those suggested.

There was only one problem: all these proposals would cost money — an estimated $900 million, or more than 10 per cent of estimated post-war National Income. "Pie in the sky," the critics said.

The Marsh Report's blueprint for the future drew enormous public interest, but the King government's initial response was indifferent or hostile. The prime minister, whose 1918 book, *Industry and Humanity*, had served as a charter for his long tenure of office, was an undoubted supporter of improvements in social welfare — when the time was ripe. But the time had never been ripe. A pay-as-you-go policy of war finance meant that taxes were very high during the war: in 1943, a married man with two children and earnings of $5,000 paid $1,062 in tax and was obliged to put $600 more into compulsory savings. Four years earlier, in 1939, tax on that income had been only $134. King feared that social welfare would carry high taxes into peacetime, and that, he thought, could only help the Opposition. Moreover, he told the Liberal caucus in Parliament, he would not buy the voters' support in wartime with their own money. King also warned his party that Marsh's social welfare proposals amounted to "a social revolution — a levelling down of those who were privileged.... That this could not be done in a day, but would take years." All of this was typical of the caution that characterized the prime minister.

After the CCF came from nowhere to run a close second behind the Conservatives in Ontario in August 1943, and after the CCF won two of four federal by-elections a few weeks later, it only needed the shock of the September opinion polls before King was ready to think again. Something had to be done to meet the popular desire for security or else the Liberals would be certain of defeat.

As a result, the National Liberal Federation called its first major wartime meeting at the end of September. The delegates enthusiastically voted for resolutions that promised massive benefits to veterans. They cheered resolutions proposing a "national scheme of social insurance" to include protection against privation resulting from unemployment, accident, ill health, old age, and blindness. They called for better old age pensions. They urged that family allowances be put in place. They pledged support for labour's right to collective bargaining. And they called for full employment through the efforts of both "public and private enterprise". The Liberals, in other words, were back in a political mainstream that had veered sharply to the left.

And the Liberals had one advantage the CCF and Progressive Conservatives

In August 1943, Churchill and Roosevelt (seated, right and centre) and the Combined Chiefs of Staff met at the first Quebec City Conference—called "Quadrant"—to plan Allied strategy in Europe and the Far East. Though Mackenzie King (seated, left) did not participate, he was on hand to play host and to pose for photographs. The empty chair was for the governor general, the Earl of Athlone.

Traitors, spies, and saboteurs made for gripping novels and films and served other propaganda purposes. In fact, however, there was not a single proven instance of wartime sabotage in Canada.

Meat rationing was a nuisance for both butchers and customers; when every ounce of meat had its price in coupons and tokens, meal planning became an art. Restaurants had meatless Tuesdays and Fridays. Alcohol was also rationed—Ontario's low point was 12 oz a month—and bootleggers sold homemade hooch whenever they could get enough sugar.

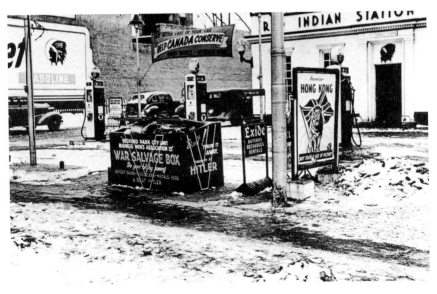

This Toronto gas station bears the "signs of the times"—for war bonds, recycling, and "making it last." With gas rationed and tires almost impossible to buy, driving became a luxury—so much so that Col. Sam McLaughlin, the president of General Motors, occasionally drove a horse and buggy to work.

One major beneficiary of the wartime mood was the Co-operative Commonwealth Federation. The social democratic party soared in opinion polls and formed the Opposition in Ontario in 1943; in 1944 it captured the government in Saskatchewan, becoming the first socialist administration in North America. Premier Tommy Douglas (centre) was extraordinarily popular, and for a brief time it seemed all Canada might go "forward with the CCF." But only for a time.

The Canadian army contribution to the D-Day assault was provided by the 3rd Division—some of its men are seen here on a Landing Craft Infantry (LCI)—and the 2nd Armoured Brigade. The LCI carried more than 150 soldiers and could drop them right on the beach.

Royal Canadian Engineers pause for a brief prayer with a chaplain just before boarding their landing craft for the D-Day invasion.

The sappers' tedious, painstaking work is in sharp contrast to the romantic image of war—as in the saturnine portrait of a Canadian sniper below.

Men of the 3rd Canadian Infantry Division, who cleared the enemy from the muddy devastation of the Breskens pocket, came to be known as "water rats." Veterans of the earlier war would have recognized the scene—and envied the array of vehicles supporting the infantry.

The Dutch liked the Canadians, and their gratitude and hospitality to their liberators remain warm to this day; the Canadians reciprocated. These men of the Fort Garry Horse seem quite at home as they work on a broken tank tread.

did not: they were in power and could implement their promises. The Speech from the Throne that opened the new session of Parliament on January 27, 1944 largely ignored the war. Instead it set out the government's "reconstruction" plans. The "post-war object of our domestic policy is social security and human welfare," the governor-general read. "The establishment of a national minimum of social security and human welfare should be advanced as rapidly as possible." The government pledged to create "useful work for all who are willing to work", to upgrade nutrition and housing, and to provide social insurance. The three main areas of its post-war planning were the demobilization, rehabilitation, and re-establishment of veterans; the reconversion of the economy to peace; and insurance against major economic and social hazards. To this end, three new departments were created: Reconstruction, National Health and Welfare, and Veterans Affairs. Moreover, the Liberals promised to introduce family allowances, and they pledged to seek the agreement of the provinces for health insurance and a "more generous" contributory old age plan. It was a virtual social revolution.

The government carried out almost all of its Throne Speech promises, although health insurance and a national contributory old age pension took more than two decades to reach fruition. And, as was so often the case, the wily Mackenzie King saw the Tories play into his hands. The issue this time was family allowances.

One of the major reasons the government had come to support the idea of the "baby bonus" was to relieve pressure on the wartime system of wage controls, as the National War Labour Board had recommended in August 1943. If the government could not remove the freeze on incomes for fear of starting the inflationary spiral again, then "we can think of no other solution for the case of the head of the family who is receiving a substandard wage, than a system of family allowances." The Cabinet considered the board's report in September 1943, but the ministers worried about the political implications. Would not English Canadians see family allowances as a devious way of helping French Canadians with their large broods? The prime minister himself was again reluctant to hand out public money: "to tell the country that everyone was to get a family allowance was sheer folly.... Great care had to be taken in any monies given out from the Treasury...." But when King talked to one of the officials in his office and learned that the man had been raised and educated on a Great War widow's pension paid to his mother, he suddenly realized that a pension differed from a family allowance only in amount, not in principle. Reassured by this fresh perspective, he turned his great energies to getting family allowances into place.

To his surprise, the prime minister found that the Department of Finance was also in favour of the plan. The deputy minister told the Cabinet that without the baby bonus Ottawa would have to find huge sums "to make possible municipally managed low-rental housing projects.... With children's allowances on anything like an adequate scale, it should be possible to avoid such a program." The bureaucrats had also come to the conclusion that money had to be distributed to people who would spend it; only in that way would there be sufficient demand for goods and services to keep the economy running at the end of the war when the munitions factories shut down. In other words, it was better to give away money than to see the country slide back into a depression. Although some powerful ministers opposed the measure on the grounds of cost (and, as the recently converted King complained, because they "still think they can go out and shoot a deer or bison for breakfast"), the Cabinet went along. To many of the ministers, the argument that family allowances might actually help the nation's children to grow up healthier and stronger did not seem as important as the financial implications.

The bill proposing the baby bonus went to Parliament in the summer of 1944, suggesting $5 a month for children up to five years of age, and rising by steps to $8 for those from thirteen to fifteen. As important, the bill directed that the money was to be paid to *mothers*; for hundreds of thousands of Canadian women, this was the first money that did not have to be extracted from sometimes grudging husbands. (In Quebec, where the dependent status of women was enshrined in provincial law, protests from the provincial government forced Ottawa to pay the baby bonus to fathers!)

The family allowances were not to begin until July 1, 1945, after the next federal election. Some Tory MPs were outraged by the plan because they felt it was designed to bolster sagging Liberal fortunes in Quebec. One Toronto MP called it a device for "bonussing families who have been unwilling to defend their country. It was a bribe of the most brazen character, made chiefly to one province and paid for by the rest." He was ejected from the House of Commons when he refused to withdraw those words. Tory leader John Bracken also called the bill a "political bribe" while Conservative Premier George Drew of Ontario said that "one isolationist province" could not "dominate the destiny of a divided Canada". Even Charlotte Whitton, the Tories' leading expert on social welfare, added her two cents' worth:

> erratic, irresponsible, bewildered of mind, and socially incapable, feeble-minded and mentally affected parents are definitely the progenitors of many of our largest families.... payments of cash grants would perpetuate this menace.

Whitton went on to say that the baby bonus would extend "the uneven rate of natural increase" of Canada's newer racial stocks at the expense of less prolific British Canadians. Some Progressive Conservatives, such as John Diefenbaker, spoke in support of family allowances, and no Conservative voted against the measure on second reading, but the damage was done. For all the lofty aims of Bracken and the Port Hopefuls, the public perceived the Tory party as against social welfare, against Quebec, and against ethnic Canadians.

Family allowances did prove to be a very potent force in the elections, and it would be naive to assume that this was not anticipated by those who charted the bill's passage. But votes were not the only motive. The baby bonus was calculated to put almost $250 million a year into the hands of women who would spend it on their children. They would buy clothes and milk, medicines and books, cribs and carriages, and every dollar spent would help keep factories and farms producing. Family allowances were in this respect similar to veterans' benefits, to assistance to industry and farmers, to funds for the construction of housing. The Liberals had accepted the economic gospel of economist John Maynard Keynes, a creed that called for government spending in hard times to keep employment up. Everyone expected post-war times to be tough, and the King government had demonstrated that it was ready to act. When the boys came home from the war this time, they really would find a Canada fit for heroes. Or so the government desperately hoped.

ON THE WORLD STAGE

If the Liberal government had created a charter for the home front with its social security package, it was taking equally revolutionary steps in international affairs.

Canada had gone to war at Britain's side, and had solidified its relations with the United States at Ogdensburg and Hyde Park. But once the United States came into the war, the necessity for close and continuous strategic and economic planning between London and Washington tended to leave Canada and the other small allies out of the picture. This was profoundly disturbing to Canada's government; politicians, exerting themselves to the utmost to win the war, felt entitled to status and recognition.

But how could the King government's desire for a share in the war's planning be accommodated, given the need for swift and efficient action? If Canada had a place at the table, then Australia, Brazil, The Netherlands, and Czechoslovakia would be entitled to seats, too. Difficult as it was, the conundrum was not insoluble. The Canadians came up with an answer they called the "functional principle".

The functional principle took advantage of Canada's strengths in some key areas. It recognized that there was little point in demanding a share in strategic planning: Britain and the United States could never concede that — and, to be honest, Canada had little to contribute there in any case. On the other hand, the United States and Britain had created the Combined Food Board in January 1942 to allocate scarce food supplies. The United States was the greatest food exporter in the world and Britain the largest importer, so their right to take decisions on the CFB was unquestioned. But the second great food-producing nation on the Allied side was Canada, and justice and logic demanded that Canada have a share in the decisions that were to govern the distribution of food produced by prairie farmers. When other countries produced food in similar quantities, Canadians said, then they should have a place as well; until then, they could sit on the sidelines. The same situation existed in other areas under the aegis of the Combined Production and Resources Board and the Combined Munitions Assignment Board.

The Canadian government pressed its case in London and Washington. The Americans generally supported the idea of Canadian representation — if London agreed. The British were upset, however, at the upstart dominion seeking a share in decisions. The Combined Food Board, Whitehall argued, was not a decision-making body and could only make recommendations — it wasn't worth much, the message seemed to suggest. On the other hand, the British argued that Canadian representation "would not make for technical efficiency". That type of two-faced argument drove officials in Ottawa's East Block wild.

For the first time, the government had some cards to play and appeared willing to play them toughly. The country had given Britain a billion-dollar gift at the beginning of 1942 to pay for the food and munitions Britain so desperately needed. London could scarcely expect further gifts if it treated Canada "as a small boy to be relegated to the sidelines", or so the governor of the Bank of Canada told the British high commissioner in Ottawa. That was a threat — and one that had to be heeded. And it marked a revolution in Canadian foreign policy. The colony that had gone to war in 1939 still firmly attached to Mama's apron-strings was growing up.

The result was full Canadian membership on the Combined Food Board and the Combined Production and Resources Board, something no other Allied nation won. Buoyed by their hard-won success with the functional principle, the government detailed its claims publicly in a major address by the prime minister in Parliament on July 9, 1943:

>...authority in international affairs must not be concentrated exclusively in the largest powers.... A number of new international organizations are likely to be set up as a result of the war. In the view of the government, effec-

tive representation on these bodies should neither be restricted to the largest states nor necessarily extended to all states. Representation should be determined on a functional basis which will admit to full membership those countries, large or small, which have the greatest contribution to make to the particular object in question....

Although that principle was never conceded by the Great Powers, it guided Canada's fight to get a seat on the directing committee of the United Nations Relief and Rehabilitation Administration, set up in 1943 to organize and run the great relief effort that would be necessary in Europe and Asia after the war. Ottawa's attempt failed, the Soviet Union proving no more amenable to Canadian claims of special status than Britain had been. But Canada did win a place on the UNRRA supplies committee, and a seat at the steering committee when supply questions were under discussion. That was more than might have been expected.

Moreover, Canadians were arguing their case in other areas. Civil air transport was going to boom after the war, and a whole series of agreements and regulations had to be worked out. Situated as it was, graced with thousands of wartime pilots, and with Trans-Canada Airlines and Canadian Pacific Airlines aspiring to world-class status, Canada demanded a role. To everyone's surprise, the country made a critical contribution to a 1944 conference in Chicago on air transport, mediating between London and Washington and drafting the charter that led to the creation of the International Civil Aviation Organization. The same thing occurred in discussions on post-war international finance: a Canadian draft plan was an important compromise document at the 1944 Bretton Woods Conference that laid out the shape of the post-war financial world. And Canada, represented by Lester Pearson and his colleagues in External Affairs, was in the midst of the fray in discussions leading to the formation of the United Nations Organization.

If Canada had bargained toughly with the Great Powers about the economic direction of the war, it did less well with the United States on continental questions. The beginning of war in the Pacific and the Japanese threat to North America had forced both Canada and the United States to pay attention to defence on the west coast. One result was American pressure for a road to Alaska, something that had been discussed in Washington and in British Columbia for years. Ottawa had resisted this intrusion onto Canadian soil, but the bombing of Pearl Harbor made it clear that both countries needed a way to move troops and equipment at will. The Americans got the go-ahead, and the all-weather gravel Alaska Highway — hastily bulldozed through some

1,500 miles of muskeg and swamp by 11,000 U.S. Army engineers and 16,000 Canadian and American civilians — was the result.

Soon there were airfields dotted across the north, helping aircraft and goods reach the beleaguered Soviet Union from North America. Oil developments at Norman Wells in the Northwest Territories, pipelines, and weather stations reflected U.S. initiatives. Over 15,000 American servicemen were in the north by the end of 1942. So large had their presence become that wits joked that the U.S. Army answered the telephone, "Army of Occupation"! But with the Japanese occupying some of the Aleutian Islands off Alaska from mid-1942, with submarines shelling West Coast installations and sinking merchant ships, the American presence had a comforting effect.

Some in Ottawa worried about the Yankee embrace, all the same. Prime Minister King fretted that the American presence "was less intended for protection against the Japanese than as one of the fingers of the hand which America is placing more or less over the whole of the Western hemisphere." But King, slow to act in almost all circumstances, had to be prodded into movement by the able and concerned British high commissioner in Ottawa. Malcolm MacDonald had served in Neville Chamberlain's Cabinet before Churchill sent him to Canada in early 1941. Two years later, he had visited the north and had been astounded to find no Canadian government representative there to watch the Americans or show the flag. For most purposes, he told Ottawa, the senior Canadian representative in the area was the secretary of the Alberta Chamber of Commerce, who was an unofficial representative of the Department of Mines and Resources.

Ottawa was finally stirred to act, and it did, appointing Brigadier W.W. Foster as special commissioner and giving him his own DC-3 aircraft to which the Red Ensign could be attached. Instructed that "no situation [must] develop as a result of which the full Canadian control of the area would be in any way prejudiced or endangered", Foster — who had directed the construction of the Canadian portion of the Alaska Highway — did his job quietly and competently. And at the end of the war, the Canadian government paid the Americans in full for every installation they had constructed in the north. Many thanks, the message was, and now go home. The Americans went, but just ten years later the Cold War would bring them back.

Even if the federal government's response to the implicit threat to its northern sovereignty had been slow and weak, something had changed in Ottawa during the war. A nation of just eleven million people, Canada had clearly come of age in a time when old and established nations were being crushed under the Nazi boot. Its diplomats moved in the corridors of power with a confidence bolstered immeasurably by the country's huge military, industrial, and agricultural contribution. Canadian representatives had new clout whenever they took their places at a bargaining table.

Moreover, the representatives Canada sent abroad to advance its interests were first class. The pre-war civil service had been small and not particularly efficient, but there were some outstanding officials in its ranks. Clifford Clark, the Deputy Minister of Finance, was a very able man; one of his key aides, Robert Bryce, was a leading Keynesian economist, and so hard-working that others stood in awe of him. The Department of External Affairs was full of men (but only a very few women) of ability: Norman Robertson, Hume Wrong, Lester Pearson, Escott Reid, and others had the respect of their British and American colleagues and the trust of their government.

The Cabinet ministers were no slouches either. C.D. Howe, the Minister of Munitions and Supply, had galvanized Canada's manufacturing industry into wartime production, and he dealt as an equal with ministers in Washington and London. J.L. Ilsley, the Minister of Finance, had a glowing reputation in Canada and abroad. Ralston, Crerar, Power, and Ernest Lapointe's successor, Louis St. Laurent, shared in one of the ablest governments Canada had ever seen in war or peace. And Mackenzie King — strange, incalculable man that he was — fought and argued for his country's place in the world. He did not always press as hard as his officials might have liked, but his experience and shrewd political sense invariably told him how far he could go. King was not cut out to be the bellicose ruler of a great power, but neither did he have the deferential acquiescence of a good colonial leader. Instead, he was ideally suited to be what he had become: the leader of the first of the wartime middle powers.

XVII
THE NORMANDY CAMPAIGN

While the war raged in Africa, Sicily and Italy, the Soviet Union, and the Pacific, the bulk of the First Canadian Army was still sitting in England. The daily routine was training: a ceaseless round of exercises by platoon, company, battalion, brigade, division, corps, army, and army group — all infinitely more demanding and realistic than before Dieppe. There were courses for snipers, engineers, artillerymen, junior leaders, senior officers, and experts of every kind. A handful of qualified soldiers slipped away to join the Special Operations Executive (SOE), the British secret agents in occupied Europe. There were hell-raising leaves in London and endless nights in the pub drinking the watered wartime version of British ale. There was sex, love, and even marriage. There was everything except action — real action, against the Germans — and that was what the men wanted. They knew action could mean death, of course, but death was something that happened to someone else, not to them and their friends.

In 1944 there would be fighting enough for everyone. President Roosevelt and the American Chiefs of Staff had been pressing since 1942 for an invasion of France at the earliest possible date. So too was Stalin, whose forces were engaged in a titanic struggle with the *Wehrmacht*; if the Allies engaged the Germans in strength in France, the Nazis would be forced to draw off troops from the Eastern Front. On Stalin's order, from 1942 on Communists and their sympathizers throughout the West beat the tom-toms for a "Second Front Now", and huge rallies filled stadiums like Maple Leaf Gardens and the Montreal Forum.

For the First Canadian Army — an army that had been told by its commander, General McNaughton, to think of itself as a dagger pointing at the heart of Berlin — the calls for a second front struck a responsive chord. That was true even after Andy McNaughton left the army in December 1943 to be succeeded, a few months later, by General Harry Crerar.

Born in Hamilton, Ontario in 1888, Crerar had graduated from the Royal Military College, served in the Great War with the artillery, and risen through the ranks of the small pre-war Permanent Force. He had been sent to London at the outbreak of war, brought back to Canada to be Chief of the General Staff in 1940, and had returned to England the next year to command the 2nd Canadian Division. Then he commanded i Canadian Corps in Britain and in Italy. Crerar was an abler technician than McNaughton, and while he was not a brilliant leader in the field, he was less likely to make mistakes that could cost lives. What he was not was an inspired leader. The men of the army loved Andy McNaughton, a man who led through example. Very few loved Harry Crerar.

Planning for D-Day

The problem of how to stage an invasion of France had been under consideration ever since the disasters of May and June 1940. Churchill and the Imperial General Staff feared the casualties that a cross-Channel assault on France could bring and looked to a strike at the alleged "soft underbelly" of Europe from the Mediterranean. By 1942 a little-known American officer, Brigadier-General Dwight Eisenhower, had produced a plan for invasion by April 1, 1943. This plan, called "Roundup", was reworked and finally accepted by the British and Americans, and the August 1942 raid on Dieppe was intended as a small dress rehearsal. The disaster of Dieppe had told the planners that it was probably impossible to seize a fortified port, and that any major assault required massive air and sea bombardment, better communications from ship to shore, and more and better landing craft of different types. The specific plan of "Roundup" was shelved. The necessity for an invasion of France remained.

The invasions of North Africa in November 1942 and Sicily in the summer of 1943 offered an opportunity to test the new amphibious doctrine that Dieppe had helped to create. The Landing Ship Tank (LST) that could carry up to twenty tanks, the Landing Craft Infantry (LCI) that carried two hundred infantry, the Landing Craft Assault (LCA) that carried almost twenty-five men, and the amphibious DUKWs that went from ship to shore and then operated on land — all these were coming off the production line and being tried in combat. While the Americans concentrated on landing ships, the British devised a number of specialized armoured vehicles inspired by the Dieppe experience — "Funnies", the troops called them. These tanks were adapted to swim, explode mines, hurl blasts of flame, and even build bridges. Everything of which human ingenuity could conceive was being readied.

Planning for the invasion was under the direction of a British officer, Lieutenant-General F.E. Morgan, Chief of Staff to the Supreme Allied Commander (Designate) or COSSAC. The new target for invasion was May 1, 1944, a date determined by the need to build enough landing craft. The ideal plan developed by COSSAC's team had envisaged five infantry divisions landing simultaneously, two more for immediate follow-up, two airborne divisions, and a further twenty divisions for build-up, but the shortage of landing craft meant that only a three-division assault seemed possible. Churchill grumbled furiously that "the destinies of two great empires seem to be tied up on some god-damned things called LSTs."

Morgan and his staff also had to determine where the landing should take place. One essential was air cover, a problem that limited the choice to the shore between Cherbourg, France and Flushing, Belgium. Suitable beaches were found only in the Pas de Calais or on the Normandy coast. The Pas de Calais was undoubtedly the best site — just twenty miles from England and with near-perfect beaches. But the Germans had been quick to realize this and their defences were very strong there. That left Normandy — specifically the Cotentin–Caen area, where the defences were comparatively light. Normandy beaches were farther from England, increasing the dangers of the crossing and the turn-around time, but on balance it seemed the better choice.

COSSAC's plan was accepted by the Combined Chiefs of Staff when they met at the Quadrant conference at Quebec City in August 1943. Also agreed to were Morgan's conditions: the *Luftwaffe* had to be shattered by a massive Allied air offensive before the invasion; the *Wehrmacht* could have no more than twelve first-class divisions in France at the chosen time and its ability to reinforce its troops there had to be limited; and some means had to be found to create an artificial port to get the invading armies' supplies ashore. With all this accepted, detailed planning for "Overlord", as the invasion of France was now to be called, went ahead. And by the end of 1943, General Dwight Eisenhower, less than two years earlier a mere brigadier-general in Washington, had been named the Supreme Allied Commander. Eisenhower had commanded the Allied forces invading North Africa, Sicily, and Italy; he was an American, and that mattered since the United States was providing the lion's share of the troops; and he had a wonderful knack for getting on with everyone and building an effective team. That was essential.

With an American in overall charge, a British officer was needed to command the armies in Normandy in the initial phase. The choice was General Bernard Montgomery, the victor of El Alamein. Montgomery was "an efficient little shit", as one British officer told an enquiring Canadian, but the important word there was "efficient". He was a victorious British general when there were few enough of those about. He had a thoroughly modern grasp of the need to inspire troops, and he ruthlessly sacked officers who failed in the field.

Monty and Ike, as the two were popularly known, immediately protested that three divisions were too few for the initial assault. The plan was reworked, more landing craft were found, and the new plan for the landing called for five divisions to land on a fifty-mile front with three airborne divisions preceding them. The First U.S. Army would land on the right, the British Second Army — incorporating the Canadians — on the left. By the evening of D-Day, the Allies intended to have eight infantry divisions and fourteen armoured regiments ashore. The new date of invasion was June 5, 1944, the day when the tides would be most favourable.

The planners had even worked out how to create the artificial harbours that would be so essential for getting supplies ashore. Immense concrete caissons would be towed from England to France and sunk into position, along with obsolete ships; the result would be a breakwater to which prefabricated piers would be attached. Cargo ships could then unload directly. Two of these "Mulberry" harbours were to be built, one for the American landing and one for the British front. The Mulberry plan was a vital secret, for the Germans had convinced themselves that the Allies had to capture a port to get ashore successfully and that, as there was nothing suitable in the Cotentin–Caen area, that area could not be the invasion site.

But if this demonstrated a rigidity of thought among the German planners, they also showed much energy and skill. The German army in France was not the strongest of the *Wehrmacht*'s forces — the real fighting, after all, was in Russia and Italy. France was more a training ground, and a resting and refitting area for units that had suffered on the Eastern Front. Even so, the Germans had 865,000 men in their Seventh Army in France, including several first-class Panzer and SS units, and these men were equipped with new weapons that were far better than anything the Allies had. The Panther and Tiger tanks could outgun and outfight the Allies' Sherman, for example, and the *Wehrmacht*'s all-purpose 88mm gun was vastly superior to any comparable British or American gun. Many of the men who made up the powerful German forces had fanatical faith in their Führer and in the Reich, and this remained unshaken, no matter what defeats their country had suffered since 1942.

The *Wehrmacht* also had a first-rate commander in France in Field Marshal Erwin Rommel. One of the most famous military men of the war, and almost as popular in Allied countries as in Germany, Rommel had been a Panzer general, a hard-driving division commander in the invasion of France in

May 1940, and a remarkably successful leader of the Afrika Korps — until he was bested by Montgomery at El Alamein in November 1942. Now he was in charge of the defence against invasion.

Rommel feared that, when the invasion came, Allied air superiority would make it impossible for reinforcements to reach the defenders on the landing beaches. The coastal divisions that manned the shore defences were not first-class troops, some units being made up of over-age or physically unfit soldiers, others of captured Soviet soldiers or conscripts from the conquered territories. If these men were to hold off an attack for any length of time, the Atlantic Wall must be reinforced by impregnable concrete blockhouses with fixed fire lanes commanding the beaches. Tens of thousands of iron "hedge-hogs" and tetrahedrons must be placed as obstacles on the shoreline and on likely sites for airborne landings, and millions of mines must be laid. The job was rushed and supplies were scarce, but Rommel's energy and shrewd assessment of the Allied possibilities made the invasion far more difficult than it might have been.

THE ALLIES LAND IN NORMANDY

While the First Canadian Army would play its role in the follow-up to the invasion, only one Canadian division was to participate in the actual D-Day assault. The formation selected was the 3rd Infantry Division, commanded by Major-General R.F.L. Keller; he would also have the 2nd Canadian Armoured Brigade under his command. Keller's division was to be directed by I British Corps in the assault phase, and from November 1943, officers from Keller's headquarters began to work with the corps headquarters. At the same time the infantry units of his division stepped up their training exercises, constantly practising amphibious assaults. The tank regiments attached to the division also had new weapons and tactics to master. The Fort Garry Horse and the 1st Hussars, regiments scheduled to land in the initial assault, had to learn how to use DD tanks — floating "duplex drive" tanks with high canvas flotation screens, and propellers to push them. All the tracked and wheeled equipment had to be waterproofed to operate in up to four feet of water.

The plan of attack for the 3rd Canadian Division called for two of its three brigades to land in the first wave on Juno Beach. The 7th Canadian Infantry Brigade, led by the Regina Rifles and the Royal Winnipeg Rifles, was to land on Mike sector; the 8th, headed by the Queen's Own Rifles and the North Shore Regiment, on Nan. In front of the landing forces would be the villages of Courseulles-sur-Mer, Bernières-sur-Mer, and St. Aubin-sur-Mer, all of which were due to be seized in the opening minutes of the invasion. To their left and right, a mile or two away, would be British divisions. Once the beachhead was consolidated, the Canadians were to move inland as far as ten miles to take and hold the high ground west of Caen. By the time this objective had been seized, the 9th Brigade and the tanks of the Sherbrooke Fusiliers would be ashore, ready to assist in beating off the expected Nazi counter-attack.

To help the invaders get ashore, the Supreme Allied Commander had brought together an overwhelming array of air and naval firepower. There were 171 squadrons of fighters and fighter-bombers to blast enemy armour, and to hit at the *Luftwaffe* if the German air force dared to take to the air. Heavy bombers would plaster the landing beaches: on Juno Beach, saturation bombing by Bomber Command of the Royal Air Force — with a very high proportion of its crews coming from the RCAF — was scheduled to begin thirty minutes before the landing. Meanwhile, destroyers and cruisers would be pounding targets ashore. Of the 7,016 ships participating in the D-Day operation, the RCN was to provide 110 of various types — destroyers, minesweepers, corvettes, and torpedo boats — including three flotillas of landing craft and the landing ships HMCS *Prince Henry* and *Prince David*, both converted armed merchant cruisers. The latter were to carry Canadian troops into action — and they would return to England with some of the first of the wounded. While the infantry and armour were going in, artillery on landing craft would add their fire to the bombardment.

Through the winter and spring the Allied air forces struck at road and rail junctions, bridges and marshalling yards, greatly restricting the *Wehrmacht*'s ability to move. To help mislead the Germans, the bombing plan took the Lancasters and B-17s all over northern France, and for every ton of bombs dropped in the Normandy region an equivalent amount was carefully targeted on the Pas de Calais.

Preceded by navy frogmen to reconnoitre beaches and clear obstacles, and by clouds of aircraft delivering the men of three airborne divisions, including the 1st Canadian Parachute Battalion, the huge Allied flotilla swept into the Baie de la Seine before dawn on June 6, 1944. Astonishingly, secrecy about the point of attack was maintained. Sailor Spud Graham took part in the D-Day invasion on HMCS *Canso*, a minesweeper. "How the Germans didn't know we were coming," he said, "I'll be Goddamned if I don't know. As far as your eye could see, there were ships. I always said that if you could jump a hundred yards at a clip you could get back to England without even wetting your feet. That's how many ships were involved."

Thorough as the planning was, there were the inevitable snafus. First, the invasion had had to be delayed one day because of poor weather. And the revised D-Day was itself a day of rain and high seas. That meant that many of the DD tanks, which had been intended to motor ashore alongside the LCAs carrying the infantry and to touch down on the beach before them, had to be landed from LSTs. A few attempted to get ashore under their own power but foundered quickly in five-foot waves. Many of the infantry, already ill from the strain of being cooped up on ship and from fear, were seasick.

The first landing craft carrying the Queen's Own Rifles hit Juno Beach at 8:12 A.M., almost half an hour late. Heavy as it was, the bombardment had not eliminated the defenders, and the queasy infantry had to run across 200 yards of open beach to the cover of the seawall under heavy fire. An 88mm gun devastated the lead platoon of A Company, and only five survivors, under command of a corporal, made it off the beach. D Company fared no better, losing half its strength in the dash for the seawall, and the riflemen who did get there had to use hand grenades to take out a nest of Germans who had survived the bombing and shelling. Rifleman Stump Gordon of Toronto had waded ashore lugging a flame-thrower that weighed almost as much as he did, somehow managing to keep the nozzle above water. "I took a shot at a pillbox, with everything whizzing around me," he remembered forty years later, "and all that came out was juice. The blasted batteries had gone."

The Regina Rifles landed on Mike sector just after 8:00 A.M.; by that time the 1st Hussars had put enough tanks on the beach to be able to provide covering fire. That was essential, as it turned out, because again the German defences were largely intact. The concrete bunkers designed to shelter machine-gun and artillery crew — they still survive virtually intact forty-five years later — were thirty-five feet across with four-foot–thick walls. The bunkers were effectively impregnable to anything but a round fired through their observation slits; some were neutralized by tanks in exactly that way. The Rifles worked their way off the beach and into Courseulles, house-clearing all the way. One of the Regina reserve companies was almost wiped out when its landing craft blew up on mines concealed by the rising tide.

The Royal Winnipeg Rifles, with an attached company from the Canadian Scottish, had as rough a time. The Scottish and two Rifles companies got ashore easily, the German gun that commanded their landing ground having been destroyed in the naval shelling. Two other companies met fierce resistance at the western edge of Courseulles, "the bombardment having failed to kill a single German", the unit war diarist noted. But the Winnipeg regiment took the beach defences, cleared mines, and established itself ashore. B Company of the Winnipeg Rifles lost almost one hundred men in a few hours.

The North Shore Regiment landed at St. Aubin. Private Joe Ryan, a signaller, had been ordered to stick close to his company commander. "He was six feet, one inch, and I am a five-foot, four-inch guy. When he stepped into the water waist-high, I thought, 'That's not so damned bad' — and jumped in — and damn near drowned." The radio he carried got drenched and did not work, and the only spare battery had been forgotten on the landing craft.

The North Shores faced a concrete bunker that had also survived the dawn shelling. Only after the bunker's hundred defenders and its anti-tank gun had caused numerous casualties and knocked out several of the Fort Garrys' tanks were the Germans eliminated. West of the town, the rest of the North Shores got into France with relative ease, though c Company had a six-hour struggle to take the hamlet of Tailleville, something accomplished with the aid of the Garrys' Shermans.

The Canadians' reserve battalions, the Canadian Scottish and Le Régiment de la Chaudière, touched down within a few minutes of the lead units. The Scottish came off the landing craft hugging bicycles that some planner had thought sure to facilitate movement inland. (They didn't.) The Chaudières suffered heavy losses from mines hidden by the tide, but still managed to take the town of Beny-sur-Mer by late afternoon, thanks to effective support from HMCS *Algonquin*, just offshore; thirteen of fifteen rounds fired landed directly atop a battery of three 88mm guns blocking the regiment's advance. By nightfall, the Canadians had pressed farther inland than any other Allied troops.

On the other D-Day beaches, the British and Americans were also getting ashore, though with difficulty. At Utah Beach on the lower end of the Cotentin peninsula the Americans landed with relative ease. But on Omaha Beach, where a golf course now amuses tourists, the U.S. 1st Infantry Division had the bloodiest landing of all, its unlucky GIs hitting a stretch controlled by effective troops operating from the high ground. The specialized British armoured vehicles, despised by the Americans, might have made a difference; instead, a total of 7,500 Americans were killed, wounded, or captured at Omaha and Utah beaches.

In the British sector things went better. On Gold Beach the 50th Division got ashore easily, and on Sword the veteran 3rd Division landed without too much difficulty but, because of fierce German resistance, failed to take its D-Day objective, the city of Caen.

Inland, the 81st and 101st U.S. Airborne divisions and the British 6th Airborne, including the 450 men of the Canadian Parachute Battalion, were scattered by heavy winds, mistakes, and evasive action by their pilots. Like many other paratroopers, Lance-Corporal Wilf De Lory of Toronto landed alone. "I'll never forget that eerie feeling of being by yourself in the middle of the night among thousands of enemy troops and not having a clue as to where the hell you were," he remembered. The Canadian battalion's task was to capture a German headquarters at Caranville, destroy a bridge over the Divette River, and hold the crossroads at Le Mesnil, atop a ridge that gave an unobstructed view of the beaches. The Canadian paratroopers accomplished their tasks. So did most of the 23,400 men in the three airborne divisions, seizing key bridges and road junctions, confusing the *Wehrmacht* high command as to the direction of the attack, and delaying German reinforcements from reaching the front. Their casualties, however, were enormous.

Canadian losses on June 6 were officially described as "light" — 340 killed, 574 wounded, and 47 captured. That was lower than the planners had feared. But to anyone who sees the row after row of graves, all dated 6 June 1944, in the Canadian military cemetery located just off the D-Day beaches at Beny-sur-Mer, "light" is not the word that comes to mind.

THE BRIDGEHEAD

By the end of D-Day, more than 130,000 soldiers had landed by sea, along with 6,000 tracked and wheeled vehicles, 600 guns, and 4,000 tons of supplies. For Eisenhower and Montgomery, for the public in the Allied countries and those nations living under Nazi tyranny, the invasion of Europe had unfolded as it should. The Allies were in France again and they were there to stay.

Their task now was to expand the bridgehead. The *Wehrmacht*'s job, of course, was to try to drive them into the sea. The first German counter-attack in strength fell upon the 3rd Canadian Division.

The North Nova Scotia Highlanders of the 9th Brigade, with the tanks of the Sherbrooke Fusiliers in support, had the task of taking the villages of Buron and Authie, on the outskirts of Caen. The Germans were in Buron, and the North Novas had to fight house to house in an effort to drive them out. At Authie, matters were worse. There the Canadian advance outstripped its artillery support and ran head on into the 12th SS Panzer Division, a crack formation made up of unblooded teenage *Hitlerjugend* led by experienced officers and non-commissioned officers, and its 25th SS Panzer-Grenadier Regiment, led by *Standartenführer* Kurt Meyer. For the first time, the Canadians encountered skilled and well-led German soldiers advancing under cover of a well-placed mortar barrage. For the first time, the Shermans faced the superior German tanks.

The result was calamitous. The Canadian battalion reeled under the assault and was ordered to pull back to Buron, itself under German attack. But disengaging proved more difficult in action than it had on exercises in England, and few managed to escape. C Company of the North Novas was wiped out, and the Sherbrooke Regiment's tanks and their green crews were unable to handle Meyer's skilled Panzer-grenadiers. Already Canadian armoured regi-

As the Canadians moved into Germany, the men were ordered not to fraternize with the enemy. Other posters, more practical, warned of VD.

House-to-house battles complete the destruction of a German town; above, German Pows wash up in a stream.

The Germans had been driven back into the shrunken Reich, but the war would not end until the Western Allies linked up with the Soviets. Hitler's dream of conquest had turned into nightmare.

VE-Day—May 8, 1945—saw joyful celebrations across most of Canada, like these revellers at King and Bay streets in Toronto.

The task of bringing the boys home was complicated. Shipping space was limited, and a complex points system determined who went when. Here, the ss *Pasteur* docks in Halifax in June 1945.

For all the VE-Day rejoicing, Canada was still at war until August 15, when Japan surrendered following the atomic bombing of Hiroshima and Nagasaki. The Japanese surrender meant freedom for the Canadians captured at Hong Kong on Christmas Day, 1941. The survivors were in appalling condition, brutalized, starving, and sick. Here, an officer from HMCS *Prince Robert* begins the inevitable paperwork before repatriation.

"Back to Civvy Street" was the goal of nearly every serviceman, and the armed services and the Department of Veterans Affairs tried to smooth the way. Rehabilitation courses began in Europe, while troops were waiting for transport; once they were home, counselling was offered on all kinds of personal and professional problems, and a variety of re-establishment grants and programs was available.

In the wake of repatriated soldiers, sailors, and airmen came more than 47,000 war brides, among them these apprehensive mothers arriving in February 1946. Here, too, the government tried to help, providing free sea and rail passage, as well as food allowances and medical attention. These young families faced some difficult adjustments, but the majority settled in and began a new life.

The Canadian War Cemetery at Calais.

ments were beginning to refer to their Shermans as "Ronsons", a bitter reference to the way their high-silhouetted tanks exploded into flames when hit. The Sherman's 75mm gun could not penetrate the front armour of the Panther tank, but the Panthers' high-powered gun could wipe out Allied armour at long range. The one consolation was that replacement Shermans were readily available; the Panthers were in short supply. Allied mass production, in other words, could swamp the Panzers by sheer weight of numbers. Tank crews, too, were expendable.

Many Canadians were taken prisoner in that day's fighting. That evening twenty-three of them, most from the North Novas and Fusiliers, were murdered by the men of the 12th ss Panzer Division. One sergeant of the Nova Scotia battalion observed the fate of some of his comrades: "I saw seven men from c Company…just sitting there…. Then I heard firing and saw some of the boys tipping over towards the road and a couple tipped over backwards. I could see the guards standing on the road firing at them…. After that they pushed the bodies towards the centre of the road." Many had previously been wounded; some had their hands tied behind their backs; some of the corpses were ground into pulp by tanks. Later the 12th ss would commit similar atrocities against officers and men of other Canadian units, and after the war Kurt Meyer was tried and found guilty of war crimes. His sentence of death was commuted to life imprisonment by a Canadian general who knew that Canadians, too, had killed prisoners.

The next day was much the same. At Putot and Cairon the ss Panzergrenadiers fell on the Royal Winnipeg Rifles and the Regina Rifles. The Winnipeg battalion, under enormous pressure and almost surrounded, retreated under fire. The Regina Rifles, with twenty-two Panther tanks to their front and rear, held their ground when their headquarters was overrun and were rescued by the timely arrival of Sherbrooke Fusiliers tanks. The Reginas' commanding officer, Lieutenant-Colonel Foster Matheson, actually killed a German riding a captured motorcycle through the Reginas' headquarters in Bretteville; his men knocked out six German tanks, three of them by PIAT. A counter-attack by the Canadian Scottish retook Putot that evening but again the cost was terrible. The Royal Winnipeg Rifles lost 257 men, including a number of POWs murdered by the ss. The Canadian Scottish lost 45 killed and 80 wounded.

The 3rd Canadian Division had been badly battered, but its lines remained largely intact. The 12th ss Panzer Division had also suffered heavily, losing irreplaceable tanks and absorbing heavy casualties. The result of the fighting thus far was a territorial standoff — the Canadians had not been driven into the sea — with the honours for combat success going to the Nazis.

The Canadians had another crack at the ss on June 12. A combined British-Canadian force took the town of Rots in a confused mêlée. There was less success at Le Mesnil–Patry, one of the objectives taken by the Canadian Parachute Battalion on D-Day but subsequently abandoned. The Queen's Own Rifles were to take the town, supported by tanks of the 1st Hussars, but inexperience left D Company hanging onto the outside of the tanks when the ss opened fire. The riflemen were decimated, a few reaching the farmhouses of Le Mesnil on sheer courage; the Hussars lost nineteen tanks of B Squadron to the enemy's tanks and antitank guns and brought only two Shermans back to the Canadian lines. Le Mesnil was a demoralizing disaster.

At this point, fortunately, the Canadians were pulled out of action for two weeks. That was just as well, for the 3rd Canadian Division had suffered 1,017 fatalities and 1,814 wounded in six days of fighting. Some 70 per cent of those casualties had been suffered by infantrymen, a rate as high as or higher than that suffered in the trench fighting of the Great War.

In a few days in Normandy, the Canadians had learned much about war, much that all their years of training had failed to teach them. They knew now about the fighting skills of the Germans. They realized that digging in was not just a tiring chore but a life-saver. They understood the requirement for coordination between infantry, armour, and artillery, and the commanders at all levels had begun to understand the necessity of prompt and accurate information. As Matthew Halton of the CBC reported to Canada on June 20, the Canadians "were new to battle. They'd never heard the screaming shrapnel before. They hadn't been machine-gunned or sniped at. They hadn't had bombs thrown in their faces. They hadn't been overrun in their slit trenches by tanks. But they have now...."

Lieutenant-Colonel James Roberts, who commanded an armoured reconnaissance regiment in Normandy, noted later that every soldier in his first action asked himself, "How will I behave under fire? Will I act in a cowardly or frightened way?" Roberts' own experience made it "crystal clear that each soldier, no matter what his rank, is deeply influenced by the presence of his comrades and knows in his heart that he must behave in a calm and courageous manner in order to retain the respect of his fellow soldiers."

But war, as an officer of the Fort Garrys said, "was 85 per cent boredom and 15 per cent sheer terror." Some soldiers could not bear the strain, and their courage snapped. There was no shame in that, or at least there ought not to have been. A man would fight well for a long period, but then some incident or near miss would finish his ability to carry on. Battle exhaustion — or shell shock, as it was popularly known — was a reality, and some 700 Canadians were diagnosed as suffering from it in July 1944. The next month, almost twice as many were designated as "neuropsychiatric casualties" — suffering from acute fear reactions and acute and chronic anxiety.

As in the Great War, many senior officers simply failed to understand the stresses the front-line soldier operated under and the reality of battle exhaustion. They tended to see the problem as cowardice. But psychiatrists intervened, as they had not in 1914–18, to insist on a medical, not a disciplinary, response. There was no cure: soldiers admitted to rest centres rarely returned to front-line service. Treated or untreated, battle exhaustion took its toll on regiments. One report by the Canadian Scottish of the 3rd Division, dated July 28, 1944, noted that the regiment had lost 569 casualties since D-Day, leaving only 336 of those who had landed on the beaches. Of 421 disabled by that date, 117 had been evacuated as battle exhaustion cases. Another 60 men had been sent to corps rest camp or pulled out of the line because their officers and medical officers thought they needed a rest. The Scottish was a good regiment, well trained and with an admirable fighting record, but there were experiences that flesh and blood could not tolerate for too long.

Evidently, war was a learning process. Soldiers had to learn how to fight, but also how to master their fear — and the process of learning to overcome fear could only take place in action. Now that the 3rd Canadian Division and the 2nd Armoured Brigade had seen battle no one had any doubts that they would go on to give an even better account of themselves.

From Caen to "Spring"

After six days the areas held by the Allies had been expanded to form a continuous deep bridgehead along the Normandy coast, and they had almost a third of a million men in France, along with 54,000 vehicles. The Mulberry harbours were nearing completion, but even without them more than 100,000 tons of supplies had been put ashore. The air forces were in operation on French soil, too — on June 10 RCAF squadrons No. 441, 442, and 443 began flying sorties from rough air strips just inland, "the first Allied squadrons to operate from French soil since the evacuation from Dunkirk," they boasted. Spitfires, Mustangs, and Typhoons were in the air continuously in daylight hours, shooting up everything that moved behind the German lines. The Typhoons, in particular, chewed up Nazi Panzers, spreading terror among the German troops. But just a week after D-Day, Hitler had launched the V-1 flying bombs at London, diverting Allied fighter resources that might have been used at the front.

The V-1s notwithstanding, the *Wehrmacht*'s strategy for the defence of the French coast had clearly failed. Rommel had had to deal with the Führer, who persisted in believing that the Normandy landings were just a feint, intended to divert attention from the Pas de Calais where the "real" invasion would soon occur. Panzer divisions continued to be held in reserve, long past the point of good sense. On the other hand, so overwhelming was Allied air superiority that Hitler's stubbornness probably saved his tanks for later battles.

Montgomery had a strategy too, though it was imperfectly understood by the Americans and was perhaps not entirely clear to Montgomery himself. The plan was to have the British and Canadians press hard to Caen, tying down the bulk of the German armour. That would allow the Americans to break out of the *bocage*, the Normandy hedgerows, in a giant wheeling movement to the south and east. The problem with the scheme was that it put the Canadian and British divisions in the hot seat, facing the best enemy divisions and the bulk of the Panthers.

While the Americans gathered strength and supplies for the breakout, the Canadians were moving on Carpiquet. The little town on the outskirts of Caen had an airfield that was, intelligence reported, defended by 150 of the teenage soldiers of the 12th ss. General Keller had learned that maximum force was necessary against the ss, and he sent out four battalions of infantry, the Fort Garry Horse, and all the artillery his division could muster.

It was not enough. Moving across ripening fields of wheat, the North Shore Regiment and Le Régiment de la Chaudière encountered heavy fire. The North Shores had forty-six killed in their worst day of the Normandy battle, leaving the fields strewn with "the pale upturned faces of the dead", as the regimental padre wrote. The Royal Winnipeg Rifles fared even worse, for their assault on the hangars and bunkers of the airfield lacked even the cover provided by waist-high grain. The riflemen tried twice to drive the ss out of the airfield, but failed; the Winnipegs who got farthest had to drive off ss counter-attacks to hold their hard-won ground. A company of Chaudières was overrun by the Nazis that night; some of the French Canadians were captured, bound, shot, and burned by their captors.

If Carpiquet could not be taken, Caen would be. The assault was preceded by a massive attack by RAF Bomber Command that destroyed much of the centre of the medieval city. Unfortunately, few Germans died in the raid, the enemy having sensibly removed almost all its men from the built-up areas; four hundred civilians were less lucky. Others sheltering in the great St. Etienne cathedral survived, though the old church was damaged, as was the centuries-old château on the hill in the centre of town. From the army's point of view, the raid was a total failure. All the bombers had done was to fill the street with rubble, impeding the advance and providing good defensive positions for the enemy.

The assault on Caen saw the 3rd Division return to some of the towns it had seen only a month before. On July 8, the Highland Light Infantry took Buron after a day-long struggle that cost it 262 men and its commanding officer. The North Novas took Authie, and the 9th Brigade captured the Abbey of Ardenne, Kurt Meyer's headquarters. The next day, the Canadians cautiously pushed their way into the city itself, astonished to be cheered as liberators by the survivors of the RAF bombing. Halton of the CBC reported the liberation to Canada:

> Amid their thousands of dead and wounded men, women and children, most of them the victims of our bombing and shelling, amid worse wreckage than I've seen in any war or campaign, amid fire and smoke and bursting shells and diving enemy aircraft, several thousand people of Caen came out of the ancient abbey church where they'd been taking shelter, to watch the flag of France broken from a masthead, and to sing the *Marseillaise* with strained and broken voices and with tears running down their cheeks....

It had taken thirty-three days to reach Caen — a city that was to have been secured by the end of D-Day.

On July 18, as the American advance was stalled at St. Lô, Montgomery launched Operation "Goodwood": three British divisions set off southward from Caen towards Bourguébus Ridge, a height of land that dominated the way south along Route Nationale 158. Again, heavy bombers were supposed to clear the way; again, the enemy remained well entrenched. From their positions overlooking the plain, antitank gunners of one of Germany's crack divisions, the SS *Liebstandarte Adolf Hitler*, calmly destroyed the Shermans of the Guards Armoured Division, one of the best formations in the British army.

Now it was the Canadians' turn. Guy Simonds' II Canadian Corps, with the 3rd Division and with General Charles Foulkes' newly arrived 2nd Canadian Division, had come into operation on July 11. Operation "Atlantic", beginning on July 18, was its baptism of fire.

The two Canadian divisions had to clear Caen's south-eastern suburbs. The 3rd Division faced hand-to-hand fighting in the ruins of a steelworks at Colombelles against a *Luftwaffe* division, and at Faubourg de Vaucelles and Giberville as well. With difficulty and at heavy cost, the objectives were largely taken, and by nightfall units of the division had crossed the Orne River and reached the city's outer suburbs. The 2nd Division had an easier day, battalions clearing Louvigny, bridging the Orne, and, the next day, taking Ifs and Fleury-sur-Orne.

On July 20, however, the 2nd Division's objective was Verrières Ridge, a 250-

foot hill that dominated the road south from Caen. Verrières, like Bourguébus, was defended by the *Leibstandarte Adolf Hitler*. The Queen's Own Cameron Highlanders of Winnipeg on the right captured St. André-sur-Orne and
held it against heavy counter-attack. On the left, Les Fusiliers Mont-Royal
managed to seize Beauvoir and Troteval farms. But in the centre there was
disaster. The South Saskatchewan Regiment, advancing in a rainstorm that
grounded the vital Typhoons, ran smack into ss Panzers and lost more than
two hundred men, including its CO. As the survivors fled with the ss in pursuit, they passed through two companies of the Essex Scottish, and panic
proved contagious.

Fortunately, the two rear companies of the Scottish held and beat back the
Germans. Not for long, however. The next morning the Germans attacked
under cover of heavy rain, overrunning the Windsor regiment's remnants and
two companies of Les Fusiliers Mont-Royal. Only the timely arrival of the
Black Watch saved the 6th Brigade from complete destruction. If there was a
lesson in this day's fighting, it was that a green Canadian division was no
match for experienced German units. German training was better, German
leadership more experienced, and the difference was simply too great.
"Atlantic", Simonds' first battle in Normandy, had been a costly failure.
Almost 2,000 men had been killed, wounded, or captured.

The Germans lost Field Marshal Rommel at this point. On July 17 a Typhoon
had strafed a staff car near Vimoutiers, grievously wounding the *Wehrmacht*
commander, and he had been replaced by Field Marshal Gunther von Kluge.
On July 20 plotters in the *Wehrmacht*, convinced that Hitler was leading Germany to total destruction, attempted to kill the Führer at his headquarters in
East Prussia. The dictator, who was bending over a heavy table at the moment
a bomb secreted in a briefcase exploded, was deafened and shaken but not
seriously hurt. His vengeance was terrible. More than 4,000 genuine and
alleged opponents of the regime — army officers and civilians both — were
tortured and killed. Senior officers were strangled on slaughterhouse meat-
hooks while film cameras recorded their agony for Hitler's later entertain-
ment. Rommel, Germany's most famous general, was implicated in the plot;
too illustrious for exposure, he was allowed a soldier's death at his own hand.

Simonds' corps moved forward again on July 24 in Operation "Spring",
another attack on Verrières. "Spring" was intended to keep the Panzers
pinned around Caen and to allow the American breakout to proceed, despite
delays, on July 25. There were complications in getting the operation under
way, in part because the Germans made skilful use of mining tunnels south
of Caen to harass the Canadians by popping up in the rear and on the flanks.
But at 3:30 A.M. the Canadians moved off, under a new tactical device from

Simonds' fertile brain: "artificial moonlight", produced by bouncing search-lights off the clouds. The drawback was that the light sometimes silhouetted the attackers, making them easy targets.

That happened to the North Nova Scotia Highlanders of the 3rd Division, who struggled forward in something that soon approached chaos. Tanks of the Fort Garry Horse coming forward to assist the North Novas were shot up as well. Barely a hundred survivors made their way back to the lines. The 2nd Division had it harder still. The Royal Regiment of Canada failed to take Rocquancourt, the concentrated fire of thirty German tanks proving too much to overcome. Then the Black Watch moved on Verrières with 325 men. The Montreal regiment surged up the slope in open order only to be slaughtered in two "killing grounds" the Germans had prepared at the summit. About 15 of them survived unscathed. And the Germans were not yet finished: an ss attack fell on the Royal Hamilton Light Infantry and its tough, determined commander, Lieutenant-Colonel John Rockingham. Rocky's Rileys (the nickname came from the regiment's initials, RHLI) used everything they had to drive off the Panzers. When three of their supporting 17-pounder antitank guns were knocked out, they continued to fight using cumbersome PIATs, and pitching grenades. The unit held but had 200 casualties. The Black Watch lost 307. It was one of the bloodiest days of the war for the Canadians.

THE CAULDRON

Operation "Spring" had achieved one of its purposes by helping to tie down the Germans — with eleven Panzer divisions around Caen — and by leaving the armour in front of the Americans — three Panzer divisions — weaker than it might otherwise have been. On July 25, Operation "Cobra", the American breakout from the *bocage*, began at last, as General George Patton's newly formed Third U.S. Army fought its first battles. In Sicily, Patton had demonstrated that he was an aggressive and flamboyant leader and a bit of a bully. But he was a superb tank commander and he pushed the Americans forward with great speed. By July 28 the GIs were in Coutances; by the 30th they had reached the Atlantic coast at Avranches.

What would the Germans do now? Good military sense suggested they should withdraw into a defensive position behind the Seine. But good military sense was in scarce supply at Hitler's headquarters, and after the failure of the July 20 assassination attempt few generals were inclined to argue with the Führer. The result was that Hitler decided on Operation "Lüttich": the Germans would gather their Panzer divisions and before the end of the first week of August they would strike at the American army — which the Führer believed would surely crumble under attack — at Mortain and Avranches. The plan was madness, as von Kluge instantly realized. "An attack, if not immediately successful," he told the High Command, "will lay open the whole attacking force to be cut off in the west." Moreover, although Hitler refused to admit it, the Panzer divisions to be employed in the attack had been battered severely by the British and Canadians and savaged from the air. Most could muster only a few battleworthy tanks.

The plan had other failings. For one thing, the Allies knew about it, thanks to Ultra — the top secret decoding effort based at Bletchley Park in England. General Omar Bradley changed his First U.S. Army's dispositions to suit. Also, the plan pressed the German armies into a potential trap. If the British and Canadians could push south to the road junction at Falaise, the Germans might be caught in a giant pocket and eliminated. Bradley, perhaps the least bloodthirsty of Allied commanders, was exultant: "This is an opportunity that comes to a commander not more than once in a century. We are about to destroy an entire hostile army."

At this stage the First Canadian Army under General Crerar became operational. Crerar had Simonds' II Canadian Corps under his command, and the weary 3rd Division, which had been in action almost without a break since D-Day, was replaced by the newly arrived, but very green, 4th Canadian Armoured Division and its thirty-three–year–old commander, General George Kitching. Crerar's army also included I British Corps and the 1st Polish Armoured Division. The Poles — tough, silent men, far from their occupied homeland — had their own scores to settle with the Nazis.

Simonds was now aiming for a breakout to take Falaise. His plan, named "Totalize", called for his men to break through the German antitank screen that had turned "Goodwood" and "Atlantic" into costly fiascos. To do this, he planned to use darkness and heavy RAF bombing. To solve the problem of transporting the infantry against the entrenched Germans, Simonds decided to take the guns out of the "Priest" self-propelled artillery that had come ashore on D-Day and turn the vehicles into Armoured Personnel Carriers. The result was the Kangaroo — the first APC, and a brilliant solution by the one tactical thinker the Canadian army had yet produced. The carriers were soon formed into a regiment commanded by Gordon Churchill, later a senior minister in John Diefenbaker's government.

"Totalize" called for regimental-sized columns to roll forward, each consisting of tanks, specialized armoured vehicles, and a battalion of infantry aboard their Kangaroos. To find their way in this wholly new kind of night attack, the vehicle drivers would follow radio beams, searchlights, and tracer fire. "We did not expect that any of these devices would be adequate,"

Simonds later explained, "but we hoped that a combination of them all would enable direction to be kept." As the armoured columns rolled forward, following units would mop up the bypassed enemy, who by then would have been shattered by the aerial bombing. And once the lead divisions had broken the German line, three divisions would exploit the breakthrough.

At 11:30 P.M. on August 7, "Totalize" was ready to roll, just hours after "Lüttich" had launched most of the Panzer divisions westward. Inevitably, the Canadian assault became confused, despite the direction-finding aids. Each of the four columns got lost and casualties were severe, but by midday on August 7 most units had taken their objectives. The villages around Caen that had proved so costly in July did so again, but Rocquancourt, May-sur-Orne, and Fontenay finally fell. Verrières Ridge was also taken at last. But the second phase of the attack slowed as the battlefield degenerated into chaos, with the dust from thousands of tanks and vehicles filling the air and with too few roads to move thousands of men. Worse, a raid by 678 USAAF aircraft dropped many of its bombs short of the Germans and atop Canadian and Polish units. Three hundred Canadian and Polish soldiers were killed or wounded, including General Keller of the 3rd Division. Two companies of the North Shore Regiment were wiped out. Few Canadians ever again trusted the bombers.

Now an old enemy arrived on the scene: Kurt Meyer's 12th SS. While heading for "Lüttich", Meyer's unit had been diverted to deal with the threat posed by "Totalize". Riding his legendary motorcycle, Meyer himself rallied the fleeing Germans, posted the fearsome 88mm guns, and sent for Tiger tanks. The already stumbling advance bogged down further; "Totalize" was in trouble.

It would get worse. On August 9 the British Columbia Regiment's tanks set off in the darkness, with the infantry of the Algonquin Regiment aboard, to take the high ground south-west of Quesnay Wood that dominated the Caen–Falaise road. The armoured commander, Lieutenant-Colonel D.G. Worthington, radioed headquarters that he had arrived on his objective; in fact he was four miles away, in an open field and almost directly under the guns of Meyer's Panzers. The two Canadian units fought a hopeless day-long battle, losing 240 killed, wounded, and captured, and forty tanks. Worthington himself had led the struggle but died in a mortar bomb explosion.

Meyer also demolished the Queen's Own Rifles and the North Shore Regiment, as they tried to clear Quesnay Wood and reach the Laison River. The Hitler Youth allowed the Canadians to emerge from the woods, then hit them with everything they had. Another 165 Canadians fell victim to the 12th SS. So did Operation "Totalize", called off by Simonds on August 11.

It was clear that II Canadian Corps had to make another major attack.

Operation "Lüttich" had lasted little more than one day before it was shattered by American air attacks and stubborn defence. While the generals pleaded with Hitler to be allowed to withdraw, the roads to the east and safety were already filling with long columns of *Wehrmacht* and ss vehicles and horse-drawn carts. The shrinking pocket of fleeing Germans had to be closed at its nearest point, near Falaise. The Canadians, as Simonds later wrote, were "to break the pivot on which the German withdrawal to the Seine must hinge."

Simonds' new plan to reach the crucial road junction at Falaise was called "Tractable". This called for two huge blocks of armour, one provided by the 4th Armoured Division, the other by the 3rd Canadian Division and the 2nd Armoured Brigade, to move off in daylight at full speed under cover of smoke. The infantry would again move in the Kangaroos. RAF bombing would precede the advance and cover the flanks. Every available gun and fighter-bomber would be used in support, though in the interests of surprise there was to be no preliminary bombardment. The plan was crude — there were no written orders, to preserve secrecy — but it might have been able to roll over the stubborn but weakened German defences had an officer carrying a marked map not got lost and been captured. The Germans were ready, after all.

The armoured columns started forward just before noon on August 14. Very quickly disaster came from the air, when RAF bombers dropped their payloads not on the Germans in Quesnay Wood but on Canadians and Poles. This time 400 were killed, wounded, or missing. Air Marshal Sir Arthur Coningham, commanding the RAF's 2nd Tactical Air Force, was behind the lines in a Staghound armoured car, almost directly under the bombers. "You know," he told General Simonds as he brushed the dust out of his hair, "I never did believe in using heavy bombers for close support." Almost no one did after that second disaster, though Simonds, the creator of the plan, maintained that without the bombing "our casualties would have been a great deal higher."

The German defenders did their utmost to stop "Tractable" by pumping shells at the armoured boxes; one fatality was Brigadier E. L. Booth of the 4th Armoured Brigade. The Laison River also proved a more formidable obstacle than expected, with tanks bogging down on the steep banks and in the gluey mud of the river bottom. But the river was soon crossed. To everyone's surprise, Germans began surrendering; not Meyer's ss, but men from two *Wehrmacht* divisions just arrived in France from Norwegian occupation duty. The Normandy battlefield was vastly different from the coffee houses of Oslo and Bergen. Meyer's division — with only fifteen tanks left — staged a night attack on the 1st Hussars, and his teenagers, fast turning into old men under the strain of the fighting, held off repeated efforts to take Versainville.

It was now more urgent than ever to take Falaise. Patton's Third U.S. Army had reached Argentan in the south, the designated inter-army boundary. There he stopped, lest his men blunder into the Canadians. Patton asked Eisenhower if he could move on to Falaise — to "drive the British into the sea", as he put it with his usual delicacy; but the Supreme Allied Commander ordered Patton to set off for Paris with the bulk of his armour, leaving just enough at Argentan to protect the bottom of the Cauldron, as the Germans now called the gap.

Cauldron it was, too. The ixth and xixth Tactical Air Commands of the USAAF, with their Thunderbolts and Mustangs, joined the British and Canadian pilots of the 2nd Tactical Air Force in their Spitfires and Typhoons as they flew thousands of strafing and bombing sorties over the retreating Germans. The roads were clogged with tanks, trucks, horses, and men, while smoke from burning supplies and trucks hung over the whole area. Pilots could smell the burning and rotting flesh even as they flew at three hundred miles an hour. "Lüttich" had turned Normandy into a charnel house for the ss and the *Wehrmacht.*

By August 16, Simonds' divisions were ready to move once more to close the eighteen-mile gap between them and the Americans and to encircle the retreating enemy armies. The 2nd Canadian Division headed for Falaise while General Stanislaw Maczek's Polish Armoured and Kitching's 4th Canadian Armoured set forth to close the Nazi escape route. Now in command of the German forces was Field Marshal Walter Model, successor to Field Marshal von Kluge, who had killed himself rather than face the Führer's wrath at the loss of the armies in France. Model was tougher; he recalled the 2nd ss Panzer Corps, which had reached safety, to smash at the Canadians and Poles, but he needed time to extricate his men from the Cauldron.

Simonds did not propose to allow Model much of that. On the 17th, the ruins of Falaise finally fell. On the 18th two American and one Free French division at last began fighting northward from Argentan towards Chambois. The 4th Armoured took Trun and set up a defence line to hold off the retreating enemy, now advancing towards them. The Poles moved east of the Canadian division to head off Model's counter-attack, most of the division taking position on a wooded hill their commander dubbed Maczuga, or "mace".

South from Trun on August 18 came a squadron of the South Alberta Regiment led by thirty-two–year–old Major David Currie, along with a company of the Argyll and Sutherland Highlanders under Lieutenant (Acting Major) Ivan Martin. Their objective was St. Lambert-sur-Dives, through which passed the last road open to the enemy. By the afternoon of August 20 two additional companies of infantry had joined Currie's little group to face waves of Germans. Currie's antitank weapons had destroyed trucks and Panthers but they proved ineffective against the largest German tank, the Tiger. The Canadian called for artillery support from the big 5.5-inch medium guns, and the heavy shells did the trick.

But the day's carnage was terrible. All Currie's officers were killed or wounded, and Currie, forced to be everywhere at once, directed the fire of his few remaining tanks and antitank guns, and knocked out a Tiger by himself. The citation for his Victoria Cross quoted one of Currie's NCOs: "We knew at one stage that it was going to be a fight to the finish, but he was so cool about it, it was impossible for us to get excited." His command had destroyed seven tanks, twelve of the deadly 88mm guns, and forty vehicles, and had killed, wounded, or captured an incredible 2,900 Germans. General Simonds recalled being unable to use a road in the area because it was piled high with German dead.

At Maczuga, the Poles were in a desperate struggle. Their tanks wreaked havoc on the Germans, as did artillery fire from the 4th Medium Regiment of the Royal Canadian Artillery; its batteries were directed onto target by their liaison officer with the Poles, Captain Pierre Sévigny, later a Cabinet minister. But the Poles had received no fresh supplies of food, ammunition, or gasoline, and their casualties were heavy under the unrelenting German attack. "Tonight," the senior survivor told his officers, "tonight we die." The survivors — the Poles lost 135 officers and 2,192 men — were relieved at noon the next day, August 21, by the Shermans of the Canadian Grenadier Guards. With Poland still in German hands, the Polish division was of course unable to fill its ranks with reinforcements. The only solution was to comb the ranks of German POWs for Poles, and to draft all found into the division!

With the Falaise Gap closed, the fighting moved rapidly eastward. The battle had been an unquestioned Allied victory, though the Canadian difficulty in closing the pocket around Model's troops had allowed many to escape. A number of senior Canadian commanders, General Kitching among them, were replaced by September. Still, the German army had lost half its men in Normandy and most of their equipment. Since D-Day, 300,000 Germans had been killed or captured, and there were 200,000 more isolated in fortified French ports on the Atlantic, certain to be taken whenever the Allies chose to assault them. Moreover, German losses in equipment were staggering: 2,200 tanks had been destroyed, countless trucks, innumerable guns. General Leclerc, commanding de Gaulle's French forces that were now leading the drive for Paris, commented that it all seemed like the spring of 1940 in reverse: "complete disorder on the enemy side." It was true, though the Germans had a capacity to reorganize and rearm that the French army in 1940 had lacked.

BACK TO DIEPPE: ON TO ANTWERP

The war was not yet won. The problem for the Allies, with their armies still driving forward, was supply. As they crossed the Seine, Eisenhower's mechanized divisions rapidly outran their logistical support. Modern armies devour vast quantities of ammunition, gasoline, and a host of supplies from bridging equipment to boot laces. The ports in Allied hands had only limited capacity, and truck convoys and improvised airlifts could not get enough fuel and ammunition to the armoured divisions now rolling forward at speed. "Inevitably we will be checked," Eisenhower admitted ruefully.

The Germans, of course, realized this and determined to defend the towns they still held on the English Channel. While the British, French, and Americans freed Paris and moved into Belgium, the First Canadian Army had the task of capturing a succession of defended and fortified ports.

For Montgomery, Allied strategy now depended on a single critical choice. If supplies were short, it was a mistake to keep all the armies moving forward; instead, a single powerful thrust should be directed at Germany. Get bridgeheads over the Rhine as soon as possible, then drive twenty divisions across the North German plain at Berlin. The result might be victory in 1944 — vital to Britain, which was out of men as well as money. Naturally, Monty claimed command of this mailed fist; the Americans would play the secondary role.

Whether his strategy was militarily correct or not, it was politically unacceptable. The American public would simply not tolerate seeing U.S. troops in a subsidiary role, and General Eisenhower and his Anglo-American staff, none too impressed with Montgomery's command of the Normandy battlefront, fully realized this. Eisenhower, a tough man when he had to be, rejected Montgomery's plan.

The task of the First Canadian Army would be the same no matter whether Ike or Monty prevailed. The Canadians had the extreme left of the Allied line and the task of opening the French ports. Their coastal advance also meant that they were forced to bridge the rivers at their mouths, the widest points. The Canadians faced a fierce fight in crossing the Seine but then the army moved quickly to liberate Rouen. By September 1, the 2nd Division was back at Dieppe, that port of bitter memories; happily, this time the defenders had gone. The 2nd Division paraded to honour its dead of 1942. Crerar attended the ceremony and was ticked off by Montgomery for missing a field marshal's conference; the unrepentant general insisted that a Canadian ceremony took precedence.

The same day, the 3rd Division took Le Tréport. But neither port had the capacity to supply more than a small portion of the Allies' needs. Antwerp, the great inland Belgian port on the Scheldt River, could, and the British captured the city, with its twenty-eight miles of docks largely intact, on September 4. The Germans were by this time, as Guy Simonds noted after the war, in "a state bordering panic...officers were deserting, commandeering cars and making for Germany, not from cowardice but in the belief it was all over...." Simonds added that his men had found a German 88mm gun in perfect working order, with ammunition stacked beside it. "When I saw that gun, I knew that we would win. It was the first time I had ever seen a German gun position abandoned without a fight." At that point, the banks of the Scheldt could have been readily cleared, freeing the port for use; unaccountably, the too-cautious British failed to move, and the opportunity was lost.

Frantic to restore a front in France and the Low Countries, on September 4 Hitler declared that Boulogne, Calais, Dunkirk, and Walcheren Island in the Scheldt estuary were fortresses to be held to the last. Canadians would pay bitterly in blood for the British slowness and for Hitler's decree.

The Canadians had to cross the wide River Somme first, and then take Boulogne in Operation "Wellhit", a task Simonds gave to the 3rd Division. Heavy bombers (called in by Simonds, who went over General Crerar's head to Bomber Command) and artillery softened the defences, but the Germans held out for six days in their strongly fortified hilltop positions. On September 23 the *Wehrmacht* finally surrendered, 9,500 prisoners going into the bag. Canadian casualties were 634. The 3rd Division then assaulted Calais on September 25. Action continued until October 1, when 7,500 Germans gave up. Donald Pearce, a lieutenant in the infantry, was not amused by the German commander after the surrender:

[He] was content enough about the defeat; it was an objective fact, no tears shed over it at all. But he was burningly interested in knowing the details of the Allied tactics: "Now why did you come in from the precise direction you did, when we were sure that you would come in from over here? What an interesting piece of tactics.... Had you come in just here, where we also expected you, do you suppose you could have succeeded? We had a warm reception prepared for you, if you had come in here...." What he was interested in was the tactical lessons.... This is not exactly stupidity, I suppose; but then, what is it, if not what the divisional commander called it — "Damned nonsense"?

The Canadians were experienced combat soldiers now, but evidently there still remained differences between a professional army and one composed largely of citizen soldiers. The Canadians simply wanted to get the whole dirty job over with so that they could go home. It would take eight more months, and thousands more dead, to complete the task.

XVIII
VICTORY

With France now all but cleared of the Nazis, the outcome of the war was no longer in doubt, though the Germans showed remarkable recuperative powers. v-1 and, soon, v-2 missiles rained down on London, beginning a terrible new era in warfare. Jet fighters, much faster and more manoeuvrable than propeller-driven aircraft, began to come off the German production lines. Despite Allied bombing, tank production in the Reich was at its peak, and Panzer units were being rebuilt. There were even units to equip; seventy divisions were being manned and armed in the West, a process that saw sixteen-year-olds inducted, training units cannibalized, and the middle-aged and infirm put into uniform. Neither the *Wehrmacht* nor the ss was as formidable as it had been a year or two before; but Hitler's legions had not yet been battered into submission.

THE BATTLE FOR THE SCHELDT

Though the First Canadian Army had barely reached Belgian soil, Montgomery's forces plunged forward into The Netherlands. The field marshal's plan was to launch a combined ground and airborne invasion code-named "Market Garden" on September 17, 1944, to secure crossings over the River Maas and the two main branches of the Rhine. Paratroopers seized several bridges and established a bridgehead at Arnhem, but then lost it again in a vicious fight. The failure of "Market Garden" was a serious loss, for the approaches to the great Belgian port of Antwerp were still held by the Germans, though the city itself was in Allied hands. Until the approaches were cleared, Allied armies would not be able to get the supplies they needed by the shortest and most direct route. Responsibility for clearing the approaches fell to the First Canadian Army, under the acting command of General Guy Simonds while Harry Crerar recovered from a serious attack of dysentery.

Antwerp lay on the Scheldt River, fifty miles from the sea. To the north of
the river's estuary was the peninsula of South Beveland, and the strongly
defended Walcheren Island. All this land was low-lying, as was the south shore
of the estuary, where the reclaimed land of the polders was below sea level
and the water was held back by fifteen-foot–high dikes topped by roads. The
dikes and two large canals would serve as solid defensive positions for the
Germans.

Simonds' plan for the Scheldt battle was straightforward. The 2nd
Canadian Division was to attack north of the estuary while the 3rd took the
south. Tough, ruthless when necessary, Simonds was just forty-one years old
in October 1944. He was one of Montgomery's favourites, almost the only
Canadian general for whose military skills the field marshal had any regard.
And Simonds, like his hero, had no qualms about firing battalion or brigade
commanders who could not or would not drive their men to achieve the
impossible.

Certainly the Scheldt battlefield verged on the impossible. The ground was
sodden and the mud thigh-deep as the under-strength infantry units of the 2nd
Division's 4th and 5th brigades headed north towards the narrow isthmus to
South Beveland. The soldiers from the Royal Hamilton Light Infantry, the
Black Watch, and the Calgary Highlanders started out on October 6 with the
object of capturing the farm town of Woensdrecht, which controlled the German land route from Beveland.

The Germans were ready for them. Their guns, mounted on the reverse
slope of the only high ground in the area, commanded the flat, muddy
approaches to Woensdrecht, and they had breached the dikes and flooded the
polders. The Royal Regiment of Canada tried and failed to take the causeway
isthmus, suffering heavy losses in the process — the casualties inevitably falling heaviest on platoon commanders and junior leaders, who had to get the
attacks moving. The Black Watch also failed, two days of fighting costing the
Montreal unit eighty-one casualties for not a yard. The Calgary Highlanders
were next, in an epic struggle against entrenched German paratroopers that
lasted from October 7 to October 10. On October 13 — "Black Friday" — the
Black Watch launched itself in a daylight attack over 1,200 yards of beet fields.
The result was tragic. Every one of the unit's company commanders was
killed or wounded. One of them, still functioning despite his wounds,
reported that he had only four men left out of the ninety who had begun the
attack. For the second time in four months, the Black Watch was wiped out as
a unit.

Not until October 16, when the Royal Hamilton Light Infantry launched a
heavily supported night attack, was the assault renewed. Jumping off at 3:30

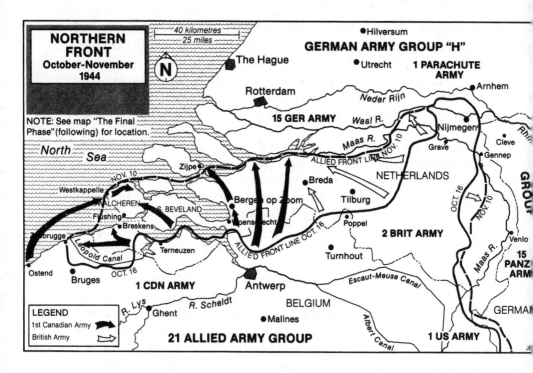

A.M. with the fire from 168 guns leading the way, the RHLI was initially successful, but the paratroopers soon counter-attacked, overrunning one company and sending its survivors fleeing to the rear. The Germans were driven off only when Major Joe Pigott, another RHLI company commander, called down a massive artillery barrage on his own positions. The 4,000 shells knocked out the German tanks and killed or wounded most of the paras. Pigott won the DSO for his actions that day. But as the RHLI's commanding officer, Lieutenant-Colonel Denis Whitaker, later noted, his battalion's estimated strength after that night and morning's fighting was only 6 officers and 157 men, barely a fifth of normal. Finally, on October 24, the job of cutting the isthmus was completed by units of the 5th and 6th brigades.

Again the cost was high. The Fusiliers Mont-Royal — under Major Jimmy Dextraze, a future Chief of the Defence Staff — suffered grievously in an attack on Nederheide, half a mile east of Woensdrecht. The FMRs also had to bear the indignity of being bombarded with leaflets: "French Canadians, Soldiers of the Regt. of Mont Royal.... You are in a country where there is nothing but rivers and canals. The English were clever enough to send you to the most difficult battlefield. You are *not* obliged to fight. Lay down your arms, helmet and belt, desert, stick your hands up, put up the white flag and you are saved." The

Wehrmacht propagandists were right about one thing—the Scheldt *was* the most difficult battlefield.

Once Beveland had been isolated, the rest of the north shore was cleared quickly, though only after hard fighting. The 4th Brigade led the assault and pressed on for forty-eight hours, until battalions of the 6th Brigade took the lead. Assisted by a seaborne assault across the West Scheldt by British troops, the 6th Brigade crossed the Beveland Canal on October 27–28. Beveland was soon cleared of the enemy, and now only Walcheren Island remained.

Walcheren was joined to Beveland by a causeway 1,200 yards long and 40 yards wide — just wide enough for a road and a railway. The Germans commanded this uninviting route with machine-gun fire, and the unlucky Black Watch, again stuck with an impossible task, suffered heavily in the first attempt to cross. An assault by the Calgary Highlanders pushed across the causeway but was then driven back by German flame-throwers. George Teasdale of the Calgarys remembered the Germans "firing shells from the other end, bouncing them off the road, and they were ricocheting back and forth all over the place.... I think I got close to the other side...." On November 2 Le Régiment de Maisonneuve managed to cross the narrow strip of land and establish a few platoons tenuously on Walcheren. Only then, after a prodigal waste of lives and courage, did staff officers recognize that the bridgehead would be a hopeless base for new attacks. At this point the Canadians were relieved by British troops under command of the First Canadian Army. Walcheren was finally cleared on November 8, after Simonds came up with a brilliant plan for a massive artillery and air bombardment to breach the dikes and flood much of the island, thus creating new beaches for amphibious assault by British commandos, army units, and the 4th Special Service Brigade — again under the First Canadian Army's command.

South of the estuary, the 3rd Canadian Division was just as heavily engaged, as it struggled to eliminate a pocket of German troops based at Breskens. The main obstacle, the Leopold Canal, was crossed only with the assistance of massed flame-throwers. The Germans continued their stubborn resistance but were eventually subdued when an amphibious assault launched with the aid of "Buffaloes" — a new troop-carrier that could carry thirty men across almost any water obstacle — completely surprised them. The historian of the North Shore Regiment recalled that the campaign was "a misery they had not known before. It was like Indian warfare, small sections taking desperate chances, probing, feeling, trying to outguess the enemy"—and all this in muddy fields where the cold and wet seeped right into the bones.

Great ingenuity was required to operate in such conditions. For example, Le Régiment de la Chaudière improvised a bridge across the Uitwaterings

Canal by driving a Bren-gun carrier into the water and piling earth, planks, and steel beams on top of the submerged vehicle. "It worked perfectly," 8th Brigade commander Brigadier James Roberts recalled, "and, next morning, the Queen's Own Rifles passed over it and through the Chaudières...." By November 3, the south bank was secure.

The Battle of the Scheldt had cost 6,367 Canadian casualties, a terribly high price for five weeks' fighting that could have been avoided. But once the German-laid mines had been cleared from the river, the port of Antwerp was opened and the supplies necessary for the final push into Germany could readily reach the front. Field Marshal Montgomery congratulated Simonds for the First Canadian Army's success: the operations had been "conducted under the most appalling conditions of ground—and water—and the advantage in these respects favoured the enemy. But in spite of great difficulties you slowly and relentlessly wore down the enemy resistance, drove him back, and captured great numbers of prisoners." More than 41,000 had been taken. Monty added that "It has been a fine performance, and one that could have been carried out only by first class troops."

THE CONSCRIPTION CRISIS

After the Scheldt battle, the First Canadian Army entered a three-month period of rest, recuperation, and light action. That was fortunate for soldiers weary from five months' unrelenting warfare and a long march from the Normandy beaches to the Dutch polders. But there were few long leaves for the men. "We knew why leaves were so scarce," Major Ben Dunkelman of the Queen's Own Rifles wrote. "Thanks to Prime Minister Mackenzie King's handling of the Conscription Issue at home...." In Italy, Brigadier Bill Murphy was even more bitter. "I personally will never cast another Liberal vote as long as King has anything to do with the party." Of all the armies, he told his family, "only that of Canada has no provisions for home leave"—and the soldiers were convinced that the reason was "that there are no men to replace them—except the Zombie army"—the derisively named home defence conscripts. "And to preserve [the Zombies'] precious skins the volunteers just have to take it." The prime minister's handling of the manpower issue was now to be tested in the greatest domestic crisis of the war.

The issue was reinforcements. The defence minister, Colonel J. Layton Ralston, had gone to Italy and north-west Europe in September 1944 to see for himself the condition of the army and to check out disturbing rumours about reinforcement shortages. To his shock, Ralston had discovered after characterically painstaking enquiry that the truth was even worse than the rumours.

There was such a shortage of infantry reinforcements that some poorly trained soldiers had been sent to the front, along with men recently recovered from wounds. That hurt morale and fighting efficiency, which in turn led to further casualties. Ralston returned to Canada determined to press the issue of conscription, determined to force Mackenzie King to honour the pledge he had made in 1942: "not necessarily conscription, but conscription if necessary". Now, Ralston insisted, conscription was demonstrably necessary to provide at least 15,000 infantry reinforcements to keep the battalions up to strength. And those men, he argued, could only be found among the 60,000 NRMA trained soldiers in Canada.

Not so, Mackenzie King replied. What he had meant by "necessary" was *necessary to win the war*. Who could doubt, with the Russians pressing west and the Allies east, that Germany would soon be compelled to give up the fight? Why tear the country apart so late in the war? As the struggle in the Cabinet intensified, suddenly it all came clear to him: the ministers opposing him on conscription were almost the same as those who had opposed the great program of social welfare that had been gradually put in place since the beginning of 1944. The push for conscription, he decided, was part of a conspiracy of reactionaries.

At this point King's thoughts turned to General McNaughton, the much-beloved soldier who had taken the 1st Canadian Division overseas in 1939 and built it up into an army. McNaughton had been recalled in late 1943 because British officers doubted his abilities, and Ralston, no admirer, had gone along with the move. The general and the defence minister had little love for each other. More to the point, McNaughton thought conscription the wrong way to recruit an army. He remained enormously popular with the troops and the public, sought by all three parties and often proposed as a first Canadian-born governor general.

On November 1, 1944 came one of the climactic Cabinet meetings in Canadian history. The conscription issue was once more rehashed at length. Then, King said, "I thought we ought to, if possible, reach a conclusion without further delay." He wanted McNaughton to be defence minister:

> the people of Canada would say that McNaughton was the right man for the task, and since Ralston had clearly said that he himself did not believe we could get the men without conscription, while McNaughton believed we could, and that he, Ralston, would have to tender his resignation...that I thought if Ralston felt in that way he should make it possible for us to bring McNaughton into the Cabinet at once—the man who was prepared to see this situation through. I said that in regard to a resignation...he had

tendered his resignation to me some two years ago and had never withdrawn it....

The axe had fallen, wielded by the brutal master of politics. But it was a gamble. Would Ralston's friends resign with him? King sat quietly while Ralston said his farewells, shook hands around the table, and left. No one departed the council chamber with him.

The news of Ralston's sacking put the conscription crisis on the front pages in screaming headlines. To King's horror, and to McNaughton's distress, the publicity created a firestorm of reaction against the once-popular general. Audiences booed and jeered when he tried to rally the country behind the no-conscription policy. Worse yet, the NRMA soldiers resisted the new appeals that their officers made to them to volunteer for overseas service. The Zombies had heard those arguments many times before and, as one put it, "If Mackenzie King wants me to go overseas, he'll have to send me. I'm damned if I'll volunteer to help out this government."

Thus, by the third week of November the reinforcement crisis remained much as it had under Ralston. The shortage of trained infantry remained, the conscriptionist ministers were again getting restive, and King faced yet another crisis. How could he get out of it this time?

The answer came on November 22, when McNaughton telephoned. "The Headquarters staff here," King recorded the general as saying, "had all advised him that the voluntary system would not get the men....it was the most serious advice that could be tendered...." At once, King said, "there came to mind the statement that I had made to Parliament in June [1942] about the action the government would necessarily take if we were agreed that the time had come when conscription was necessary." Now conscription *was* necessary — not to win the war, but to save the government — and King prepared to reverse the course he had held so steadfastly.

But how could the prime minister justify the switch to himself—and to Louis St. Laurent, the Minister of Justice since late 1941 and the key Quebec minister? That was no problem for a mind so agile. The advice of the generals, he rationalized, constituted nothing less than a revolt, "the surrender of the civil government to the military", a "palace revolution". Better to yield to conscription than to see democracy destroyed. Tough and clear-minded as he always was, St. Laurent nonetheless went along with this fiction. Air minister Power would not, however, and promptly resigned to keep faith with his promises to Quebec.

The crisis was effectively over. King told the Cabinet of his *volte-face*, and the ministers passed an order-in-council sending up to 16,000 NRMA soldiers overseas. Across the country, reverberations rattled a few windows. Quebec newspapers and politicians railed against the government, while many English Canadians called for King's head for all the delays. But King survived a vote of confidence in Parliament, likely helped by the fact that both a conscriptionist, Ralston, and an anti-conscriptionist, Power, had left his government. After all, what better illustrated the essential moderation of his policy?

At Terrace in British Columbia — inland from Prince Rupert — a brigade of NRMA men mounted guns on the single rail line and announced that they were on strike. Senior officers, who had been attending a conference in Vancouver, returned and quietly restored order. Despite a large number of desertions, 12,908 NRMA men went overseas before the end of the war, and 2,463 were posted to units of the First Canadian Army. As it happened, the predictions of "wastage" that had provoked the reinforcements crisis had been incorrect. The three-month hiatus between the Battle of the Scheldt and the army's return to action prevented thousands of casualties. The transfer of I Canadian Corps from Italy to north-west Europe in February 1944 also provided a respite. Further conscription measures therefore proved unneeded, and it could be argued that the whole crisis had been unnecessary—but no one, in November 1944, could foresee that.

INTO GERMANY

If the First Canadian Army was in a static period, the war nevertheless went on. In December 1944 the Germans suddenly struck at the First U.S. Army in enormous force through the heavily forested and lightly manned Ardennes. Hitler's aim was to reach Antwerp, trapping huge armies and creating a second Dunkirk. The First Canadian Army was not directly involved in this titanic struggle; had the *Wehrmacht* made it to Antwerp, the Canadians too would have been caught in the trap, but General Eisenhower quickly moved his armies to counter the threat. Although units of the Yanks dissolved in scenes of great chaos, others held on, especially at the critical road junction of Bastogne, and the line was soon restored. The Ardennes attack may have been Hitler's last offensive gasp, but it demonstrated that the *Wehrmacht* remained a formidable foe even with its back to the wall.

A wily foe, too. On Christmas Eve, as Ben Dunkelman remembered, the Germans sang carols and fired tracers into the air, "as good as any display of fireworks". The Canadians opposite them in the line relaxed, left their slit trenches, and watched. "At this point, without warning, the enemy let loose a tremendous barrage of fire at our positions."

On New Year's Day, RCAF squadrons were among the targets for the *Luft-*

waffe's counterpart to the Battle of the Bulge. Eight hundred planes, including a captured Spitfire, tried to catch the Allied flyers with New Year's Eve hangovers. Scores of Allied aircraft were wrecked and burned — but so were *Luftwaffe* planes when the Allies responded. RCAF squadrons had some of their best days, and — unlike the Germans — they could make good their losses.

By February 1945 the Canadians were back in action. With General Crerar again in command, the First Canadian Army participated in massive operations to destroy the remaining Nazi armies west of the Rhine. Under Crerar were thirteen divisions, including nine British divisions and units of Belgians, Dutch, Poles, and Americans. It was the largest force ever commanded in operations by a Canadian officer. The plan was for Crerar's army to strike south-east to clear the land between the Maas and Rhine rivers.

The Canadians faced three lines of German defensive works: a strong line of outposts; the Siegfried Line, or West Wall, running through the wooded area of the Reichswald; and the fortified Hochwald area, again heavily forested and protecting the Rhine crossings at Wesel. The plan to break these lines was code-named "Veritable".

"Veritable" began on February 8 with a massive air and artillery bombardment. "I don't know what effect [the bombardment] had on the enemy," one Canadian remembered, "but, by God, [it] frightened me." Then came the tanks and, behind them, the Canadian infantry, cracking the outpost line — held by a scratch German division — with fewer casualties than expected. But in the Reichswald forests the going was slower, the resistance stronger, as the *Wehrmacht* fought stubbornly and with cunning on German soil. Donald Hough, a photo interpreter with the Royal Canadian Engineers, remembered the way the Germans used dummy artillery to draw fire and mislead the attackers—one battery was "heavily camouflaged and had a flash simulator in it which sent off flashes for two rounds ranging and ten rounds gunfire."

The Germans, who were desperate to delay the advance while they rushed in reinforcements of high quality parachute and Panzer troops, had flooded the low-lying ground, creating the familiar quagmire that Canadian soldiers had been obliged to deal with in the Scheldt fighting. When the 3rd Canadian Division faced a weak Grenadier Regiment, they reported that the floods were the "greatest enemy", and one officer remembered that he had had to help two short men through the deep spots, holding their battledress collars so their chins stayed out of the freezing water. Even so, by February 10 the 9th Canadian Infantry Brigade had broken through the Siegfried Line defences and fulfilled the promise of the popular 1939 song "to hang out the washing on the Siegfried Line". Hough recalled that the troops put up a sign and "on a line suspended on poles hung the proverbial washing." In fierce fighting, the Reichswald was cleared by February 13.

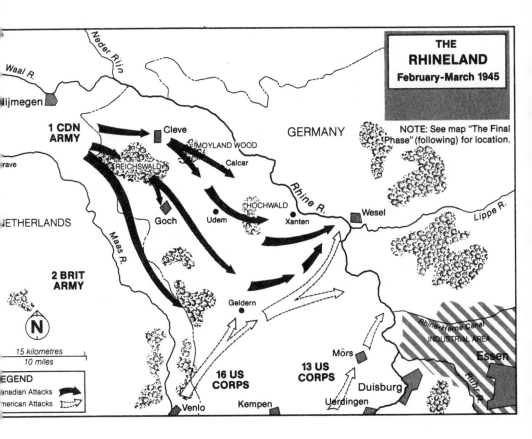

Then strong pockets of resistance had to be eliminated in Moyland Wood and along the Goch–Calcar road, a task entrusted to units of II Canadian Corps. Infantry of the Royal Winnipeg Rifles, the 1st Canadian Scottish, the Royal Hamilton Light Infantry (Rileys), the Royal Regiment, and the Essex Scottish did the job. The Canadian Scottish suffered especially heavy losses against German paratroopers; they had 140 casualties on February 18–19, including 53 taken prisoner after a counter-attack. The Winnipeg Rifles lost even more, but finally crushed enemy resistance in Moyland Wood on the 21st.

The Hochwald was next. Situated on a ridge in front of the ancient town of Xanten, the forest was to be the object of Operation "Blockbuster" on February 26. Although German paratroop units launched an attack on the jumping-off point of the 2nd Division just hours before the planned start of "Blockbuster", the enemy was driven back by a company of Rileys and tanks of the Fort Garry Horse. As a result, "Blockbuster" started on schedule at 3:45 A.M., the troops moving in Kangaroos or aboard tanks and finding their way with the aid of artificial moonlight. The Cameron Highlanders of the 6th Brigade, assigned a critical objective, almost faltered when their commanding officer was killed. Major D.M. Rodgers, one of the Winnipeg regiment's company commanders, took over, personally cleared three houses of snipers, and ensured that the assault took the ground as planned. The major won the DSO for his gallantry.

On the 3rd Division's front, the Queen's Own Rifles had a difficult time attacking Mooshof, where they were forced to cross an open slope studded with pockets of paratroopers. The German tactics were very effective, as Major Dunkelman explained:

> No rigid defence: under attack, they hold on as long as possible in their excellently concealed slit trenches, then withdraw to prepared positions a little further back. Instantly, previously ranged mortar and artillery fire is poured on the positions they've just vacated—even if a few of their own men are still there. The shelling is coordinated with infantry assaults to retake the ground they've lost. Superb tactics.

Twice the QOR's leading platoon was driven back by German fire, and a Nazi counter-attack left the platoon with only five unwounded survivors. Sergeant Aubrey Cosens took command, ran twenty-five yards in the open to a tank of the 1st Hussars that had finally arrived to lend support, and—sitting exposed in front of the turret—directed fire against the German position. Then he broke up another counter-attack by plunging the tank directly into the midst of the Germans. Next Cosens organized a counter-attack by his men and directed the tank to ram one of the farm buildings that had been turned into a fortified German position. He then cleared the building and two others, winning the awe of his riflemen. Cosens had killed at least twenty Germans, and captured as many more. But the sergeant was not invincible, and as he went to report to his company commander he was cut down by a German sniper. The Victoria Cross was posthumously awarded to Sergeant Cosens.

On the last day of February, the Canadians attacked the Hochwald proper, losing scores of men to enemy mines and fire before finally clearing it on March 4. Xanten fell on the 8th, and on March 10 resistance ceased west of the Rhine. Canadian casualties in operations "Veritable" and "Blockbuster" numbered 5,304. The Germans had lost untold numbers of dead and more than 22,000 prisoners.

I Canadian Corps, fresh from the Italian front, now joined Crerar's First Canadian Army. The new arrivals were astonished at the endless air cover, the profusion of armour, and the flow of supplies that the north-west European front received. For the first time all major Canadian units were under one command. The expanded First Canadian Army crossed the Rhine on March 23 in Operation "Plunder". The troops were ferried across the great river in Buffaloes under cover of a massive artillery barrage, and the resistance was comparatively light, the Germans clearly having consumed their last effective resources west of the Rhine. "It begins to look as if the Hun has lost all his fight and confidence," the Irish Regiment's padre wrote home. "The general picture certainly indicates the fall of all organized resistance. What is making them continue?"

By the beginning of April, the Canadian army was driving rapidly northwards. Its task was to clear the north-eastern Netherlands, the German coast east to the Elbe, and the western Netherlands. II Canadian Corps handled the first two tasks, while I Canadian Corps undertook the latter.

The fighting was never easy—even *in extremis* the German soldier remained the best fighting man in the world—but the advances were rapid. II Corps cleared Deventer, Zwolle, Groningen, Emden, Wilhelmshaven, and Oldenburg. Some units found and enjoyed the spoils of war. Trooper Bill McDowell of the 8th Reconnaissance Regiment wrote home that "we took a lot of boats off a canal, and they were full of wine, candy and food." His unit "sure did a lot of wine drinking and had a good time as we could get anything we wanted with the candy."

I Corps captured Arnhem and Appeldoorn — where, Farley Mowat wrote, "the only shots fired were those fired into the air by the [Hastings and Prince Edward Regiment] C.O.'s pistol as he sought to clear a path through the civilian throngs." The Canadians were preparing to assault the German defences around Utrecht when the Nazi *Reichskommissar* in The Netherlands offered to permit food to be brought in to feed the starving Dutch—the official daily ration in April of that "hunger winter" amounted to 320 calories—if the Canadians stopped their advance. Field Marshal Montgomery agreed, and a *de facto* truce went into effect on April 28. One soldier of the Saskatoon Light Infantry remembered that first night: "It was too quiet. You were so used to sleeping with shells landing all about you," Bob Stier recalled, "that when it became quiet that night, nobody could fall asleep." Food was carried into this heavily populated area of Holland by truck convoys, or dropped from the air. A pilot officer in Bomber Command, Colin Friesen, recollected that "Thank you, Canadians!" had been painted on the rooftops — but he also recalled that, in accordance with the truce, the aircraft had to keep to routes and heights agreed to by the Germans. "I remember watching the German ack-ack guns and I can recall them following our progress.... And then the Dutch people would appear everywhere in the vicinity of the drop...everywhere waving banners and caps—and I'm sure of it, you felt you could hear them cheering." You could, too.

By the end of April, the war in Europe truly seemed to be drawing to a close. On April 25, American and Soviet soldiers, happy but already a little wary of each other, had met at Torgau, cutting the remnants of the Third Reich in two. The Russian armies were crushing everything in their path. Soviet tanks and grenadiers were already inching their way through the rubble of Berlin against fanatical resistance from old men and young boys. The American, British, and Canadian armies were moving eastwards with speed, now rounding up prisoners by the tens of thousands as German will at last began to collapse. The Soviets were so feared, their desire for revenge against the Nazis who had slaughtered millions in the Soviet Union so obvious, that the main aim of German soldiers—and civilians—was to end up on the Allied side of the final armistice line.

The Germans had reason to be afraid. By now, the Allies had liberated concentration camps in Eastern Europe and on German soil. For years there had been rumours of horrible atrocities, but most Canadians had tended to discount them as propaganda. Now the truth was there for everyone to see. The pitiful survivors, dressed in their striped rags, were literally skin and bones. General Georges Vanier, the Canadian ambassador in Paris, reported after seeing the camp at Buchenwald that he could actually see "how [their] knee and ankle joints held together." In death camps such as Auschwitz, the "showers" that had produced not water but Zyklon-B gas, the ovens used to dispose of millions of corpses, stood as mute testimony to the Nazis all-too-successful attempts to eliminate the Jews, gypsies, and other *Untermenschen* of Europe. Outraged Allied commanders rounded up local townsfolk and marched them through the camps. In future, they believed, no one would ever be able to deny that such atrocities had occurred. Soviet commanders unleashed their soldiers on the population, and the rape of both young and old became a daily occurrence.

There was sporadic fighting and still more death. As late as May 4, an officer and the padre of the Canadian Grenadier Guards left their lines to try to assist German wounded. Both were killed. They were almost the last Canadians killed in action in the European theatre, as General Crerar called off all operations the moment he learned that surrender negotiations were in progress. The war *was* drawing to a close.

The Führer of the Third Reich, the man responsible for the great war that had devastated the continent and caused misery around the world, was now living a mole-like existence in his deep bunker in the centre of Berlin. On April 29, Adolf Hitler married his mistress, Eva Braun, and the next day the Nazi leader and his bride committed suicide. While most of the Führer's personal staff took part in a wild orgy, others in the entourage killed themselves and their children. Hitler's body was taken to the surface and burned with the aid of gasoline.

A few days later, on May 2, the German armies in Italy surrendered. In Germany, however, Grand Admiral Karl Dönitz — Hitler's choice as successor — delayed the surrender as long as possible to permit more troops and civilians to reach the Allied lines. Surrender negotiations in north-west Europe began at last on May 4, to conclude only in the early morning hours of May 7. Effective at 8:00 A.M. May 7, the war in Europe was over.

At the front, the reaction was not one of jubilation. "I think we were all a bit numb," Major-General Harry Foster of the 1st Canadian Division recalled. "Six and a half years is a long time for any man to be thinking about just trying to stay alive.... I think everyone was just too bloody tired to get excited." Lieutenant John Bennett, who was with his artillery unit near the German naval base at Emden, remembered "a tremendous feeling of relief. They issued us two rations of rum that morning." And a navy man explained, "The stress level we had maintained for so long was replaced by a feeling that can only be described as subdued and a little sad."

Robert Rintoul, a corporal in the Royal Canadian Dragoons, had more profound feelings of relief. Just before the surrender, his squadron had been pinned down by German artillery fire, and he and his comrades at first refused to believe the good news. "Ah, that's all bunk, propaganda," was their initial reaction; the war was supposed to be over "but the Germans were still using shells."

Farther away from the front, the joy was unconfined. John Gray, an army intelligence officer, helped liberate a Dutch city after Nazi surrender. His jeep passed a house full of German soldiers "waving and yelling excitedly, as joyously as the liberated Dutch."

This we weren't quite in a mood for yet, and we hurried by with only a perfunctory acknowledgement of this forgive-and-forget gesture. It wasn't just a rough hockey game we had all been playing, and even if these men had not committed the mindless bestialities of the Nazis... they could not expect us to stop thinking them loathsome just because pieces of paper had been signed saying the shooting would stop.

A Dutch teenager in The Hague remembered the arrival of the liberating troops:

...I saw a tank in the distance, with one soldier's head above it, and the blood drained out of my body, and I thought: *Here comes liberation.* And as the tank came nearer, I had no breath left, and the soldier stood up, and he was like a saint. There was a big hush over all the people, and it was suddenly broken by a big scream, as if it was out of the earth. And the people climbed on the tank, and took the soldier out, and they were crying. And we were running with the tanks and the jeeps all the way into the city.

Such moments almost made up for the war's suffering.

The celebrations in Paris were, well, French. Barney Oldfield, a soldier on leave, was decorated with kisses by pretty *jeunes filles*. "We knocked on a house door and were invited in to celebrate with a family." Another soldier, Charlie Cunningham, was in Paris on a three-day pass on May 8. "I think I kissed and hugged half the women in Paris that day. All ages. And I don't think I had two drinks out of the same bottle all day." In London, celebrants mobbed Piccadilly Circus, while more solemn crowds gathered in front of Buckingham Palace waiting for Churchill and the king.

At home in Canada, the celebration got out of hand. Not in Toronto, where thousands danced in the streets and three Mosquito bombers dropped tickertape. Not in Ottawa, where enthusiasm was likely dulled by Mackenzie King's address of thanksgiving. Not in Vancouver, where people remembered that the war with Japan had still to be won. But in Halifax it was different.

Halifax had nearly doubled in size during the war, with some 60,000 servicemen added to the Nova Scotia capital's peacetime population of 65,000. Many of the newcomers, in addition to chafing under military discipline, hated the town, disliked the locals, and bitterly resented the antiquated liquor laws. The resentment boiled over when VE-Day came and businesses, restaurants, and stores – including liquor stores — shut down for the holiday. Despite plenty of notice, service commanders had done nothing to plan for the VE-Day mood. Nor had civil authorities. Milling, frustrated sailors and some soldiers and airmen, joined by civilians, sacked Keith's Brewery and attacked liquor stores, "liberating" 65,000 quarts of booze. One participant remembered coming across a sergeant "who had a full case of Canadian Club. He had already emptied one bottle and was selling the others at fifty cents each." Certainly there was alcohol enough to fuel rioting and the looting of more than five hundred businesses, including restaurants and taverns. While some celebrated the coming of peace by coupling on Citadel Hill, other women were raped, three rioters died, and two hundred more were arrested. The mayor blamed the navy, and declared, "It will be a long time before the people of Halifax forget the great crime." The navy took the lesson to heart. When VJ-Day came in September, things were different, as Chief Engine Room Artificer Walt Farrell recalled. "They had a real party. There was no rough stuff. They had orchestras and everything [at the base]. Had a real good time. Everybody had all the booze they could drink.... There wasn't a window broken in Halifax...."

POLITICS AT HOME

The silencing of the guns in Europe meant that domestic politics picked up steam. Mackenzie King had already announced that a federal election was to take place on June 11, not at all coincidentally the same day that a provincial election was scheduled for Ontario. But Premier George Drew, a fierce opponent of the federal Liberals, moved his election up one week to June 4. A Tory victory in Ontario would help John Bracken's federal Progressive Conservatives.

At the beginning of the federal campaign few expected a Liberal win. The memories of the conscription crisis the previous November were still strong, and the general feeling was that there had been too much death and suffering, too long a period of high taxes, too much Mackenzie King. Or so everyone thought.

But who were the voters to cast their ballots for? In Quebec, no federal politician stood high in the public estimation. In English Canada the CCF had clearly peaked at least a year before and though M.J. Coldwell, the party leader, was admired, a business-backed propaganda campaign depicted his party as "national socialists, eager to nationalize everything that moved". After all the wartime regimentation, that did not sit well with many. The Tories, expecting to be swept to power on a wave of anti-government sentiment, vowed to use conscripts in the war against Japan, and continually harked back to such Liberal failures as the wartime reinforcements crisis. Bracken was uninspiring as a speaker, and his promises roused little enthusiasm at a time when most people were worrying about the impact of peace on the economy. Did the end of the war mean another economic collapse like that of the Great Depression?

Mackenzie King's campaign was pitched to deal with this widespread fear. Liberal posters promised "a New Social Order", a CCF future without socialism. King talked little about the war, urging one London, Ontario audience to "Remember, it is with the future, not with the past, that you should be concerned." His government had implemented social welfare; "We have already placed on the statutes of Canada, law after law to deal with the situations that will have to be met through the coming years." One measure was family allowances, the centrepiece of the King campaign; every month, said one piece of Liberal election literature, family allowances would pour $132,981 into Cochrane, Ontario, and $153,891 into Welland. Such numbers, replicated across the land, translated into jobs and sales for merchants. Social welfare was a guarantee that, even if the economy slipped, no one would starve.

The result of the balloting on June 11 was unaffected by George Drew's Ontario triumph a week before. The King Liberals won 41 per cent of the popular vote and 127 seats while the Tories took only 28.5 per cent and 67 seats. The CCF drew 14.7 per cent of public support and won 28 seats. In the armed forces' vote, the Liberals won 35 per cent of the total, the CCF 32 per cent, and the Tories, despite their eagerness for conscription, only 26 per cent. That was perhaps the most astonishing result of the voting. J. Douglas Harvey, a young RCAF bomber pilot, remembered a large crowd of officers and airmen booing the prime minister in England:

"Who is this guy?" Many didn't know but we were booing lustily. Finally a ground crew flight sergeant enlightened me.

"It's Mackenzie King," he said.

"Who's he?" I asked.

A look of disdain came over the flight sergeant's face. "Our prime minister, you asshole."

I really hadn't known, nor had half the crowd in that hangar. Yet we all booed vigorously. It took several years before I fully understood how much the Canadian serviceman detested the man and his weak-kneed war policies.

Still, there could be little doubt that Quebec, as one writer noted, "saved our King". Quebeckers gave King more than 50 per cent of their votes and 53 seats. Presumably the French-speaking electorate had remembered that King had, after all, fought against conscription, a memory undoubtedly sharpened by the way the Conservatives kept harping on the reinforcement question.

Mackenzie King was duly grateful to the nation. As he wrote in his diary, "The relief of mind that I experienced is indescribable.... almost as if I had had a bath after a dusty and dirty journey, with the storm of lies, misrepresentations, insinuations...which I have had to pass during the past few weeks.... I felt a real vindication in the verdict of the people...."

Whatever the reason, Mackenzie King had won once more. The great magician of Canadian politics had conjured victory out of certain defeat. Perhaps he won because Canada's war effort had been so impressive in military, economic, and industrial terms. Whatever their political allegiance, Canadians had to recognize that the main job — the job that *had* to be done — had been done well.

THE ATOMIC AGE BEGINS

By May 1945, the Japanese Empire had shrunk to a small portion of its vast extent at the floodtide of victory in 1942. Then Tokyo had threatened Australia and India; now, aside from remnants of once-great armies struggling against the inevitable in Burma and garrisons on a few Pacific atolls, only the home islands remained. Japan's wooden cities were being torched in massive American bombing raids, and the once-mighty Imperial Japanese Navy had virtually all been sunk. But the Japanese soldier remained a daunting foe, and no one expected an easy or unopposed invasion of the home islands.

Canada was to participate in that invasion with army, navy, and air contingents. In September 1944, the Cabinet War Committee had decided that "as a basis for planning, but without any commitment", the Canadian army would provide one division and ancillary troops to operate with the Americans. Up to 30,000 battle-experienced troops, to be found from men serving in the European theatre, would make up the force. And, as the prime minister told Parliament on April 4, 1945, the force would be chosen "from those who elect to serve in the Pacific theatre". No conscription, in other words. Moreover, each volunteer was entitled to thirty days' home leave before posting to the Pacific.

In the RCN, with the cruiser HMCS *Uganda* already in the Pacific and HMCS *Ontario* under orders, the volunteers-only rule caused serious problems. Officers and ratings serving in Europe or Canada who volunteered for the Pacific were posted immediately to the cruiser *Ontario*. But those sailors already on the *Uganda* also had the right to decide if they wished to volunteer for Pacific service. *Uganda* had been engaged in operations off Okinawa and Japan; despite appeals by its officers, the majority of the ship's crew decided not to volunteer, and the cruiser embarrassingly had to return to Canada on July 27, 1945. In Canada, Petty Officer Earle Johnson remembered, with delight unaltered after forty years, that he had volunteered for the Pacific to get the thirty days' leave. "But...we beat them out — we got the leave, but didn't have to go to Japan," because the war ended before his ship was ready. "We were sent home instead!"

The army division for the Pacific war, the 6th Canadian, was organized on

American lines with regiments instead of brigades. In command was Major-General Bert Hoffmeister, who had been a successful armoured division commander in Italy and north-west Europe. His men were to concentrate at training camps across Canada, then move to Kentucky for further exercises.

The plans were in hand, and 24,000 officers and men had been posted to the Canadian Army Pacific Force, when the war against Japan came to its sudden conclusion in August. The atomic bombing of Hiroshima on the 6th and of Nagasaki on the 9th forced Japan to sue for peace and ended the Pacific war on August 14. Only a few realized that the A-bomb had changed warfare for ever. Even fewer had known that much of the wartime research into the secrets of the atom had been carried out in Canada, largely by British and French scientists, under the aegis of the National Research Council, and that Canadian uranium had been a vital resource. With the end of wartime secrecy, the government was quick to make its part known. Curiously, Ottawa kept silent until the 1980s about code-breaking work run by the National Research Council's "Examination Unit". The unit had cracked some Japanese army codes, as well as eavesdropping on German ship traffic — and on the Vichy French legation that had stayed in Ottawa until November 1942.

The survivors of the Hong Kong force and a few additional Canadians were among the thousands of prisoners of war held by Japan. All had suffered unspeakable treatment in their prisons, with beatings a regular occurrence and starvation the norm. After the surrender, remembered John Stroud, one of those captured when Hong Kong fell on Christmas Day, 1941, American aircraft flew over the POW camp at Niigata and dropped "everything we needed". Included were large pails of ketchup, one of which hit a tree and exploded, showering Stroud with red. "I thought, 'I've survived all this and now I've been wounded.'"

Without any logistical support in the Pacific, the Canadian government had to rely on the British and American forces in its efforts to help Canadian POWs. Leading the effort to rescue the 1,085 Canadians held in Japan was Brigadier Richard S. Malone, attached to General MacArthur's staff. In a CBC broadcast to Canada, Malone said, "It was hard for the prisoners to believe that they were now free. Some of them had just about given up hope in their prisons." Malone then quoted a prayer written by a Canadian officer after he had been locked up in Hong Kong for three years and was "beginning to wonder if we were really coming."

You know Lord how one has to strive at Sanshepow to
    keep alive.
And how there isn't much to eat —

Some rice and greens at Argyle Street.
It's not much, God, when dinner comes,
To find it's boiled chrysanthemums....
So what I really want to say is if we soon don't get
    away,
From Sanshepow and Argyle Street,
Then please Lord could we have some meat —
A luscious fragrant heaped up plateful.
And also Lord we would be grateful
If you would grant a living boon and send some Red
    Cross parcels soon.

A Grateful Nation

Canada was fully intending to grant a "living boon" to all its veterans. Nowhere were bitter memories of the Great War more pronounced. Ian Mackenzie, King's Minister of National Health and Pensions, had made a career as an advocate for his fellow veterans. He could remember the old complaints about pensions, settlement, and the "soldiers' bonus". Everything that had been sought by the men who returned in 1919 was included in the new "Veterans' Charter". But first a scheme had to be developed to bring them from Europe. The army worked out a complicated point system to determine priority for repatriation. Soldiers received two points for each month of service in Canada, three for each month overseas, and a 20 per cent bonus if they were married. Points were deducted for periods of non-performance of military duty, such as time spent in detention for infractions against military law. A high score got you home faster, though top priority was given to those who volunteered for the Pacific war. As General Harry Crerar told his men, shipping space was in terribly short supply, and Canadians were competing for that space with their Allies. That was why the battalions and regiments that had fought together through Italy, France, and the Low Countries could not go home as units.

Once the men and women got home, each received thirty days' leave. Discharge then followed; at the peak of demobilization, in the winter of 1945–46, 3,000 men and women were being returned to "civvy street" each day. Thanks to the efforts at reconstruction planning that had got under way at the very beginning of the war, and to the Department of Veterans Affairs (DVA), created in 1944, each veteran received $100 to buy civilian clothing and a war service gratuity of $7.50 for each thirty days' service, plus an additional 25 cents for each day overseas. In addition, veterans drew one week's pay for each six months' service outside Canada. In all, these gratuities went to just under one million men and women and amounted to an average of $488 each. Since compulsory savings had been deducted from men overseas, to deter overspending and British resentment, most veterans had a tidy nest egg.

In addition to that benefit, the government paid unemployment insurance premiums for more than half a million ex-service personnel. It passed the Veterans' Land Act to help settle 33,000 on the land as farmers and assisted thousands more in purchasing land. It offered loans to those who wanted to set themselves up in business. The DVA oversaw a vast training program that sent tens of thousands to vocational programs and helped rehabilitate the wounded and injured. Those who declined further education or vocational training or did not seek assistance settling on the land received instead a "re-establishment credit". This did not come in the form of cash; instead it could be used for the acquisition, repair, or modernization of a home; purchase of furniture; or to help start a business. (NRMA men who had not gone "active" did not receive this credit.) And there was a generous scheme of pensions for widows and dependants and for those whose lives had been permanently altered by physical or mental wounds. Canada wanted to be generous. By most contemporary standards, and certainly in comparison with 1919, a rich array of benefits awaited the veterans. It was no more than they deserved.

Tens of thousands of qualified veterans went to university to enrol or to finish degrees interrupted by the war. The universities, small, understaffed, and underequipped, had to prepare for this flood of veterans. At the University of British Columbia, President N.A.M. MacKenzie solved the housing and classroom needs of his campus by moving in 370 army huts from bases all across the province. Other universities followed suit, and veterans who had hoped that they had seen the last of H-huts now found themselves living and attending class in them. Toronto opened a new engineering school in abandoned war factories in the suburb of Ajax. Ottawa's Carleton University was virtually created by veterans.

Improvisation was the order of the day, but thousands of vets — most of whom had learned to discipline themselves and to organize their time in the service — became lawyers, doctors, engineers, and teachers as quickly as they could. Some universities speeded up their programs: UBC helped by giving veterans a year's worth of classes in four months.

However many grants and programs there were for the men and women who came home, the transition to peace was harrowing to many. Some Canadian soldiers had been overseas since December 1939 without once returning home, longer, they joked, than any soldiers since Alexander the Great's. Servicemen had worked in trades where killing was necessary, where cruelty often outweighed compassion. Now they were to return to a society where, thank goodness, the war's devastation had never touched down, where different mores prevailed, and where few who had not seen service overseas could understand the horror that air crew, infantrymen, or survivors of the U-boat war had come through.

Worse still, the veterans had not seen their wives or watched their children grow up. The strain that such prolonged separation placed on families and marriages was inevitable and immense. As Brigadier James Roberts wrote in a memoir, "I had left Canada in November 1941 and written regularly" to his wife once a week. "Like other Canadians, I had known several women in England during our three years of training there, but it had never even remotely crossed my mind that I would not return to Canada and resume my life with Helen." But Roberts fell in love with a woman he met in The Netherlands, and when he returned to Toronto, it was to a difficult situation.

> I found Helen waiting for me at the Union Station and I was very glad to see her again, after an absence of nearly four years. We took a taxi to her apartment, made coffee, and settled down to talk about our personal affairs. As to the war years, they never seemed to have happened; she did not seem to be interested, and I found little to talk about with her except the important question of what we were going to do.... I told her openly that I had fallen in love and that I wanted a divorce....

That happened to many veterans. Many others found that their wives had made other arrangements while they were overseas.

Still other soldiers, sailors, and airmen faced the problem of integrating British, French, Dutch, or Italian war brides into their families at home. Many had exaggerated the extent of "Daddy's ranch in Toronto", as one "Herbie" cartoon teased. The brides themselves had to adjust to a new culture, and while they were generally greeted with kindness and warmth, there were hostile moments.

Harder still was the effort faced by those who had lost a husband or father overseas. Private Elmer Johnson of the Loyal Edmonton Regiment died on the Senio River in Italy just days before 1 Canadian Corps pulled out of the line to rejoin the First Canadian Army in north-west Europe. Years later his son, who had been just three years old in 1945, wrote of what it meant to grow up without a father:

> I can't remember how I felt when told of his death, not knowing the meaning of the word. But as I grew in consciousness, his absence became a fact

of my life — like being a boy and not a girl, or living with people who were my family and not somebody else's. I came to realize I would never see him, but it wasn't something I could rationally get my mind around.

Because everybody else I knew had a father, I felt set apart, like one of the strange people hidden in backrooms or attics. It also meant I didn't have an obvious and recognizable identity: I didn't belong to Dr. X or Shift Boss Y. However, I did have a privileged spiritual link. While my classmates uttered abstractions during the daily rote muttering of the Lord's Prayer, I had a picture in my mind of "Our Father, who art in Heaven"....

The return to normalcy was hard indeed; the astonishing thing is that so many veterans managed so successfully to pick up the pieces of their lives and to begin to earn a peacetime living.

XIX
A NATION FORGED IN FIRE

The Canada to which the veterans returned in 1945 and 1946 seemed like God's country. Compared to the devastation that was Germany, Japan, and Italy, compared to the ruination and privation that hung over Europe and Asia, Canada really was blessed. The nation had escaped the destruction that war had brought to most of the rest of the world. In fact, war had brought unparalleled prosperity to a country that in 1939 had been trapped in the Great Depression. A new Canada had emerged, forged in the fires of war.

For the men and women who returned from overseas there were the veterans' benefits, there were jobs, there was care for the wounded and pensions for the maimed in body and mind. The country made what amends it could for the dislocation of all these lives.

For those who did not return, the nation maintains military cemeteries scattered across Britain, France, Belgium, The Netherlands, Germany, Italy, Hong Kong, and a dozen other locations where Canadians fought and died. The beautiful grounds, lovingly tended—the stark headstones with their simple messages from parents, wives, or children — cannot fail to bring tears to the eyes of all who visit their quiet precincts.

We should weep for the dead of the Second World War. Some Canadian soldiers, sailors, and airmen died while performing acts of high courage. But the Aubrey Cosens and Andy Mynarskis were always few in number. Many died while simply trying to carry out the orders they had been given. Take that hill, bomb that factory, guard that convoy — such objectives, multiplied by ten thousand instances, were the war for most servicemen who came under fire. Countless other men and women trained for war but spent their time in the multitude of essential, unglamorous jobs that make every modern military machine operate.

Some of those who died or were wounded were victims of bungles, incompetent planning, and inadequate equipment. Seamen suffered horrible deaths because the Canadian navy was forced to use inferior equipment. Soldiers killed or captured on Hong Kong's steep hills had found themselves there because planners in London underestimated the Japanese and because their counterparts in Ottawa occasionally suffered spasms of misguided imperial loyalty. Those who bombed Germany in underpowered and underarmed aircraft suffered from the government's sins of omission and commission. We try to forget these mistakes today, papering over the guilty memories with assurances that all who died were brave, that all showed great courage under fire, that the defeats and the disasters, recorded with a care that suggests a kind of pride, were almost things of beauty. They weren't. The dead of the Second World War deserve to be remembered with more clarity than that provided by history glorified with romance.

Many have also forgotten other, equally important facts about that war. All these young Canadians (and we should not forget that the great majority were in their late teens and early twenties) fought for some important goals. Words like "freedom" and "democracy" tend to make Canadians blush and scrape their toes in the dirt in embarrassment. But the war against fascism was about freedom and democracy. There is too much naivety afoot these days, a feeling that no war can be a just war, that no cause can be worth dying for. The horrors of the Vietnam War and the ominous shadow of the nuclear arms race have made most Canadians unable to realize that once it was different.

The Second World War was a just war. The war against the unspeakable evil of Hitler's Germany, the savage buffoonery of Mussolini's Italy, and the sinister militarism of Tojo's Japan had to be fought, and had to be won. If the Axis had triumphed, the outcome could only have been unspeakable tyranny and institutionalized horror. The Second World War, Canadians should always remember, was fought to determine whether the world was to be slave or free. Those young Canadians, along with their comrades from the United States, Britain, and the other Allied nations, fought and won the most important battle of the modern era.

Many of those who served only dimly realized the importance of the struggle in which they fought. Not all were politically sophisticated, and the war's bloody horror — to say nothing of the obscene jockeying of politicians and generals for national or personal advantage — often made it nearly impossible to realize that noble ends were sought. Nor were they easier to see after victory left half of Europe under a Soviet tyranny as odious as Hitler's. But those ends were there and, at root, the men and women in uniform or at home in the factories and on the farms knew it.

Gerard Adriaenssens was with the Belgian Resistance when the Canadian army liberated his family farm near Knokke in October 1944. Thirty years later he started an annual march on November 1 to commemorate the liberation. When he was asked why, Adriaenssens said that a platoon of men had bedded down in his barn for one night in that hard October, and that their demeanour had remained fixed in his mind:

> They were not Rambo soldiers, as one now imagines, but rather quiet, simple boys with a dull look in their eyes, who mourned their comrades who fell that day. They sat there quietly and knew that it might be their turn to offer their lives the next day so that we here in Europe might live in freedom, friendship and peace.
>
> That is what we must tell the youth: the sacrifice these young Canadian soldiers freely gave for us.... they will always be remembered.

They should always be remembered — and not just by Europeans.

The death and destruction unleashed by the Second World War was unparalleled. Those men and women who gave their lives might have written great books, discovered cures for disease, or, more likely, simply have lived out their days in peace in their native land. They lost the chance for a full life because of forces beyond their control, beyond their country's control — forces most of them comprehended only dimly.

Canada and Canadians have had freedom and the fruits of victory since 1945. It is true that we have had precious little peace in that time — the victors moved into the Cold War before the ruins of Germany and Japan had ceased smouldering. But freedom has remained — and had we not fought, freedom would have been lost.

Was it worth it? Was it worth the death, the maiming, the unending pain? That is a terrible question if posed by someone who lost a son, a husband, or a father at Ortona, on HMCS *St. Croix*, or in a Lancaster over the Ruhr. Even so, there can be only one answer. Was it worth it? Oh, yes.

APPENDIX A

1st Canadian Division

Artillery:

1st Brigade, C.F.A.
  1st Field Battery
  3rd Field Battery
  4th Field Battery
  2nd Howitzer Battery

2nd Brigade, C.F.A.
  5th Field Battery
  6th Field Battery
  7th Field Battery
  48th Howitzer Battery

1st Division Ammunition Column

Engineers:

1st Brigade, C.E.
  1st Battalion
  2nd Battalion
  3rd Battalion

1st Division Signal Company

Infantry:

1st Infantry Brigade
  1st (Western Ontario) Battalion
  2nd (Eastern Ontario) Battalion
  3rd (Toronto Regiment) Battalion
  4th (Central Ontario) Battalion
  1st Trench Mortar Battery

2nd Infantry Brigade
  5th (Western Cavalry) Battalion
  7th (1st British Columbia Regiment) Battalion
  8th (90th Rifles) Battalion
  10th (Western Canadians) Battalion
  2nd Trench Mortar Battery

3rd Infantry Brigade
  13th (Royal Highlanders of Canada) Battalion
  14th (Royal Montreal Regiment) Battalion
  15th (48th Highlanders of Canada) Battalion
  16th (The Canadian Scottish) Battalion
  3rd Trench Mortar Battery

Machine Gun Corps: 1st Battalion, C.M.G.C.

Army Service Corps: 1st Divisional Train, C.A.S.C.

Army Medical Corps: 1st, 2nd, 3rd Field Ambulances, C.A.M.C.

2nd Canadian Division

Artillery:

5th Brigade, C.F.A.
  17th Field Battery
  18th Field Battery
  20th Field Battery
  23rd Howitzer Battery

6th Brigade, C.F.A.
  15th Field Battery
  16th Field Battery
  25th Field Battery
  22nd Howitzer Battery

2nd Division Ammunition Column

Engineers: 2nd Brigade, C.E.
    4th Battalion
    5th Battalion
    6th Battalion

2nd Division Signal Company

Infantry: 4th Infantry Brigade
    18th (Western Ontario) Battalion
    19th (Central Ontario) Battalion
    20th (Central Ontario) Battalion
    21st (Eastern Ontario) Battalion
    4th Trench Mortar Battery

5th Infantry Brigade
    22nd (French Canadian) Battalion
    24th (Victoria Rifles of Canada) Battalion
    25th (Nova Scotia Rifles) Battalion
    26th (New Brunswick) Battalion
    5th Trench Mortar Battery

6th Infantry Brigade
    27th (City of Winnipeg) Battalion
    28th (Northwest) Battalion
    29th (Vancouver) Battalion
    31st (Alberta) Battalion
    6th Trench Mortar Battery

Machine Gun Corps: 2nd Battalion, C.M.G.C.

Army Service Corps: 2nd Divisional Train, C.A.S.C.

Army Medical Corps: 4th, 5th, 6th Field Ambulances, C.A.M.C.

3rd Canadian Division

Artillery:

9th Brigade, C.F.A.	10th Brigade, C.F.A.
31st Field Battery	38th Field Battery
33rd Field Battery	39th Field Battery
45th Field Battery	40th Field Battery
36th Howitzer Battery	35th Howitzer Battery

3rd Division Ammunition Column

Engineers: 3rd Brigade, C.E.
    7th Battalion
    8th Battalion
    9th Battalion

3rd Division Signal Company

Infantry: 7th Infantry Brigade
    The Royal Canadian Regiment
    Princess Patricia's Canadian Light Infantry
    42nd (Royal Highlanders of Canada) Battalion
    49th (Edmonton Regiment) Battalion
    7th Trench Mortar Battery

8th Infantry Brigade
  1st Canadian Mounted Rifles Battalion
  2nd Canadian Mounted Rifles Battalion
  4th Canadian Mounted Rifles Battalion
  5th Canadian Mounted Rifles Battalion
  8th Trench Mortar Battery

9th Infantry Brigade
  43rd (Cameron Highlanders of Canada) Battalion
  52nd (New Ontario) Battalion
  58th (Central Ontario) Battalion
  60th (Victoria Rifles of Canada) Battalion
    (replaced, April 1917, by 116th [Central Ontario]
    Battalion)
  9th Trench Mortar Battery

Machine Gun Corps: 3rd Battalion, C.M.G.C.

Army Service Corps: 3rd Divisional Train, C.A.S.C.

Army Medical Corps: 8th, 9th, 10th Field Ambulances, C.A.M.C.

4th Canadian Division

Artillery: 3rd Brigade, C.F.A.   4th Brigade, C.F.A.
               10th Field Battery   13th Field Battery
               11th Field Battery   19th Field Battery
               12th Field Battery   27th Field Battery
               9th Howitzer Battery   21st Howitzer Battery

       4th Division Ammunition Column

Engineers: 4th Brigade, C.E.
               10th Battalion
               11th Battalion
               12th Battalion

       4th Division Signal Company

Infantry: 10th Infantry Brigade
               44th (Manitoba) Battalion
                 (redesignated "New Brunswick", August 1918)
               46th (South Saskatchewan) Battalion
               47th (British Columbia) Battalion
                 (redesignated "Western Ontario", February 1918)
               50th (Calgary) Battalion
               10th Trench Mortar Battery

       11th Infantry Brigade
               54th (Kootenay) Battalion
                 (redesignated "Central Ontario", August 1917)
               75th (Mississauga) Battalion
               87th (Canadian Grenadier Guards) Battalion
               102nd (North British Columbians) Battalion
                 (redesignated "Central Ontario", August 1917)
               11th Trench Mortar Battery

                 12th Infantry Brigade
                   38th (Ottawa) Battalion
                   72nd (Seaforth Highlanders of Canada)
                     Battalion
                   73rd (Royal Highlanders of Canada) Battalion
                     (replaced by 85th [Nova Scotia Highlanders]
                     Battalion, April 1917)
                   78th (Winnipeg Grenadiers) Battalion

Machine Gun Corps: 4th Battalion, C.M.G.C.

Army Service Corps: 4th Divisional Train, C.A.S.C.

Army Medical Corps: 11th, 12th, 13th Field Ambulances, C.A.M.C.

Canadian Corps Troops

Cavalry: Canadian Light Horse

Artillery: Corps Heavy Artillery

1st Brigade, C.G.A.	2nd Brigade, C.G.A.
1st Siege Battery	1st Heavy Battery
3rd Siege Battery	2nd Heavy Battery
7th Siege Battery	2nd Siege Battery
9th Siege Battery	4th Siege Battery
	5th Siege Battery
	6th Siege Battery

3rd Brigade, C.G.A.	5th Divisional Artillery
8th Siege Battery	13th Brigade, C.F.A.
10th Siege Battery	52nd Field Battery
11th Siege Battery	53rd Field Battery
12th Siege Battery	55th Field Battery
	51st Howitzer Battery

                 14th Brigade, C.F.A.
                   60th Field Battery
                   61st Field Battery
                   66th Field Battery
                   58th Howitzer Battery

                 5th Division Ammunition Column

Engineers: Anti-Aircraft Searchlight Company
                 3rd Tunnelling Company
                 Corps Survey Company
                 1st Tramways Company
                 2nd Tramways Company

                 Corps Signal Company

Machine Gun Corps: 1st Motor Machine Gun Brigade, C.M.G.C.
                 2nd Motor Machine Gun Brigade, C.M.G.C.

Army Service Corps: Corps Troops Motor Transport Company C.A.S.C.
                 1st, 2nd, 3rd, 4th Division Motor Transport
                   Companies, C.A.S.C.

	5th Divisional Artillery Motor Transport Detachment
	Engineers Motor Transport Company, C.A.S.C.
	Motor Machine Gun Motor Transport Company, C.A.S.C.
	5th Divisional Train Detachment, C.A.S.C.
Army Medical Corps:	1st, 2nd, 3rd, 6th, 7th, 8th General Hospitals, C.A.M.C.
	2nd, 3rd, 7th, 8th, 9th, 10th Stationary Hospitals, C.A.M.C.
	1st, 2nd, 3rd, 4th, 5th, 6th Forestry Corps Hospitals
	1st, 2nd, 3rd, 4th Casualty Clearing Stations. C.A.M.C.
	14th Field Ambulance, C.A.M.C.

Miscellaneous Units

Canadian Cyclist Battalion
Corps Reinforcement Camp
Corps Schools
Corps Signal Company

Canadian Cavalry Brigade

Cavalry:	Royal Canadian Dragoons
	Lord Strathcona's Horse (Royal Canadians)
	Fort Garry Horse
	R.N.W.M.P. Squadron
Artillery:	Royal Canadian Horse Artillery Brigade
Army Medical Corps:	7th (Cavalry) Field Ambulance, C.A.M.C.

Army Troops (Attached to the British Expeditionary Force)

Artillery:	8th Army Brigade, C.F.A.
	24th Field Battery
	30th Field Battery
	32nd Field Battery
	43rd Howitzer Battery
	8th Army Brigade Ammunition Column
	"E" Anti-Aircraft Battery
Engineers:	1st, 2nd, 3rd, 4th, 5th Army Troops Companies
Railway Troops:	Canadian Overseas Railway Construction Corps (1st to 13th Battalions)
Forestry Corps:	58 companies, C.F.C.

(No reference is made to formation headquarters or to many small units which performed important services.)

APPENDIX B

CANADIAN EXPEDITIONARY FORCE ENLISTMENTS AND CASUALITIES

	Officers	Other Ranks	Total
Enlisted as Volunteers	21,616	455,432	477,048
Enlisted under the Military Service Act		142,588	142,588
TOTAL	21,616	598,020	619,636
Killed in action	1,777	33,148	34,925
Missing, presumed dead	157	4,273	4,430
Died of wounds	602	11,658	12,260
Died at sea	28	105	133
Died of disease or injury	425	7,371	7,796
TOTAL DEATHS	2,989	56,555	59,544
Wounded in action	5,496	121,098	126,594
Gassed	361	11,211	11,572
Injuries	1,279	33,505	34,784
TOTAL NON-FATAL CASUALTIES	7,136	165,814	172,950

APPENDIX C

SOCIAL AND ECONOMIC CHANGE IN WARTIME CANADA

A. **Labour:**

Year	Wage Index (1949 = 100)	Union Members (thousands)	Time lost in strikes (thousands of days)
1911	24.0	133	1,821
1914	25.8	166	491
1915	26.0	143	95
1916	27.8	160	237
1917	31.9	205	1,124
1918	37.4	249	648
1919	44.0	378	3,401

APPENDIX C

B. Inflation by Price Indices: (1937 = 100)

Year	Total	Food	Rent	Clothing	Fuel/light
1913	79.5	88	74	88	76
1914	80.0	92	72	89	74
1915	81.4	93	70	97	73
1916	88.1	103	71	110	74
1917	104.3	133	76	130	83
1918	118.1	153	80	152	91
1919	129.8	164	87	175	99
1920	150.4	188	100	213	119
1925	120.8	127	118	141	121

C. Public Finance:

Year	Budgetary Expenditure ($ million)				Budgetary	National
	Defence	Transportation	Veterans	Total	Revenue	Debt
1911	10	63	—	136	136	463
1914	72	79	1	246	133	750
1915	173	85	1	338	172	974
1916	311	69	3	497	233	1410
1917	344	94	8	574	261	1871
1918	439	86	30	696	313	2638
1919	347	61	75	740	350	2978
1925	14	74	46	356	383	

APPENDIX D

ORDER OF BATTLE: FIRST CANADIAN ARMY, 1945*

1st Canadian Infantry Division

4th Reconnaissance Regiment (Princess Louise Dragoon Guards)

1st Infantry Brigade
  The Royal Canadian Regiment
  The Hastings and Prince Edward Regiment
  48th Highlanders of Canada
2nd Infantry Brigade
  Princess Patricia's Canadian Light Infantry
  Seaforth Highlanders of Canada
  Loyal Edmonton Regiment
3rd Infantry Brigade
  Royal 22e Régiment
  Carleton and York Regiment
  West Nova Scotia Regiment

Saskatoon Light Infantry (MG)

1st Field Regiment RCHA
2nd Field Regiment
3rd Field Regiment
1st Anti-Tank Regiment
2nd Light Anti-Aircraft Regiment

2nd Canadian Infantry Division

8th Reconnaissance Regiment (14th Canadian Hussars)

4th Infantry Brigade
  Royal Regiment of Canada
  Royal Hamilton Light Infantry
  Essex Scottish Regiment
5th Infantry Brigade
  The Black Watch (Royal Highland Regiment) of Canada
  Le Régiment de Maisonneuve
  The Calgary Highlanders
6th Infantry Brigade
  Fusiliers Mont-Royal
  Queen's Own Cameron Highlanders
  South Saskatchewan Regiment
  Toronto Scottish Regiment (MG)

*The authors regret that space limitations require the omission of some Arms and
  Services of First Canadian Army.

4th Field Regiment
5th Field Regiment
6th Field Regiment
2nd Anti-Tank Regiment
3rd Light Anti-Aircraft Regiment

3rd Canadian Infantry Division

7th Reconnaissance Regiment (17th Duke of York's Royal Canadian Hussars)

7th Infantry Brigade
 Royal Winnipeg Rifles
 Regina Rifle Regiment
 1st Bn, Canadian Scottish Regiment
8th Infantry Brigade
 Queen's Own Rifles of Canada
 Le Régiment de la Chaudière
 North Shore (New Brunswick) Regiment
9th Infantry Brigade
 Highland Light Infantry of Canada
 Stormont, Dundas and Glengarry Highlanders
 North Nova Scotia Highlanders

Cameron Highlanders of Ottawa (MG)

12th Field Regiment
13th Field Regiment
14th Field Regiment
3rd Anti-Tank Regiment
4th Light Anti-Aircraft Regiment

4th Canadian Armoured Division

29th Reconnaissance Regiment (South Alberta Regiment)

4th Armoured Brigade
 21st Armoured Regiment (Governor General's Foot Guards)
 22nd Armoured Regiment (Canadian Grenadier Guards)
 28th Armoured Regiment (British Columbia Regiment)
10th Infantry Brigade
 Lincoln and Welland Regiment
 Algonquin Regiment
 Argyll and Sutherland Highlanders of Canada (Princess Louise's)
 Lake Superior Regiment (Motor)

15th Field Regiment
23rd Field Regiment (Self-Propelled)
5th Anti-Tank Regiment
4th Light Anti-Aircraft Regiment

5th Canadian Armoured Division

3rd Armoured Reconnaissance Regiment (Governor General's Horse Guards)

5th Armoured Brigade
  2nd Armoured Regiment (Lord Strathcona's Horse) (Royal Canadians)
  5th Armoured Regiment (8th Princess Louise's New Brunswick Hussars)
  9th Armoured Regiment (British Columbia Dragoons)
11th Infantry Brigade
  Perth Regiment
  Cape Breton Highlanders
  Irish Regiment of Canada
  Westminster Regiment (Motor)

  17th Field Regiment
  8th Field Regiment (Self-Propelled)
  4th Anti-Tank Regiment
  5th Light Anti-Aircraft Regiment

1st Armoured Brigade

11th Armoured Regiment (Ontario Regiment)
12th Armoured Regiment (Three Rivers Regiment)
14th Armoured Regiment (Calgary Regiment)

2nd Armoured Brigade

6th Armoured Regiment (1st Hussars)
10th Armoured Regiment (Fort Garry Horse)
27th Armoured Regiment (Sherbrooke Fusiliers)

I Canadian Corps Troops

1st Armoured Car Regiment (Royal Canadian Dragoons)

7th Anti-Tank Regiment
1st Survey Regiment
1st Light Anti-Aircraft Regiment (Lanark and Renfrew Scottish Regiment)

II Canadian Corps Troops

18th Armoured Car Regiment (12th Manitoba Dragoons)

6th Anti-Tank Regiment
2nd Survey Regiment
6th Light Anti-Aircraft Regiment

First Canadian Army Troops

25th Armoured Delivery Regiment (Elgin Regiment)
1st Armoured Personnel Carrier Regiment

1st Army Group, Royal Canadian Artillery
  11th Army Field Regiment
  1st Medium Regiment
  2nd Medium Regiment
  5th Medium Regiment

2nd Army Group, Royal Canadian Artillery
  19th Army Field Regiment
  3rd Medium Regiment
  4th Medium Regiment
  7th Medium Regiment
  2nd Heavy Anti-Aircraft Regiment (Mobile)

Royal Montreal Regiment
Canadian Parachute Battalion (with 6th British Airborne Division)

APPENDIX E

PRINCIPAL SHIPS OF THE ROYAL CANADIAN NAVY
1939–1945

Class	Ship
Cruiser	Ontario
	Uganda
Escort Carrier	Nabob
	Puncher
Armed Merchant Cruiser	Prince David
	Prince Henry
	Prince Robert
Destroyer	Algonquin
	Annapolis
	Assiniboine
	Athabaskan
	(sunk 29 Apr. '44)
	Buxton
	Chaudière
	Columbia
	Fraser
	(sunk 25 June '40)
	Gatineau
	Haida
	Hamilton
	Huron
	Iroquois
	Kootenay
	Margaree
	(sunk 23 Oct. '40)
	Niagara
	Ottawa
	(sunk 14 Sept. '42)
	Ottawa
	Qu'Appelle
	Restigouche
	Saguenay
	St. Clair
	St. Croix
	(sunk 20 Sept. '43)
	St. Francis
	St. Laurent
	Saskatchewan
	Sioux

Class	Ship
	Skeena
	(sunk 25 Oct. '44)
Frigate	Annan
	Antigonish
	Beacon Hill
	Buckingham
	Cap de la Madeleine
	Cape Breton
	Capilano
	Carlplace
	Charlottetown
	Chebogue
	Coaticook
	Dunver
	Eastview
	Ettrick
	Fort Erie
	Glace Bay
	Grou
	Hallowell
	Inch Arran
	Joliette
	Jonquière
	Kirkland Lake
	Kokanee
	La Hulloise
	Lanark
	Lasalle
	Lauzon
	Lévis
	Loch Achanalt
	Loch Alvie
	Loch Morlich
	Longueuil
	Magog
	Matane
	Meon
	Monnow
	Montreal

Class	Ship	Class	Ship
	Nene		Barrie
	New Glasgow		Battleford
	New Waterford		Beauharnois
	Orkney		Belleville
	Outremont		Bittersweet
	Penetang		Bowmanville
	Port Colborne		Brandon
	Poundmaker		Brantford
	Prestonian		Buctouche
	Prince Rupert		Calgary
	Ribble		Camrose
	Royalmount		Chambly
	Runnymede		Charlottetown
	St. Catharines		(sunk 11 Sept. '42)
	Saint John		Chicoutimi
	St. Pierre		Chilliwack
	St. Stephen		Cobalt
	Ste. Thérèse		Cobourg
	Seacliffe		Collingwood
	Springhill		Copper Cliff
	Stettler		Dauphin
	Stone Town		Dawson
	Stormont		Drumheller
	Strathadam		Dundas
	Sussexvale		Dunvegan
	Swansea		Edmundston
	Teme		Eyebright
	Thetford Mines		Fennel
	Toronto		Fergus
	Valleyfield		Forest Hill
	(sunk 7 May '44)		Fredericton
	Victoriaville		Frontenac
	Waskesiu		Galt
	Wentworth		Giffard
Corvette	Agassiz		Guelph
	Alberni		Halifax
	(sunk 21 Aug. '44)		Hawkesbury
	Algoma		Hepatica
	Amherst		Hespeler
	Arnprior		Humberstone
	Arrowhead		Huntsville
	Arvida		Kamloops
	Asbestos		Kamsack
	Athol		Kenogami
	Baddeck		Kincardine

Class	Ship
	Kitchener
	Lachute
	La Malbaie
	Leaside
	Lethbridge
	Lévis
	(sunk 19 Sept. '41)
	Lindsay
	Long Branch
	Louisburg
	(sunk 6 Feb. '43)
	Louisburg
	Lunenburg
	Matapedia
	Mayflower
	Merrittonia
	Midland
	Mimico
	Moncton
	Moose Jaw
	Morden
	Nanaimo
	Napanee
	New Westminster
	Norsyd
	North Bay
	Oakville
	Orangeville
	Orillia
	Owen Sound
	Parry Sound
	Peterborough
	Petrolia
	Pictou
	Port Arthur
	Prescott
	Quesnel
	Regina (sunk 9 Aug. '44)
	Rimouski
	Rivière du Loup
	Rosthern
	Sackville
	St. Lambert
	St. Thomas
	Saskatoon

Class	Ship
	Shawinigan
	(sunk 25 Nov. '44)
	Shediac
	Sherbrooke
	Smiths Falls
	Snowberry
	Sorel
	Spikenard
	(sunk 10 Feb. '42)
	Stellarton
	Strathroy
	Sudbury
	Summerside
	The Pas
	Thorlock
	Tillsonburg
	Timmins
	Trail
	Trentonian
	(sunk 22 Feb. '45)
	Trillium
	Vancouver
	Ville de Québec
	West York
	Wetaskiwin
	Weyburn
	(sunk 22 Feb. '43)
	Whitby
	Windflower
	(sunk 7 Dec. '41)
	Woodstock
Minesweeper	Bayfield
	Bellechasse
	Blairmore
	Border Cities
	Brockville
	Burlington
	Canso
	Caraquet
	Chedabucto
	(sunk 21 Oct. '43)
	Chignecto
	Clayoquot
	(sunk 24 Dec. '44)
	Comox

Class	Ship	Class	Ship
	Coquitlam		Oshawa
	Courtenay		Outarde
	Cowichan		Portage
	Cranbrook		Port Hope
	Daerwood		Quatsino
	Digby		Quinte
	Drummondville		Red Deer
	Esquimalt		Revelstoke
	(sunk 16 Apr. '45)		Rockcliffe
	Fort Frances		Rossland
	Fort William		St. Boniface
	Fundy		St. Joseph
	Gananoque		Sarnia
	Gaspé		Sault Ste. Marie
	Georgian		Stratford
	Goderich		Swift Current
	Granby		Thunder
	Grandmère		Transcona
	Guysborough		Trois-Rivières
	(sunk 17 Mar. '45)		Truro
	Ingonish		Ungava
	Kalamalka		Vegreville
	Kapuskasing		Wallaceburg
	Kelowna		Wasaga
	Kenora		Westmount
	Kentville		Winnipeg
	Lachine	*Armed*	Ambler
	Lavallee	*Yachts*	Beaver
	Llewellyn		Caribou
	Lloyd George		Cougar
	Lockeport		Elk
	Mahone		Grizzly
	Malpeque		Husky
	Medicine Hat		Lynx
	Melville		Moose
	Middlesex		Otter
	Milltown		(sunk 26 Mar. '41)
	Minas		Raccoon
	Miramichi		(sunk 7 Sept. '42)
	Mulgrave		Reindeer
	New Liskeard		Renard
	Nipigon		Sans Peur
	Nootka (Nanoose)		Vison
	Noranda		Wolf

APPENDIX F

Home War Establishment

No. 1 Fighter Squadron (renumbered 401, 1 Mar. '41)
No. 2 Army Co-operation Squadron (disbanded 16 Dec. '39)
No. 3 Bomber Squadron (disbanded 5 Sept. '39)
No. 4 Bomber Reconnaissance Squadron WAC
No. 5 Bomber Reconnaissance Squadron EAC
No. 6 Bomber Reconnaissance Squadron WAC
No. 7 General Purpose Squadron (disbanded 10 Sept. '39)
No. 8 Bomber Reconnaissance Squadron WAC
No. 9 Bomber Reconnaissance Squadron (disbanded 1 Sept. '44) WAC
No. 10 Bomber Reconnaissance Squadron EAC
No. 11 Bomber Reconnaissance Squadron WAC
No. 12 Composite Squadron
No. 13 Seaplane and Bomber Reconnaissance Training Squadron (disbanded
    9 Nov. '42) WAC
No. 14 Fighter Squadron (renumbered 442, 8 Feb. '44)
No. 110 Army Co-operation Squadron (renumbered 400, 1 Mar. '41)
No. 111 Fighter Squadron (renumbered 440, 8 Feb. '44)
No. 112 Army Co-operation Squadron (renumbered 402, 1 Mar. '41)
No. 113 Bomber Reconnaissance Squadron (disbanded 23 Aug. '44) EAC
No. 115 Bomber Reconnaissance Squadron (disbanded 23 Aug. '44) WAC
No. 116 Bomber Reconnaissance Squadron EAC
No. 117 Bomber Reconnaissance Squadron (disbanded 15 Dec. '43) EAC
No. 118 Fighter Squadron (renumbered 438, 18 Nov. '43)
No. 119 Bomber Reconnaissance Squadron (disbanded 15 Mar. '44) EAC
No. 120 Bomber Reconnaissance Squadron (disbanded 1 May '44) WAC
No. 121 Composite Squadron EAC
No. 122 Composite Squadron WAC
No. 123 Army Co-operation Squadron (renumbered 439, 1 Jan. '44)
No. 124 Ferry Squadron
No. 125 Fighter Squadron (renumbered 441, 8 Feb. '44)
No. 126 Fighter Squadron EAC
No. 127 Fighter Squadron (renumbered 443, 8 Feb. '44)
No. 128 Fighter Squadron (disbanded 15 Mar. '44) EAC
No. 129 Fighter Squadron (disbanded 30 Sept. '44) EAC
No. 130 Fighter Squadron (disbanded 15 Mar. '44) EAC
No. 132 Fighter Squadron (disbanded 30 Sept. '44) WAC

(EAC = Eastern Air Command; WAC = Western Air Command)

No. 133 Fighter Squadron WAC
No. 135 Fighter Squadron WAC
No. 145 Bomber Reconnaissance Squadron EAC
No. 147 Bomber Reconnaissance Squadron (disbanded 15 Mar. '45) WAC
No. 149 Bomber Reconnaissance Squadron (disbanded 15 Mar. '44) WAC
No. 160 Bomber Reconnaissance Squadron EAC
No. 161 Bomber Reconnaissance Squadron EAC
No. 162 Bomber Reconnaissance Squadron (served in Coastal Command) EAC
No. 163 Fighter Squadron (disbanded 15 Mar. '44) WAC
No. 164 Transport Squadron EAC
No. 165 Transport Squadron WAC
No. 166 Communications Squadron WAC
No. 167 Communications Squadron EAC
No. 168 Heavy Transport Squadron
No. 170 Ferry Squadron

RCAF Overseas

No. 400 Army Co-operation (later Fighter-Reconnaissance) Squadron 2 TAF
No. 401 Fighter Squadron
No. 402 Fighter Squadron 2 TAF
No. 403 Fighter Squadron 127 Wing 2 TAF
No. 404 Coastal Squadron
No. 405 Bomber Squadron (a Pathfinder squadron)
No. 406 Night Fighter/Intruder Squadron
No. 407 Coastal Squadron
No. 408 Bomber Squadron 6 Group
No. 409 Night Fighter Squadron 2 TAF
No. 410 Night Fighter Squadron
No. 411 Fighter Squadron 2 TAF
No. 412 Fighter Squadron 2 TAF
No. 413 General Reconnaissance Squadron (disbanded 23 Feb. '45)
    (served in Ceylon)
No. 414 Fighter Reconnaissance Squadron 2 TAF
No. 413 Torpedo Bomber Squadron
No. 416 Fighter Squadron 2 TAF
No. 417 Fighter Squadron (served in Middle East, Italy)
No. 418 Intruder Squadron 2 TAF
No. 419 Bomber Squadron 6 Group
No. 420 Bomber Squadron 331 Wing (served in North Africa, Italy)
No. 421 Fighter Squadron 127 Wing 2 TAF 6 Group
No. 422 Coastal Squadron
No. 423 General Reconnaissance Squadron 6 Group
No. 424 Bomber Squadron (flew North Africa, Italy) 331 Wing
No. 425 Bomber Squadron (the French-Canadian "Alouette" squadron)
No. 426 Bomber Squadron 331 Wing 6 Group

No. 427 Bomber Squadron 6 Group
No. 428 Bomber Squadron 6 Group
No. 429 Bomber Squadron 6 Group
No. 430 Fighter-Reconnaissance Squadron 2 TAF
No. 431 Bomber Squadron 6 Group
No. 432 Bomber Squadron 6 Group
No. 433 Bomber Squadron 6 Group
No. 434 Bomber Squadron 6 Group
No. 435 Transport Squadron (served in Burma)
No. 436 Transport Squadron (served in Burma)
No. 437 Transport Squadron
No. 438 Fighter Bomber Squadron 2 TAF
No. 439 Fighter-Bomber Squadron 2 TAF
No. 440 Fighter-Bomber Squadron 2 TAF
No. 441 Fighter Squadron 2 TAF
No. 442 Fighter Squadron 2 TAF
No. 443 Fighter Squadron 2 TAF
No. 664 Air Observation Post Squadron, 1st Cdn Army
No. 665 Air Observation Post Squadron, 1st Cdn Army
No. 666 Air Observation Post Squadron, 1st Cdn Army

(6 Group = 6(RCAF) Group, Bomber Command; 2 TAF = 2 Allied Tactical Air Force)

INDEX

348